WESTERN EUROPE AND ITS ISLAM

INTERNATIONAL COMPARATIVE SOCIAL STUDIES

VOLUME II

WESTERN EUROPE AND ITS ISLAM

BY

JAN RATH

RINUS PENNINX

KEES GROENENDIJK

ASTRID MEYER

BRILL
LEIDEN · BOSTON · KÖLN
2001

This book is printed on acid-free paper.

Library of Congress Cataloging-in-Publication Data

Nederland en zijn Islam. English
    Western Europe and its Islam / by Jan Rath... [et al.].
        p.   cm. — (International comparative social studies, ISSN 1568-
4474 ; 2)
    Includes bibliographical references and index.
    ISBN 9004121927 (cloth : alk. paper)
    1. Muslims—Netherlands—Social conditions. 2. Muslims—Belgium—
—Social conditions. 3. Muslims—Great Britain—Social conditions. 4.
Islam—Netherlands. 5. Islam—Belgium. 6. Islam—Great Britain.
7. Netherlands—Ethnic relations. 8. Belgium—Ethnic relations.
9. Great Britain—Ethnic relations. I. Rath, Jan, 1956- II. Title. III. Series.

DJ92.M86 N4413 2001
305.6'97104—dc21   2001025217

Die Deutsche Bibliothek – CIP-Einheitsaufnahme

Western Europe and its Islam / by Jan Rath .... – Leiden ; Boston; Köln :
Brill, 2001
    (International comparative social studies ; Vol. 2)
    ISBN 90–04–12192–7

ISSN   1568-4474
ISBN   90 04 12192 7

CONTENTS

PART TWO

THE INSTITUTIONALIZATION OF ISLAM AND
THE STRUGGLE FOR RECOGNITION AT THE
LOCAL LEVEL

PART THREE

AN INTERNATIONAL COMPARISON

PREFACE

The widespread introduction of Islam into Western Europe occurred with the arrival of immigrants from regions such as North and West Africa, Asia, and the Caribbean. For some time the Islamic religion led a 'hidden existence' in countries such as Great Britain, Belgium and the Netherlands, but this has gradually altered with the growth of a whole range of Muslim institutions. From Muslim communities there is a constant demand for the recognition of their religion and its institutions; however, the responses of the receiving societies have seldom been straightforward, despite freedom of religion being firmly established in law. In fact we know very little about the precise reactions of society at large, about the ways in which society has created opportunities or thrown up obstacles for the development of these institutions, and about how such reactions should be accounted for.

In 1988 Kees Groenendijk and Rinus Penninx set up a research project to examine these issues at the Institute for the Sociology of Law at the Catholic University of Nijmegen, financed by that University's Research Fund and Law Faculty. This post-doctoral project rapidly became an inter-university project with Penninx's appointment to a post at the Free University in Amsterdam, while Jan Rath was recruited in Nijmegen. In the course of the project, contributions were made by a number of Masters students from the Catholic University of Nijmegen, the Free University of Amsterdam and the University of Utrecht. Niek van der Dungen, Jeroen Feirabend, René Hampsink, Christa van Marrewijk, Astrid Meyer, Judith Roosblad and Hasan Yar all researched parts of the subject and delivered their reports; they have all been awarded their degrees in the interim. In addition, Jeanne van der Voort contributed to the work while she was resident in England.

With the departure of Penninx and Rath to the Institute for Migration and Ethnic Studies (IMES), the University of Amsterdam also became involved in the project, and shortly afterwards Astrid Meyer was appointed by IMES to the research team. In the last stages of the work, Heleen Ronden of IMES took charge of the manuscript, and carried out the final editing. Yoost Penninx provided technical support in the editing process.

The end-product of this project was published in Dutch in book form as *Nederland en zijn Islam*, of which the present edition is a translated and partially revised version. Michael Wintle, with Alastair and Cora Weir, carried out the translation into English; we are grateful to the Netherlands Organization for Scientific Research (NWO), which made the translation possible.

Our thanks is due to all those who have contributed, in whatever way, to the realization of this book.

Amsterdam/Nijmegen, December 2000

CHAPTER ONE

WESTERN EUROPE AND ITS ISLAM

Introduction

Islam on the political agenda

On a very rough estimate there are at least five to six million Muslims living in Western Europe today.[1] Their presence results mainly from the massive influx of workers and other migrants from former colonial territories in Africa, Asia and the Caribbean region, and from such countries as Turkey. Although there have been Muslims in Europe since time immemorial,[2] they have never had such a large presence as they do now. Some therefore like to refer—though from a historical point of view mistakenly—to the '*New* Islamic presence' (Gerholm & Lithman 1988).

Among immigrants in Western Europe, Islam appears to be an important mobilizing force: from the start Muslims have devoted themselves to setting up institutions in the public sphere, in order to guarantee the profession of their faith in the long term. Muslims organize themselves in many ways, and go on to establish institutions varying from mosques, *halâl* butchers, schools, broadcasting organizations, and political parties right through to cemeteries, having worked for the routine appointment of Muslim spiritual advisers in hospitals, prisons, the armed forces, and similar organizations. Some of these institutions have been established with a minimum of fuss, others after conflict with the government or other interested parties, and at times with their support.

---

[1] The figures are far from precise, since in most countries there is no central registration of residents by religion, and the data are therefore based on the number of migrants from countries where Islam is the most important religion. This gives around 200,000 Muslims in Belgium, 2.5 million in France, between 0.55 and 1.5 million in Great Britain (Nielsen 1987: 25–34; Peach 1990), 1.7 million in the Federal Republic of Germany (Thomä-Venske 1988: 78) and almost 628,000 in the Netherlands (CBS 1996: 53).

[2] Cf. Waardenburg 1983: 253.

One way of identifying the development of Islamic religious communities outside the core areas is by looking at Islam itself. Islam is then perceived as a normative system, as a system of norms and values giving direction to everyday life. According to this view, wherever Muslims may be, both in the Muslim world and in the diaspora, they will constantly strive to arrange their lives as much as possible in accordance with this normative system, because such is the way of Islam. So it is hardly surprising that the adherents of this view are primarily concerned with the formal aspects of religion. However, this point of view is open to a great deal of criticism: it is deterministic and static.

Another approach view is possible, one which concentrates on the interaction between Muslim immigrants and the society in which they find themselves. Practising Muslims do not shape the development of Islamic religious communities in isolation; the society around them also influences the process. The final form which Islam—with all its variants—assumes can be viewed as the result of consultation and conflict between all the different parties involved. Many factors play a role in this interaction, including some which in themselves have little to do with Islam. The scope gained by Muslims to practise their own religion and to develop their own institutions then becomes the product of political decisions, today or in the past, about the recognition of religious institutions.

Most West European societies form in principle secular nation states, though in some countries, such as Denmark or Great Britain, there is a national or established church. In the other countries, church and state are kept strictly separate, at least in theory, though in practice the dividing line is sometimes blurred. In all cases we encounter social formations which in religious or ideological respects are permeated with Christian or Humanist elements. Whether this is a matter of the Christian or Humanist ethic being reflected in legislation, or of more everyday public matters such as the celebration of official holidays, these issues are all informed in part by Christianity or by a specific denomination within it. In addition, despite the separation of church and state in these nation states, the government offers certain facilities to established religious communities, both in the strictly religious sphere and in the public or semi-public spheres of education, social security and the like. The presence of people who adhere to a non-Christian religion puts this historically determined system to the test.

We are here concerned with what Taylor (1994) described as *the politics of recognition*, the process of recognition of Muslim identities, and their public forms of expression. The politics of recognition is intrinsically ambivalent. On the one hand it refers to *equal* distribution of rights and provisions to all citizens, regardless of their identity. Here Taylor speaks of *a politics of universalism*, since it assumes the equal dignity of all citizens. 'What is to be avoided at all costs is the existence of "first-class" and "second-class" citizens' (Taylor 1994: 37). On the other hand, the politics of recognition can also refer to the distribution of *special* rights and provisions. This is based on the assumption that individuals or groups possess a unique identity, which distinguishes them from other people. The politics of recognition then revolves around giving status to something that is not universal, but specific. There is a certain tension between the two forms. For someone seeking special rights and provisions, the granting of equal rights will be perceived as a disregard of his specificity, and perhaps even as an unwelcome attempt at homogenization. Based on 'difference-blind liberalism', neutral ground can be offered in this way to Muslims, for example to form their identity within the framework already existing for everyone. However, as Taylor claims (1994: 62), many Muslims are aware that,

> Western liberalism is not so much an expression of the secular, post-religious outlook that happens to be popular among liberal *intellectuals* as a more organic outgrowth of Christianity. (. . .) The division of church and state goes back to the earliest days of Christian civilization. The early forms of the separation were very different from ours, but the basis was laid for modern developments. The very term *secular* was originally part of the Christian vocabulary.

Whatever the exact issues, Europe is currently faced with the question of how the politics of the recognition of Islam should be dealt with.

At first, neither the government nor the political parties in any of these countries paid very much attention to the institutionalization of Islam. To the extent that they did, their attention focused on its expressions which were perceived as problematic, or were considered to be part of the ethnic identity of the newcomers. Now, however, greater significance is being ascribed to Islam, which does not mean that it is automatically recognized as an important spiritual movement. On the contrary, some see only the spectre of a 'clash of civilizations' (Huntington 1997), or of advancing fundamentalist groups who would engulf the achievements of West European or national culture. They see in Islam a danger that must be driven out or at the very least controlled by society. This interpretation is founded in part on centuries-old anti-Islamic images and sentiments. However, the intensity of the moral panic against the wearing of headscarves by women and girls, and the reactions to the Rushdie affair and the Gulf War, illustrate that this is not a minor issue, but a fear or rejection of Islam—albeit not always clearly defined—which is experienced by many people. It would be too simplistic to describe the reaction to the advent of Muslims and their institutions exclusively in such terms, since at the same time many people show themselves to be more tolerant and respectful of Islam, and are prepared to facilitate its observances.

In a general sense the institutionalization of Islam is taking place all over Western Europe, but if one looks more carefully at the individual countries, important differences can be discerned. In each nation state the process of institutionalization, and its recognition, takes a different and specific form. Let us take the example of the headscarf. The supporters in France of a ban on Muslim women wearing headscarves in public places invoke the secular ideology of the French state, which has ruled supreme since the French Revolution.[3] Consequently they take the debate to a level of principle in which compromise is virtually excluded in advance. In Germany, the government and civil servants are also expected to maintain the norm of religious neutrality (Häussler 1998). In July 1988 the Minister of Education in Baden-Württemberg refused to appoint a teacher to a primary school. She was a practising Muslim and wanted to wear a headscarf while she was teaching. Although she had worn her headscarf without problems during her teaching practice, it was now judged that her behaviour would breach religious neutrality. In Great Britain the supporters of a ban cannot invoke any constitutional ruling. Here the debate is about the obligation to wear traditional school uniform. Some of the justifications for compulsory uniform are to

---

[3] In Article 2 of the 1958 Constitution it is laid down that France is a secular republic. The Educational Acts of 1881 and 1882 envisaged completely secular primary education. In introducing it, according to the Minister, account should nonetheless be taken of the 'sensibilities' of the population. Some people invoked this again in the debate about headscarves (Blaise & De Coorebyter 1990: 70–72).

prevent the outward signs of social inequality and to promote loy-
alty to the school community. There the question is less easily linked
to anything as weighty as constitutional principles, and consequently
is resolved in a simple and pragmatic way: headscarves are allowed,
provided they are in the colour of the school uniform (Poulter 1990:
90–91). Finally, in the Netherlands, the Secretary of State for Education
has repeatedly made clear that the objections to wearing headscarves
are not important enough to impose a ban. Headscarves are in the
domain of civil liberties.

Another example is the funding of mosques. In the Netherlands,
local and national leaders debate the question of the extent to which
the key institutions of Islamic religious communities—the mosques—
should be supported financially by the government. The supporters
invoke the right of equal treatment, and point to a series of legal
rulings which until the mid-1970s applied to Christian churches. In
France, on the other hand, the question of subsidizing mosques does
not really arise. There have already been several cases of mayors
authorizing the bulldozing of mosques, although such reactions are
not common. In short, in spite of the fact that the problems are the
same in the different countries, and that there is both support and
opposition, it appears that the discussion, its ideological grounds and
the political outcome, can all show marked differences.

This much is clear: Islam and its adherents, and more recently
the presence of Muslims in various West European societies, have
gradually gained a place on the political agenda and in public discussion. These societies react at all levels to what has by now become
the emphatic presence of this religion and its followers.

Social-science researchers at first paid little attention to the religious aspects of migration and their sociological significance. They
saw immigrants primarily as guest workers, foreigners, blacks or ethnic minorities, depending on the specific point of view current in
their country. Whenever any research was directed at their religion,
it was mainly about Muslims, the development of their identity, the
formation of their organizations, and other aspects of the 'internal'
culture or structure of their religious communities. Although we have
dealt with the attitudes of the Muslims themselves, the focus here is
decidedly on the way in which society creates opportunities for the
development of these institutions, or opposes them. Here we start
from the premise that Muslims and the society around them maintain dynamic relationships, in which it is even possible that some

Muslim institutions have sprung up at the instigation of the surrounding society itself.

The specific character of these relationships can perhaps best be
revealed by comparing the situation in different countries. Various
international publications on Islam have recently appeared in Western
Europe.[4] However, these publications vary in nature and quality,
and there has been no comparative study determined by a well-
defined theoretical perspective. We intend to fill this gap with this
book, in which we describe, analyse and compare the process of the
recognition of Islam in Western Europe.

The reactions of society: a framework for analysis

Institutions and institutionalization

By institutionalization we mean the social process of the origin and
development of institutions. In accordance with Buiks and Van Tillo
(1980: 29), we see institutions as 'more or less standardized patterns
of human actions and ideas which possess a normative validity within
the society in which they are rooted'.[5] Institutions are therefore social
phenomena, not directly dependent on individuals. To define the
concept more narrowly, the emergence of Muslim places of worship
and the establishment of organizations for that purpose are forms
of institutionalization. In many countries this is possible thanks to
other institutions, such as the freedom of religion embedded in the
Constitution, or the government guaranteeing this freedom and providing funds for certain activities such as education. There are institutions with a wide reach, such as the Constitution, the educational
system or the political system, and there are institutions with a relatively small coverage, for instance the ritual circumcision of boys
according to the Islamic rite.

We are particularly interested in the process of institutionalization
where the established society is involved in it, or feels the effects of

---

[4] See Anwar & Garaudy 1984; Nielsen 1987; Gerholm & Lithman 1988; Shadid
& Van Koningsveld 1991, 1995.
[5] An even shorter definition is provided by Beerling (1978: 293): an institution
is 'an accepted and structured communal action in a socio-cultural context'. It concerns therefore a pattern of behaviour carried out in a specific context and with a
specific ideology.

it. When adherents of a particular religion come to live in a new
society and try to set up their religious institutions there, they can
do so within the closed confines of their own community, if need
be underground. In such cases the institutions constructed by the
group have a restricted range and validity within the group itself.
These institutions attain no formal recognition within society, they
are not adopted, accepted or integrated into the totality of society's
institutions. A reason for this could be that the established society
has fundamental objections to certain organizations,[6] but this is not
always the case. The point is that these forms of institutionalization
occur in the private sector, and that there is no direct inducement—
either for the religion's adherents or for the society at large—to draw
up rules or take other kinds of action in the public sector.

Adherents of a given religion, on the other hand, can choose or
be forced to work towards the recognition of their institutions within
the established society. Such efforts may be inspired by considerations of the principle of equality, and by the desire to be treated on
an equal footing with other institutions which are already accepted
by society. They can also be based on material considerations: recognition can bring with it the right to financial support by society.
Finally, it is also possible that established forces in society, like government, demand that these institutions be run in a specific way, in
other words more in accordance with what is considered normal and
desirable in the receiving country. In all cases adherents of a religion and their organizations have to act in consultation and nego-
tiation with the established society if they are to achieve recognition
for their institutions, which can result in a more *public institutionalization*. The form this public institutionalization takes can vary for
Muslims from the recognition of an institution exclusive to them, to
the rather challenging example of a 'Muslim section' within a Christian
Democratic party, or the recognition of equivalence between the
electronically amplified call to prayer and the ringing of church bells.

The most important difference between internal and public institutionalization is therefore recognition by society. The struggle for
recognition can have both positive and negative outcomes. When
the decision is positive, the new institution is integrated into society,

---

[6] For example, as regards female circumcision, to the extent that it can be considered an Islamic ritual.

sometimes subject to strict conditions. The form this recognition eventually takes, and the degree to which it has to be fought for, can
vary widely. Among other things it depends on the institutional
context of society: some new institutions can be integrated relatively
easily because comparable institutions already exist for other groups.
For other institutions the process of recognition is appreciably more
difficult, and the struggle for recognition can even result in failure.

These considerations have led to the following three key research
questions:

- To what extent is there evidence of the creation of Muslim institutions, old or new, in West European countries, and in what
  spheres of life does this occur?
- Which factors and agents play a role in this institutionalization?
- How is the discussion about institutionalization conducted, and
  how is it related to the political actions of the agents involved?

Range and density of institutions

The first question is descriptive in nature. We have already stated
that the development of Muslim institutions is in full swing in a
number of spheres of life. For this research we distinguish seven
spheres in which the process of institutionalization can take place,[7]
listed in random order.

- *The religious sphere.* This concerns the recognition of freedom of
  religion and of religious organizations, and the equal treatment
  and recognition or acceptance of key religious institutions: spiritual leaders, religious festivals, places and provisions for worship,
  the public call to prayer, and the prescriptions or usages based
  on the religion (such as ritual slaughter, diet, and funeral customs).
- *The legal sphere.* This refers to the recognition of practices rooted
  in religion or religious tradition, including such elements as Islamic
  family law.
- *The educational sphere.* The central issue here is the transfer of knowledge and values (including religious ones), covering both the social-
  ization of children and knowledge transfer and diffusion among

---

[7] This framework of spheres is constructed on the basis of the very extensive
Dutch form of institutionalization of religions in society: the pillar model, as defined
by Lijphart (1982).

adults: provisions for Islamic training and education, theological courses, religious instruction in and outside schools, and the media.

— *The socio-economic sphere.* Within this sphere we look at economic institutions based on Islamic principles, such as slaughterhouses, financial institutions on an interest-free basis, enterprises controlling Muslim foundations, Muslim employers' and employees' organizations, and corporations or co-operatives for the building and management of housing.

— *The socio-cultural sphere.* This includes bodies for Muslim socio-cultural, women's, children's and old people's activities; recreation, hobby, musical and sports clubs and suchlike; and the possibility of their recognition, support and funding, for example by providing premises for their activities.

— *The sphere of health and social care.* This involves Muslim foundations for social work, home nursing, hospitals, homes for the elderly and suchlike.

— *The political sphere.* This concerns the formation of Muslim political organizations or parties, the recognition of Muslim organizations as dialogue partners, and their participation in advisory and management structures at all levels.

A systematic listing of Muslim institutions and organizations, and of the extent to which they are recognized by society, gives us a first insight into where, within these various spheres, institutionalization is taking place. In addition it can reveal the presence of networks of institutions, and organizations within the spheres. This will enable us to compare the extent of institutionalization in the various countries, and to determine whether and to what extent a national situation has specific characteristics. We will then investigate whether this national situation is dependent on the structural characteristics of that society, or whether it is part of a general phenomenon associated with the settlement of immigrants with a specific religion which is unfamiliar in the receiving country.

Factors and agents

To determine the course of the institutionalization process and who is involved in it, we first listed a number of factors and agents, which can be found in the model reproduced below. On the basis of this we also formulated a number of assumptions about the factors and agents and their mutual interrelationships. The arrows in Figure 1 show the direction of the links.

Figure 1: Potential factors and agents

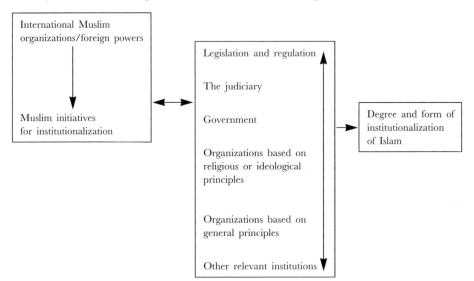

In the actual research this model was not used as a test frame in the strict sense, but as a heuristic model: the assumptions served as reminders and guiding ideas, and above all structured the collection of material and the choice of areas of study. Here we give a brief explanation of the model and its assumptions.

In the first place there is the dependent variable, *the degree and form of the institutionalization of Islam* (its occurrence in the various spheres, and its density). If this factor was the descriptive variable in the first question, in the model it became the one to be explained. The other factors are included as independent variables, though we accept that some of them are not fully independent in relation to each other.

The first factor discussed here, *initiatives by Muslims,* is in practice a necessary condition for starting a process of institutionalization. From the existing literature we know that there are many of these initiatives, even if in some cases they have had an impetus from the established society. Particularly among first-generation Muslim immigrants, Islam forms an important organizing principle. Some people consider this a significant development, because to some extent it is contradictory to developments within Europe as a whole, where the dominant influences appear to be secularization and the rise of the individual. Of paramount importance here is the sphere in which initiatives and claims to recognition by the Muslim communities occur.

Most Muslims in Europe maintain international links. Not only have most of them come to Europe as immigrants, or have been born into an immigrant family, but the vast majority of Muslims in the world live outside Europe, which is why the global centre of gravity of the Islamic religious faith is not in Europe. These international links are expressed in at least two ways which are important for our research: links with *foreign powers*, and links with *international Muslim organizations*. In some countries where Islam is the most important religion, the separation of church and state is not so pronounced as it is in many European countries, or is even entirely absent. In such countries the government is closely involved with the religious life of its subjects, an involvement which can extend to its subjects abroad. An example is the Turkish Presidium for Religious Affairs, the *Diyanet*, which appoints and pays imams abroad.[8] In a few cases the government assumes responsibility for the Muslim 'diaspora' wherever it may be in the world, and regardless of whether they are in fact its subjects (examples are Libya and Saudi Arabia). In addition to the involvement of foreign powers with Muslims in Europe, there is the intervention of more or less private Muslim organizations which set up local offices, sometimes with the aim of carrying out missionary activities. Thus direct or indirect external influence can be exerted on Muslims in Europe to deploy specific initiatives, and there is also the possibility of material and other kinds of support.

All the other factors concern the receiving society. Here institutions are involved which we assume to be of significance for the institutionalization of Islam. Although we are aware that individuals sometimes play an important part, for instance, as brokers, agents or identity entrepreneurs (Lal 1997), we concentrate here on the institutional level. Institutions can react in three different ways to the presence of Islam, its adherents and their claims: they can actively promote or support the formation of new Muslim institutions; they can be passive and adopt a more or less neutral attitude; or they can actively oppose the development of new institutions, for instance by the literal application of regulation, and by delays in putting them into force, or by laying down new restrictions.

---

[8] See, *inter alia*, Den Exter 1990.

An important framework within which these processes are played out is that of *legislation and regulation*. In the Netherlands, freedom of religion and ideology is regulated to the extent that every ideological or religious group can invoke opportunities and facilities anchored in legislation. In Belgium, however, there is a general and explicit recognition of religious communities by the government, while England has an established church which has a privileged position in law.[9] The legislation and regulation itself can influence the formulation of claims for facilities or the taking of initiatives. This applies in particular to those facilities for which the government can provide resources, such as schools and welfare activities. Since the Muslim community does not form a monolithic block, there is every chance that claims and campaigns for facilities and financial resources become the subject of internal strife between movements within that community, and this does in fact happen.[10] The acquisition of facilities and resources strengthens the internal position of movements within the Muslim community, but also the status of those movements from the point of view of parts or the whole of the host society. It therefore makes sense to distinguish between forms of institutionalization which develop with this material support from the government, and those that occur without it.

Although we started from the assumption that existing legislation and regulation can influence the degree and nature of initiatives, influence in the opposite direction is also conceivable. It serves well to remember that the legal structure of various European countries is historically determined. For non-Christian religions and ideologies this may mean that the nature and practice of the organization or the needs of new groups for their own institutions are not accommodated by the rules. In such cases a debate may arise, appealing to the principles of freedom of religion and of equality, about changing the rules. This can result in an adjustment of the legislation and regulation, but also in the introduction of new rules to prevent the development of certain institutions.

The next factor is *the judiciary*. Originally we had not listed this institution separately, but during the research it became clear that the courts had an important and very special role to play.[11] The

---

[9] Cf. Rath *et al.* 1991.
[10] Cf. Landman 1992.
[11] Cf. Rath *et al.* 1992: 28–30.

help of the judiciary was called in when normal procedures ended in an impasse; for instance, when those involved were not sympathetic, or when they were unable or afraid to exercise their responsibilities. In practice the courts sometimes proved to have anticipated new legislation, or to have set the parameters within which future decisions could be taken.

Then there is *government*, here defined in the sense of the whole system of official bureaucracies and representative bodies, with the exception of the judiciary. The authorities are bound in their attitude and actions by existing legislation. If the initiatives and claims of new groups comply with these rules, in principle the authorities should honour them. Legislation and regulation are, however, continuously subject to change, and some changes restrict opportunities for religious groups to set up their own institutions. A drastic example is the change to the Dutch Constitution in 1983, which resulted in the severance of the links between church and state, and withdrew from the authorities the ability to provide a range of facilities for religious communities.

Another aspect we have to take into account is that the attitude of the government authorities is not exclusively legalistic when it comes to implementation. Although they are bound by the existing legislation, and are obliged by the Constitution to treat similar cases equally, they may have various options. To start with, the scope for flexibility in applying the rules is not always the same. For instance, in honouring claims for spiritual care for Muslims in prisons, hospitals or the armed services, flexibility is far greater than in the founding of private Muslim schools, at least in the Netherlands. Particularly when implementation is decentralized—on the grounds that local circumstances and preferences are more likely to be given their due weight—the rules and procedures are far from explicit, and lack detail. It is not always the intention to provide those responsible for implementation with more freedom of action, but the rules are often ambiguous. Politicians or civil servants who have to apply these rules in actual cases can use their judgement. In legal sociology it is accepted that application of the law often occurs within 'semi-autonomous social fields'. This refers to social systems which exist between the legislator and the individual, and which produce their own rules (Moore 1973). The intervention of the authorities is therefore influenced by political and ideological assumptions, as well as by the organizational environment of the agents involved in the

implementation of law and regulations. The attitude of the authorities can also change in the course of time. What was unthinkable
at one moment can later become normal practice. In this regard it
serves to remember that politicians and civil servants are in turn
exposed to the influence of other semi-autonomous social fields.
Political pressure from outside, or conflict within or among departments and higher and lower levels of authority, are factors which
can influence their attitudes and scope for action. Particularly at the
local level, municipalities can adopt divergent attitudes and apply
their political flexibility in different ways.[12]

In this connection, the development of policy in other areas is
also important. In most European countries the authorities have a
specific policy of integration for categories which they define as 'ethnic minorities' or 'immigrants'. These categories and those of Muslims
sometimes overlap each other considerably. It is likely that the aims
of integration policy may influence the attitude of the authorities
towards Muslim institutions. For this reason it is important to analyse
the possible interaction between different forms of policy (and the
associated definitions of target groups and problem formulations).
In view of the preoccupation of many government bodies with the
curtailment of national expenditure, we also assume that initiatives
and claims which have financial implications—sometimes considerable ones—will generally tend to arouse more opposition from the
authorities.

The government may be an important agent, but it certainly does
not act in isolation. Countless other interested parties feel called upon
to intervene in word or deed in the recognition of Muslim institutions, and so influence the attitude of the authorities. Examples are
interest groups, political parties and trade unions, but also residents
associations, businesses, and organizations for animal protection.
Within this diverse collection of organizations and institutions, we
distinguish between those founded on religious or ideological principles, and more generally based organizations. For it is likely that
both types—with their different views of the ideal society and the
role religion should play in it—attribute a fundamentally different
significance to the foundation of Muslim institutions.

---

[12] Cf. Feirabend & Rath 1996; see also: Hampsink 1992; Landman 1992; Rath
& Meyer 1994.

Although in recent years society has become much more secular, and many people no longer feel the need to lead their lives exclusively within the provisions and structures of their own religious community, organizations *based on religious or ideological principles* can still be an important power factor. Their attitude to the recognition and institutionalization of Islam can take several forms. It seems plausible that they will take a positive view of the emergence of new institutions based on religious principles, either from ideological considerations, or from political or strategic ones (the strengthening of organizations based on religious principles against other power blocs in society). But it is equally plausible that they will be in fierce opposition, for example on the grounds of orthodox religious arguments (the de-Christianization of society), or because of considerations of competition (drawing customers away from them). This much is certain: such organizations and institutions try to exert influence in their own interest, both on the maintenance or amendment of legislation, and on the attitude of the authorities.

The attitude of *organizations based on general principles* can also vary. Neutrality can be expected with respect to claims and initiatives which lie outside the sphere of public interest and which have few or no financial repercussions for society. Initiatives and claims which, if honoured, would have consequences in the public or semi-public sphere, can on the other hand expect opposition, resulting from the fear that society's dominant secular values may be questioned.

Finally we have included *other relevant institutions* in the model. This is a residual category in which we place institutions such as the media and academia. We assume that the influence they bring to bear on Muslims and their institutions will focus on the attitude of the authorities, but it may also fall on the initiatives which Muslims may take. Negative examples are the articles by some journalists on 'the advance of the Islamic threat' or the 'clash of civilizations'. On the positive side might be the effects—which may be interpreted as encouraging to some Muslims—of academics such as Klop (1982), who argued in the Netherlands for the inclusion of Islam in the Christian Democratic Party (CDA).

So far we have discussed the development and recognition of Muslim institutions in various spheres and the different factors which might play a role. With the model we have explained here, we are in a position to determine which legal and political processes take place and who or what institutions are involved. If, however, we

want to gain some insight into the question of why certain initiatives by Muslims succeed in gaining support, or are at least tolerated, and others not, this model is not sufficient. For that we must
move a step further and address the third key question of our research:
how is the debate about institutionalization conducted, and how do
those involved justify their actions? How do they view the legislation in force? To what extent and subject to which conditions do
they consider it to apply in the cases in question? What idealized
image of society, of Islam, and of Muslims is hidden behind all this?
With these questions we come to the ideological context in which
the process of institutionalization and the recognition of Muslim institutions takes place.

Ideological concepts

The ideological context shows how people perceive reality, and how
they give meaning to it. Their ideological conceptions, or representations, need not form any coherent or reasoned views about human-
ity. They usually take the form of a system of common-sense notions
about how society, and the social relationships within it, should operate. Such ideological assumptions have a two-fold social significance.
They not only give direction to social life, and form a guideline for
actions, but they also give legitimacy to a specific course of events.
The primary expression of these assumptions, however inconsistent
or unreasoned they may be, occurs in written and spoken language:
in a discourse.

The discourse carried on therefore informs us about the ideological assumptions of the agents, and at the same time provides insight
into the causes of their actions. This does not mean that their ideological conceptions and actions have to be in complete accordance
with each other. To some extent this is associated with legal or political circumstances, in the sense that the law or political forces can
command or forbid certain actions. Thus an official or politician
might be a supporter or opponent of the foundation of schools based
on religious principles, but depending on the legislative context current at the time, he or she may be obliged to assist in their advancement or, alternatively, to oppose them. It is also the case that a
discourse is often ambiguous, and can consist of different, sometimes
contradictory ideological conceptions. Civil servants or politicians
may accept the foundation of Muslim schools because schools based

on religious principles are clearly a constitutionally based and generally accepted institution, but they may have considerable problems with the fact that the pupils almost without exception come from immigrant families.

To gain an insight into the interaction between the ideological conceptions and the actions of the agents involved, we pose the following central questions. Which subjects and arguments are advanced in the debate about Islam? Who introduces them, how, when, why, and to what effect? We assume that we will encounter three dimensions in this discourse. Most of the conceptions can be reduced to the first dimension: ideologies about the nation state and the internal distribution of rights and obligations, and the related social goods and services. The second dimension concerns the ethnic-cultural distinctions in society; the third, religious differences.

Distribution of rights and obligations within the state

Who is a full member of the community of the state, and for that reason has full rights and duties? Is that membership mainly or exclusively granted to individuals, or is there also a role for groups? Opinions differ, and we distinguish three variants: an ideology of citizenship, an ideology of residence, and an ideology of a plural society in which group rights play a dominant role.

The *ideology of citizenship* assumes that members of a nation have certain common features (such as origin, culture, religion and so on). The imagined commonality, and the distinction from others inherent in it, is expressed in the notion of citizenship, a formalized criterion for the distinction between 'full members' of the nation state and 'foreigners'. This becomes clear, for example, when the state employs the self-assumed right to decide on the admission or deportation of citizens of foreign states. The granting or withholding of rights for foreigners living legally in the state's territory (such as political rights, but also the right to provisions from the state, or to the acquisition of citizenship) forms another clear instance of this conception. That the commonality is only an ideological assertion should be clear; it takes no account, for instance, of class or gender differences. This ideology can, however, have consequences for Muslims living within the frontiers of the nation state. If they are regarded primarily as foreigners, they have *de jure* an inferior position in law, and can consequently make less claim on social goods and services. As a result they also receive less support from the authorities for the realization of their own institutions. By extension, Islam as such can be regarded as an alien religion.

The *ideology of residence* assumes that it is not the common possession of certain characteristics, but residence, that is the decisive factor for membership of the state. In this view social goods and services are not reserved for citizens, but are available for all long-term residents, regardless of nationality. In the welfare state as it has developed in recent years in many European countries, this ideology has clearly gained in importance. Equal rights and minimum economic standards are guaranteed to all residents, including foreigners who are admitted into the state. In practice we see that once they are admitted as immigrants, and the longer they stay, the fundamental equality of all residents gains in significance. This does not mean that differences do not remain between the various countries.

Both these ideologies place the distribution of rights and obligations, and of social goods and services, firmly at the level of the individual. Citizens and residents in this respect are in a direct relationship with the state. However, this is by no means self-evident. It is also possible to distribute goods and services to collectivities within the state, and to do so through intermediary institutions associated with these collectivities. The 'pillarized system' in the Netherlands is an outstanding example of this. Over a long period an extensive system of legislation, regulation, and other institutions was developed within which the state distributed financial and other provisions among the various religious or ideological 'communities'—the pillars. The implementation of government policy therefore lay partly in the hands of organizations within these pillars. For Muslims and Islam such an *ideology of a plural society* offers opportunities based on group rights because it is founded primarily on religion and collective organizations.

Ethnic-cultural diversity
The second dimension is related to the question of how the position of immigrants in society is perceived. In current public discussion the concept of 'integration' is a popular one. The content of this concept, and the political conclusions associated with it, are closely linked to ideas about the way in which the imagined community of the nation is ideally seen, about the place immigrants should have in it, and about the role their culture should play in it. It should be noted that this is no longer an analytical concept of integration, but a normative one.

Within this dimension at least two typical opposite poles can be distinguished. The first is a *pluralist ideology*, in which society, now and in the future, is perceived as culturally heterogeneous. In such a society respect for separate cultural identity goes together with equal rights and opportunities, although this is not automatically the case (as shown by the former apartheid system in South Africa). Groups of immigrants, like indigenous cultural groups, should be able to form their own organizations or institutions. In this view strong emphasis is placed on the level of the collective.

Diametrically opposed to this is an *ideology of assimilation*. The ideal type of society is in this case an individualized and explicitly culturally homogeneous society. Each individual in it has equal rights and opportunities, and the government guarantees this equality in the public sphere with universally applicable rules. Immigrants should, like everyone else, comply with these common rules which are implicitly or explicitly regarded as universal. Group formation on the basis of a separate cultural identity, with separate organizations and institutions, is in this view considered undesirable or even a threat to national unity or to the position of others. (The only group formation which is acceptable in this point of view is that of the nation itself.)

There are a large number of variants between these two ideal types. In each sphere the emphasis is sometimes laid on the individual, and then again on the collective of which people are assumed to make up a part. We can define this chaos of variants by the term *integrationism*, which is exclusively reserved for the mixed forms.

Religious diversity
This dimension refers to the function that religion in general, and Islam in particular, occupies in society: Is an important place allotted to it, or do people favour the exclusion of religion from public life as much as possible? In the first case it is conceivable that people might only want to give room to specific religions; for instance because they consider one particular faith superior, and all the others mere heresies. When they see certain perceived norms and values as being in conflict with important perceived norms and values of the 'modern Western' or 'liberal Christian' society, they will try to restrict the scope for institutionalization as much as possible.

With the analytical framework explained in this section, we have formulated the basic assumptions for our research into the reactions of the host society to the intitutionalization of Islam. In the next and final section of this chapter we explain how we have applied these assumptions to our research in practice.

Method and structure of research

We have divided the research into three levels: national, local and international. First of all national discussions and reactions, and the emergence of national institutions are investigated. Although important, these national developments do not always indicate what happens at the local level, for general rules have to be applied in practice, and all kinds of local political and ideological influences play a role. Moreover, Muslims are locally concentrated to some extent which may influence their relative power position. The total picture gained in this way within a single society only comes into focus when a comparison is made with what is going on in other countries.

By carrying out research at three different levels, the area to be covered is very extensive. We have therefore opted to focus on a number of well-defined subjects and partial studies. Within them we have collected specific material through a literature search, archive research, and interviews with those involved. We have also concentrated on the situation in a few countries: the centre of gravity of the research is in the Netherlands, with comparisons on a more aggregated level with the situation in Belgium and the United Kingdom.

The case of the Netherlands is interesting. In an earlier period of history a society emerged in which religion and ideology were among the most important social determinants.[13] The social groupings made up on the basis of religion or ideology formed 'pillars'; these were more or less closed communities, within which the whole of social life was played out from the cradle to the grave. Each pillar had its own institutions, ranging from hospitals, daily and weekly papers, broadcasting networks, schools and universities, to trade unions, small-business associations and political parties, and even choral societies. There was virtually no social interaction between the pillars, except at the top where accommodation between them was arranged, and where the political leaders carried on close mutual consultation, avoided threatening conflicts and secured their own interests. In the

---

[13] See, for example, Lijphart 1975; Van Schendelen 1984.

developing welfare state, pillarized organizations were closely involved in the creation and implementation of government policy, not least in the distribution of social goods and services to citizens, which justified their existence. This state of affairs was embedded both in social and political practice, and in legislation and regulation. Although there was opposition to pillarization while the system was being built up, its influence was limited. Not until the 1960s, with the process of secularization and the decline in church influence, did the pillarized organizations lose their dominant position, and see their automatic involvement in policy diminish. Legislation was accordingly altered on a number of points, with, as its provisional culmination, the constitutional amendments of 1983. These involved the redemption of a large number of government obligations (including financial ones) to the churches, and the separation of church and state entered a new phase. The individual, rather than the religious or ideological collective, acquired a central importance.

Although the two processes of the advance of Islam and the decline of pillarization occurred more or less simultaneously, they were in a sense contradictory. This historical accident was unfortunate for the Muslims, not least because the automatic way in which religions acquired a recognized place in society was affected. On the other hand, the process of depillarization is still far from complete, if indeed that were possible. Many of the old social, political and legal practices and structures are still wholly or partially intact. The question now is to what extent Muslims have demanded and acquired in this arena opportunities to shape their identity and institutions according to their own agenda.

For our research in the Netherlands at the *national level* (Part 1) we collected all the available documentation on Muslim institutions and the reactions to them: articles in newspapers and journals, brochures, parliamentary papers, theses and academic papers. On the strength of this we provide in Chapter 2 a bird's-eye view of how Dutch society and government have reacted to the increasing presence of Muslims. The material collected enabled us to obtain an overall picture of Muslim institutions in the Netherlands, and the spheres or domains in which they occur. On the basis of this review we chose three spheres, which have been studied with the help of additional material, and on which we can therefore report more comprehensively in this book: the spheres of religion (Chapter 3), education (Chapter 4), and politics (Chapter 5, first section).

The spheres of religion and education in particular are examined in more detail, since it is here that numerous initiatives have been deployed at the national level. This applies rather less to the political field. The four other domains (the legal, socio-economic, and socio-cultural spheres, and health and social services) are dealt with in a short summary, since there is much less development of Muslim institutions in these areas (Chapter 5, second section).

For a few specific studies on the institutionalization of ritual circumcision for boys, financial support for Muslim places of worship, and the national political representation of Islam we received assistance from Masters students Niek van den Dungen, René Hampsink and Hasan Yar respectively.[14]

The research in the Netherlands at the *local level* (Part 2) was mainly carried out in two cities, Rotterdam and Utrecht. The choice of these cities was based on prior general knowledge: Rotterdam appeared to have a relatively active and explicit policy for Muslim organizations and institutions, while this did not seem to be the case in Utrecht. Moreover, there were indications that Utrecht had a rather reserved attitude in such matters. A comparison of the two cities should, it was thought, be able to provide more insight into the political and ideological contexts to the way in which the established society reacted to Muslim institutions, and its sociological significance.

In these cities we carried out the research in the three spheres listed above, though focusing on specific subjects. We begin this part with the political domain, concentrating on the recognition of Muslim organizations as dialogue partners in local politics (Chapter 7). In the sphere of religion attention is paid to places of worship (Chapter 8), and in that of education to the introduction of Islamic religious instruction (Chapter 9) and the emergence of Muslim schools (Chapter 10).

For part of the research in Utrecht we have had the assistance of two Masters students at the University of Utrecht: Jeroen Feirabend and Christa van Marrewijk.[15] In addition, Judith Roosblad made a special study of the foundation of a Muslim primary school in Amsterdam.[16]

---

[14] See Hampsink 1991, 1992; Van den Dungen 1993; Yar 1993.
[15] See Feirabend 1993; Van Marrewijk 1993; Feirabend & Rath 1996.
[16] See Roosblad 1991, 1992.

Finally we carried out *comparative international research* on a limited scale (Part 3). When it came to choosing countries, Belgium (Chapter 12) was obvious, because both the Netherlands and Belgium have a recognizably pillarized structure, and the Muslim populations in both countries display strong similarities. Most of the Muslims consist of Turks and Moroccans, who arrived in both countries at the same time and for the same reasons, and now find themselves in roughly similar circumstances. Of the countries researched by us, Belgium is the only one in which the government can on the basis of existing legislation officially recognize a religious denomination with a single stroke of the pen. The government of Belgium can also grant the most direct financial support.[17] On the strength of an article of the constitution, the government pays the salaries and pensions of spiritual leaders, without any obligations being incurred in exchange. To be eligible for this financial support the denomination involved must be recognized legally. When this occurs, a commission is set up by legislation or by royal decree to supervise the religion's temporal goods, and also to function as a liaison between the denomination and the civil authorities. In addition, local religious communities can submit a request for formal recognition, which may be granted by royal decree. The criteria used by the authorities for this process are not established in law and can therefore vary, so that there is room for political and ideological manoeuvring.

Besides Belgium we chose Great Britain (Chapter 13) as an example of a country virtually without pillars. Furthermore, the Muslim population there is different, as was the history of their arrival. Unlike Belgium, legislation in Great Britain is not based upon the concept of recognition (Nielsen 1987: 27). In England there is an *established church*. Its position is reflected in such things as the status of canon law, the procedures for the appointment to high ecclesiastical office, the organization of church courts, and in the representation of the church in the House of Lords (Commissie-Hirsch Ballin 1988: 168). Moreover, the monarch is also the head of the Church of England. Other faiths have a different, usually less privileged status. There are special *Acts of Parliament* for the older Christian denominations and for the Jews, but the rest are, as it is formulated, free to function

---

[17] The financial relationship between church and state is laid down in the Constitution (Commissie-Hirsch Ballin 1988: 143–146; Blaise & De Coorebyter 1990: 21 ff.).

within the limits of the law. However, the existing general legislation does not always take account of 'alien' religions such as Islam. Most legal provisions are based *implicitly* on the Christian faith or the Christian ethic, and therefore sometimes are an obstacle to the free practice of the Muslim religion.

As in the case of the Netherlands, in both countries we pay attention to the political, religious and educational spheres, and the four subsidiary themes within these domains. Linked to the recognition of Muslims as partners in the political debate, we also take a brief look at the recognition of Islam in the wider sense.

The international comparative research is mainly based on secondary literature, which entails a number of limitations. For instance, in the available literature, information about specific subjects or areas is not evenly distributed. We could not focus attention in the same systematic way that we could in the Netherlands on the ideological assumptions and arguments which might have been important. Therefore we can only make a few general observations on the international comparison in the concluding chapter (Chapter 15).

For part of the research in Great Britain we had the assistance of Jeanne van den Voort. In 1992 and 1993 she collected material on Islam and education, and the attempt to gain recognition for a Muslim school, the Islamia Primary School in London. In addition, at the international level we have drawn on Hasan Yar's MA thesis, referred to earlier, in which he makes a comparative study of the political recognition and representation of Islam at the national level in the Netherlands and Belgium. The collection of data for the book as a whole was completed in 1995.

We end each level, and so each part of the book, with a chapter bringing together the most important conclusions for the three key research questions for each level (Chapters 6, 11 and 14). The three levels are finally brought together again in the form of general conclusions in Chapter 15.

PART ONE

THE NETHERLANDS: THE INSTITUTIONALIZATION AND RECOGNITION OF ISLAM AT THE NATIONAL LEVEL

CHAPTER TWO

GOVERNMENT, SOCIETY AND ISLAM:
A BRIEF HISTORY

The Netherlands first came into contact with Islam at a time when
its people, as a nation of traders and a colonizing power, roamed the
world's oceans. Consequently their contact with this religion was an
indirect result of commercial and diplomatic involvement with the
Ottoman Empire, and Dutch colonial rule in the Netherlands East
Indies.[1] It was indirect, because these early contacts had little significance for the vast majority of Dutch society, and hardly induced any
reaction from its members.[2] This changed, and Islam acquired more
direct significance with the settlement of increasing numbers of
Muslims in the Netherlands. This chapter discusses how Dutch society
and the Dutch government first reacted to their growing presence.

The history of this reaction can be roughly divided into three periods. The first runs up to the early 1980s. Until then Islam had, as
it were, led a hidden existence in the Netherlands, and the reactions
of society and of the government were only *ad hoc* and of a frag-
mentary nature. The second period began around 1983, when Muslim
organizations started to attract notice, formulating their requirements
and claims with increasing clarity, demanding recognition and a more
consistent policy from society and the government. In this period
the government too, for a variety of reasons, found it necessary to
regulate several matters. The recognition emerging at this stage was
mainly a case of recognizing issues as they came up. The third and
most recent period set in towards the end of the 1980s. The prominent presence of Muslims and their growing institutionalization led
from this time onwards to a wider and more fundamental discussion about the place of Islam in Dutch society, now and in the
future. Before describing this institutionalization in each separate
sphere, this opening chapter will sketch out the main lines of that
development and its consequences.

---

[1] For contacts with the Ottoman Empire see: Theunissen *et al.* 1989.
[2] This led to specialized academic knowledge about Islam, albeit very much in
the service of the interests of colonial policy (Shadid & Van Koningsveld 1990a).

A hidden existence

The presence of Muslims in the Netherlands dates from before the Second World War. In its early stages this only affected a few local authorities and communities, such as The Hague, where small concentrations of Muslims had settled (Landman 1992: 20 ff.). Landman traces the first formal organization of Islam in the Netherlands back to 1932, when Indonesians in The Hague set up their first Muslim association. In the 1950s and early 1960s, new groups of Muslims, though limited in size, settled in the Netherlands. Some of the Moluccan soldiers from the Dutch East Indies Army, arriving in 1951, were Muslims, and there were small numbers of ex-Indian Muslims among the early immigrants from Surinam. They wanted and eventually obtained their own residential areas and facilities for religious activities.[3]

After 1965 the number of Muslims began to rise rapidly, with the arrival of ever increasing numbers of foreign workers from North Africa and Turkey. In 1971 the estimated number of Muslims was about 50,000; in 1975 it was already around 100,000, and by 1992 more than 414,000.[4] The Central Bureau of Statistics (CBS 1996:

---

[3] In 1956 a mosque was built in the Wyldemerk camp near Balk. The Dutch government paid for its building and maintenance, as well as for the salary of its spiritual leader, until the transfer of responsibility put an end to such payments in the 1980s. Moluccan Muslims in Ridderkerk and Waalwijk had to wait much longer for an official mosque: the number of Muslim families there was far too small (fewer than 35) for an official church building subsidy from the Ministry of Culture, Recreation and Social Work (Landman 1992: 32 ff.).

[4] Knippenberg (1992a, 1992b) estimated the number of Muslims in the Netherlands in 1992 at 414,000, around 2.7 per cent of the population. Their distribution over the Netherlands is, however, very uneven: in the west of the country, and particularly in the large towns, there are large concentrations. Outside the urban agglomeration in the West (the Randstad), the areas with the largest concentrations are the Brabant conurbation, Twente and central Gelderland. The figures given vary. The 1994 CBS *Statistical Yearbook* gives a total of 483,000 for 1 January 1992, or 3.2 per cent of the population (CBS 1994: 49). These differences apply particularly to recent years, because since the 1971 national census, no formal records are kept of religious affiliations, and the estimates are therefore based largely on the countries of origin of immigrants (see Beets & Oudhof 1982). They therefore cover mostly Turks and Moroccans, with smaller groups of Surinamese, Pakistanis, Indonesians, Tunisians and Egyptians. However, in these estimates account should be taken of the consequences of secularization and the decline of churchgoing, and the fact that not all immigrants from 'Islamic' countries are Muslims. There is also a group of Christian Turks, and there are political refugees from Iran. Taking this into account, and in view of the growth in the number of naturalizations, the number of 'Muslims' in the statistics can be expected to fall.

53) estimated the number of Muslims on 1 January 1995 at almost 628,000. These figures show that within a few decades Islam had become the second religion (or rather, the largest non-Christian religion) in the Netherlands. That sounds more spectacular than it really is: in fact it forms less than 3 per cent of the population in the Netherlands, and it often includes non-practising Muslims and even non-Muslim immigrants.

The growth in numbers has *not directly* led to a reaction by Dutch society or to its adoption of a particular stand. In the first period of increasing immigrant labour, the religious aspect was virtually hidden from society. Although prayer rooms were arranged within businesses for Muslim employees, there were few signs of Islam outside the work environment. The belief that these guest workers were only temporarily present in the Netherlands undoubtedly contributed to the scant attention paid to Islam.

This view is also reflected in the policy papers of this period. The 1970 *Memorandum on Foreign Workers* only devoted two sentences to Islam.[5] Religious provisions for these temporary foreign workers were defined in the Memorandum as a small part of the policy for the welfare of this group. Their faith may have been respected in principle, but there is no hint of any recognition which might have had consequences for Dutch society.

The related 1974 *Memorandum in Reply*, four years later, did not devote a single word to religious provisions. After various pressure groups objected to this silence,[6] the centre-left Den Uyl government proposed in the discussion of the Memorandum that grants for activities on Muslim festivals, and financial support for houses of prayer, should be considered, adding that exploratory research should first be undertaken.[7]

The research was conducted, and in the following period some facilities were made available and practical provisions arranged.[8] In

---

[5] After a sentence about the pastoral care for Catholic Italian and Spanish workers, the Memorandum continued: 'For those who are adherents of another religion, such as the Muslims, attempts will also be made to meet the needs expressed for pastoral care, including the observance of certain rites and customs. This can present difficulties, because in the Netherlands there has so far been so little contact with Islam' (*Handelingen van de Tweede Kamer der Staten-Generaal* (*Hand.* TK) 1969–1970, 10504, no. 1, p. 13).

[6] See: *Bijlagen Handelingen* (*Bijl. Hand.*) II 10504, no. 1, p. 3.

[7] *Bijl. Hand.* II TK 1974–1975, 10504, no. 12, p. 10.

[8] The survey of what was required resulted in the publication by Samuels and

1976 the Ministry of Culture, Recreation and Social Work announced a grant scheme for places of worship, and the Ministry of Public Health and Environmental Hygiene altered the Meat Inspection regulations, making ritual slaughter possible.[9] For the time being, however, such provisions were only a marginal phenomenon. Everything was based on the temporary nature of the immigrants' stay, for which a few welfare facilities were made available to help them maintain their identity.[10]

Towards the end of the 1970s, the tension between the 'fiction of temporality' and the actual long-term presence of many immigrants steadily increased. Family reunion took place on a large scale, and communities of immigrant groups were formed, in most cases Muslims. Gradually Muslim institutions emerged, at least in outline. Increasingly they set up their own organizations, and religion proved to be an important mobilizing force for Turks and Moroccans.[11] These organizations began to press harder for recognition of their own culture and religion.

In 1979 this tension between image and reality was set down in the report of the Scientific Council for Government Policy on *Ethnic Minorities* (*Etnische Minderheden*, WRR 1979), and in 1980 led to a major reformulation of policy planning in the government reaction to this report (Ministerie van BiZa 1980), and in the *Draft Minorities Memorandum* (*Ontwerp-Minderhedennota*, Ministerie van BiZa 1981). How-

---

Gransbergen (1975). The whole text of it is included as an appendix in Werkgroep-Waardenburg (1983: 137–183).

[9] See respectively: *Nederlandse Staatscourant* 1976, no. 75, p. 1, and *Staatsblad* 1977, no. 28. The second regulation had a mainly technical and organizational background: the prevention of the annual problems involved with the *Eid ul-Adha* (Festival of Sacrifice). The General Regulation concerning Subsidies for Places of Worship was integrated into the Policy for Cultural Minorities, as the former Department for Migrant Groups of the Ministry of Culture, Recreation and Social Work had been called since 1976.

[10] The actual survey into what was required, the recommendations arising from it, and the formulation of the 1976 subsidy arrangements, used the following phrases in turn, 'cultural minorities', 'cultural identity' and 'cultural-religious perceptions and needs of immigrants', to describe concepts to which in the context of 'environmental advancement justice should be done' (Samuels & Gransbergen 1975: 27; see also other documents in the appendices of the Waardenburg Working Party (Werkgroep-Waardenburg 1983)).

[11] For data on the relative importance of Muslim organizations within the totality of forms of organization among Turkish and Moroccan immigrants in particular, see: De Graaf 1983, 1985; De Graaf *et al.* 1988. For a description of the development of organizations of and within different Muslim groups, see: Landman 1992; for Turks, see also: Doomernik 1991.

ever, it is noticeable that religion in general and Islam in particular were hardly mentioned in these three papers.[12]

In short, in these years there was no question of Islam being integrated among the religious institutions in the Netherlands, and neither the administration nor politicians saw any need for a discussion on the principles involved.[13]

Breakthrough: de facto recognition and co-operation

Slowly Muslims began increasing their demands for the scope to exercise their freedom of religion, a fundamental right guaranteed by the Dutch Constitution. They based this on the following specific points: the establishment and funding of places of worship; entry to the country of spiritual leaders (imams); funeral arrangements; ritual slaughter; recognition of Muslim feast days; the public call to prayer; ritual circumcision of boys; religious instruction both within and outside the regular curriculum; establishment of their own schools; their own network and broadcasting time on radio and television; spiritual guidance and observance of dietary prescriptions in the armed forces, prisons and hospitals; recognition of Islamic family law; and participation in advisory bodies. All in all Muslims were working

---

[12] The report of the Scientific Council for Government Policy states that 'both in the law and in the rules and practice for their implementation, and in government and private institutions, many adjustments to the situation of a multi-ethnic society are still necessary and possible, without the cultural achievements of our society being affected: such adjustments are even in line with the constitutional rights mentioned previously' (WRR 1979: xxii). With some good will this pronouncement can also be interpreted in favour of religious rights, without actually referring to them as such. In the *Draft Minorities Memorandum*, Islam is mentioned four times: Muslims have freedom, within certain limits, to give form to their own internal relations; in doing so they must, like everyone else, keep to the general rules: for instance, civil marriage has precedence over religious marriage; family law will not be adapted (Ministerie van BiZa 1981: 283). Account must be taken of the dietary customs and religious festivals of members of minority groups in detention (ibid.: 280). Under the heading, 'improving relations', it states that the culture of foreign workers is very different to the Dutch, and is largely determined by the Muslim background of those involved (ibid.: 217). Finally, the *Draft Minorities Memorandum* states that Islam makes it particularly difficult for women to orient themselves in Dutch society (ibid.: 259).

[13] Among the reactions to the *Draft Minorities Memorandum* (Ministerie van BiZa 1982) were those of three Muslim organizations (A9, A10 and A17). They all commented on the absence of Islam from the Memorandum, and stated that what mention there was, was negative.

hard at developing their own institutions within Dutch society, in order to give shape to their religious communities.

The visible signs of this could soon be observed in many places. In 1975 the first 'real' mosque was opened in Almelo, complete with minaret, built with financial support from the government in accordance with the Church Building Subsidy Act. In 1975 a Muslim cemetery was opened in Rotterdam.[14] For anyone wishing to be buried in their country of origin, but unable to afford it, since 1986 there has been a Fund for Religious Services, which also offers occasional scholarships and supplements to welfare benefits. In 1977 the government legalized ritual slaughter according to the Islamic rite. In 1980 the first home for the elderly with provision for Muslims was created in Sint Michielsgestel. In 1986, with official approval and a government subsidy, the Islamic Broadcasting Foundation went on the air, to be followed in 1993 by the Netherlands Muslim Network. In Amsterdam, Rotterdam, The Hague and Eindhoven, the first schools based on Islamic principles opened their doors; by the end of the 1990s there were 30 such schools. An imam training course has been in existence for some time, since 1983 in The Hague. In 1984, at the instigation of a Dutch agent, the extension of the suffrage to non-Dutch nationals led to the formation of a Muslim political party in Rotterdam. In addition, there are now in various places Muslim conference centres, boarding schools, rehabilitation centres for drug addicts, libraries and shops. Islam in the Netherlands is now out in the open, active in many places and in various domains.

From 1983 onwards Islam attracted greatly increased attention as a result of a number of developments in certain areas. Muslim organizations not only became more prominent, but more attention was paid to Islam by the authorities, both in the minorities policy and in the discussions on the separation of church and state in the 1983 revision of the Constitution.

With an eye to the expiry of the temporary 1976 grant scheme for places of worship, the Interdepartmental Committee on Minorities Policy recommended in 1980 that the Ministry of Culture, Recreation and Social Work should temporarily continue the scheme. They also proposed,

---

[14] This provision had existed in The Hague since 1932, albeit intended primarily for Indonesians.

following further appropriate research, to advise on the desirability of arriving at arrangements for grants for religious provisions for the benefit of ethnic minorities in the context of the minorities policy.[15]

As a result, the ministry set up the Waardenburg Working Party, taken from outside the civil service, in August 1982.[16] This was given a closely-defined task: to make recommendations on the desirability of government subsidy for the provision of premises for religious minority groups (Werkgroep-Waardenburg 1983: 204). The Working Party itself enlarged this remit by basing its considerations not only on matters relevant to the minorities policy, but also on the constitutional principle of freedom of religion.[17] It published its recommendations in 1983, proposing that in future religious organizations be regarded as 'a very natural form of "interest organization" for people coming from cultures permeated by religion' (ibid.: B). In addition they argued for a range of facilities and arrangements in a variety of fields. The argument of equality of rights for all religions may well have played a certain role in their recommendations, but the dominant framework was that of 'ethnic minorities'. Islam was presented as just one of the cultural expressions of this category.[18]

In the definitive *Minorities Memorandum*, religion was given an explicit place for the first time (Ministerie van BiZa 1983: 110–123)—a place, admittedly, which again was formulated from the perspective of the minorities policy. Account was taken of the existence of new religions: amendments were announced to legal prescriptions which until then had been obstructive (on ritual slaughter and funerary arrangements). In addition the practice of religion was to be made possible by licensing religious leaders and by provisions for schools, in prisons and in the army. Finally, religious organizations were recognized as potential partners in implementing the minorities policy.

---

[15] Letter from the Minister of Culture, Recreation and Social Work to members of the Working Party on Religious Provisions for Minorities, dated 7 June 1982 (DWM-U-27854). See also: Werkgroep-Waardenburg 1983: 206 ff.

[16] The Working Party, under the leadership of Professor Waardenburg of Islamic Studies, was made up of seven academic experts and practitioners from welfare organizations. There were also several members from the target groups of the Minorities Policy.

[17] See letter submitting the report to the Minister in: Werkgroep-Waardenburg 1983: 0027X/I.

[18] One of the consequences—probably not intended by the Working Party—was to leave uncertain whether Muslim organizations of groups not recognized by the government as ethnic minorities, such as Pakistanis or Palestinians, were also eligible for the facilities.

Although the authorities now apparently had a more mature understanding that space must be created for Islam and other new religions, the implementation of the Waardenburg Working Party recommendations came up against political opposition, particularly the arrangements for new places of worship.[19] To understand this apparent contradiction, it is first necessary to describe a completely separate development which was taking place at about the same time: the separation of church and state in the Netherlands. Let us briefly examine its history.

Until late in the eighteenth century there was a close link, which was also a financial one, between the Dutch Reformed Church and the state.[20] This changed under the influence of the philosophy and institutions of the French Revolution. From the Batavian Revolution of 1796, a slow process began of separating church and state, which resulted in the status of the Dutch Reformed Church becoming 'normalized', while Roman Catholic and Jewish citizens were officially given equal rights with other citizens.[21] After 1946 there were discussions on ending the financial ties—the so-called silver strings—between some Christian churches and the state. This led to an agreement in 1981, and a law buying out the salaries and pensions of clergy and abolishing their rights to free postage.[22] In 1983 the relevant sections of the Constitution of the Netherlands were completely revised. In Article 1 new emphasis and recognition was given to the principle of equal rights, and in Article 6 equal protection was explicitly granted to religions and ideologies. The 1983 revision of the Constitution strengthened the bargaining position of Muslims, but at the same time the separation of church and state and the cutting of the 'silver strings' meant that direct financial links with any denomination, and so also with Islam, had to be avoided or ended. Therefore a separate grant arrangement for places of worship for minorities became a debatable matter.

---

[19] TK 16102, nos 55 and 99; Commissie-Hirsch Ballin 1988: 81; see also Chapter 3.

[20] The government appointed and paid the salaries of some Reformed Church ministers. Non-members of the Reformed Church were virtually excluded from many government offices (Commissie-Hirsch Ballin 1988: 22–23).

[21] It was not until the twentieth century, however, that Roman Catholic and other churches gained equal rights in education. Government funding of schools based on religious principles was only based on the principle of equal rights from 1917 onwards. This decision, arrived at after a long period of political strife, was a milestone in the construction of the pillarization of Dutch society (Stuurman 1983).

[22] Cf. Commissie-Hirsch Ballin 1988: 21–26.

However, this did not mean that the government now refrained from offering any form of support. On the contrary, it continued to create conditions for religious observances. To determine in more detail how various matters should be regulated after the amendments to the Constitution, in 1983 the ministers involved entered into discussions with representatives of Christian churches and of Humanist, Hindu and Muslim groups. The participation of Muslims in these discussions can be regarded as an important milestone in the actual recognition of Islam.

As a result of these discussions, in early 1986 the government set up the Advisory Committee for the Provision of Support for (Church) Communities, generally known as the Hirsch Ballin Committee.[23] It was given the task of making recommendations on some of the unresolved issues of previous discussions, and also on the possible subsidizing of places of worship.[24] The second Lubbers government thought that there was still a need for further discussion on these matters, despite earlier objections in the Second Chamber. The Hirsch Ballin Committee's report (1988) included in its recommendations the provision of spiritual facilities for Muslims (and Hindus) in public institutions, and the granting of subsidies for building and equipping places of worship.

The definitive reaction of the government to the recommendations of this Committee came from a new administration, the third led by Lubbers, in which Hirsch Ballin was one of the ministers. Unlike the Committee, and the Cabinet that had set it up, this government considered that a special grant arrangement for places of worship for 'ethnic minorities' was not necessary because the availability of places of worship was considered to have improved since the ending of the last arrangement in 1984. It did, however, agree to the proposals for spiritual care (Hampsink 1992: 25).

The surprising thing about the developments outlined above is that the discussions generally took place in a restricted circle made

[23] The chairman, Professor Hirsch Ballin from Tilburg, was later to become Minister of Justice in the third Lubbers Cabinet. The Committee consisted largely of lawyers. Prof. Waardenburg, chairman of the Waardenburg Working Party referred to above, was a member of the committee. See also Chapter 3.

[24] The Committee was asked to advise on 'the criteria for granting government finance and facilities to churches and other communities based on religious principles, with particular reference to the areas of spiritual care and the maintenance of buildings used by these communities' (Commissie-Hirsch Ballin 1988: 218).

up of the politicians, officials and organizations directly involved.
There was no question of a wide public discussion. The subjects
were rarely if ever explicitly on the agenda of political parties.
Meanwhile a practice developed by which ministers and officials recognized religious organizations *de facto* as important partners in the
minorities policy, and entered into consultation with them. The same
occurred in the context of the separation of church and state.

As far as the wider public was concerned the institutionalization
of Islam took place more or less behind closed doors, and very gradually. In certain circles the emergence of such institutions caused a
predictable uproar. Sometimes initiatives by Muslims found support
from individuals, organizations and institutions in society, and coalitions were formed on opportunistic or principled grounds. But often
they came up against opposition and obstruction. At a local level,
Dutch residents in a number of areas opposed the arrival of a mosque
in their neighbourhood. Applications to establish a Muslim school
unleashed many a furious debate and sometimes met with obstruction. Dutch organizations and institutions did not always welcome
Muslim initiatives, and offered resistance with a variety of arguments.
In the Second Chamber, certain orthodox Calvinist members opposed
the extension of the local suffrage to non-Dutch nationals, fearing
that Muslims would form their own political parties. The Society for
the Protection of Animals campaigned against the regulations allowing ritual slaughter, with the argument that animals should not suffer
unnecessary pain. Local authorities in a number of municipalities for
a long period opposed the opening of Muslim schools.

Political debate

Dramatic events in the 1980s and early 1990s provided concrete
occasions for the debate on Islam. There was the *fatwa* issued by
the Iranian leader Khomeini against Salman Rushdie for his *Satanic
Verses* in 1989, and the Gulf War in 1990. These events suddenly
made large sections of Dutch society aware that a substantial group
of Muslims lived among them in the Netherlands, and the political
and religious attitudes of Muslims were closely scrutinized.[25] But not
only that: these developments aroused anti-Islamic tendencies, and

---

[25] Cf. Shadid & Van Koningsveld 1992b; Rath & Sunier 1993.

also led to fundamental discussions on the place of Islam in the Netherlands.[26] By now individuals were advancing their opinions at every opportunity. In the early 1980s two professors, Couwenberg and Chorus, put the 'fundamental stumbling block of the Islamic religion' on the agenda. Couwenberg (1982) was of the opinion that,

> we can hardly be asked to accept the application of capital punishment, or the amputation of parts of the body as a punishment, or discrimination as a matter of principle against women; things which are regarded as entirely normal in Muslim circles.

Chorus (1981: 42–43) predicted that 'as soon as Muslim guest workers can act as a bloc, they will demand and achieve their own system of law as a way of life', adding ominously, 'and with OPEC behind them it is not easy to resist such demands'. According to this author, the Muslim 'militant religion' would infect the Dutch democratic system by measures such as the introduction, or re-introduction, of capital punishment and blood feuds. However, these writings still did not lead to wide public debate about the place of Islam.

This occurred 15 years later. The conservative liberal politician Bolkestein (1991a, 1991b) warned against the Muslim threat to European civilization, from a world characterized by bloody excesses, intolerance and oppression. His primary platform was the international debate about the economic and strategic military situation in Europe, after the disappearance of the traditional enemy, Soviet communism. This political leader had scented the change in the political wind correctly: shortly afterwards, in February 1995, the NATO ambassadors decided on new objectives, directed against advancing Muslim fundamentalism on the south flank of the NATO area. What gave Bolkestein special publicity was that he extended his fear to Muslim immigrants in the Netherlands. He expressed his anxiety that 'backward' Muslim culture was just around the corner as a result of the 'massive immigration' from Muslim countries. Muslims would never embrace Western liberal democratic principles, putting the unity of the nation at risk. Society should therefore seriously ask itself how much room should be given to Muslims to build up a

---

[26] Anti-Islamic views were expressed in a highly distasteful form in *De ondergang van Nederland. Land der naïeve dwazen* (*The Decline of the Netherlands. Land of Naïve Fools*), published in 1990 by Mohamed Rasoel. For an analysis of this affair, see: Shadid & Van Koningsveld 1992b: 5–23.

religious community according to their own ideas. Bolkestein's warn-
ings brought about a spate of reactions.

One of the more fundamental issues in the debate involved the
question of how much freedom the Muslim newcomers should be
given for setting up and running their own institutions. The positions taken on this demonstrate the two different perceptions of the
'imagined' Dutch society.[27] On one side were the leaders of the
Christian Democratic Party (CDA) such as Lubbers and Brinkman,
who supported traditional 'pillarization' as a model for the social
participation of Muslims, thereby allotting an important role to religion and institutionalization. On the other side were the political leaders of the Liberal Party (VVD) and Democrats 66 (D66), such as
Bolkestein and Van Mierlo. They opposed this confessional thinking, and considered religion to be an obstacle to emancipation.
Bolkestein publicly challenged the notion that the practice of the
Islamic faith was compatible with membership of Dutch society.

In addition to politicians, in recent years academics have also aired
explicit opinions on the place of Islam in Dutch society, and on the
possible formation of a new Islamic pillar as a route to emancipation
at a time when the dominant trend was towards de-pillarization.[28]
Klop, on the staff of the research office of the Christen Democratic
Party (CDA), acknowledged that differences in the national origins
of Muslims had a role to play in the formation of a possible Islamic
pillar, but he predicted that within a few generations these would

[27] For a more detailed description of the positions taken, see: Rath *et al.* 1992.
[28] Cf. Rath *et al.* 1992. That Islam in the Netherlands for a long time existed
in concealment is reflected in academic research. The first scholarly publications
only appeared in the late 1970s. For three reviews of research into Islam in the
Netherlands, see Strijp 1990; Tennekes 1991; Rath *et al.* 1992. There is a biblio-
graphical review in Van Ooijen *et al.* 1991. Earlier publications are: Theunis 1979;
Wagtendonk 1982; Waardenburg 1983, 1986. Originally these were almost all theological publications, in which Islam, as a religion, occupied an important place.
These were often intended to help inform the Dutch about this 'new' religion. Not
until the late 1980s did interest grow in social-science circles, particularly among
anthropologists. The development of organizations and institutions among the various Muslim groups from different countries then became a central issue. A third
point of interest for researchers was the development of the image of Islam in society, and its consequences (Shadid & Van Koningsveld 1990b, 1992b; Shadid 1994).
The research of Shadid and Van Koningsveld was mainly based on an examination of negative images of Islam, in which they tended to reduce the whole debate
about immigrants from Turkey and Morocco to an anti-Islamic tirade (see Rath &
Sunier 1993).

be reduced to a 'flourishing folklore'. Islam and Hinduism would become established as religious communities and cultural influences. He called on the authorities not to waste time on whether they wanted an Islamic pillar in the Netherlands, but to give serious thought to how it could be achieved as advantageously as possible (Klop 1982). The Reverend Slomp wrote in reaction to this that Klop's reasoning was utterly false. In his view there was no Islamic religious community; just an enormous ideological and organizational internal diversity. Moreover, Muslim customs were quite different from those of either Roman Catholics or Protestants. In Slomp's view (1983: 107), Klop was mistakenly trying 'to impose a Dutch stamp on the *corpus alienum*, the foreign body of Muslim minorities, which had settled within Dutch society'. Others felt that applying the classical pillarization model presented problems, and produced several reasons for this, such as the small number of Muslims, their heterogeneity, lack of leadership and changed political and economic circumstances.

The point of view of the sociologist Van Ree (1995) was of a different order. He claimed that Dutch culture had undergone a drastic historical development: in the last two centuries the process of secularization had advanced, while public morality had shifted towards permissiveness at the expense of Christianity. In his view the Dutch now benefited from

> a historically unprecedented free climate in which homosexual televi-
> sion presenters enjoy general popularity, blasphemous books can be
> published without anyone turning a hair, and husbands publicly claim-
> ing that their wives belong in the kitchen can count on a compas-
> sionate smile.

These liberties we have gained will soon be lost, he wrote, as a result of the arrival of immigrants from regions which

> still bear a much stronger religious stamp, and where in the areas of
> relations between the sexes, education and sexuality, views still domi-
> nate which we have long ago abandoned (ibid.).

In particular the advent of Islam as a religious community would produce fundamental problems on this point. However, this sociologist thought there was little to be done about it. As a democratic state the Netherlands should continue to allow all its citizens the same rights, and we would as a result find traditional Muslim ethics gain-ing a democratic counterpart in the form of all kinds of institutions.

The arguments which were exchanged in the many discussions seemed very diverse. Some emphasized prejudices, rooted in history, against Islam, and stressed the universal nature of the debate. Others put the accent on matters of principle, such as whether the norms and values of Islam and Muslim groups were compatible with those of the basically Christian society of the Netherlands. Others again saw the position of religious and other minorities in the Netherlands as the central issue. They argued about whether and how the Dutch tradition of pillarization could serve as a model for the emancipation of Muslim immigrant groups.

Three fundamental legal principles were always central to both the general debate about the position of Islam and the particular discussions on the recognition of separate institutions of that faith: freedom of religion, equality before the law, and the separation of church and state. Article 6, Section 1 of the Constitution guarantees the right to profess a religion or philosophy of life freely as individuals or in the company of others, obviously subject to every citizen's responsibility before the law. Article 1 of the Constitution decrees equal treatment and forbids discrimination on grounds of religion. Alongside these two principles stands the separation of church and state. Scholars of constitutional law are in agreement that in any event this principle implies that the state may not interfere in the internal affairs of churches, although their opinions differ on the precise interpretation of Article 6 of the Constitution. Some, like Hirsch Ballin (1983)[29] and Den Dekker-Van Bijsterveld (1988), believe that it goes further than simply guaranteeing freedom of religion. They think that the Constitution has a social component: everybody, including the weaker socio-economic members, should be able to exercise their freedom of religion to the full. The authorities therefore have a duty to make provisions for its observance, and Hirsch Ballin had this to say on the responsibility of the state:

> The state can, and in some circumstances must, give help (subsidies) for the realization of the conditions for freedom of religion when full exercise of that freedom would otherwise be prevented (1983: 275).

A more restrictive interpretation of the principle of the separation of church and state comes from the Council of State's Department

---

[29] In his capacity as constitutional lawyer, not as a Minister.

for the Administration of Justice. In 1987 it determined that no financial claims on the authorities could be derived from Article 6 of the Constitution.[30] It should be noted that the Department made no pronouncement on the possible *acceptability* of state support: it stated only that support by the state could not be claimed as a right.

While the debate continued in all kinds of circles, the actual consolidation and expansion of the institutionalization of Islam was taking place in a number of areas. The next three chapters discuss how this institutionalization was achieved. This is done in terms of the spheres outlined in Chapter 1. As already stated, attention at the national level is mainly focused on the spheres of religion and education, and to a lesser degree on that of politics. Within these spheres four themes are covered: places of worship, Islamic religious instruction, Muslim schools, and the participation of Muslims in consultative structures.

---

[30] The cause was the question of whether a municipality ought to subsidize a Protestant institution for social work, when they had already voted to extend subsidies to a single general institution in which all religions and ideological tendencies were represented. The Department of Justice approved the municipality's actions (Administratiefrechtelijke Beslissingen 1987, no. 287; see also Hampsink 1992: 9, note 2).

CHAPTER THREE

THE SPHERE OF RELIGION

The sphere of religion covers a range of key religious institutions such as places of worship, the clergy, religious festivals, the public call to prayer, and the prescriptions and usages founded on religion or religious practices for ritual slaughter, diet and funeral rites. This chapter describes the development of these key institutions of the Islamic religion.

Places of worship

Places of worship rank among the central public institutions of the Muslim faith. They fulfil not only religious functions, but also specific social, cultural and political ones.[1] Muslims have seen reason enough to take their establishment energetically in hand. They built their first mosques in the Netherlands in the 1950s: in The Hague (1955) and in Balk in Friesland (1956).[2] From the early 1960s onwards they created small simple places of worship in numerous commercial and domestic buildings. Over the years, more and more larger places of worship have also appeared. These have sometimes been purpose-built, as in Almelo, Ridderkerk and Eindhoven; more often, however, they were established in former churches or synagogues, school buildings, shops or factories. Landman (1992: 331) put the number of places of worship in 128 municipalities at 'more than 300' by early 1988;[3] six years later he estimated the total to be more than 380 (see also Table 1).[4]

---

[1] See, *inter alia*, Theunis 1979; Wagtendonk 1982; De Graaf 1985; Shadid & Van Koningsveld 1990a; Doomernik 1991; Landman 1992.
[2] For Pakistani and Moluccan Muslims respectively. See Theunis 1979: 379; Waardenburg 1983; Landman 1992: 30–35.
[3] Landman actually arrived at several different estimates: on page 43 he talks of about 300 mosques in 1990, while on page 331 of 'about 300 mosques in 128 municipalities'. Assuming that the latter estimate is based on his inventory by municipality, then the date should be fixed in early 1988. According to Shadid and Van Koningsveld (1990a: 25), 'on the basis of data supplied by the appropriate national organizations, the total number of places of worship and mosques in the Netherlands [can] be estimated at about 300'. They do not elaborate on these 'data' or where they can be consulted.
[4] In the course of a paper delivered at an NWO symposium, on 25 November 1994.

Even in the early stages, the Muslims who generated plans for places of worship were already thinking in terms of their being financed—wholly or partly—by the Dutch authorities. This is hardly surprising: in the post-war period the national government provided grants on a large scale for building churches. Under the terms of the Church Building Subsidy Act (*Wet Premie Kerkenbouw*) alone, almost 112 million guilders was disbursed for this purpose between 1961 and 1975, a sum almost completely absorbed by Christian congregations.[5] The 1980s, however, saw an acceleration in the efforts on the part of the authorities towards the total separation of church and state, a tendency which was completely at odds with the provision of financial support for building new places of worship—including mosques.

In the past 30 years the legislation has been subject to so many changes that building places of worship for any denomination, including Islamic ones, has sometimes qualified for subsidy and sometimes not. This legislation will be discussed briefly,[6] as will two reports calling for grant schemes.

Table 1: Estimated numbers of Muslims and Muslim places of worship in selected municipalities in 1988

	Total population × 1,000	Total Muslims × 1,000	%	Registered places of worship
Amsterdam	695	60	8.6	28
Rotterdam	576	48	9.2	29
The Hague	444	28	6.3	20
Utrecht	231	22	9.5	10
Arnhem		6		3
Nijmegen		5		4
Breda		4		1
Venlo		3		2

Source: Landman (1992: 287–305).

---

[5] *Bijl. Hand.* II 1981–1982, 16559, no. 5, p. 3. This sum was disbursed for 770 church buildings in total, for which permits were issued to contractors between 1 March 1961 and 1 March 1975.

[6] Those stipulations which are not directly relevant to Muslims will not be dealt with, such as the Regulation on War Damage to Church Buildings (*Oorlogsschaderegeling Kerkelijke Gebouwen, Nederlandse Staatscourant* 1949, no. 92), the Regulation on Financing

Grant regulations

The Church Building Subsidy Act (1962–1982)
In the early 1950s some local authorities subsidized the building of
churches, while others emphatically refused to do so. From the point
of view of consistent administration, the national government considered this situation irregular and unacceptable. The first step towards
a more uniform arrangement followed in 1954 when Minister Beel
for Internal Affairs (a member of the Catholic People's Party, KVP)
spoke out against the refusal by the Provincial Executive of the
Province of Gelderland to grant the municipality of Nijmegen the
power to subsidize a Roman Catholic church.[7] By Royal Decree it
was ruled that in this case the granting of a subsidy should in fact
be permitted.[8] Of more fundamental importance in this decision was
the recognition that local authorities were competent to grant subsidies for building churches. Beel's contribution to the affair was nevertheless a national rather than a local competence: in 1955 he duly
appointed a Committee, chaired by the Catholic Sassen, to investigate the extent to which, and how, uniform subsidies for church
congregations should be provided by the government.[9]
   Two years later this so-called Sassen Committee brought out a
report in which it proposed a legally framed, nationwide government
contribution towards the church building costs (Commissie-Sassen
1957). Four years later, in February 1961, the government submitted
a bill, based on this report, comprising a grant scheme for places of
worship.[10] In 1962 a majority in parliament voted in favour of the
Church Building Subsidy Act, which came into effect that same year.[11]

Church Buildings in the Noordoostpolder (*Regeling Financiering Kerkenbouw in de
Noordoostpolder*) of 31 March 1955 (*Hand.* II 1953–1954, pp. 3351 & 3362; *Bijl. Hand.*
II 1953–1954, 3200 B, no. 6 en 7), the Regulation on Financing Church Buildings
in the IJsselmeerpolders (*Regeling Financiering Kerkenbouw in de IJsselmeerpolders*, Ministerie
van Verkeer en Waterstaat, 28 June 1962), and the Flood Damage Act (*Wet op de
Watersnoodschade*, Staatsblad 1953, no. 661).
   [7] *Provincieblad* 1953, no. 185; *De Gemeentestem* 1954, no. 5261.
   [8] Koninklijk Besluit (KB) of 9 August 1954, no. 12, *Administratiefrechtelijke Beslissingen*
1954, pp. 603–606; *De Gemeentestem* 1954, no. 5296, pp. 164–165.
   [9] Order of the Minister for Internal Affairs, 14 December 1955, no. U 19752.
   [10] *Bijl. Hand.* II 1960–1961 & 1961–1962, 6260. In contrast to the proposals of
the Sassen Committee, in the bill local authorities were forbidden to make financial
contributions to churches.
   [11] *Hand.* II, 22 May 1962, pp. 3851–3918; *Staatsblad* 1962, no. 538. The Catholic
Party (KVP) was unanimously in favour of the bill, the Communists (CPN), the

Although the Sassen Committee, the government and parliament had primarily Christian denominations in mind, during parliamentary discussions on the bill it was agreed that legally recognized bodies based on religious principles, such as the Humanist Society or the 'Mohammedans', would be equated with the churches. This equivalence was the result of the amendment moved by MP Scheps (Labour, PvdA) who, based on the principle of equality before the law, wanted other religious faiths besides Christianity to be considered for support.[12]

In 1971 the period of the Act's validity was extended,[13] but in 1982 it was repealed without any similar arrangements to succeed it.[14] Just before its repeal, use was made of the Church Building Subsidy Act to build just one mosque, that in Almelo.[15]

General Regulation concerning Subsidies for Places of Worship (1976–1981)
In the *Memorandum on Foreign Workers* of 1970, Minister Roolvink of Social Affairs and Public Health (Calvinist Anti-Revolutionary Party, ARP), wrote that the government should try to meet the requirements for spiritual care of 'those who are members of another religion, such as the Muslims'.[16] In the interim report following this Memorandum, the views of members of the government were requested on the possibility of support by the authorities for the spiritual care of Muslims and on the 'probably essential subsidization of the costs of provision of accommodation, buildings, etc., which are no doubt necessary for the practice of this religion'.[17] The *Memorandum of Reply* to the interim report, however, was silent about any form of support by the authorities.[18] During the discussion, members of the Catholic People's Party (KVP) and the two main Calvinist parties (ARP and CHU) returned to this point. They regretted that there was no mention at all in the *Memorandum of Reply* of the 'emphatic

Pacificists (PSP), and most Calvinist parties (ARP, GPV & SGP) were all unanimously against it, while Labour (PvdA), the Liberals (VVD), and the Christian Historicals (CHU) were divided.

[12] *Bijl. Hand.* II 1961–1962, 6260, no. 12; *Hand.* II, 24 May 1962, p. 3916.

[13] *Staatsblad* 1971, no. 169.

[14] *Staatsblad* 1982, no. 538; *Bijl. Hand.* II 1980–1981 & 1981–1982, 16559.

[15] A subsidy of Fl. 57,650 was obtained. For an account of this case, see Hampsink 1992: 31 ff.

[16] *Bijl. Hand.* II 1969–1970, 10504, no. 1, p. 13.

[17] *Bijl. Hand.* II 1970–1971, 10504, no. 5, p. 20.

[18] *Bijl. Hand.* II 1973–1974, 10504, no. 9.

need to create more and improved opportunities for spiritual care',
which they had stressed in the interim report. The Labour Party
(PvdA), too, pressed for subsidies for 'the provision of premises which
could serve as mosques'.[19] In defining their position, they emphasized the many functions of a place of worship for Muslims.[20] Minister
Van Doorn of Culture, Recreation and Social Work (Radical Party,
PPR), spoke positively about direct grants for building Muslim places
of worship,[21] but decided that an investigation into what was needed
should be carried out first.[22] As a result of this investigation the
General Regulation concerning Subsidies for Places of Worship (*Globale
Regeling inzake Subsidiëring Gebedsruimten*) was announced in 1976.[23] The
central objective of this temporary scheme was 'to facilitate the process
of integration into Dutch society (while retaining their own cultural
values and religion)' (Werkgroep-Waardenburg 1983: 64). According
to an official of the Ministry's Section for the Welfare of Foreign
Workers, charged with the implementation of the General Regulation,
this was a necessary part of winning Muslims over to the integration policy. Were it not for the scheme, they would never have
agreed to discuss anything else. The official also ventured that integration would benefit from the creation of a kind of Dutch Islam,
independent of finance from abroad.

The scheme in fact applied only to those Muslims who had in
the past been recruited as guest workers, and their families; not to
Surinamese Muslims. This restriction, according to the same official,
was because there was a difference of opinion concerning subsidies
between the Section for the Welfare of Foreign Workers and the
Section for the Welfare of Moluccans, Surinamese and Caravan
Dwellers, both part of the Ministry of Culture, Recreation and Social
Work. In an apparent attempt to allow as many Muslims as possible to make use of the scheme, it was decided that any Muslim legal
entity could be considered for financial support, provided that all
Muslims were allowed access to the place of worship to be built as
a result. In view of the religious and political differences between

---

[19] *Bijl. Hand.* II 1973–1974, no. 11.
[20] *Bijl. Hand.* II 1973–1974, no. 11, p. 3.
[21] *Hand.* II 24 October 1974, p. 794.
[22] Resulting in Samuels & Gransbergen 1975, as previously mentioned; see also
Bijl. Hand. II 1974–1975, 10504, no. 12, p. 10.
[23] Letter W.B.-46649, 13 April 1976; *Nederlandse Staatscourant* 1976, no. 75, p. 1.

Muslim organizations, this soon proved to be a very unrealistic expectation.[24] The General Regulation expired in 1981.[25]

Temporary Regulation concerning Subsidies for Places of Worship for Muslims (1981–1983)
The General Regulation had resulted in Muslims from the Mediterranean area being able to take advantage of the grant scheme, but not those from the Moluccas or Surinam. This was in spite of the fact that attention to the culture and religion of cultural minorities was at that time seen as one of the mainstays of minorities policy, and that the authorities had included all these categories of Muslims, along with other groups, under the heading of 'cultural minorities'.

While waiting for a report on the desirability of subsidies, the Minister of Culture, Recreation and Social Work announced a Temporary Regulation concerning Subsidies for Places of Worship for Muslims (*Tijdelijke Regeling Subsidiëring Gebedsruimten voor Moslims*), which came into effect in March 1981 and lasted up to the end of December 1983.[26] In reality this scheme was a continuation of the previous one, so that it was still only those Muslims from Mediterranean areas who could apply for a grant.[27]

Bill containing powers to set up a Foundation for the Maintenance of Moluccan Churches (1983)
In 1983 a separate bill aimed at compensating Moluccan Muslims for this deficiency. In the context of attempts to normalize relations with Moluccan residents, and to separate church and state, the government pursued a policy of transferring the ownership of Moluccan church buildings and mosques to their local users. One of the promises made by the Minister of Welfare, Health and Culture, Brinkman (Christian Democratic Party, CDA) to the Moluccans was that each Moluccan community of more than 30 families would obtain its own

[24] Cf. Landman 1992: 163; Hampsink 1992: 17.
[25] A total of Hfl. 1,657,650 was disbursed in subsidies for the establishment of 31 places of worship; the average subsidy was about Hfl. 53,500 (Werkgroep-Waardenburg 1983: 66 & 105).
[26] On the basis of this Temporary Regulation, around 69 places of worship received a contribution, ranging from Hfl. 2,760 to Hfl. 30,000 (Commissie-Hirsch Ballin 1988: 80).
[27] Applications were indeed entered by the Surinamese community. See *Nederlandse Staatscourant* 1982, no. 1 & no. 172, p. 6.

place of worship, and in addition the Ministry would contribute to
the maintenance costs.[28] To this end the Minister was authorized to
set up the Foundation for the Maintenance of Moluccan Churches,[29]
and according to Article 2 of its statutes, 'churches' were understood
to include mosques, which in practice meant those in the towns of
Ridderkerk and Waalwijk.[30] In a report to the Queen the Minister
stated that in view of the historical background of the arrival and
settlement of the Moluccans in the Netherlands, no precedent could
be derived from this scheme.[31] The Christian Democrats (CDA),
Labour (PvdA), the Liberals (VVD), and two minority Calvinist parties (GPV and SGP) generally agreed with this policy, though in fact
it was never the subject of open debate in parliament.

Report of the Waardenburg Working Party (1983)
In line with the minorities policy the Minister of Culture, Recreation
and Social Work, De Boer (Christian Democratic Party, CDA), set
up the Waardenburg Working Party in August 1982. It was commissioned

> to advise on the need for premises in which members of cultural
> minorities can carry out their religious practices, the desirability of gov-
> ernment support for this, and the conditions under which this support
> might be granted.[32]

In their report the Working Party gave a review of the current provision of places of worship in the four major cities (Amsterdam,
Rotterdam, The Hague and Utrecht) and concentrated its attention
on the need for places of worship. The financing of existing mosques
had largely been arranged by Muslims themselves, although here
and there local authorities had made accommodation available free
of charge (Werkgroep-Waardenburg 1983: 22–29).[33] One of the
Working Party's recommendations was that subsidies should be given

---

[28] For this purpose the Ministry reserved the sum of Hfl. 12,600,000 for a 10-
year period (Hampsink 1992: 19).
[29] The bill to this end was introduced on 4 November 1983. See *Bijl. Hand.* II
1983–1984 & 1985–1986, 18151.
[30] See *Memorie van Antwoord, Bijl. Hand.* II, 1985–1986, 18151, no. 5. For the construction and maintenance of the mosque in Ridderkerk alone, the state paid out
Hfl. 2,130,000 (Hampsink 1992: 19).
[31] *Bijl. Hand.* II 1983–1984, 18151, B-C.
[32] Besluit W.B.-U-29470 II, in Werkgroep-Waardenburg 1983: 204, appendix 21.
[33] Cf. Liefbroer 1985: 34–36: Waardenburg 1988.

for establishing mosques, at least for the target groups of the minorities policy.[34] This implied that Turkish, Moroccan, Surinamese and Moluccan Muslims could apply for support from the government, but that Pakistani, or Palestinian Muslims, for example, could not. The Working Party also recommended that in the granting of subsidies, Muslims should be distinguished by country of origin and religious sect. In addition there should no longer be any question of a maximum subsidy, as had been the case under the Temporary Regulation. Subsidies would encourage the integration of Muslims into Dutch society, not least because in the future financial assistance from abroad would no longer be needed. During the symposium on Islam in Rotterdam on 28 May 1983, representatives of all the Muslim organizations indicated that they stood fully behind the recommendations of the report (Van Bakelen 1984: 22).

The government's reaction to the Working Party's recommendations are to be found in the *Minorities Memorandum* (*Minderhedennota*, Ministerie van BiZa 1983), in which the first Cabinet led by Lubbers, comprising Christian Democrats (CDA) and Liberals (VVD), stated that an active minorities policy could not overlook the fact that the level of material facilities for religious minorities was lower than that for other groups, despite the fact that religious facilities were an essential component of the way in which minorities functioned in Dutch society.[35] During the discussions on the *Minorities Memorandum* in parliament in the spring of 1984, MP Krajenbrink (Christian Democratic Party, CDA) tabled a motion calling for agreement with the recommendations of the Waardenburg Working Party. However, a majority of the Social Democrats and Liberals rejected the motion.[36] In September 1984 Minister Rietkerk (VVD) for Internal Affairs, in reply to questions from MPs Wiebenga and Hermans (both Liberal, VVD) and Van Ooijen and Buurmeijer (both Labour, PvdA), stated that there were no pressing constitutional obstacles to do with the separation of church and state against a temporary and limited grant

---

[34] The Working Party called additionally for subsidies in aid of the provision of social and educational activities, the inclusion of Islamic religious instruction in the education curriculum, the recognition of Muslim religious holidays, the setting up of 'communication channels' between the government and Muslims, and for a series of regulations concerning the media, ritual slaughter, funerals, and the like.

[35] *Bijl. Hand.* II 1982–1983, 16102, no. 21, p. 110.

[36] *Bijl. Hand.* II 1983–1984, 16102, no. 55; *Hand.* II, 10 April 1984, p. 4326.

scheme.[37] The Minister also reported that consultations were currently in hand about the desirability of such a scheme. Parliament's
acceptance of the Wiebenga/Dales motion (VVD/PvdA) made clear
that these consultations were in fact unnecessary. This motion rejected
financial support for certain ethnic minority groups on the grounds
of the separation of church and state and the principle of equality.[38]
Minister Brinkman (Christian Democratic Party, CDA), for Welfare,
Health and Culture then announced that the Cabinet had decided
against a new, separate subsidy scheme. Instead he had decided to
set aside Fl. 400,000 up to 1989 for granting 'a one-off government
contribution or subsidy towards the capital cost of establishing accommodation for socio-cultural/religious purposes'.[39]

This proposal came just before the first local elections in which
non-Dutch citizens were allowed to take part, in March 1986, and
for the opposition this was reason enough to treat it as a cheap vote-
grabbing stunt. A second Wiebenga/Dales motion, of the same tenor
as the first, finally destroyed the initiative.[40] The repeated rejection
by parliament certainly made it plain that the political balance of
power was changing: the non-confessional parties were apparently
capable of determining the relationship between church and state.

This did not mean that the fate of the Waardenburg Working
Party's proposals was completely sealed. Some of them are in fact
to be found again in a 1988 report on the provision of support to
religious denominations.

The report of the Hirsch Ballin Committee (1988)
In 1983, government ministers were already holding discussions with
representatives of Christian denominations, the Humanist Society,
and representatives of Muslim and Hindu groups, in order to determine how subsidies should be arranged after the constitutional revi-
sions of that year. During the talks it transpired that many things
were far from clear, and as a result in February 1986 the government appointed an Advisory Committee concerning Subsidies to

---

[37] *Aanh. Hand.* II 1984–1985, no. 19.
[38] *Bijl. Hand.* II 1984–1985, 16102, no. 99.
[39] *Bijl. Hand.* II 1985–1986, 16102, nos 133 & 139; *Bijl. Hand.* II 1986–1987,
16102, no. 144.
[40] *Bijl. Hand.* II 1986–1987, 16635, no. 11. Carried on 28 October 1986 with
opposition from the CDA, PPR and PSP; *Hand.* II 28 October 1986, p. 832.

Churches and other Religious Societies, otherwise known as the Hirsch Ballin Committee.[41] In their report the Committee pronounced the following:

> In general it is not the task of government to give general financial support to societies for founding, maintaining, and exploiting or restoring their buildings. When a church or other society has need of a building for conducting religious or philosophical activities it should itself provide the costs involved. However, special circumstances which restrict the free practice of a religion or philosophy of life can create occasions in which the authorities may decide to offer support (Commissie-Hirsch Ballin 1988: 52).

The Committee judged that such special circumstances did in fact exist in the case of Muslims, and recommended creating a one-off and temporary subsidy scheme as a successor to the Temporary Regulation of 1981. Such a scheme was particularly intended to 'reduce the disadvantages of the denominations among minorities vis-à-vis the Christian churches' (ibid.: 11).

In its report on Immigrants Policy, the Scientific Council for Government Policy (WRR 1989: 50) declared itself in favour of granting material support. According to Weerts (1989), the MP Krajenbrink (Christian Democratic Party, CDA) also stated that his party was in complete agreement with the thrust of the Hirsch Ballin Committee's final report. However, his colleague Jabaaij (Labour, PvdA) let it be known that her party, after reading the report, was not in favour of 'subsidizing church buildings for minorities'.[42] Minister Van Dijk for Internal Affairs (Christian Democratic Party, CDA), stated in November 1989—in the final days of the second Lubbers Cabinet (Christian Democrats and Liberals)—that he supported the Committee's conclusions, 'subject to a few marginal comments'.[43] He was even prepared to propose a one-off subsidy scheme for a limited period. However, the next—third—Lubbers Cabinet (Christian Democrats

---

[41] *Nederlandse Staatscourant* 1986, no. 51, p. 9.

[42] *Hand.* II, Uitgebreide Commissie Vergadering van de Tweede Kamer (UCV) no. 7 on 31 October 1989, TK 1989–1990, p. 17.

[43] *Bijl. Hand.* II 1989–1990, 20868, no. 2. The Minister had stated earlier that in view of the disadvantages borne by Muslims in this matter, the granting of subsidies would be appropriate. However he thought a general regulation to be undesirable, and was of the opinion that government assistance should only be secondary and subsidiary. See *Nederlandse Staatscourant* 1989, no. 192, pp. 1, 6 & 7; and *Nederlandse Staatscourant* 1988, no. 63, p. 2.

CDA and Labour PvdA) took a different view. An ironic detail is
that a number of the protagonists in the earlier discussions, including Hirsch Ballin (CDA) and Dales (PvdA), had meanwhile become
members of the new Cabinet. Dales, who as a Member of Parliament
had twice tabled a motion against a subsidy scheme for places of
worship, now indicated in writing in March 1991 in her capacity of
Minister for Internal Affairs, that discussions with nationwide minority organizations based on religion had shown that there was no
longer any shortage of places of worship.[44] In her view, therefore,
there was no need for a new scheme. The Ministry of Welfare,
Health and Culture was taken by surprise by this point of view—
indeed, they had a new draft for a subsidy scheme ready—but in
the end Dales' plans won the day (Hampsink 1992: 25).

Other religious institutions

As well as places of worship, a number of other institutions have
become established in recent decades. The most important are briefly
discussed here.

Imams

With the increase in the number of mosques, the need for spiritual
leaders or imams has also increased. These were (and still are)
recruited mainly from the countries of origin of the Muslims concerned. It was in 1980 that the Secretary of State for Justice first
set out rules for the admission of imams.[45] Since then there have
been several changes of policy, but the main line of approach has
been held: the organization inviting the imam is responsible for his
housing and maintenance; there must be no objection to the admission of the imam concerned on grounds of public order or national
security; and before he arrives in the Netherlands he must be granted
authority for temporary residence. The Ministry tries to prevent the

---

[44] *Bijl. Hand.* II 1990–1991, 20868, no. 3. Spokespersons for the Islamic Foundation
of the Netherlands, which claimed to be the largest Islamic organization in the
country, maintained that they had not been consulted on this matter. In their view
there was still a severe lack of places of worship (Hampsink 1992: 25).
[45] Circular of 10 June 1980, AJZ 1334/E-633–A-360. In the Netherlands, a
Secretary of State (*staatssecretaris*) is a deputy minister, junior to the Minister him/her-
self. In the UK the Secretary of State is the head of the Ministry.

admission of undesirable ('fundamentalist') imams by this last requirement, though this is actually an infringement on freedom of religion,
for it limits religious communities in their choice of leaders.

While the Ministry of Justice supervises the admission of imams,
their position under the labour laws is heavily dependent on the
leadership of the community concerned. A series of judicial pronouncements in the 1980s have strengthened this dependency.[46] For
instance, it has been decided that imams have no right to social
security, that for them—just as for the spiritual leaders of other religious groups—it is not necessary to apply for permission to dismiss
them, and that they have no right to any family allowance, or un-
employment, disability or sickness benefit. The imam is therefore in
practice excluded from the Dutch social security system. Since the
early 1980s there has been talk, both within the Muslim communities and outside them, of the desirability of training courses for imams
in the Netherlands. This is discussed in more detail in Chapter 4.

The call to prayer

In the mid-1980s the *adhân* or *ezan*, the call to prayer, became an
item on the local and national political agenda. In several towns
those in charge of the mosque requested leave to broadcast the call
to prayer, or proceeded to do so without obtaining permission. These
Muslim initiatives provoked considerable discussion locally. Some
people were afraid that it might hinder integration and increase tension in the neighbourhood.[47] However, freedom of religion and the
principle of equality were important arguments in favour of allowing this institution.

This last argument also played a central role in 1987 in the discussions at the national level during the passage of the Public
Demonstrations Act (*Wet op de Openbare Manifestaties*). This Act grew
out of the new pronouncements on freedom of religion and philosophy of life in Article 6 of the 1983 Constitution. In parliament,
Van Otterloo (Labour, PvdA) tabled an amendment in which he
wanted to emphasize the obligation for equal treatment of Christian

---

[46] Hoge Raad 30 May 1986, *Nederlandse Jurisprudentie* 1986, no. 702; AB 1989,
no. 475, 1990, no. 36 & 1991, no. 669; Jurisprudentie ABW 1983, no. 14; see also
Den Dekker-Van Bijsterveld 1988: 255–264.
[47] For local discussions, see *Trouw*, 9, 20 & 21 May, 5 June & 11 July 1987.

residents and Muslim immigrants.[48] This amendment was accepted
with the support of all the major parties, with the three small Calvinist
parties voting against.[49] Consequently a majority consisting of Labour
(PvdA), the Liberals (VVD), and Democrats 66 (D66) forced through
statutory recognition of the equal treatment of Muslims on this point
and broke through the opposition of the Christian parties. The new
Act gave local authorities the power to lay down their own regulations on bell ringing and the call to prayer. According to Landman
(1992: 289 ff.), this power entailed that the regulations and their
practical implementation could differ from one local authority to
another. Thus some local authorities, such as Utrecht, remained
opposed to the broadcast of the call to prayer, while in other areas
a system of licensing had been in place even before the introduction
of the new Act, for instance in Leiden and Amsterdam. The practical solution worked out by the Amsterdam authorities for the call
to prayer probably served as a model for other local authorities.

Ritual male circumcision

Ritual male circumcision is an institution which has become established in the Netherlands without attracting notice. In contrast to
female circumcision—which had provoked great opposition and was
finally forbidden, partly on the grounds of widely held notions in
the Netherlands about the integrity of the human body[50]—male circumcision is a generally accepted operation in the case of boys.[51]
The phenomenon of circumcision in the Jewish community, to which
people were already accustomed in the Netherlands, and considerations of hygiene already current in the world of medicine, particularly in the United States, played a role in this.

These circumcisions were increasingly carried out in hospitals, and
such problems that occurred were mainly concerned with practical
matters such as the high cost of the operation in a hospital, and the
capacity available.[52] Nevertheless there arose a demand from some

---

[48] TK 1987–88, 19427, nos 17 & 19. For an account of the debate, see Groenendijk
1994.
[49] *Hand.* TK 26–28 January 1988, pp. 2198–2282.
[50] Cf. GHI 1994: 14; Struijs 1995: 233–234.
[51] Cf. Van den Dungen 1993: 37–40.
[52] These issues have occasionally been the subject of summary legal proceedings,
which have sometimes led to new arrangements. For example, as a result of sum-

of the Muslim communities for a more formal arrangement. In 1985 there were consultations on the matter between the Ministry of Welfare, Health and Culture and a number of Muslim organizations, which led to a survey being undertaken into Muslim circumcisions. The most important recommendation to come out of it was that there should be a training course for Muslims carrying out the operation (Hoffer 1990). The government considered such a course desirable, particularly from a medical point of view. The condition was that the Muslim community should arrange for a proper organizational structure, which in turn required a body representative of the various Muslim groups (ibid.: 42–44). This requirement produced a remarkable silence on the subject of a possible training course for those performing circumcisions. In 1992 some local initiatives in Rotterdam, in which medical professionals performed multiple circumcisions outside hospitals on an experimental basis, breathed new life into the plans, and in 1995 the Netherlands Centre for Foreigners worked out a national scheme for the regularization of Muslim circumcisions, at the request of the Ministry of Health, Welfare and Sports.[53] The condition requiring a representative body seemed to have been abandoned.

Religious festivals

The recognition of Muslim festivals has been the subject of discussion for a number of years and has led to the modification of the legislation in a number of areas. The first official ruling was made in 1981 for Muslims in the armed services. The Facilities Rule (*Faciliteitenregeling*), which already existed for Jewish servicemen, was then supplemented by the recognition of several Muslim holy days, and with a rule designating Friday as the day of rest for Muslim servicemen instead of Sunday (Beune & Hessels 1983: 220). Claims for special leave associated with Ramadan, however, did not seem to be in the realm of possibilities.[54]

---

mary proceedings, the medical insurance group Het Zilveren Kruis has adopted the same policy towards circumcision for religious reasons as towards the same operation for medical reasons (*de Volkskrant*, 21 August 1993).

[53] See, *inter alia*, Spalburg 1993: 7; *de Volkskrant*, 21 December 1994; *De Eenheid* 15 (1995): 7.

[54] *Aanh.* TK 1986–87, no. 809; *Tijdschrift voor Ambtenarenrecht* 1990, no. 243.

In the prison system there was a longstanding informal practice recognizing other festivals besides Christian ones. A 1976 report resulting from an investigation by the Ministry of Justice stated that in fact this could cause 'bad blood' among other prisoners, because those concerned also benefitted from Christian festivals (Mesman Schultz & Methorst 1976: 15).

In several other areas existing legislation was replaced by a more open rule. This applies, for example, to the 1976 Shop Closing Act (*Winkelsluitingswet*), which now includes the provision that shopkeepers may observe a day other than Sunday as their weekly closing day. Another example is the 1988 Civil Service Act (*Ambtenarenwet*). This includes a general rule that a civil servant is not obliged to work on 'days which are for him festivals or days of rest on grounds of his religion or principles, unless duties make it unavoidable'.[55] The occasion for this amendment was the clause on freedom of religion in the new 1983 Constitution.

In industry a claim of unfair dismissal led to a declaration of principle by the Supreme Court,[56] which laid down in 1984 that festivals of other religions could not be put on the same footing as the generally recognized festivals which applied to everyone in the Netherlands regardless of faith or nationality. But if an employee asked in good time for a day off in connection with a religious festival which was important to him or her, such a request could only be denied if it caused serious damage to the firm's interests. Moreover, the employer was not permitted to draw a distinction between different religions.[57] This declaration of principle determined the direction of future political and judicial discussion, and played a role, for instance, in the discussion on the 1988 Civil Service Act referred to above.[58]

In 1985 the government decided not to give Hindu and Muslim festivals legal equivalence with Christian festivals. The difference in the treatment of members of Christian churches and of Muslims or Hindus was in fact acknowledged, but the government saw a justification for the differential in the general social function these

---

[55] *Staatsblad* 1988, no. 229, art. 125b.
[56] This concerned a case in which an employee had not obtained permission to take a day off for the *Eïd ul-Fitr* (Festival of Breaking the Fast). She was summarily dismissed when she did not appear for work on the day in question.
[57] Hoge Raad 30 March 1984, *Nederlandse Jurisprudentie* 1985, no. 350.
[58] TK 11.12.1988, p. 2625.

Christian festivals had acquired.[59] Nonetheless, the recognition of Muslim festivals has continued to be a subject of debate.[60]

Dietary rules

In the 1980s there was another subject on which Muslims requested an adjustment of the legislation: the ability to comply with their dietary rules in penal institutions and in the armed forces. In the case of the latter the 1981 Facilities Rule, referred to earlier, had already introduced measures for Muslim, Hindu and Jewish servicemen. It stipulated that a serviceman whose pay was subject to deductions by the authorities for his rations, and who wished to observe the religious dietary rules which applied to him, had a right to compensation for expense incurred each day that he provided his own food.[61] The serviceman would have to inform his commanding officer which religion he observed. The regulation gave no entitlement to the provision of ritually prepared food.

In 1986 the fixed deduction for rations lapsed and all servicemen could eat outside their lines if they wished, once they were off duty. Provision of a ritual diet was not practical for reasons of perishability, or expense.[62] Three years later vegetarian meals were introduced, 'taking due account of the dietary rules applying to ethnic groups',[63] and this solution had the additional advantage of extending the freedom of choice for all servicemen. Instead of special treatment for a small group, the variety was increased for all servicemen. In spite of this it seemed in the early 1990s that the provision of appropriate food for Hindu and Muslim servicemen was still presenting problems (Choenni 1995: 194 ff.).

Within penal establishments, too, there are still problems surrounding the observation of dietary rules, although, according to a working party of the Ministry of Justice (1976), this has been taken into consideration as much as possible since the 1970s. In 1981 the same Ministry issued a circular regarding the ritual diet of Jewish

---

[59] TK 1985–86, 16102, no. 128, pp. 22–25.
[60] See for example UCV no. 47 on 22 June 1993, TK 1992–1993; Shadid & Van Koningsveld 1992b: 97–98.
[61] Article 5 of the Facilities Rule (*Faciliteitenregeling*).
[62] *Aanh.* TK 1988–1989, no. 62.
[63] TK 1988–1989, 20821, no. 4, p. 1.

prisoners.[64] A year later a prison governor, after a complaint from a Muslim prisoner, stated that his budget did not allow for special diets. Both the local Complaints Committee and the Appeals Committee of the Central Council for the Prison System rejected this point of view: Jews and Muslims in detention had a claim to equal treatment.[65]

In 1984, apparently on financial grounds, a new circular was issued which from that point on gave Jews and Muslims in detention only the right to procure a ritual diet at their own expense.[66] When this new regulation met with protests—the Coornhert League for legal reform judged that the measure was in conflict with freedom of religion—the Secretary of State Korte-Van Hemel (Christian Democratic Party, CDA) withdrew the circular a fortnight later.[67]

Ritual slaughter

An institution which attracted attention relatively early is that of ritual slaughter. The lack of any legal arrangements whatsoever led to problems at abattoirs every year around the time of the *Eid ul-Adha* (Festival of Sacrifice), and to much illegal slaughtering. In the late 1960s and early 1970s there were several court cases against Muslims who had slaughtered a goat or a sheep on their own initiative, in breach of the law. In 1969 a defendant in one of these cases pleaded freedom of religion. The judge discharged him on this ground. The Supreme Court, however, decided that freedom of religion was not a licence to ignore the prescriptions of the legislation on meat inspection.[68] At the same time the Advocate General commented on the constitutional obligation to treat all religious communities alike.

As a result of a request by the Federation of Muslim Organizations in the Netherlands to introduce regulations for ritual slaughter according to Islamic rites, similar to those which had been in existence since 1920 for the Jewish community, the Ministry of Public Health and Environmental Hygiene announced in 1975 that the Meat Inspection Order (*Vleeskeuringsbesluit*) would be amended (Van den Berg-Eldering

---

[64] Circular of 26 October 1981, no. M 3/07, Penitentiaire Informatie 1982, p. 4.
[65] Beroepscommissie Centrale Raad van Advies voor het Gevangeniswezen 27 September 1982, *Rechtspraak Vreemdelingenrecht* 1983, no. 114, with a note by Groenendijk.
[66] Circular of 25 April 1984, no. 443/384 concerning dietary rules for prisoners.
[67] Letter to the Second Chamber, 9 May 1984, TK 1983–84, 18100, VI, no. 50.
[68] Hoge Raad 4 November 1969, *Nederlandse Jurisprudentie* 1970, no. 127.

1978: 148; Wagtendonk 1982: 129). Anticipating the amendment, Secretary of State Hendriks (Catholic People's Party, KVP) gave permission for ritual slaughter in specified abattoirs for two days during the 1975 *Eid ul-Adha*. Exemptions were also granted the following year. These measures provoked protests from animal protection organizations and gave rise to questions in the House.[69] MP Koekoek of the Farmers Party (BP), asked (in vain) that the exemptions be withdrawn in view of the objections from the animal protestors.[70] Meanwhile the prosecutions for illegal slaughter continued. In late 1976 a public prosecutor in a case in Rotterdam stated that the absence of a legal ruling was asking for the law to be broken.[71]

In 1977 the Meat Inspection Order was finally amended.[72] To the general rule that an animal must be stunned before being slaughtered, the same exceptions were made for the Islamic rite as for the Jewish one. In both cases a range of additional provisions were applied to prevent the animals suffering unnecessary pain. Moreover, all slaughter had to take place in abattoirs specified by the Minister. Annual consultations take place with representative Muslim organizations at the national level, after which the chief veterinary inspector of public health lays down national guidelines for slaughter every year at the time of the *Eid ul-Adha*, and specifies designated abattoirs. Meetings are also held on the subject at local level between local Muslim organizations, the abattoir, and the appropriate local government officer.

In the early 1980s ritual slaughter again became the subject of fierce debate in national politics. The immediate cause was the European Treaty on the protection of slaughter animals. This treaty expressly allowed the slaughter of animals in accordance with religious rites without prior stunning, but prescribed previous immobilization.[73] Members of the Labour and Radical Parties (PvdA and PPR) were afraid that the purchase of the necessary equipment would

---

[69] For the protests, see *de Volkskrant*, 9 & 12 December 1975.

[70] *Aanh.* TK 1976–77, no. 714. The Farmers Party (Boerenpartij) started as a small right-wing interest group but gradually developed into a more general radical-right movement which had several electoral successes in the mid-1960s (see Van Donselaar 1993).

[71] The accused received a token sentence from the magistrate, in the form of a suspended fine of Hfl. 100 (*de Volkskrant*, 17 November 1976).

[72] *Staatsblad* 1977, no. 28.

[73] Articles 13 and 17 of the European Treaty on the Protection of Slaughter Animals, *Tractatenblad* 1981, no. 76.

make ritual slaughter too expensive, and they demanded urgent discussion of the treaty in parliament. In the discussion, the Liberals (VVD) and Christian Democrats (CDA) laid stress on the equal treatment of the Jewish and the Islamic rite, while opponents raised the actual content of the Muslim tradition: both the far-right-wing Centre Party and the Netherlands Society for the Protection of Animals claimed that slaughter with prior stunning was not at variance with the Jewish and Islamic prescriptions.[74] This pressure from the opposition was not without effect. Thus Secretary of State for Agriculture Ploeg (Liberal Party, VVD), in answer to questions from the Centre Party, stated that requests for exemption from the ban on exporting ritually slaughtered meat would in future be refused.[75] In an interview with the weekly *Vrij Nederland* some time later, Ploeg stated:

> In deprived areas, feelings have been raised against the Turks by this ritual slaughter. There are balconies there dripping with blood. (...) For my part, Jews and Muslims may slaughter their beasts in the traditional way, but they can't do so any more for export (43 (1984) 3).

With these pronouncements Ploeg evoked fierce opposition, particularly from the Jews,[76] and in reaction to their protests, the Secretary of State resigned in 1985. In a letter to parliament he explained that, subject to strict conditions, he was again prepared to grant exemptions for the export of ritually slaughtered meat.[77] Although animal protection organizations still made a number of attempts through the courts to end ritual slaughter for export,[78] public discussion subsided after the treaty was approved in early 1986.

The wearing of headscarves

For some Muslim women and girls, wearing a headscarf out of doors is an important sign of their religious identity. Usually this causes no problems, but sometimes it can lead to conflicts.[79]

---

[74] TK 1982–1983, 17011, no. 10, p. 3; *de Volkskrant*, 1 June 1984; *NRC Handelsblad*, 5 January 1985.

[75] TK 1982–1983, 17011, no. 11, p. 4.

[76] R.M. Naftaniel in *de Volkskrant*, 6 December 1984 and Rabbi Van der Kamp in *NRC Handelsblad*, 5 January 1985.

[77] TK 1984–1985, 18600, XIV, no. 84.

[78] See *de Volkskrant* and *NRC Handelsblad*, 30 April 1987; Chairman Afdeling Rechtspraak 18 April 1989, ARB 1989, no. 546.

[79] Cf. *Rechtspraak Vreemdelingenrecht* 1989, no. 293; Shadid & Van Koningsveld 1985, 1990b: 108–114; Coppes 1994.

One often quoted case is the 'headscarf affair' in Alphen aan den Rijn. In early 1985 the Alderman for Education there decided to forbid the wearing of headscarves at school. An expert from Leiden, who had been asked for advice by the local authority, was of the opinion that a headscarf was not essential for observance of the Muslim faith.[80] This point of view provoked protests from Muslims and from the Netherlands Centre for Foreigners and led to questions in the House by Van Ooijen (Labour, PvdA). Minister of Education Deetman (Christian Democratic Party, CDA), thereupon stated that 'forbidding pupils to wear a headscarf is not compatible with our modern society'.[81] Meanwhile the ban in Alphen was withdrawn under pressure of the protests.

Nevertheless the Minister's position did not lead to an unequivocal policy in practice. In some schools headscarves were not an issue, whereas in others wearing them remained forbidden. Since the Alphen affair, wearing headscarves has continued to be a cause of conflict on several occasions between parents and school managements and between employers and employees.[82]

Spiritual care in public institutions

There is a long tradition of government responsibility for the spiritual care of those who live, whether voluntarily or not, in 'total' or intramural institutions. There are a number of rules designed to guarantee their freedom of religion. This involves an 'open' regime which takes account of the religious pluriformity of the population of institutions such as the armed services, prisons, detention centres and children's homes.

In 1976 the spiritual care of Muslims and Hindus in penal institutions was the subject of the investigation referred to earlier, carried out at the request of the Ministry of Justice (Mesman Schultz

---

[80] The expert who had been called in the Alphen headscarf affair returned to the subject in a later publication. He had been asked by the local council 'whether it was true, as had been alleged by a number of Moroccans in that municipality, that the prescription of headscarves for Muslim women and girls was based on the Koran, which was the reason that their daughters could not take them off in class'. The answer was in the negative, 'because headscarves are not mentioned in the Koran' (Brugman 1991: 70–71).

[81] *Aanh. Hand.* II 1984–85 no. 700.

[82] See, *inter alia, De Gelderlander*, 10 November 1988; *Trouw*, 13 February 1990 & 16 December 1993; *Contrast* 12 (1994); *de Volkskrant*, 9 August 1995.

& Methorst 1976). A ministerial working party confirmed that there
was evidence of unequal treatment of detainees in the practice of
their religion, and made several recommendations (Ministerie van
Justitie 1976). Some 10 years later, the Hirsch Ballin Committee
reached a similar conclusion on Muslims and Hindus in the armed
forces, and therefore argued for the institution of two spiritual services, one for Muslims and one for Hindus, in the armed services
and in penal institutions (Commissie-Hirsch Ballin 1988: 10). This
would be subject to the groups involved setting up some form of co-
operative body to represent their interests in discussions with the
government, and to act as a 'missionary agency'.[83] It was precisely
these conditions which proved to be the obstacle to putting the two
spiritual services into effect.

Pending a definitive arrangement, the Ministries of Justice and
Defence took various temporary measures.[84] Claims by Muslims in
this context were supported by spiritual advisers of other denominations, who have also played a role in introducing new imams into
penal institutions. In 1994 the government tabled a bill which was
intended to provide general rules concerning the access to and availability of spiritual care in caring institutions (hospitals, nursing homes
and old people's homes) and in penal institutions. The proposal was
for an 'open' regime that would make it possible for people in these
institutions to have contact with 'the spiritual adviser of the religion
or life-philosophy of their choice'.[85] On the basis of this summary
law, further rules can be made concerning the availability, organization and remuneration of this spiritual care. Given its open character, the arrangements could also apply to the spiritual care of
Muslims.

Funeral arrangements

A subject that has scarcely led to any discussion is the adjustment
of legislation on funerary practices. There are various interrelated
reasons for this. First of all, the religious traditions of Islam for funer-

[83] TK 1989–1990, 20868, no. 2, p. 19.
[84] See for example Circular of 7 September 1982, no. 459/382, Penitentiaire
Informatie 1982, p. 202; UCV, 22 June 1992, pp. 47–21; Circular on spiritual care
of Muslims and Hindus in judicial institutions, Ministry of Justice, 10 June 1993.
[85] Ontwerp van de Wet Geestelijke Verzorging Zorginstellingen en Justitiële
Inrichtingen, TK 1993–1994, 23720, nos 1–2.

als have not necessitated any drastic changes. The most important differences are that the deceased should be buried within 24 hours, without a coffin and with their head pointing towards Mecca. Secondly, undertakers appear to have been reasonably quick in meeting the wishes of this new group of customers. In practice they have acted as intermediaries between the Muslims and the host society. In addition, a bill for the complete revision of the old 1869 law was tabled as early as 1971, although it took two decades to get it made law. At various moments during this period, the Labour (PvdA), Liberal (VVD) and Democrats 66 (D66) parties asked whether burial in accordance with Islamic rites was possible and would remain so.[86] This was finally positively confirmed in 1982.[87] When the new Funerary Arrangements Act (*Wet op de Lijkbezorging*)[88] and the order for its implementation finally came into effect in 1991, actual practice had for years been adapted to the customs of Muslim migrants, and in various places in the Netherlands (including Rotterdam and Amsterdam-Osdorp) there were already Muslim cemeteries (Wagtendonk 1982: 130).

Swearing oaths on the Koran

The last institution to be covered here has also led to very little discussion. Adjustment of the legislation did not appear to be necessary, since the 1911 Oaths Act (*Eedswet*) gave sufficient scope for an oath to be taken in a way other than that prescribed by the law if the person involved 'derives from his religious denomination the obligation to swear his oath, make his promise or his confirmation in some other way'.[89] The Act came into existence at a time when it was unclear whether and how an oath should be taken by atheists and agnostics.

In the 1990s questions were again raised about oaths. This occurred during the installation of a Muslim in a local council, and the swearing in of an officer cadet from Morocco.[90] In both cases it was decided that in accordance with the 1911 law it was possible for the oath to be sworn on the Holy Koran.

---

[86] TK 1977–1978, 11256, no. 9, p. 5.
[87] TK 1981–1982, 11256, no. 17, p. 11.
[88] Act of 7 March 1991, *Staatsblad* 1991, no. 130.
[89] *Staatsblad* 1911, no. 215.
[90] See *de Volkskrant*, 15 April 1994; *Het Parool* and *NRC Handelsblad*, 8 September 1994.

CHAPTER FOUR

THE SPHERE OF EDUCATION

Among the organizations involved in passing on values and standards, and which therefore contribute significantly to the continuance of Muslim customs, a key role is played by the media and educational institutions. There are sound reasons for all mosques having Koran schools attached to them where children learn the scriptures and practices of Islam. The national education system also offers various opportunities, such as the attention given to Islam in the curriculum on geography, history or religious movements, or in the programme of education in community language and culture.[1] This chapter concentrates on Islamic religious instruction in state and private primary schools and on the establishment of Muslim primary schools. In addition other educational institutions will be reviewed, such as Muslim broadcasting organizations and theological courses.

Islamic religious instruction

Legislation

Since the introduction of the Primary Education Act (*Wet op het Lager Onderwijs*) in 1920, religious instruction has been a regular, if optional, component of the curriculum of *state schools*.[2] Nowadays numerous clergymen and humanist councillors take Bible classes or humanist education for several hours a week, and so contribute to the 'active pluriformity' of state education.[3] As early as the 1970s, Muslim organ-

---

[1] Cf. Lkoundi-Hamaekers 1987: 97; Voorbij 1987; Shadid & Van Koningsveld 1989b: 1310–1315, 1990a: 110. Particularly in Muslim schools, this curriculum was to have a religious character.

[2] Since the separation of church and state was made law under the Batavian Republic, religious instruction has occupied a special position in state schools. State education has to respect the religious beliefs of its pupils, yet at the same time it must maintain a neutral position, so that as an interdenominational school system it is open to all pupils without discrimination between religious beliefs (Drop 1985: 221–227).

[3] The Association for State Education (VOO 1992: 7–12) in particular is very

izations were arguing for the introduction of Islamic religious instruction.[4] There seemed to be no legal objections. The government stated on several occasions that this right also applied to the 'religions of ethnic minority groups' (Ministerie van BiZa 1983: 112; see also WRR 1989: 51).

The status of religious instruction is laid down in the Primary Education Act (*Wet op het Basisonderwijs*) which came into effect on 1 August 1985.[5] This law imposes a duty on the competent authority to help arrange religious instruction in accordance with the wishes of parents for their children. However, the competent authority, in this case the municipality, bears no responsibility for the content of any such instruction, for the way in which it is delivered, or for the choice of teachers and teaching material. Responsibility for these things lies with institutions such as religious congregations, local churches, or other competent legal entities which according to their statutes aim to provide religious instruction. These institutions cannot, however, make any financial claim on the municipality on the basis of the Primary Education Act; grants for religious instruction are discretionary. If a local authority does indeed wish to subsidize it, this must be done on the basis of a universal regulation (Drop 1985: 224).[6] The provision of a grant in such cases thus appears to be an instrument capable of imposing supplementary and specific conditions on religious instruction, including that of the Islamic faith.

An example of a supplementary condition of this type is the language of instruction. This requirement has not gone unchallenged, since the law gives no definite ruling on it. The most usual interpretation is that the lessons should be given in Dutch. Article 29 of the Primary Education Act lays down that state schools must be

keen on this 'active pluriformity'. For a discussion of this in the Humanist League, see Beckeringh *et al.* 1986.

[4] Cf. FOMON s.a.; Lkoundi-Hamaekers 1987: 102: Triesscheijn 1989b; Landman 1992: 245.

[5] The relevant passages are Article 3, Sections 1 and 2, and Articles 29, 30, 31, at least in so far as religious instruction in state schools is concerned. Act of 2 July 1981, containing the Primary Education Act, *Staatsblad* 1981, no. 468. The relevant articles were amended by the acts of 4 July 1985, *Staatsblad* 1985, no. 393, and 12 May 1993, *Staatsblad* 1993, no. 270.

[6] Some municipalities have in fact done this. According to Drop (1985: 225), however, many municipal councils withdrew from their voluntarily undertaken financial burdens in 1985—the year in which the Primary Education Act came into force.

accessible for all children, without any distinction on grounds of religion or ideology. If this article is interpreted to mean that *all lessons*
in a state school must be accessible to *all children*, this excludes any
other language than Dutch. Inspectors of the Ministry of Education
and the Association of Dutch Local Authorities have interpreted the
law in this way.[7] However, the Council of Churches maintains that
the competent authority should not lay down requirements which
are not feasible,[8] and argues that most teachers of Islamic religious
instruction were not educated in the Netherlands and have only a
limited mastery of the Dutch language.[9] If local authorities are
adamant in their requirement that Dutch should be the language of
instruction, many Muslim children in state schools will be deprived
of religious instruction. Here the Council draws a comparison with
the education in community language and culture programme, which
according to the law does not have to be given in Dutch either. In
June 1990, in a meeting about this problem between the Association
of Dutch Local Authorities and the Council of Churches, both parties expressed the wish that local authorities should for the moment
show some flexibility on this point, and as a result of this meeting
a Memorandum was drawn up for the Education Committee of the
Association.[10] The Committee subscribed to the content of the

---

[7] Letter from the head of the Department of Education, Culture, Sport and
Recreation of the Association of Dutch Local Authorities to the Council of Churches
in the Netherlands, dated 15 March 1990 (from the Association's own records). The
Association put forward three arguments for their point of view: 1) the Primary
Education Act explicitly states when instruction need not be given in Dutch, and
this is not the case with religious instruction; 2) ideological persuasions are a relevant criterion for religious instruction, but the language or country of origin are
not; 3) religious instruction in schools is not directed at the worship or the practice of a religion, but at communicating knowledge about the religion, its scriptures,
customs and traditions. Therefore the use of a language other than Dutch is not
necessary.

[8] Letter from W.R. van der Zee, General Secretary of the Council of Churches
in the Netherlands, to the Board of the Association of Dutch Local Authorities,
dated 29 June 1988 (from the Association's own records). Bosma (1983) uses similar wording in the VOO journal.

[9] The Council of Churches seems to be in agreement on this point with the
tenor of the discussion about the content of the curriculum for education in community language and culture. Some are of the opinion that religious education is
self-evidently a part of this curriculum. Muslim organizations have at times offered
to provide education in community language and culture, according to their own
definition (Gemeente Rotterdam 1982a: 47).

[10] *Memorandum on Islamic Religious Instruction in State Schools*, OC 20/46. The Hague:
Association of Dutch Local Authorities.

Memorandum, but saw no reason to change the Association's line of advice. They did express agreement on the need to be flexible about the language requirement in practice.[11]

According to the Association an 'important but often unvoiced argument' for the requirement of Dutch as the language of instruction is that it enables local authorities to check what is going on during religious instruction periods. They might have no formal responsibility for the content of these lessons, but

> ... the possibility of limited checks is indeed thought necessary to prevent opinions being promoted during religious instruction which are in conflict with Dutch law and order. The Rushdie affair has demonstrated that this is not an imaginary risk.[12]

In the Association's opinion, municipal authorities could limit this risk by only temporarily allowing religious instruction in national languages 'when local groups have united in a platform', such as the Interdenominational Network on School Affairs, in which various Protestant Christian churches and religious communities worked together.[13] The Association was unforthcoming on the possibility of having checks carried out by Turkish or Arabic-speaking inspectors. Other criteria sometimes applied by local authorities are concerned with the relationship with the school curriculum and the pedagogic-didactic approach (VOO 1992: 15).[14]

The discussion outlined so far concerns religious instruction in state schools, where approximately half the total number of Moroccan and Turkish children are educated (Karagül 1994: 125). The other half are in *private schools*, where the situation is of course different. The most important difference is that Islamic religious instruction in

---

[11] Letter from the Association of Dutch Local Authorities, dated 12 May 1995, to the authors (authors' own records).

[12] *Memorandum on Islamic Religious Instruction in State Schools*, OC 20/46. The Hague: Association of Dutch Local Authorities. The Working Party which in Amsterdam in 1981 drew up the conditions for subsidizing Islamic religious instruction formulated it even more strongly: 'The staff should act in accordance with the norms and values applying in the Netherlands' (Lkoundi-Hamaekers 1987: 102; see also Van Rijsewijk 1984a: 196).

[13] *Memorandum on Islamic Religious Instruction in State Schools*, OC 20/46. The Hague: Association of Dutch Local Authorities.

[14] A parallel is sometimes drawn with Koran schools, which have acquired a dubious reputation in this respect. Cf. Kriens 1981; Ergün 1982; Van Rijsewijk 1984b; Van der Elst 1989; Roovers & Van Esch 1987: 41; Wagtendonk 1991: 156.

non-Muslim private schools is not a right but a privilege.[15] As a rule
the school management obliges children of other religions to attend
Catechism or Bible classes, though they do not always go so far as
to force these children to join in prayers or singing.[16] The introduction of Islamic religious instruction has seldom featured on the
agenda of Catholic or Protestant school boards, for managements
keen to retain the identity of a school have usually seen this as going
too far (Van Rijsewijk 1984a: 198; Bierlaagh 1988: 91). Rather than
religious instruction, they would consider offering ideological and
socio-cultural instruction in which attention is also paid to other religions. But this alternative has also come up against obstacles.[17] The
issue has been discussed by representatives from private schools on
study days and in steering groups, while national education study
centres have set down their views in memoranda and reports.[18] In
some cases the discussion has focused on the principle of whether
non-Catholic or non-Protestant children should really be admitted
to these schools.[19] The orthodox schools seem to be more strict in
their faith than those which encourage more open discussion or dialogue (Hilhorst 1985: 30–31).

Muslim initiatives
The development in some places of one form or another of Islamic
religious instruction, or at least a discussion about it, encouraged a
number of Muslims to concern themselves with the establishment
and quality of instruction for Muslim children. In the 1980s Muslims

---

[15] Act of 2 July 1981, containing the Primary Education Act, *Staatsblad* 1981, no.
468, Article 37. This article has been amended by the Acts of 4 July 1985, *Staatsblad*
1985, no. 393, and 12 May 1993, *Staatsblad* 1993, no. 270.

[16] In the Muslim schools founded by the Islamic Foundation of the Netherlands
for Education and Upbringing, non-Muslim children are exempted from Islamic
religious instruction and given the opportunity to take instruction in their own religion. In practice, however, this rule means very little; there are no non-Muslim children in Muslim schools (Shadid & Van Koningsveld 1991: 112–113).

[17] In March 1992 Bishop Gijsen of Roermond decided that 22 Limburg secondary schools could no longer call themselves Catholic. These schools had refused
to adapt their statutes in accordance with the General Regulations for Catholic
Education in Roermond. One of the points at issue was the scope offered by these
schools for other religions, such as Islam. The Bishop thought this was left too open
(*de Volkskrant*, 11 March 1992).

[18] There is an impression that private education takes a more active and principled view on this question than state education (cf. Roovers & Van Esch 1987:
44–45; Bierlaagh 1988; Wartna 1991).

[19] See, for instance, *Reformatorisch Dagblad*, 9 April 1983.

were involved in the development of a syllabus for Islamic religious instruction (Gerritsen 1991). In 1989 the Institute for Syllabus Development attempted a dialogue on the subject with the Christian Pedagogic Study Centre, of which the National Discussion Group Muslims and Christian Education in the Netherlands were members. However, to their dissatisfaction—as those involved told the authors—the Muslims in this Discussion Group were only allocated a secondary role.

After that the Islamic Foundation for the Advancement of Integration took the initiative in 1991 and set up the Islamic Pedagogic Centre (Triesscheijn & Geelen 1991). In June 1993, at the invitation of the Ministry of Education and Sciences, talks were held about the role of the Centre, in which the Ministry indicated its wish to discuss the subject further with representatives of Muslim primary schools. Those who had taken the initiative decided to hand over the further development of the Centre to the Islamic Schools Managements Organization (ISBI 1994: 2–3). Because of the Organization's lack of resources there were further delays, but in April 1995 the Islamic Pedagogic Centre at last became a reality.

Practical results

In practice, Islamic religious instruction has very rarely been provided in the state school system. In 1976 the Federation of Muslim Organizations in the Netherlands assessed the willingness of local authorities to provide opportunities for Islamic religious instruction. From the 70 local authorities approached they received 27 replies: some referred the Federation to the managements of private schools (FOMON s.a.: 26–29). Although most of the replies were positive, the enquiry did not trigger off a large-scale introduction of Islamic religious instruction. Wagtendonk (1991: 156) ascribed this to the local authorities' fear that the quality of the religious instruction would be as poor as the alleged quality of the Koran schools.[20]

---

[20] Wagtendonk maintains that at this time the Federation of Muslim Organizations in the Netherlands was dominated by the Süleymanlı movement, an orthodox stream within Turkish Islam. In Germany this movement tried to monopolize Islamic religious education. Both the 'left wing' and the Turkish 'Kemalists' protested at this situation, which eventually led to what was called the *Koranschule Debat*, in which Koran education in German mosques gained a poor reputation. The arguments were later transposed to the Netherlands. Wagtendonk believes that it was this bad reputation in particular which led to the reluctance of local authorities to render assistance in introducing Islamic religious education.

In some towns—Amsterdam, Deventer and Leiden—proposals were submitted, but the language requirement proved to be an insuperable obstacle (Roovers & Van Esch 1987: 40–44; Shadid & Van Koningsveld 1990a: 111–112). Nevertheless the Primary Education Act gave scope for a range of interpretations, as is evident from the fact that in Tiel Islamic religious instruction was actually provided in Arabic and in Turkish, and was subsidized.[21] In the 1993–1994 school year, Islamic religious instruction was also provided in Rotterdam, Apeldoorn and Ede (Karagül 1994: 110). In Ede, the language requirement was once again controversial. In the 1994–1995 school year, Islamic religious instruction was withdrawn from state schools there because objections were raised in one school against the subject being taught in Turkish. The municipal council was no longer willing to allow religious instruction in foreign languages, and adopted the view that state education must be accessible to everyone (*Trouw*, 17 June 1995). Although the Schools Inspectorate shared this view, according to one Inspector a policy of tolerance was followed in practice: lessons might be given in the children's mother tongue provided the teaching staff were at all times capable and willing to give an explanation of the content of the lessons in Dutch.

The absence of Islamic religious instruction in practice indicates that Muslims are by no means making obvious use of their rights to it, or are even able to do so. Experience has certainly not strengthened their faith in the state or church school system. In Wagtendonk's view (1991: 55), this has encouraged Muslims to attempt to establish their own denominational schools.

---

[21] An official of the Tiel Education Department explained, when asked, that it was up to the religious bodies concerned whether or not the Dutch language was used. After all, it was the quality of the teaching staff which mattered, and the local authorities should not interfere with that. Moreover, he continued: 'I am 100 per cent certain that we would block Islamic religious education with a regulation of that kind.' The 'minimal likelihood' that a Dutch Muslim would not be able to take the course was in his view not a strong counter-argument. Religious instruction in Tiel is provided by an imam. See also: Gemeente Tiel 1986; Roovers & Van Esch 1987: 41.

Muslim schools

Legislation

In the Netherlands parents and guardians have the constitutional right to plan the education of their children in accordance with their own religious or ideological beliefs. Article 23 of the Constitution guarantees freedom of foundation, denomination and organization, as well as of the appointment of teachers and choice of teaching materials. Moreover, the Constitution guarantees equal financial treatment of private and state education: both are funded from the public purse according to the same criteria. To qualify for funding, schools must satisfy a range of conditions concerned with quality, public order, morality, the competence of teaching staff and the public interest (Drop 1985: 180–208).

The procedure for founding or obtaining funds for new primary schools was laid down in the Primary Education Act referred to earlier.[22] Since 1992 new additional legislation has been in force, linked to economies of scale in primary education, which should eventually lead to a decrease in the total number of primary schools.[23] The procedure for starting a school begins with a request to the local authority to include the proposed school in the authorities' 'new schools plan',[24] and this request should, in addition to indicating the school's denomination, include the following: an estimate of the expected number of pupils, based on such things as written declarations by a sufficient number of parents; a description of the catchment

---

[22] Notably in Articles 51–64 of the Act of 2 July 1981, containing the Primary Education Act, *Staatsblad* 1981, no. 468, pp. 1–28. The provision of premises for the educational institution is regulated in Articles 65–91.

[23] The Act of 1 July 1922, containing a temporary regulation for the funding of new primary schools, pending comprehensive amendments to the system of criteria for founding or closing down primary schools (Temporary Act on Funding New Primary Schools), *Staatsblad* 1992, no. 365, pp. 1–10, and the Act of 15 December 1993, containing amendments to the system of criteria for founding and closing down primary schools in the Primary Education Act, and of the organization of accommodation in the Primary Education Act and the Interim Act on special education and special secondary education, *Staatsblad* 1993, no. 716.

[24] Until 1992 local councils had to submit a new plan before 1 October each year for review by the Provincial Executive. Since 1992 that plan has to be submitted by 1 August, and it is no longer the Provincial Executive, but the Minister of Education, who reviews it. A request for inclusion in the 'new schools plan' must be submitted before 1 February (Article 8, Temporary Act on Funding New Primary Schools).

area; an indication of the location in the municipality where the schooling will be provided; and finally a proposed date for the commencement of funding.[25] Based on this forecast, the local authority or the Minister decides whether the school is viable. The forecast must demonstrate convincingly that within five years of the proposed start of funding, and for at least the following 15 years, the school will have at least 200 children in attendance.[26] A tighter criterion for foundation is applied in many municipalities, such as 315 pupils in Amsterdam, 302 in Rotterdam, 333 in The Hague, and 312 in Utrecht. In drawing up the forecast, other schools of the same denomination need to be taken into account. If there is a similar school within three kilometres of the proposed catchment area, children for whom there would be sufficient places in the other school may not be counted.[27] After the local authority has made its decision on the new schools plan, it is submitted for approval to the Minister.[28]

Other important requirements with which the new school must comply are concerned with the settlement of labour disputes and employee participation issues.[29] All in all the rules for funding and the legal position of staff are laid down in great detail, with the result that politicians and officials are restricted in their range of policies.[30]

---

[25] Articles 5 and 12, Temporary Act on Funding New Primary Schools.

[26] Article 6, Temporary Act on Funding New Primary Schools.

[27] This rule contained a source of conflict about the actual interpretation of the concept 'denomination' (*richting*). This comes up, for instance, when those founding a school believe themselves to be of a denomination which differs from that of a neighbouring school, while the authorities reject the alleged differences as not material. The foundation of a second Muslim school in Den Bosch, or rather the associated legal tug-of-war, provides an illustration (Shadid & Van Koningsveld 1992a: 232–233). In Rotterdam, indeed, the Schools Inspector stated that as far as the Inspectorate was concerned, a Muslim school was a Muslim school, in order 'to prevent schisms'.

[28] The Minister has to give a decision before 1 December. See Article 8, Temporary Act on Funding New Primary Schools.

[29] See respectively Articles 40–42 of the Act of 2 July 1981, containing the Primary Education Act, *Staatsblad* 1981, no. 468, and Article 9 of the Act of 16 December 1981, containing basic regulations with regard to the representation of staff, parents and pupils within schools for pre-school, primary and secondary education, *Staatsblad* 1981, no. 778.

[30] Thus Akkermans (1986: 402–403) stated that the legislation on education was more of a safeguard than an instrument to control social processes.

Freedom of education

During the parliamentary discussion on the Primary Education Act in the mid-1970s, the issue of separate schools for different nationalities was touched upon in the course of discussions about the possible founding of Muslim schools. The government's response in its explanatory Memorandum to the Act made clear that Dutch legislation did not allow for any funding for separate national schools; however:

> This [Article 7] does not therefore cover, for example, schools for Muslim children in which the Dutch system of education is followed. Such schools should be treated on an equal footing with those for other denominations.[31]

In parliament, members of the Labour Party (PvdA) enquired whether this reasoning also applied if such a school was attended exclusively by children of Turkish nationality.[32] According to the government, however, the actual composition of the student body was not important:

> If it should happen that a Dutch school is attended entirely by children not of Dutch nationality, that does not necessarily mean that the school is intended exclusively for such children. Schools located in the Netherlands, and governed by Dutch legislation on education, are not directed at any specific nationality, nor should they be.[33]

In this response the government confirmed the freedom to found Muslim schools and their right to funding, subject to compliance with the conditions laid down by law.

In 1989 they repeated this point of view again in a special Policy Memorandum from Secretary of State Ginjaar-Maas (Liberal Party, VVD) for Education, in which she stated that Article 23 of the Constitution was intended to offer protection against arbitrary action by the authorities: 'For instance, it prevents an authority opposing the foundation of a school because its "denomination" is unwelcome to them.'[34] In her view, the article did not mean that the authorities

---

[31] *Explanatory Memorandum to the Primary Education Act*, TK 1976–1977, 14428, nos 1–4, p. 41.

[32] *Preliminary report on the Primary Education Act*, TK 1979–1980, 14428, no. 11, p. 36.

[33] *Memorandum in Reply on the Primary Education Act*, TK 1979–1980, 14428, no. 12, p. 24.

[34] Foundation of primary schools on Hindu or Islamic principles, TK 1988–1989, 21110, no. 1, p. 2.

must always assist with the funding. This obligation was only present if schools fell within the scope of the Primary Education Act. According to Article 7, Section 1 of the Act, this was expressly not the case for 'schools exclusively intended for children not of Dutch nationality'.

During the parliamentary discussion of the Temporary Law on the Funding of New Primary Schools (*Tijdelijke Wet Bekostiging Nieuwe Basisscholen*), the possible founding of Muslim schools came up in passing. Three members, representing orthodox Calvinist parties (Van der Vlies (SGP), Schutte (GPV) and Leerling (RPF)), indicated that they considered the stricter criteria a further infringement of the freedom of foundation, particularly for smaller religious groups.[35] The Secretary of State for Education, Wallage (Labour, PvdA) replied as follows:

> If I look at how many schools have been founded and I look at how denominations over a number of years have been able to take advantage of the low threshold, the assumption must be that in the great majority of cases, I will mention one exception, the founding of schools has to a large extent been possible, and so it is reasonable to ask all denominations to mark time. (. . .) Certain denominations have begun to catch up. The Muslims, who have not been in the country so long, are concerned to found their own schools, and they could well be affected by this foundation criterion. Certainly, Muslim sections of the population are often concentrated in certain areas, and it is quite likely that there will be sufficient children in such areas to satisfy the criterion. On practical grounds I therefore see no problem in principle for these denominations.[36]

It is difficult to judge how far this circumstantial argument holds water.[37]

According to the Islamic Schools Managements Organization, the new legislation made it impossible to found Muslim schools. On 23 March 1995 the Organization held a meeting with Secretary of State

---

[35] See Funding of Primary Schools, TK 83, 27 May 1992, pp. 83–5082 – 83–5092. We may assume that they were here thinking not of Muslim but of Christian groups. This is also clear from the election manifestos, in which they argued for the maintenance of the Christian character of Dutch society.

[36] Ibid., p. 83–5092. Muslim schools are mentioned once more, in a review of new primary schools founded in the period 1987–1991. Of the 347 new schools, 20 were Muslim, 23 ultra-orthodox Calvinist, 39 non-confessional private, 43 Roman Catholic, 58 Protestant and 143 state schools (TK 1991–1992, 22468, no. 5, p. 3).

[37] But if we recall that two-thirds of the Muslims in the Netherlands live outside the four main cities, it looks as if they again chose a historically unfavourable moment for their claims, as they did in the financing of their places of worship.

Netelenbos (Labour, PvdA) and various officials on this issue. The co-ordinator made the following comment on the meeting:

> We had the impression we were not being taken seriously. She [Netelenbos, Secretary of State] had little understanding of our disadvantaged situation. The general point of view was that the legislation was the same for everyone and that we had to make the best of it.

Wide-ranging discussion in society

Although the principle of freedom of education is subscribed to by all sides—at least officially—the emergence of Muslim schools has repeatedly caused debates to break out about their desirability. Opinions vary widely. A public opinion poll held in January 1992 showed 57 per cent of the Dutch population willing to allow Muslim schools, with 34 per cent against.[38] The general discussion led Secretary of State Ginjaar-Maas (Liberal Party, VVD) to set out her position in a Policy Memorandum—already mentioned above—in which she judged Muslim (and Hindu) schools

> on the basis of general social and educational criteria, and on criteria derived from specific policies, such as the minorities policy and the priorities policy in education.[39]

They are a speculative undertaking, in view of the fact that separate schools

> reinforce the self-awareness of pupils and improve their school results. (. . .) Such developments should be applauded, in the judgement of the government. But a different development is also conceivable: isolation may be intensified, for example because not only is there a common religious or ideological infrastructure, but also group formation based on nationality, or nationality of origin, and language. One may regret this happening, but in the first instance it is their own choice. Moreover, if the language of the country of origin plays an important role in or around the teaching process, this can be an obstacle to the acquisition of Dutch as a second language. (. . .) This would be an undesirable development in the government's view.[40]

---

[38] InterView, commissioned by *Veronica Nieuwslijn*, 'Nederlanders over de islam', January 1992. The research also showed that 60 per cent of the Dutch population thought that Muslim immigrants should be able to continue following their own religious practices and customs; 32 per cent wanted some of these practices banned.
[39] Foundation of Primary Schools on Hindu or Islamic Principles, TK 1988–1989, 21110, no. 1, p. 6.
[40] Ibid.

In the end it was the prospect of potential segregation which worried the Minister. Surprisingly enough her successor, Wallage (Labour, PvdA), argued three years later in favour of setting up separate single-sex classes for girls, to prevent Muslim girls dropping out of school (Ministerie van O & W 1992);[41] however, they never materialized.

Oddly enough, Ginjaar-Maas's policy document, endorsed by the Education Council, was never discussed in parliament.[42] As was customary, however, it was laid before the Central Committee for Consultation on Education, the body through which the government meets the representatives of the interest groups or co-ordinating organizations in education. Within the Central Committee, the Dutch Protestant Christian School Council Foundation and the Dutch Catholic School Council agreed with the Secretary of State's conclusions. The Contact Centre for the Advancement of State Education and the Association of Dutch Local Authorities thought that sufficient light had still not been shed on the social consequences of founding these schools.[43]

At a conference a few weeks later, the chairman of the Contact Centre, Tieleman, expressed objections to setting up Muslim schools which in his view could lead to tensions in society:

> We are on the wrong road with this increased fragmentation. It leads to the isolation of cultural minorities. It leads to fragmentation into subsidiary cultures which have fewer and fewer points of contact with each other (quoted in Sikkes 1989: 26).

After a few more weeks, on the occasion of the official opening of a Muslim primary school in Eindhoven, Minister of Education Deetman (Christian Democratic Party, CDA) expressed his 'sympathy' for the school in a letter to the management: 'The school can make a contribution to increasing mutual tolerance and respect for each other's beliefs' (quoted in *de Volkskrant*, 24 March 1989).[44]

---

[41] Although the Memorandum mentions 'Turkish and Moroccan girls', the classes Wallage had in mind were in fact meant for Muslim girls.

[42] By the time this was to happen, the Cabinet had resigned. It was not considered an appropriate time to put this Policy Memorandum on the agenda. In January 1992, however, the Memorandum came up for discussion indirectly as a result of questions in the House by MP Franssen about Hindu and Islamic primary schools: see note 47.

[43] Foundation of Primary Schools on Hindu or Islamic Principles, TK 1988–1989, 21110, no. 1, p. 1.

[44] The Alderman for Education and the Schools Inspector also spoke at the same

The Research Office of the Calvinist Reformed Political League (GPV) did not share this view because Muslim schools 'could encourage discrimination and the formation of ghettos', though it did acknowledge the constitutional right of Muslims to found their own schools (Groen van Prinsterer Stichting 1984: 106–108). The Study Centre Foundation of the Political Reformed Party (SGP) put forward another argument: the foundation of a 'Koran school' in their view conflicted with the intent of the 1917 'pacification', with which half a century of strife over education had been finally settled between the secular and religious parties. The 'Schools Question' had after all been fought 'for the freedom of Protestant education' (Mulder *et al.* 1988: 73–74). Furthermore, the Study Centre thought that 'education in its various forms should be in accordance with the Word of God', meaning the God of the Bible (and more precisely, of the Dutch Authorized Version) (ibid.: 62–63). The Labour Party (PvdA 1992: 13) in its turn acknowledged the right to found denominational schools, but was still in principle in favour of state education.

In parliament opinions were just as divided. The Christian Democrat Huibers (CDA) thought that Muslim schools could make a contribution to integration, provided they oriented themselves towards Dutch society and complied with the normal legislation on education (Niedekker 1992). Like his colleague Hermes (Christian Democratic Party, CDA), he drew a parallel in the *NRC Handelsblad* (17 January 1989) with the emancipation of Catholics and Calvinists. However, Van Leijenhorst (also of the Christian Democrats), in the same *NRC* article, was apprehensive about extending the language deficiency among Muslim children, while Lilipaly (Labour, PvdA) was afraid that the dialogue 'between Dutch and immigrant groups about each other's cultural customs was being avoided'. Lankhorst, of the Green Left Party (GroenLinks), expressed the view in *de Volkskrant* (24 March 1992) that Muslim schools had as much right to exist as Roman Catholic and Protestant ones. As far as he was concerned, however, the whole of private education could be jettisoned, since he was in favour of 'a pluriform school'.[45] Franssen, of the Liberal Party (VVD), following in the footsteps of his party leader, Bolkestein, implied in

opening ceremony. Both warned parents not to force their children into isolation (Lammers 1989: 7).

[45] Lankhorst was supported during a discussion forum by De Cloe (Labour, PvdA) and Nuis (Democrats 66, D66).

January 1992 on an IKON radio programme that Muslim schools did not comply with Dutch law.[46] In the *NOS-Laat* television programme of 15 January 1992 he expressed himself as follows:

> What worries me primarily is that we are putting Muslim children into quite separate schools, when they are part of a minority group in Dutch society which is in a most vulnerable position socially, economically and from the point of view of the community, and which we are trying hard through a minorities policy to integrate into Dutch society, and to give the same opportunities the Dutch have. I am very much afraid that with a further growth in the number of Muslim schools to a hundred or so, also continued in secondary education, this segregated development within a closed-in culture, which is in no way related to Dutch society, will lead to tensions in the future. (. . .) Is this a desirable development, and are we not right to launch a debate about it, particularly because a number of the reasons for which parents want to found those schools arise from criticisms of the way Muslim children are treated in the Dutch education system? And would we not do better to improve Dutch education, rather than encouraging this separate development?

He even tabled questions for the government on this issue.[47] In addition to the points listed above he also raised the spectre of possible 'indissoluble links (. . .) with fundamentalist or non-democratic organizations in their countries of origin'. He also appealed to the government to carry out a closer inspection into the functioning of these schools, as well as developing a policy to prevent Muslim schools. The Secretary of State categorically refused these demands.[48] He stated plainly that the schools satisfied all the legal and educational criteria. To Franssen's suggestion that there might be unacceptable contamination by fundamentalist or non-democratic organizations, the Minister replied:

> There is absolutely no reason even to suspect a penal offence when a school simply applies to be considered for funding. Any measures taken on such grounds would be evidence of prejudice against the organizations involved.[49]

---

[46] Cf. *NRC Handelsblad*, 13 January 1992; see also Rath & Sunier 1993.

[47] Questions in the House by Member of Parliament Franssen about Hindu and Muslim primary schools. (Submitted 21 January 1992.) Reply by Secretary of State Wallage (Education and Sciences). (Received 29 January 1992.) Appendix TK 1991–1992, pp. 719–721.

[48] The Schools Inspectorate had reported on the functioning of Muslims schools as early as 1989 and 1990. From these reports it appeared that these schools functioned 'normally' in every respect.

[49] Appendix TK 1991–1992, pp. 719–721. As a result of Franssen's public pro-

It was not only members of the indigenous Dutch population who took part in the exchange of views, although they dominated the public discussion. Voices were also heard in opposition from immigrant organizations. For instance, the Committee of Moroccan Workers in the Netherlands (KMAN 1989: 4) maintained that Muslim schools would be responsible for the creation of 'educational ghettos, even worse than black schools'. Moreover, children in those schools would be exposed to an ideology 'which did not tally with the real situation of the migrants in the Netherlands'.

The Türk Eğitimen Birliği (TEB), an organization for Turkish teaching staff, thought that 'Muslim schools could not provide a solution to education problems, whether from the pedagogic point of view, or culturally and socially'. According to the TEB, concerns about 'religious ideology' carried more weight in the founding of Muslim schools than concerns for 'other problems', and what is more, in principle the TEB was in favour of 'migrant and Dutch children learning together and playing together' (Doğru 1990: 17). The Turkish Federation of Democratic Social Associations also thought problems could arise if Muslim children rarely mixed with Dutch children.[50] Kabdan, a Turkish academic, expressed his opinion in *de Volkskrant* (17 November 1987) that some Turkish Muslim leaders, masquerading behind national identity, were just trying to increase their own power and to serve their own commercial interests.

It is undoubtedly the case that Muslim schools are a controversial subject in the political and ideological climate of the Netherlands. Besides arguments in favour of founding Muslim schools, such as freedom of education and the principle of equality, plenty of objections have been put forward: the fear of segregation and of ghetto formation, negative consequences for integration, and interference by fundamentalist or non-democratic organizations.

Administrative integration

The founding of Muslim schools is not only influenced by the attitude of the local community, which can sometimes be sceptical and

nouncements, a letter in *de Volkskrant* (18 January 1992) drew attention to the Convention on Children's Rights. The writer claimed that this 1989 UN Convention contained at least seven articles justifying the foundation of Muslim schools.

[50] Triesscheijn 1989a; Teunissen 1990: 49; see also: reader's letter in *Samenwijs* 10 (1990) 5: 199.

suspicious. The administrative integration of these schools, which includes complying with the legal obligation to be affiliated to an appeal board, a surety organization and an arbitration committee, can produce further problems. Most appeal boards and surety organizations are linked to organizations of school managements, which in their turn are affiliated to co-ordinating organizations. These are run on religious or ideological lines, and operate in a strongly 'pillarized' structure of management and control. This arrangement has proved to be a deterrent to the entry of a new denomination. In the early days, the existing management organizations refused to accept Muslim school managements as members, using the argument that this would be an unacceptable breach of their founding principles.[51] The alternative was to set up their own management organization, but this came up against the legal requirement that at least 50 schools must be affiliated. There were not that many Muslim schools. Under pressure from the Ministry of Education, the Association of Private Schools for Education on General Principles, and to a lesser extent the Managements Association for Protestant Education, finally accepted Muslim school managements, but only on a temporary basis, a single year at a time, and as special non-voting members (Leeuwis 1988: 5; Shadid & Van Koningsveld 1990a: 125–126). Both organizations restricted their efforts to administrative and legally required activities, and excluded the affiliated Muslim school managements from anything to do with policy. Secretary of State for Education Wallage (Labour, PvdA) finally released them from their obligations. On 13 October 1989 he announced that the legal minimum number of schools for an appeal board was lowered from 50 to 10 (Shadid & Van Koningsveld 1992a: 230). This decision smoothed the way for a Muslim management organization and on 27 February 1990 the Islamic Schools Managements Organization was set up.

The Muslim school managements were not exactly falling over each other to set up their own co-ordinating organization. They were, however, put under pressure from various sides to take steps in this direction. To quote the co-ordinator:

---

[51] One example is the Foundation for Islamic Schools in Eindhoven, which in 1981 tried in vain to gain membership of a schools managements organization. The aloof attitude of, in this case, the Association of Private Schools for Education on General Principles was in fact partly due to the fear of becoming entangled in the web of extreme nationalist groups such as the Grey Wolves and the Amicales (Coppen & Ural 1982: 40).

At the outset we did not really welcome the prospect. Let us be honest. We really doubted that we were ready for it. The problem is, you haven't got a firm base. You can't employ anyone. But you are a co-ordinating organization and must carry out certain tasks. The other co-ordinators ... even the smallest has several hundred schools. If we had been able to get the things we have to get now at the same level and in the same quantity from another organization, then it [setting up the Islamic Schools Managements Organization] would probably not have been necessary. But that option was not available.

In accordance with the requirements of the law, the Managements Organization provided its own surety fund, an appeals board and an arbitration committee for employee participation issues.[52] All Muslim primary schools became members. However, the Islamic Foundation of the Netherlands for Education and Upbringing (ISNO)—which set up three schools—left the Islamic Schools Managements Organization in 1991 when their representative was dismissed from the chairmanship of the Managements Organization. In the autumn of 1993 the Islamic Foundation disbanded itself, and the three schools acquired three separate school managements. Since 1994 one of them has formally rejoined the Islamic Schools Managements Organization; the other two have until now been associated with the Managements Organization on an informal basis.[53]

A side-effect of the foundation of the Managements Organization was that its Muslim school members made their entry on the political scene. Like the other co-ordinating organizations, the Islamic Schools Managements Organization had the right to participate in the numerous consultative and administrative bodies in the field of education, such as the influential Central Committee for Consultation on Education, on which members of government from the Ministry of Education also sat. As a small organization the Islamic Schools Managements Organization is not in fact in a position to stir things up very much. They do not themselves participate in the Central Committee, and for information about the world of education they are very dependent on the other co-ordinating bodies. To quote the Managements Organization co-ordinator on this position:

---

[52] *Appendix* TK 1991–1992, pp. 719–721; Landman 1992: 266.
[53] Oral information from the Secretary of Islamic Foundation of the Netherlands for Education and Upbringing and Co-ordinator of Islamic Schools Managements Organization.

We have very close contacts with Catholic and Protestant managements organizations. We have good contacts with them, have pretty generous access to documentation and information, and we also discuss matters. With the others, such as the Association of Private Schools for Education on General Principles, we also have good contacts and we even make use of some of their services. But we are up against mega-organizations. That can also be very awkward. We are not kept fully informed about everything. There are many things we don't hear about until after they have been settled. Agreements, regulations, consultation with the Directorate-General for Education, etcetera, we only hear afterwards that we, too, could have taken part in them. But we're not really seen as a full partner in the first place. As a result we're automatically excluded from certain activities. In itself that's not such a bad thing, because if you want to take part in everything then you have to devote capacity, expertise and staff to it and be able to send people along everywhere. So long as you're small and have no financial backing, you can't do that.

At the March 1995 meeting with Secretary of State for Education, Netelenbos (Labour, PvdA) the Islamic Schools Managements Organization raised the point of the deficiencies in the flow of information reaching them, and the fact that the Managements Organization was never involved. The Secretary of State promised to improve matters. In future the Managements Organization hopes to be able to participate fully in the Central Committee.

Practical results

The first Muslim primary schools started in 1988. By 1994 there were 29 Muslim primary schools in the Netherlands—out of a total of 8,139.[54] Three of them had been launched on the initiative of the Islamic Foundation of the Netherlands for Education and Upbringing before its demise in 1993. This Foundation was linked by its statutes to the Islamic Foundation of the Netherlands (Hollanda Diyanet Vakfi), which from the start had pursued the establishment of Muslim primary schools.[55] The majority of present-day Muslim

    [54] Numbers for the school year 1993–1994. Source: Central Bureau of Statistics (CBS) (table produced on request) and Islamic Schools Managements Organization (written overview of Muslim schools).
    [55] The Islamic Foundation of the Netherlands was officially set up on 10 December 1982. See for the Diyanet, the Islamic Foundation of the Netherlands and the Islamic Foundation of the Netherlands for Education and Upbringing: De Graaf 1983: 13–17, 1985: 25–29; Den Exter 1990; Teunissen 1990: 48–49; Landman 1992: 101–113; Shadid & Van Koningsveld 1992a: 228.

schools have, however, been founded by local organizations with divergent backgrounds.

In 1993 only a small minority of children from a Muslim background—about 4 per cent—were educated in a Muslim school.[56] Their numbers (4,360 in the 1993–1994 school year) pale into insignificance when compared to the 1,426,533 primary schoolchildren in that year.[57] As far as is known there is not a single non-Muslim pupil in a Muslim school (Shadid & Van Koningsveld 1991: 112). On the other hand it is still the case that the majority of the teachers are non-Muslims.

The increase in the number of Muslim schools does not mean that the applications of Muslim organizations are always granted. Since 1988 several applications have been refused or declared unacceptable. The grounds vary: because data were lacking; because it was thought that more than one Muslim school in a radius of five kilometres was unnecessary; or because the school in question was considered to be a 'nationality school' (Wagtendonk 1991: 167). Where Muslim schools have at long last been placed on a municipality's 'new schools plan', it has often happened with bad grace. This will be discussed more extensively in Chapter 10, dealing with the establishment of Muslim schools in Rotterdam and Utrecht.

Other educational institutions

In addition to Islamic religious instruction and Muslim schools, there are two other institutions within the field of education requiring attention. These are Muslim broadcasting networks, and training for imams and other theological courses.

Muslim broadcasting networks

Muslims first raised the question of a Muslim broadcasting network in the 1970s. Initially the authorities were very dismissive. The first applications for transmission time were refused because the Ministry

---

[56] *Handboek Minderheden* 5/1050 (1993): 27. A year earlier Shadid and Van Koningsveld (1992a: 229) calculated a total of 3.7 per cent. The percentages for Turkish and Moroccan children would be 2.5 and 3.1 per cent respectively.

[57] CBS (table produced on request) and Islamic Schools Managements Organization (written overview of Muslim schools).

of Culture, Recreation and Social Work took the view that the organizations applying were not sufficiently representative (Landman 1992: 256). The 1983 *Minorities Memorandum* said nothing about communication channels specifically for Muslims, in spite of the recommendations of the Waardenburg Working Party (Werkgroep-Waardenburg 1983: 57), from which it was obvious that a clear need was felt among Muslims for such channels. However, in 1986, after repeated refusals, the Ministry was apparently no longer able to ignore the demand for a Muslim network. In that year the application by the Turkish-Islamic Cultural Federation Foundation was granted, on condition that the transmission time was assigned to the Islamic Broadcasting Foundation.[58]

It was not only representativeness that played a role in the allocation of transmission time to the Islamic Broadcasting Foundation. In contrast to earlier applications for transmission time by Muslim organizations, the Board of Welfare for Minorities at the Ministry of Welfare, Health and Culture were increasingly involved in this application, alongside the Board of Radio, Television and Press. The Minorities board eventually played a major part in the final judgement on the application for transmission time. In the context of the minorities policy, the Board of Welfare for Minorities thought the introduction of a Muslim network of great importance, particularly because of the role such a network could play within Dutch society. This argument is reflected in the speech by Minister Brinkman (Christian Democratic Party, CDA) of Welfare, Health and Culture, at the inauguration of the Islamic Broadcasting Foundation, in which he stated that 'one of the most important functions of the Foundation consists in informing Dutch society about Islam in the Netherlands'.[59]

On several occasions after 1986 the argument of not being representative enough still played a role in decisions on the allocation of transmission time to Muslim networks. This was the reason for the Media Commission withdrawing transmission time from the Islamic Broadcasting Foundation in 1993 to allocate it to the Netherlands Muslim Council, which afterwards set up the Netherlands Muslim

---

[58] Decree RTP/ZAZ/U-87515 II by the Minister of Welfare, Health and Culture, dated 16 April 1986.
[59] *Handboek Minderheden*, Snelle Berichtgeving 5 (1987): 8.

Network.[60] A request by the Council in 1995 for more transmission time was refused for the same reason.[61]

Training for imams and other theological courses

In spite of the existence of a few private courses for imams,[62] up to now Muslim organizations have recruited their religious leaders mainly from abroad. The desirability of a Dutch course for imams has, however, been the subject of discussion since the early 1980s, both within Muslim communities and outside them. The concept of a 'Dutch Islam' seems to play a role in this. Imams trained in the Netherlands would obviously be more familiar with the Dutch situation. They would also be able to act as a bridge between the Muslim communities and Dutch society, and so could contribute to the integration of Muslim migrants. An additional advantage of a course for those already in the country is that it would avoid the problems to do with admission. On these grounds the Waardenburg Working Party (Werkgroep Waardenburg 1983: 53) argued in the early 1980s for a Dutch course for imams, recognized and subsidized by the authorities.

In 1983 there were several exploratory meetings about an imam course at academic level between representatives of the co-ordinating group Muslim Organizations in the Netherlands and the management of the Faculty of Theology at the University of Amsterdam. For various reasons the proposed course was not forthcoming.[63] Since 1983, however, arguments for a Dutch imam course have repeatedly been advanced at various times in parliament, mainly by the Christian Democrats (CDA).[64]

---

[60] *Nederlandse Staatscourant* 1993, no. 121.

[61] Letter from the Commissariat for the Media, JV/1924/TV, to the Netherlands Muslim Council, dated 10 May 1995.

[62] The Jamia Madinatul Islam, a course mainly taken by young Indian and Pakistani Muslims, started in The Hague in 1983. There is also a part-time course in Utrecht run by the Federation Ahmaddiyah Anjuman Isha'at Islam Netherlands, which trains adults to be assistant and auxiliary imams. After this relatively modest course they can take a further three-year imam training course in Lahore, Pakistan (Wagtendonk 1990: 118; Landman 1992: 269–270; Onderwijsraad 1994: 39).

[63] Muslim Organizations in the Netherlands ceased to exist a short time after the discussions. In addition, the Faculty of Theology at the University of Amsterdam was reorganized, and it was not clear how many students would be interested in an imam course at academic level (Karagül & Wagtendonk 1994: 22).

[64] See, *inter alia*: Handelingen TK 1989–1990, UCV 48, p. 51.

Ten years later, in 1993, an imam course was again the subject of discussion. Mulder-Van Dam, a Christian Democrats member of the House, tabled a motion on the subject in which she asked the government to investigate whether and how the authorities could create conditions for the Muslim community itself to provide the opportunity for training Muslim spiritual leaders if there was a requirement for this. She considered the creation of such a provision desirable 'in the context of the integration process'.[65] MP Apostolou (Labour, PvdA), supported the motion. Van den Berg (Political Reformed Party, SGP), however, announced that his party saw no reason at all for such a request: 'We cannot see that any obligation lies with the authorities in this area.'[66] Nevertheless the motion was accepted. A few weeks later Minister of Education Ritzen (Labour, PvdA) replied that in principle it was possible for 'an applied, professionally oriented imam course to be grafted onto an existing educational institution'.[67] Following this a project group on imam training was set up in the Ministry. In early 1994 it began consultations with representatives of the Turkish consultation body, the Turkish embassy, the Diemen College, several experts and, at a later stage, with representatives of several Muslim organizations (Onderwijsraad 1994: 2).

The project group established that in secondary education there was no provision whatsoever for the professional training of imams. There were some possibilities in further and higher education, but no clear policy in existence.[68] Ritzen asked the advice of the Education Council on the need and desirability of an imam course within secondary education.[69] In its advice, which appeared in October 1994, the Council concluded that the national government could play a limited role in creating conditions for setting up a preliminary course in secondary education. Their concrete proposal was that secondary schools wanting to co-operate with an imam course should allow for a maximum of seven hours a week for this in the options area of the basic curriculum. A large part of the preliminary training, how-

---

[65] TK 1993–1994, 23409, no. 8.
[66] *Hand.* TK, 1993–1994, UCV 19, p. 27.
[67] TK 1993–1994, 23409, no. II.
[68] Colleges can register their courses with the Central Register of Courses in Higher Education. Recognition of their application can be expected once it is clear there is a social need for them. As for academic education, reference was made to the University of Leiden (TK 1993–1994, 23409, no. 14).
[69] TK 1993–1994, 23409, no. 14.

ever, would have to be the responsibility of the Muslim groups themselves in the form of extra-curricular activities (Onderwijsraad 1994:
10–11).

Early in 1995 Secretary of State for Education Netelenbos (Labour,
PvdA) declared that she agreed with the Education Council's views.
She indicated that she would give secondary schools the opportunity
of training their Muslim pupils to be imams.[70] Bolkestein, chairman
of the Liberal Party (VVD), thereupon commented in the Christian
daily *Trouw* (4 February 1995) that from the point of view of the
'integration of our Muslim fellow-citizens' a Dutch imam course was
so important that the authorities should give financial support to it.
Some time later, in the same newspaper (9 and 17 February), the
Platform of Islamic Organizations in Greater Rotterdam and the
Turkish-Islamic Cultural Federation Foundation voiced criticisms of
Netelenbos's and Bolkestein's pronouncements, which they claimed
gave the wrong impression of an imam's training. 'You can't do it
in just a few hours at school. In involves far more,' remarked a representative of the Platform.

Meanwhile the Turkish-Islamic Cultural Federation, in co-operation with the Islamic Foundation of the Netherlands, had already
developed an imam course at secondary level in Turkey, intended
for Turkish boys who had completed their primary education in the
Netherlands (Karagül & Wagtendonk 1994: 23–24).

Islam has recently gained ground in higher vocational and university education. In 1992 the University of Leiden started a three-
year degree course in Islamology, and after some stirrings in Muslim
circles the University of Amsterdam acquired the first Special Chair
of Islam in Europe, an initiative of the Amsterdam Centre for
Foreigners which enjoyed wide political support.[71] In addition, a start
has recently been made on a higher vocational course for teachers
of religion/Islam at the Diemen College.

---

[70] *Contrast* 2 (1995) 4: 6. The Second Chamber of Parliament was informed on
31 January 1995 (TK 1994–1995, 23901, no. 9).
[71] In the Committee of Recommendation the most important political parties
(Labour (PvdA), Christian Democrats (CDA), the Green Left Party (GroenLinks,
Liberals (VVD) and Democrats 66 (D66)) were represented.

CHAPTER FIVE

POLITICS AND OTHER SPHERES

The political sphere

Participation in politics by Muslims

In recent decades, Muslims have appeared on the political scene at various times and in different ways, deriving their right to do so in the first instance from the Dutch Constitution.[1] The most important limitations on the political rights of many Muslims stem from Article 4 of that Constitution, which states that every *Dutch national* has an equal right to choose the members of general representative bodies, or to be chosen as a member of such bodies. Residents without Dutch nationality are excluded from elections for the States General or Parliament (Articles 54 and 56) and for the Provincial Councils (Articles 129 and 130), though they do have the right to take part in elections for municipalities and municipal districts (Article 130). The exclusion is primarily a question of citizenship; in itself it has little to do with religion or race, although such considerations are not completely absent. During parliamentary discussion on the proposed law on voting rights for non-Dutch residents, for example, spokesmen for the small Calvinist parties expressed their fear that this would give political power to Muslims or allow them to set up their own parties (Rath 1988: 26).[2] Partly because of this they later (in the second instance) voted against extending the franchise.

Although Muslims have *de jure* equality, their political activities are very closely watched. In the 1970s, when the first Muslim organizations made their appearance, they were very quickly accused of being fascist or crypto-fascist, and of being involved in the violent oppression of guest workers. It was rumoured that they had links

---

[1] The Constitution lays down, for example, that all residents of the Netherlands—and hence Muslim residents of foreign nationality—enjoy the fundamental democratic right of appeal (Article 5), together with freedom of speech (Article 7) and freedom of association, of assembly, and of demonstration (Articles 8 and 9), within the limits of the law.

[2] See also *Hand.* TK 1978–1979, pp. 3696–3697.

with far-right and nationalistic organizations such as the Turkish Grey Wolves and the Moroccan Amicales.[3] Today the image of Muslim organizations is certainly less crude, though some are still associated with political extremism.[4]

According to De Graaf (1983, 1985), Muslim organizations in the mid-1980s concerned themselves little, if at all, with Dutch politics. In the 1990s, however, they have engaged in all kinds of political activities, either through their own more or less autonomous organizations, or—on occasion—through existing organizations in society, such as trade unions or political parties.[5] Although no political parties are known to exclude Muslims by statute, it appears that the possible membership of Muslims can arouse fierce controversy, to say nothing of their possible adoption as candidates. The adherents of the Christian parties in particular find this a problem.

The key question here is whether it is possible for Muslims to engage in 'Christian politics'. Supporters of parties of principle such as the Calvinist SGP, GPV and RPF, and some of the more orthodox among the Christian Democrats (CDA), reject this out of hand. In their eyes public life and politics is based on the Law of God, and they recognize only one Almighty God. All other divinities, including Allah, are banished to the realms of idolatry and false religions, and could never therefore guide Christian policies.[6] Within the Christian Democratic Party (CDA), however, a more liberal outlook prevails. Their mainly pragmatic approach in part goes back to the agreements struck on political matters in 1978—that is to say

---

[3] Cf. Penninx 1979; Theunis 1979: 449; LAKAF 1980.

[4] Mohammed Rabbae, then director of the Netherlands Centre for Foreigners, claimed in the spring of 1993 that the Union of Moroccan Muslim Organizations in the Netherlands was a cover organization for the Moroccan authorities. He alleged that the Union employed intimidating practices to bring 'dissident' Moroccans into line. The Union thereupon asked the courts to forbid the Netherlands Centre for Foreigners making further public statements of this kind, but their request was refused. The Centre had made sufficiently plain that it had good grounds for its allegations (Koolen 1993a, 1993b; Rabbae 1993; KMAN 1994: 43–44; *ACB Nieuwsbrief* 4 (1994) 1: 13–17). The Intelligence Services warned in 1992 that the presence of Muslims would be a threat to state security if violent fundamentalist movements were to extend their activities to the Netherlands. A university department was commissioned to carry out research on this subject, and the researchers concluded that fears of Muslim extremism were based on fantasy (Latuheru *et al.* 1994).

[5] For the activities of independent organizations, see Doomernik 1991; Landman 1992.

[6] Cf. Groen van Prinsterer Stichting 1984; Verburgh 1989; see also *Reformatorisch Dagblad*, 8 August 1992; *Trouw*, 13 August 1992.

at the time of the fusion of three confessional parties (the Catholics, and two Calvinist parties (KVP, ARP and CHU) into a single Christian Democratic party (CDA). The party may be founded on the gospels, but this was operationalized into a programme of political principles and four rather abstract core concepts: justice, shared responsibility, solidarity, and stewardship. This applies to all members of the party, regardless of their personal source of inspiration, for they do not 'judge one other'. The discussions and arguments on this question were not in fact concerned only with Muslims; Hindus, marginal cults, agnostics and 'career-obsessed yuppies' were also the subject of debate.[7]

Muslims or their organizations have been represented with varying emphases in municipal and district municipal elections.[8] Muslim parties have appeared here and there, but without much effect (*inter alia* Rath 1986). Leaders of Muslim organizations have also stood as candidates for the regular parties, such as the left-wing Green Left Party (Groen Links), or the Christian Democratic Party (CDA) (Sunier 1994). To encourage the political participation of Muslims, the Islamic Foundation for the Advancement of Integration took the initiative of setting up a national association for Muslims with political interests: the Debating Club '94 (DC'94). In addition to organizing management training and other courses, DC'94 strives for integrated consultations with the existing political parties (ISBI 1994). In 1996 the Ministry of Internal Affairs refused a request for a subsidy for these activities because they did not concern any matter covered by the current rules on political parties.[9]

---

[7] The discussions took place at the time the Christian Democratic Party (CDA) was formed (1978). After that they were raised again on the establishment of the Intercultural Council (1983) and the 1986 municipal elections; on the occasion of Ramlal, a Hindu, taking his seat as a Member of Parliament, and in the somewhat unfortunate remarks by the party chairman, Van Velzen, in 1992; and finally when the Programme of Basic Principles was revised (1993). See *inter alia*: *Bestuursforum*, January 1982; *de Volkskrant*, 22 February 1986; *Het Binnenhof*, 29 August 1992; Letter from Mr O.W.A. Baron van Verschuer, chairman of the Commission on Basic Principles and Political Activities, to the Chairman of the CDA, Prof. Dr P.A.J.M. Steenkamp, dated 30 October 1978; Letter from Wim van Velzen, party chairman, to the members of the CDA party executive, no. A1–751/92/HD, dated 2 September 1992.

[8] See Rath 1981, 1982, 1985 and 1990; Pennings 1986; Rath & Buijs 1987.

[9] Letter from the Minister of Internal Affairs H.F. Dijkstal to the Debating Club '94, dated 17 April 1996, ref. Cim 96/557.

Partners in the political debate

In the 1970s contacts between the national authorities—in particular the Ministry of Culture, Recreation and Social Work—and organizations of Muslims were sporadic and limited to discrete subjects
such as the Temporary Regulation concerning Subsidies for Places
of Worship for Muslims, and practical matters such as regulating ritual slaughter. As far as the government was concerned, there was
no need (as yet) for an integrated partner in the political debate.
Given a little flexibility, problems still seemed capable of being resolved
without official representation.

From the early 1980s this attitude slowly began to change. There
was an increase in the contact between Muslim organizations and the
Ministry of Welfare, Health and Culture (and within it notably with
the Board of Welfare for Minorities). This resulted not only from the
fact that the Muslim organizations themselves were co-ordinating
more and more socio-cultural and other activities, but also from a
growing awareness that with their widespread following they could
play an important role in implementing the minorities policy. To
quote a Ministry of Welfare spokesman: 'It was clear, for instance,
that through these organizations people could be reached who would
have been beyond the reach of other organizations.'

At first the Board of Welfare for Minorities maintained contacts
which were mainly concerned with the subsidy of social and cultural
activities.[10] After some time this framework was widened: for instance,
the Board played an important role in the establishment of the
Islamic Broadcasting Foundation, by lobbying the media departments
within the Ministry. The need to arrive at some form of representative dialogue grew, but its realization was still a long way off.

In addition to the Ministry of Welfare, Health and Culture, the
Ministry of Internal Affairs actively started looking for a dialogue
with Muslim organizations from 1981 onwards. The reason for this
was that they wanted to set up a national framework for the involvement of minorities, a National Advice and Consultation Structure,
an arrangement first suggested in the 1981 *Draft Minorities Memorandum*
(*Ontwerp-Minderhedennota*, Ministerie van BiZa 1981: 45–48). The most

---

[10] This became possible after the statement of principle in the *Minorities Memorandum*
that Muslim organizations should also be considered eligible for financial support
for socio-cultural work (Ministerie van BiZa 1983: 110–111).

important minorities would have separate seats arranged by their
countries of origin or combinations of them. In this context, in 1981
the Ministry began to bring together, in principle, all the organizations of Surinamese and Antilleans (those from the Dutch West Indies
islands) into a single platform. And according to an official of the
Ministry, 'the religious wing was very deliberately not omitted'. For
example, the World Islamic Mission was also approached when it
came to Surinamese organizations.

A Turkish consultation body was set up two years later, and here,
too, the Ministry of Internal Affairs was closely involved. From the
start two Muslim organizations took part in setting up the Turkish
Consultation Body; they were the Turkish-Islamic Cultural Federation
Foundation and the Netherlands Islamic Centre Foundation. Eventually
both of these also became part of the Turkish Consultation Body. The
Ministry played a less prominent role in setting up the Co-operative
Association of Moroccans and Tunisians a little later, although it
continually pressed for the participation of the Union of Moroccan
Muslim Organizations in the Netherlands in the Co-operative Associa-
tion, but without success.

The efforts of the Ministry of Internal Affairs were mainly aimed
at making the proposed co-operative associations as representative
as possible.

> And if you talk about the degree of representativeness, in principle
> you should involve all supra-regional organizations and groupings, and
> therefore the religious organizations as well,

said one of the officials involved. Apparently the idea that Muslim
organizations were indispensable for the implementation of the minorities policy had meanwhile taken root. One of the consequences was
that the government received a number of recommendations on religious affairs from a sub-committee of the National Advice and Consultation Structure (*inter alia* IOT 1992).

During the Rushdie affair the Ministry used the contacts it had
built up with the National Advice and Consultation Structure to
arrange consultations between all known organizations and Minister
Van Dijk (Christian Democratic Party, CDA). The two meetings
which took place on this subject[11] were meant primarily to prevent

---

[11] The first meeting was with the Co-ordination Director of the Minorities Policy,
followed a few days later by a personal meeting with the Minister.

any possible damaging consequences to the minorities policy resulting from the Rushdie affair, by reaching agreements and clarifying
the position of both sides. In addition the Ministry wanted to create a structure for consultation, so that in similar circumstances they
could communicate easily and quickly with all leading figures in
Muslim circles. During the discussions the Muslim organizations were
given a three-part message:

> Obey the law; you have plenty of scope within the law to express your
> opinions; and if anyone interferes with your rights then you will find
> the government on your side, backing you.[12]

On the eve of the Gulf War the same Ministry again arranged a
meeting with Muslim organizations, not with all of them this time,
because of the short notice, but only with the larger ones. The main
aim of this initiative was also to prevent undesirable developments.[13]

A representative body

Meanwhile the report of the Hirsch Ballin Committee (Commissie-
Hirsch Ballin 1988) had been published. On the subject of the spiritual care of Muslims and Hindus in public institutions, the Committee
argued for two spiritual services to be set up. The condition was
again that the groups involved would set up a form of co-operative
association which could function as a partner in dialogue with the
authorities and, like the Christian churches, act as the organization
sending out the spiritual advisers.[14] The Ministry of Internal Affairs
again organized meetings with Muslim organizations. However, unlike
the setting up of the consultation bodies, or the meetings occasioned
by the Rushdie affair and the Gulf War, the Ministry did not push
the initiative. According to one of the civil servants involved, spiritual care was regarded as an internal matter for the churches, in
which the authorities could and should not take an active part, on
the grounds of the principle of the separation of church and state:

> All we can do is to send the signal, "We need a partner in the dia-
> logue from your side, but you will have to set it up yourself". All we
> can do after that is make sure that we think the partner put forward
> is sufficiently representative.

---

[12] Interview with a civil servant in the Ministry of Internal Affairs.
[13] Idem.
[14] TK 1989–1990, 20868, no. 2, p. 19.

By 1989 it was already plain that a representative body would not be immediately forthcoming. During the meetings at the Ministry at the time of the Rushdie affair it became obvious that there was some kind of schism; one section of the Muslim organizations refused to sit around the same table as the rest. Late in 1989, when the definitive government position on the proposals of the Hirsch Ballin Committee was put to parliament, there was as yet no suggestion of setting up a representative body. In March 1991 Minister Dales (Labour, PvdA) wrote to parliament to the effect that two broad platforms, one for Muslims and one for Hindus, were expected to be formed within six months. The Muslim platform would be the Islamic Council of the Netherlands. However, groups such as the Shiites and the Ahmadis were not represented in it. The Minister explained that the available posts for spiritual care for Muslims in the armed forces and in penal institutions could perhaps be shared proportionately between the Islamic Council and the Ahmadis: 'This would accord with religious pluriformity.'[15]

However, the creation of a representative co-ordinating organization to supervise this proved complicated. An Islamic Council of the Netherlands was formed, soon followed by an 'umbrella' of organizations which were not actually part of it—the Netherlands Muslim Council. Four years later there was still no sign of a representative organization recognized by the government. In early 1995 the new Minister for Internal Affairs, Dijkstal (Liberal, VVD), informed parliament that it had always been plain that in the short term the Muslim movements in the Netherlands would not be able to arrive at a single representative co-operative body.[16]

In the autumn of 1995 there seemed to be a fresh opportunity. According to a report in *de Volkskrant* of 12 October 1995, the Islamic Council of the Netherlands and the Netherlands Muslim Council had set up a committee to look into the problems which had until then prevented the various organizations from working together.

Other spheres of activity

In addition to the areas discussed in more detail in this part of the study, we distinguished four other spheres in Chapter 1: the socio-

---

[15] TK 1990–1991, 20868, no. 3.
[16] TK 1994–1995, 20868, no. 5, p. 2.

economic and socio-cultural spheres, health care and social services, and law. We also indicated that in these cases there was much less evidence of Muslim institutions being set up. Moreover, those institutions which have been created, or initiatives towards them, have led to hardly any interventions by the national authorities. There has been no question at all of discussion at the national level, as there was about the introduction of Muslim schools. There are, however, several exceptions to this general picture.

The socio-economic sphere

One institution which has featured on a fairly wide scale in this sphere is the Muslim butcher. The first butcher's shops were set up towards the end of the 1960s in the large towns, often without valid papers and in premises which did not bear much resemblance to a butcher's shop. In 1968, by means of an exemption regulation, the Ministry of Economic Affairs offered Muslim butchers who had not undergone a Dutch butcher's training the opportunity to establish butcher's shops legally.[17] This meant that Muslim butchers gained a similar position to Jewish butchers, for whom special arrangements already existed in the form of exemptions.

Exemption was possible if the applicant fulfilled an urgent need for a product which other businesses could not adequately supply. At first the criterion was applied of one butcher's shop per 1,000 single Muslims or heads of Muslim families.[18] In addition, prospective Muslim butchers would have to pass a test of professional competence. This test proved too exacting for most of the candidates: the Dutch language was too great a barrier and the section on pork proved an intractable problem (Tunderman 1987: 23). In 1975 the test of professional competence was replaced by the 'trade test compatible with the Mohammedan rite'.[19] That same year, for the first time a small number of butchers received special licences giving them permission to slaughter in the Muslim manner (Bakker & Tap 1985: 35).

---

[17] The exemption ruling was based on Article 15, Section 1b, of the 1954 Companies Act (*Vestigingswet Bedrijven*). Since 1971 authority to decide on claims for exemption has been delegated to the Trades Sectoral Board (Bakker & Tap 1985: 35–36).

[18] In the interim this criterion has been raised to 2,000 Muslim residents for the first butcher, 3,000 for the second, 5,000 for the third, and so on (*Handboek Minderheden* 3/1100–8 (1994)).

[19] A separate regulation was drawn up for this purpose, and approved by the Ministry of Economic Affairs in 1977 (Bakker & Tap 1985: appendix III).

The demand for ritually slaughtered meat increased steadily in the 1970s, while the number of Muslim butchers remained relatively small. For the Muslim butchers who were already established this was a golden opportunity: on Fridays and Saturdays they had customers queuing at their doors. In 1985 the Butchery Sectoral Board commissioned research into Muslim butchers in the Netherlands. The investigation led to a number of recommendations, including a Muslim butchery training course (ibid.: 155), and eight years later, in 1993, it was actually established. The advent of this three-year vocational course marked the end of the provisional policy on Muslim butchers, though the need to supply an essential service meant that there was still good reason to grant exemptions.[20] In early 1996 there were, according to a report in *De Gelderlander* (25 April 1996), a total of 325 specialized Muslim butchers who were members of the Butchery Sectoral Board.

In addition to the butchers, a number of other Muslim institutions appeared in the course of time, such as Muslim wholesalers, a Muslim bank, and mosque shops. With the exception of these last, their arrival went almost unnoticed. The appearance of mosque shops sometimes led to action being taken by the local authorities (Landman 1992: 302), but there was never any question of the national government getting involved.

One further initiative should be mentioned, and that is the Türk Hollanda İadamlar Vakfı, the Turco-Dutch Employers Foundation, which was set up in 1995. The initiative was taken mainly with the objective of organizing Turkish employers, which has remained an elusive aim to date.[21]

The socio-cultural sphere

In the 1983 *Minorities Memorandum*, religious organizations were treated in the same way as those of a non-religious nature. Consequently religious organizations could be considered for subsidies on the strength of the subsidy arrangements for non-confessional organizations. It was argued that:

---

[20] Exemption is now, however, linked to the condition that the butcher in charge has passed the Trade Test in Muslim Butchery, and that the manager has followed and completed a course in business methods (*Handboek Minderheden* 3/1100–8 (1994)).

[21] Information from Adem Kumcu, IMES.

It would be unfair if the religious organizations of minorities, which set themselves the objective of carrying out activities of a socio-cultural nature, were in certain cases denied an opportunity for subsidy because they had been organized on religious principles. In any decision on granting a subsidy, the nature of the activity for which the subsidy is requested should be the criterion, rather than whether or not the applying organization has a religious basis (Ministerie van BiZa 1983: 110–111).

The number of Muslim organizations which have made use of subsidies granted by the Ministry of Welfare is very small.[22] Moreover, since 1985 only activities such as the promotion of interests and publicity through national organizations still come under the direct purview of the Ministry. Financial support for local socio-cultural work was in that year decentralized to the municipalities, who according to Landman (1922: 286 ff.) have not always adopted an unequivocal stance on the initiatives of Muslim organizations. The extent of the variety in practice at the local level will be made clear in Part 2 of this study, when the state of affairs in Rotterdam and Utrecht is discussed.

Health care and social services

Local initiatives have also been developed in health care and social services. To date they have seldom led to the establishment of specific Muslim institutions or to the involvement of the national authorities. One exception is the Turkish Islamic Union for the Elderly, set up in 1993, which looks after the interests of elderly Turkish Muslims in a variety of ways. This initiative was welcomed by the Minister of Welfare, Health and Culture, d'Ancona (Labour, PvdA), and has received occasional subsidies from that Ministry.[23]

The Union formed the basis of a national interest group for all Muslim pensioners in the Netherlands which was actually set up two years later: the Netherlands Islamic Association for the Elderly.[24]

[22] In 1991 35 national organizations received grants under the minorities policy. Only two of them were Muslim organizations: the Netherlands Islamic Centre Foundation and the Turkish-Islamic Cultural Federation Foundation (Commissie Doelmatigheid Landelijke Minderhedenorganisaties 1992, appendix 3: 5–6).
[23] Address on the occasion of the presentation meeting of the Turkish Islamic Union for the Elderly, 27 November 1993.
[24] Turkish, Moroccan, Surinamese, Palestinian, Jordanian, Egyptian, Indonesian, Javanese and Dutch Muslims were represented on the executive of the Netherlands Islamic Association for the Elderly (*NISBO Magazine* 1 (1995) 6: 19).

Moreover, in late 1995 the Netherlands Foundation for Islamic Welfare and Care was set up, which in co-operation with the Netherlands Islamic Associations for the Elderly promoted several projects, including some for elderly Muslims.[25]

Muslim young people have also formed associations. There is, for instance, a young people's section of Milli Görüş, and in May 1995 the National Islamic Turkish Youth Organization was set up. Since then some 30 local Turkish Muslim youth organizations have joined it. The Youth Organization concentrates particularly on promoting the interests of Turkish Muslim young people, and organized a national conference to that end in January 1995 in The Hague.[26]

The legal sphere

In 1981 in the *Draft Minorities Memorandum* the government devoted brief attention to the religious law of minority groups, Muslim or otherwise. The government recognized that members of minority groups regarded Dutch family law 'as deviating from their own cultural identity' (Ministerie van BiZa 1981: 283). However, they saw no occasion to put in hand 'special family law provisions for members of minority groups'. Citizens could arrange their mutual relationships within the bounds of current Dutch family law according to their own understanding and so in accordance with their own conception of what was right. An example is that in drawing up a marriage settlement, account could be taken of a dowry. The government also laid down two parameters: the equality of man and woman, and the separation of church and state. 'Just as no departure from these precepts can be accepted for Catholic or Jewish Dutch citizens, so no exception can be made for members of Muslim minority groups' (ibid.).

Islamic family law therefore only applies in the Netherlands to the extent that it is incorporated in the national law of the individual involved. A limitation to this is that the result must not conflict with public order in the Netherlands, that is to say, with the fundamental principles of Dutch law. This restriction has come into play in two matters affecting Moroccan immigrants: repudiation and polygamy.

---

[25] *NISBO Magazine* 2 (1996) 7.
[26] Information by telephone from the chairman of the National Islamic Turkish Youth Organization.

The Supreme Court decided in 1986 that repudiation based on the unilateral declaration of the husband, and without the involvement of a judge, conflicted with the principles of Dutch law and could not be recognized in the Netherlands.[27] Polygamous marriages are recognized as valid, but the second wife and the children of that marriage have no right to family reunion in the Netherlands. Moreover, polygamy is an obstacle to naturalization as a Dutch citizen.[28]

[27] Supreme Court 31 October 1986, *Nederlandse Jurisprudentie* 1986, no. 702; see also Bolten 1984: 122–129, 1987: 55–63; Rombout 1990: 155–162; Vestdijk-Van der Hoeven 1991: 286.
[28] See Ministry of Justice, Naturalisatie, DVZ Thema no. 4, The Hague 1993, and the letter from the Secretary of State for Justice to the Second Chamber of Parliament, dated 12 March 1996, TK 1995–1996, 23594, no. 27.

CHAPTER SIX

CONCLUSIONS AT THE NATIONAL LEVEL

The previous chapters make clear that the institutionalization of Islam is taking place in many spheres of life. Full consideration has been given to the areas of religion, education, and politics in particular, because it is here that a number of initiatives have been developed—though to a lesser extent in the political sphere at the national level. The other areas—the socio-economic and socio-cultural spheres, health care and social services, and law—were discussed more briefly, since there was much less evidence here of Muslim institutions being set up.

This chapter relates our findings to the three central questions of this study. In turn it deals with the range and the density of Muslim institutions, the factors and agents involved in the process of institutionalization, and finally, the ideological concepts in the debate.

Range and density

Within the religious sphere a range of institutions can be distinguished which have been set up in recent decades and which have in one way or another achieved recognition in the host society. The most striking is the increase in the number of Muslim places of worship. The first were built in the early 1950s; by 1994 their total number was estimated at 380. Recognition in principle of this institution was recorded in 1962 in an amendment to the Church Building Subsidy Act. After that various subsidy schemes for the establishment of places of worship, including mosques, came into force. However, such schemes came to an end in 1983. Though there were two subsequent official reports on the possible granting of support for the establishment of Muslim places of worship, no fresh schemes for subsidies were forthcoming. In spite of the lack of direct financial support from the government, the density of mosques is high—one mosque for about every 1,250 Muslims.

In addition to the establishment of places of worship, arrangements have been made covering ritual slaughter, Muslim holy days, dietary requirements, funerals, and the admission of imams, mainly from abroad. Ritual circumcision of boys takes place on a relatively large scale. Pending the formation of a representative body, temporary arrangements have been made for the spiritual care of Muslim prisoners and for Muslim members of the armed forces. The possibility of taking an oath on the Koran has been confirmed and reconfirmed. These arrangements did not all come into effect at the same time; ritual slaughter was possible as early as 1976, whereas oaths on the Koran only became acceptable (once more) in the 1990s.

In the sphere of education there are also a number of new Muslim institutions. A start—albeit on a very limited scale—has been made with Islamic religious instruction in the primary state school system, Muslim schools have been founded, and Muslim broadcasting organizations have gone on the air; in addition to the introduction of a limited number of courses for imams, Islamic theology is gradually gaining ground in further and higher education. Here, too, developments have not occurred synchronically. Initiatives for the implementation of Islamic religious instruction and for the introduction of a Muslim broadcasting network date from the 1970s, while the first Muslim broadcasts were only realized in 1986. Muslim schools first opened their doors in the late 1980s, and theological courses within the Dutch educational system are of an even more recent date, in the 1990s. Moreover, the density also varies: whereas 29 Muslim schools were started within a relatively short time, Islamic religious instruction is only provided in a very limited number of primary state schools.

Over the years individual Muslims and their organizations have also taken on a political role. They have done this through their own organizations or through social organizations such as trade unions or political parties. Here and there Muslim parties have stood in elections for municipalities and municipal districts, if without much success. The potential membership of Muslims has given rise to a certain amount of controversy within the regular political parties, and particularly within the Christian Democratic Party (CDA). Muslim organizations have also begun to play an official role in dialogue with the authorities. At first the contacts were occasional in nature and limited to specific problems, such as ritual slaughter. However, in the mid-1980s the idea took root in official circles that there was a role for Muslim organizations in the implementation of the minorities policy. Contacts then became more intensive and acquired a more structured character. Moreover, in the context of spiritual care for Muslims, the authorities pressed for the formation of a national representative body.

Within the other spheres there is hardly any sign of institutionalization at the national level. To the extent that it has occurred, it has led to little or no involvement of the national government. Exceptions to this are the establishment of Muslim butchers, a national interest association for elderly Muslims, and the recognition of Muslim organizations involved in carrying out socio-cultural work. In 1983 they were put on an equal footing with secular organizations in the arrangements for subsidizing activities of a non-religious nature. In practice, however, there are only a few organizations who actually make use of this at a national level.

Factors and agents

It is clear that *initiatives taken by Muslims* are of decisive importance in the process of institutionalization. In all kinds of fields Muslims have attempted to establish Muslim institutions, and have in many cases succeeded. In other cases, their efforts have not achieved the desired result: Islamic religious instruction is only encountered on a limited scale, and there is still no course for imams funded by the Dutch government, nor a spiritual care service for Muslims in the armed services or in penal institutions. Occasionally the initiative has not come from Muslim circles, but from others who put pressure on Muslims to create a Muslim institution. This applies, for example, to the establishment of a co-ordinating organization for Muslim schools, and for a national representative body (yet to be set up) for Muslim organizations responsible for the spiritual care of Muslims in public institutions; these were initiated by the Ministries of Education and of Internal Affairs respectively.

In a number of areas we see that *foreign powers* and/or *international Muslim organizations* influence the process of institutionalization. They have played a role, for instance, in the appointment and training of imams and in the establishment of Muslim schools by the Islamic Foundation of the Netherlands for Education and Upbringing. They have also occasionally extended financial support to establish places of worship. In particular the Diyanet, the Turkish presidium of religious affairs, has been involved in many initiatives.

At the same time there is a *fear* of the intervention of these two agents. At times this fear has led to opposition to the advent of Muslim institutions. It caused a Liberal (VVD) Member of Parliament to ask the Minister of Education for a policy barring Muslim schools, and in the 1970s the activities of Muslim organizations were watched very closely. At other times the fear of intervention appears actually to have encouraged institutionalization. A good example is the General Regulation concerning Subsidies for Places of Worship. An important argument for this regulation was that subsidies for Muslim places of worship would render foreign support unnecessary, and so promote the 'integration' of Muslims.

Legislation and regulation has influenced the institutionalization of Islam in various ways. In some cases these proved favourable to Muslim initiatives. They could make use of existing legislation to set up Muslim schools and their own broadcasting network, and to obtain recognition of these institutions. In other cases the rules are formulated in more general terms, and the question has arisen of whether and how far these 'open' rules also apply to Muslims (or Hindus). This was the case with the Sunday opening of shops, the recognition of Muslim holy days in penal institutions and for Muslim civil servants. In yet other cases, such as ritual slaughter and the call to prayer, initiatives by Muslims were in fact hampered by existing legislation.

In the course of time legislation has been adjusted in various areas. Sometimes these adjustments followed infringements by Muslims, such as illegal slaughtering associated with the *Eid ul-Adha* (Festival of Sacrifice), opening Muslim butchers without the necessary papers, and not turning up for work on religious festivals without permission for leave or a day off. Changes in legislation or in the way it is applied mean that these activities are no longer illegal. In addition, some existing regulations have been changed under the influence of legislative processes which of themselves had nothing to do with initiatives for setting up Muslim institutions. For instance, the new rules on religious freedom in the 1983 Constitution led to bills which in turn gave rise to discussion on the adaptation of existing rules in accordance with the wishes of Muslims or Hindus. Examples are the Public Demonstrations Act, the Civil Service Act, and the Spiritual Care in Caring and Penal Institutions Act, which regulate the call to prayer, the recognition of Muslim festivals for civil servants, and the appointment of imams for spiritual care. Something similar occurred with the bill for the new Act on Funerary Arrangements.

The bill for the approval of the European Treaty on the Protection
of Slaughter Animals, on the other hand, gave fresh arguments to
the opponents of ritual slaughter, which had meanwhile been permitted to Muslims.

No evidence has been found of the opposite—the adaptation of
existing rules to prevent claims by Muslims. At most there have been
a few attempts in this direction, for instance in the areas of dietary
requirements and the export of ritually slaughtered meat. Of more
interest, perhaps, are the general processes mentioned earlier, which
sometimes have a damaging effect on initiatives. An example is the
'cutting of the silver strings' which influenced the decision to give
no more financial support for the establishment of mosques after
1983, and ·new legislation concerning the increase in scale of primary education which seems to have made it more difficult to set
up Muslim schools.

In addition to legislation, *the judiciary* appears to play an important
role in the recognition of Muslim institutions. In a large number of
issues, conflicts about the recognition of freedom of religion for
Muslims have led to court proceedings. Sometimes judicial pronouncements have determined the direction of the political solution to the
problem. The Supreme Court's judgements on ritual slaughter (1969)
and on time off for employees on Muslim festivals (1984) to a large
extent dictated the content of later regulations; this last ruling played
an important role in the discussion of the 1988 Civil Service Act.

Court cases or judicial pronouncements have sometimes served as
an incentive for the Muslims involved to enter discussion with the
relevant organizations, which in turn has led to new agreements or
regulations. Ritual slaughter was one such issue, as was the question
of whether the cost of the circumcision of boys for religious reasons
should qualify for reimbursement by health insurers.

The *national government* is an important agent in the institutionalization process. Its attitude to Muslim institutions has not always
been consistent over the past decades. Sometimes the government
has encouraged the formation of Muslim institutions (as, for instance,
with the creation of a representative body for Muslims, and the
participation of Muslim organizations in the National Advice and
Consultation Structure for the minorities policy). At other times they
have taken a legalistic stand, as with the establishment of Muslim
schools. On yet other occasions they have tried to guide or direct
the formation of Muslim institutions (for instance, a Muslim broad-

casting network) or decided on a total ban (the ritual circumcision of girls). Often, too, government attitudes have been influenced by the minorities policy, as in the active interventions by the Ministry of Internal Affairs to include Muslim organizations in the contributing councils of the National Advice and Consultation Structure, and also in the decisions on possible financial support for Muslim places of worship, on subsidies for the socio-cultural activities of Muslim organizations, and on the allocation of transmission time to a Muslim broadcasting network.

Moreover, we can see that the attitude of the government on certain issues has changed over time. Financial support for places of worship offers a good example. While in the 1970s finance was provided on the basis of the argument for equal treatment, in the mid-1980s it was decided on the basis of the same argument to stop further grants for mosques. The authorities have not always been all of one mind. In the allocation of transmission time to the Islamic Broadcasting Foundation, various interests came into play: whereas the Board of Radio, Television and Press were against granting transmission time on the grounds that the Foundation was not sufficiently representative, the Board of Welfare for Minorities exerted pressure in favour of it in the context of the minorities policy.

Apart from the government, many other organizations have been involved in the process of institutionalization. Involvement of *organizations based on religion or ideology* was evident particularly in the area of education and in the field of spiritual care for Muslims in public institutions. The Council of Churches worked in favour of achieving Islamic religious instruction, and the claims of Muslims were supported by the clergy of several other denominations, who were also in favour of the recruitment of new imams in penal institutions.

More *generally based organizations* have also played their part. Some supported Muslim initiatives, but there were also fierce protests. Ritual slaughter gave rise to some of these. Animal protection organizations made various attempts to have a ban imposed on this institution through political influence and the judiciary, though in fact none were successful. Various organizations also opposed the establishment of Muslim schools. As well as the Contact Centre for the Advancement of State Education and the Association of Dutch Local Authorities, various secular immigrants' organizations spoke out against schools based on Islam.

Among the *remaining relevant organizations*, apart from the influence of the media on the process of institutionalization, academics were sometimes involved: one municipality justified its ban on wearing headscarves by calling on the advice of an expert. In general both the media and academia have contributed to the full attention given to Islam over recent years, whether in a positive or a negative sense.

Ideological concepts

Many arguments have been put forward in discussions on the various points at issue. Nearly all of them appear to fall within one of two ideologies: that of residence and that of pluralism. Arguments concerned with citizenship are hardly ever encountered. Moreover, certain arguments return time and again: the separation of church and state, freedom of religion, the principle of equality, efforts to integrate Muslims, and the representativeness of their organizations.

The *separation of church and state* has played a role in the discussion particularly since 1983. In several cases this argument has been used to refuse financial support for Muslim organizations, as in the discussions on the Hirsch Ballin Committee's report on material support for places of worship. On the basis of this argument, the Ministry of Internal Affairs also refrained from active involvement in setting up a representative body. At the same time these government authorities have applied this same principle more flexibly in other cases, becoming actively involved with Islam and its organization, as in the selection of imams, and in the participation of Muslim organizations in the contributing councils of the National Advice and Consultation Structure.

The argument of *freedom of religion* has often been grounds for recognition or for financial support. In several cases this freedom has been balanced against or limited by other values or interests, such as a restrictive admissions policy (for imams), protection of animals (ritual slaughter), the equal status of women, and the protection of the physical integrity of the individual (ritual circumcision). In the discussion on female circumcision this last value in the end carried considerably more weight than freedom of religion.

The *principle of equality* has been used in two ways, depending on the reference group. On the basis of this argument all kinds of rights or facilities which have been extended to Christians or to Jews were also granted to Muslims. This applied to the establishment of mosques, the call to prayer, the recognition of festivals, spiritual care in public institutions, and ritual slaughter. In these cases it was particularly the secular parties (Labour (PvdA), Liberals (VVD), and Democrats 66 (D66)) which invoked the principle of equality in parliamentary debates. Certainly in the early stages these parties ensured that Islam was recognized in principle as being on an equal footing with other religions. The first indication of this tendency was the Scheps amendment (Labour, PvdA) during the passage of the Church Building Subsidy Act. Christian Democrat Members of Parliament and Ministers sometimes acted with rather more reserve: they laid more stress on the differences between the 'new' religions and those which had been present historically. However, when it came to financing spiritual care by the government, the Christian Democrat politicians, too, maintained the principle of equality for Muslims and Hindus. But Labour (PvdA) and the Liberal Party (VVD) for their part used the same principle of equality in 1984 as an argument for stopping further financial support for the establishment of Muslim places of worship.

In some cases it has been difficult to determine what the claim for equal treatment precisely involved. The recognition of their own festivals, for example, led to Muslim prisoners having more days off work than other prisoners. On the other hand, jealousy at the provision of a special diet in the forces was prevented by giving all servicemen more choice in their field rations. In this way servicemen who preferred vegetarian food for other than religious reasons had the opportunity to opt for it.

Efforts towards integration were also two-edged. Those who opposed the granting of rights and facilities used this argument in the discussion on Muslim schools. They feared negative consequences for integration because Muslim schools might lead to segregation and, in the opinion of some, even to the creation of ghettos. Fears of adverse effects on integration were also expressed in discussions about the call to prayer and the admission of imams, on the grounds that this might arouse opposition in the indigenous population or might create the risk of 'fundamentalism' in mosques or prisons. Such arguments were used particularly, but certainly not exclusively, by parties on the extreme right. The argument that according to the Koran or to liberal Muslims certain customs were not obligatory, can also be regarded as an implicit employment of the integration argument.

Liberal, 'more integrated' Muslims would appear to be enjoying official recognition, but not the 'hardliners'.

On the other hand, the efforts towards integration were also used to justify granting rights and facilities. This applied, for instance, to the 1976 subsidy scheme for mosques, which was based on the idea that the integration of Muslims would benefit from the creation of some kind of Dutch Islam, independent of finance from abroad. This argument also played a part in the discussions about a Dutch training course for imams.

Finally, the *representativeness of the organizations* involved in the decision-making process, or to whom certain rights are granted, has sometimes been regarded pragmatically, and at other times treated as an insuperable barrier, as in the case of the appointment of spiritual advisers in the armed forces and in penal institutions. This argument also came up in the decisions about the allocation of transmission time to Muslim networks. Time was at first refused on the grounds of allegedly insufficient representativeness, and recently the same argument was a reason for not honouring a request for an extension of transmission time. But the national and local authorities were less stringent in their requirements for ritual slaughter in 1977, for the admission of imams for penal institutions in 1981, for the training scheme for carrying out circumcisions, and for the training or further training of imams. When the government itself has identified a clear interest, such as keeping the peace in prisons, or maintaining public order at the time of the Rushdie affair or the Gulf War, the lack of a representative body has not proved any obstacle to going ahead with the existing variety of Muslim organizations.

PART TWO

THE INSTITUTIONALIZATION OF ISLAM AND THE
STRUGGLE FOR RECOGNITION AT THE LOCAL LEVEL

INTRODUCTION

There are many ways in which local authorities may be involved with Muslims. They can range from granting permission for a Muslim cemetery to be put into use, subsidizing language and orientation courses for imams, or involving Muslim organizations in employment projects. At the local level we shall also concentrate on the spheres of religion, education and politics, and within these spheres on four separate topics: places of worship, religious instruction, schools, and organizations as partners in the political process. We have studied these four subjects in detail in two municipalities, Rotterdam and Utrecht.

In 1988 Landman (1992: 290 and 297) estimated the number of Muslims in those cities at 48,000 and 22,000 respectively. In that year there were 29 mosques in Rotterdam and 10 in Utrecht. In both towns the numbers of Muslims and of mosques have increased quite rapidly since the early 1980s. In October 1981 Rotterdam had 'only' 27,000 Muslims within its borders and 13 mosques (Gemeente Rotterdam 1981b: 1), while Utrecht in 1982 had 14,513 Muslims and five mosques (Gemeente Utrecht 1992).[1]

Rotterdam's concern with immigrants, and particularly Muslim immigrants, dates from the early 1970s. Irregularities in lodgings for guest workers—often unregistered—and riots in the working-class neighbourhood Afrikaanderwijk in 1972 forced the city government to take notice of the presence of guest workers. The attention of the Alderman responsible for foreign workers at first concentrated on their accommodation, but gradually came to cover wider and more social aspects. The Migrants Office was set up. In 1978 the *Memorandum on Immigrants in Rotterdam* (*Nota Migranten in Rotterdam*, GR 1978) was published, the first policy document in which a comprehensive view on the integration of immigrants into the city was formulated. Seven years later the report was followed by *Minorities Policy in a Changed Situation* (*Minderhedenbeleid in een gewijzigde situatie*, GR 1985a). Various Aldermen have had the minorities policy, or what passed for it, in their portfolio. Since 1990 this policy has been a 'facet' policy,

---

[1] In the following pages we indicate the documents of the Rotterdam municipality with 'GR', and those from Utrecht with 'GU'.

outlined by a small staff, while its implementation has been in the
hands of municipal services and organizations. Traditionally Rotterdam
has followed a policy aimed strongly at integration, if not assimilation. Special provisions for 'ethnic minorities' have always been dis-
couraged. This policy was reinforced again in 1992 in the executive
document *The New Rotterdammers* (*De nieuwe Rotterdammers*, GR 1992b).

In Utrecht, the city published in 1981 its *Outline Memorandum on
Minorities Policy* (*Rompnota minderhedenbeleid*, GU 1981), outlining its policy. The general policy attempted to conform as much as possible
with existing procedures and consultation structures. Where there
was a question of specific policy, the Utrecht municipality claimed
to allocate an important role to the minority groups' interest organizations. At first responsibility for minorities policy was in the hands
of the Alderman for Social Affairs, and the Alderman for Welfare.
There was no separate office for this policy in the municipal organization. But there was an Official Co-ordinating Group for Minorities.[2]
Above this Co-ordinating Group there was an Administrative Co-
ordination and Consultation on Minorities, in which administrators,
officials and external interested parties were involved in consultation,
and made policy. Since 1986 care for minorities has been integrated
into general services, albeit with earmarked funds. Like Rotterdam,
Utrecht tends towards a policy leading to assimilation.

Following this brief outline of the general minorities policy of Rotterdam
and Utrecht, in the next four chapters we shall examine local policy
and local reactions to Muslim institutions in these municipalities more
specifically, starting with the sphere of politics because of its crucial
significance at the local level for developments within the spheres
both of religion and education. In succession we will examine Muslim
organizations as partners in the political debate (Chapter 7), the
establishment and funding of places of worship (Chapter 8), Islamic
religious instruction in public primary schools (Chapter 9), and Muslim
schools (Chapter 10). We will end this part of the book with a summary of the three key questions, and a comparison between Rotterdam
and Utrecht.

---

[2] This Co-ordination Group consisted of a project manager, a policy co-ordinator and various representatives of the services and policy sections involved. In 1985
the position of project manager was dropped, and his duties transferred to the co-
ordinator of the minorities policies in the Welfare Service.

CHAPTER SEVEN

RECOGNITION AS PARTNERS IN THE POLITICAL DEBATE

Muslims join political parties at the local level, and can stand for election for one of the existing parties. They can also form a local Muslim party; for instance, in Rotterdam the Muslim party, Hakyol, fought the 1984 municipal district elections.[1] In Utrecht the announcement of the formation of a Muslim party caused a considerable stir in 1993.

However, we will concentrate on another form of political participation: the role played by Muslim organizations in municipal consultation structures, advisory and executive committees, and suchlike. Our attention is directed particularly towards the way in which Muslim organizations are involved in the political decision-making process in Rotterdam and Utrecht.

Rotterdam

The 1970s: a wide gulf

In the 1970s there was a wide gulf between the municipality of Rotterdam and Muslim organizations. The council denied in principle any responsibility towards 'church congregations'. Moreover, it had no wish to become involved with organizations within the sphere of influence of the Grey Wolves or the Amicales. It may have recognized that Muslim organizations could contribute to the mutual integration of Muslims and other Rotterdammers, but it granted them no influence at all in formulating municipal policy (GR 1978: 71–72).

On the other hand, progressive, secular, immigrant organizations were given free rein to take part in politics. Around 1980 the municipality itself supported the formation of a co-ordinating body, the Platform for Foreigners in Greater Rotterdam, although there was no question of separate provisions for consultation. This Platform was intended as a 'counterweight' to the Foundation for Foreign

---

[1] Cf. Rath 1985.

Workers in Greater Rotterdam, which was managed more by native Dutchmen; or organizations such as the Action Committee on behalf of Guest Workers. Organizations wanting to affiliate themselves with the Platform had to satisfy two criteria: the ability to actively promote their own interests, and a 'democratic' character. According to the Platform, Muslim organizations did not satisfy this second criterion, and therefore could not be admitted (De Graaf 1985: 37). This exclusion meant that they were deprived of an opportunity to express political opinions, and that secular, progressive forces monopolized the contacts between interest organizations and the authorities.

A wind of change: discussions through the Migrants Office

In the early 1980s the municipal Migrants Office opened a debate about the role of Muslim organizations with its *Mosques Memorandum.* Although the debate was centred on the possible subsidization of mosques, the justification for the political exclusion of Muslim groups also came under discussion. The municipality would be able to address these organizations about their responsibilities more effectively if they were recognized as 'by far the most important interest organizations'. The municipal council would have to abandon its 'anxious reticence towards the most important group-formation among the migrants', and did not need to fear the violation of the separation of church and state, or involvement with the extreme right-wing Turkish Grey Wolves or Moroccan Amicales (GR 1981b: 1).

According to the claims of an official of the Migrants Office, Alderman Schmitz (Labour, PvdA), who was responsible for Special Groups, was not altogether keen on a reversal of policy. At the same time the conviction was growing in the municipal council that Muslim organizations could form an important link in the integration of newcomers into Rotterdam society. The symposium on Islam held in Rotterdam in September 1982 gave strength to this argument, and provided opportunities for personal contact between officials and the Turkish leaders of the Muslim community. In addition the Minister for Culture, Recreation and Social Work, De Boer (Christian Democratic Party, CDA), was arguing for a more open approach towards Muslim organizations.[2] Schmitz's successor, Simons (Labour, PvdA),

---

[2] The Minister for Culture, Recreation and Social Work declared during the opening session of the symposium that Dutch society must take a sympathetic atti-

cautiously followed words by deeds: immediately after taking office in 1982 he initiated a series of personal meetings with leaders of Muslim organizations, and visited several mosques (GR 1983: 1).[3] A special circumstance favouring this development was that just at that time several leaders had emerged from Muslim circles who, in the opinion of officials of the Migrants Office, 'had the right idea'. They posed questions about social matters such as education and employment, and seemed able to bring about the links the council wanted with a section of the newcomers.

In 1983 the Migrants Office submitted a new Memorandum to the Board of Mayor and Aldermen entitled *Mosque Groups as Interest Organizations* (*Moskeegroepen als zelforganisaties*), in which they argued for a more pro-active attitude. The council should no longer wait to see which 'clubs' approached it, but should seek out co-operation with 'the groups which lie closest to the hearts of the immigrants themselves. For Turks and Moroccans those are the mosques' (GR 1983: 1). This Memorandum brought the recognition of Muslim organizations as partners in the political debate a step closer, as, for the first time, there was explicit mention of Muslims taking part in political decision making as a distinct group. Support and recognition of Muslim organizations would create 'social partners in the immigrant policy' for the municipality (ibid.: 4–7).

It was proposed that Muslim organizations should be treated in the same way as other interest organizations in such areas as management training courses, and that a secretariat be set up, modelled on

---

tude to the needs of Muslims. By this the Minister alluded, among other things, to the provision of mosques. He referred to the subsidy scheme for places of worship, and to the Waardenburg Working Party he had recently set up to advise him on religious provisions for ethnic minorities. He also conjectured that Muslims might seek engagement with the social reality they met in the Netherlands, and that they might reconsider their religious position in that light (De Boer 1982).

[3] The Alderman for Special Groups actually paid fairly frequent visits to immigrant organizations. A Memorandum stated that such 'tours' served a 'useful purpose'. They could contribute to 'mutual trust' and the 'formulation of policy nuances', though they should not be seen as a '*replacement* for the desired participation of immigrants' in policy-making institutions (GR 1982b: 38; emphasis added). To prevent possible misunderstandings, the municipal council immediately pointed out that the formation of 'a separate consultation frame for immigrants' was undesirable because that would only give sanction to the special position of immigrants. It is notable that in this Memorandum the municipality makes no mention of Muslim organizations, let alone of a visit to them. There is a reference to the separation of church and state, and some appreciative words are devoted to the initiatives of church organizations in that matter (ibid.: 43).

the Platform for Foreigners in Greater Rotterdam. The idea was that there should be a co-ordinating body for Muslim organizations, able to react appropriately to the policies of the municipal authorities on employment, reuniting families, accommodation and discrimination.

In September that year the Memorandum was discussed by the Board of Mayor and Aldermen, which after exhaustive discussion decided on a change of policy.[4] In future the local authority would be less reticent with regard to Muslim organizations. The Alderman for Special Groups was asked to make further proposals for the material implementation of this policy.

Elaboration of the revised policy

In early 1984 the Alderman for Special Groups and some of his officials held three exploratory meetings with eight Turkish imams, all associated with the Turkish Diyanet. Imams of other nationalities, or other, more orthodox, Turkish Muslim movements, such as the Süleymanlı or the Milli Görüş, were not invited.[5]

Many subjects were covered in the discussions, including the responsibilities of the imams, their view of the situation of Turks in the Netherlands, and the participation of Turks in the forthcoming municipal district elections.[6] During the second meeting the imams were invited to represent their communities in discussions with the council. The spiritual leaders voted in favour of this, at least in so far as it would make clear to the Turks what rights they had. They had in advance opposed any potential attempts at imposing Dutch policy.[7]

---

[4] Report on the meeting of the Board of Mayor and Aldermen, dated 16 September 1983. Rotterdam Municipal Council.

[5] The one-sided selection of dialogue partners was undoubtedly the result of the good contacts which the municipality, in this case the Migrants Office, had maintained since the Islam Symposium (1982) with influential Turkish Muslims, particularly with an executive member of the Turkish-Islamic Cultural Federation Foundation. In this regard the prominent presence of the co-ordinator of the Diyanet imams in Greater Rotterdam was of great significance: he functioned as a confidant of the member of the executive of the Turkish-Islamic Cultural Federation Foundation.

[6] Report of the discussions between the imams of mosques affiliated to the Federation of Turkish Islamic Cultural Associations, officials from Special Groups, and Alderman Simons. Rotterdam Municipal Council, Migrants Office. During the first meeting the co-ordinator of the imams handed over a letter, in which on behalf of the other Turkish imams he asked the municipality to lend its support to a series of orientation visits by a group of imams to a large number of social institutions and businesses.

[7] Report of discussions between imams of mosques affiliated to the Federation

During the last meeting an official asked for their views on 'the process of co-operation *to be expected*' between Muslims of different nationalities (emphasis added). The imams avoided a direct answer to the question and referred to the Federation of Muslim Organizations in the Netherlands (FOMON).[8] Finally the imams agreed to play a role in the forthcoming municipal district elections on 16 May. Obviously they would themselves refrain from taking any political position, so they said, but they could certainly point out the general importance of taking part in the elections.[9]

In a Memorandum to the Board of Mayor and Aldermen the Alderman for Special Groups next proposed that the council must prevent or minimize the isolation of Muslim organizations by creating working links with them (GR 1984b). The specific proposals in the Memorandum included the following: the Alderman for Special Groups should arrange a series of meetings with the leaders of Muslim organizations,

> in which not only could their wishes and ideas be put forward, but in which it would also be made plain to the mosques precisely what the council did or did not have in mind (ibid.: 2).

This 'critical dialogue' would have to concentrate on education; the Migrants Office should recruit a member of staff who would maintain contacts with Muslim organizations and in particular should see to it that the 'critical dialogue' was implemented; the municipal council should ensure that imams could make an 'orientation tour of

---

of Turkish Islamic Cultural Associations and the Special Groups department of Rotterdam Municipal Council, dated 31 January 1984. Rotterdam Municipal Council, Migrants Office.

[8] Report of the discussion between imams of mosques affiliated to the Federation of Turkish Islamic Associations and the Special Groups department of Rotterdam Municipal Council, dated 14 February 1984. Rotterdam Municipal Council, Migrants Office. An official of the Migrants Office explained that the Board of Mayor and Aldermen must first decide its position before a start could be made with orientation visits by imams to Dutch institutions. The imams demanded for an early start to a special Dutch language course, but the official insisted on following procedures. Clearly he wanted confirmation of the Board's approval; the closer approach to Muslim organizations was after all a politically sensitive matter.

[9] It is interesting that a few weeks after this meeting the Hakyol political party was proclaimed in three municipal districts as a participating political group. It presented itself as the Interest Group for Islamic Minorities and was the brain-child of the same member of the executive of the Turkish-Islamic Cultural Federation Foundation who had good contacts with the Migrants Office. The party leadership was recruited through the mosques linked to the Diyanet (Rath 1985: 64–73).

Dutch institutions', and take a Dutch language course, so that they could improve their knowledge of Dutch society, and the council should treat Muslim organizations in the same way as 'the other interest organizations'. The Memorandum concluded that 'the conditions are now in place for a positive relationship between mosques and the Dutch community' (ibid.).

The municipal council, or at least a majority of the Committee for Special Groups, subscribed to these proposals.[10]

The search for a single representative partner in the political debate

Under the guidance of the municipality's Migrants Office, recognition of Muslim organizations as partners in the political debate slowly took shape, with the 'critical dialogue' as an interim achievement.[11] The representatives of the Migrants Office, however, appeared to be dealing with quite a large, heterogeneous and changing constituency. The need for a single body to act as spokesman increased. Urgent representations were repeatedly made to the Muslim leaders that they should hold discussions among themselves about who should speak for them. Some kind of co-ordinating organization would also be a good idea, they were told.[12]

In December 1985 Muslim organizations arranged a meeting in the Gültepe mosque to discuss the position of Muslims in Rotterdam. Some 12 to 14 leaders of Turkish and Moroccan groups attended.[13] Further meetings followed, but they came up against the problem that some of the leaders had insufficient mastery of the Dutch language, so that the discussions lasted a very long time, which was

---

[10] Public meeting of Co-ordinated Welfare Policy/Welfare Planning/Special Groups, dated 5 June 1984 (SG Affairs), agenda item 8. Rotterdam Municipal Council, Secretariat Department of Cultural Minorities.

[11] It seems that the municipality had also found other ways of contacting Muslim organizations. One was the Ufuk project, an education project for which students could be recruited via Muslim organizations. In the *Memorandum concerning the Minorities Policy in the 1990s*, this project was reported to be a success, which '[mainly] was based on the co-operation of *interest organizations*' (GR 1988: 10; emphasis added).

[12] In the recent past Muslims in Rotterdam have in fact tried to unite. In 1977 Muslims of different nationalities and belonging to different Islamic sects set up a foundation with the object of building a colossal 'true' mosque. This prestigious project, for which several of the oil states would have provided funds, ran aground on internal disputes. An interesting detail is that one of the Muslims involved in founding the international mosque joined the municipal Migrants Office in the mid-1980s as a policy officer on 'mosque policy' (interview with the persons concerned).

[13] Interviews with those concerned.

irksome for some of the participants. In 1986 it was therefore decided that in future each nationality would meet separately. The idea was to create co-operative links with each nationality,[14] but the practical realization of the scheme was a long time in coming.

Not until the spring of 1988 did the Co-operative Turkish Mosques in Rotterdam emerge.[15] The pioneers, three young Turkish imams from the most important groups, the Süleymanlı, Diyanet and Milli Görüş, sounded out other non-Turkish Muslim organizations on whether they wanted to join. By 19 June 1988 they were ready: at a meeting they set up the Platform of Islamic Minorities in Rotterdam, later called the Platform of Islamic Organizations in Greater Rotterdam. This Platform was officially baptized exactly three months later. The Alderman for Cultural Minorities and a senior official of the Ministry of Internal Affairs were present at the ceremony. At that time the Platform consisted of 21 Rotterdam Muslim organizations (SPIOR 1989: 5); in 1994 there were 39 (SPIOR 1995).

Recognition of the Platform of Islamic Organizations in Greater Rotterdam

The Platform tried in the first instance to become recognized by the municipality as a co-ordinating organization, at least equal in standing to the Platform for Foreigners in Greater Rotterdam. Such recognition at the political level implied financial support for a professional secretariat.

Some officials of the Migrants Office, who had been closely involved in setting up the Platform of Islamic Organizations, once again offered their services. As early as March 1988 one of them had already been pressing for the support of this 'alternative platform'.[16] However, the Alderman for Cultural Minorities showed no inclination to sever the financial ties between church and state immediately. In his view the Foundation for Foreign Workers in Greater Rotterdam should make a post available,[17] although he did offer moral support to the

---

[14] Ibid.

[15] One of their first acts was a letter to the Inspector of Direct Taxation about the problem that, suddenly, gifts to mosques were apparently no longer deductible (letter from the Co-operative Turkish Mosques in Rotterdam to the Inspector of Direct Taxation in Rotterdam, dated 7 March 1988). Rotterdam Municipal Council.

[16] Brief annotation on the Platform of Islamic Minorities Rotterdam, dated 28 March 1988. Rotterdam Municipal Council, Migrants Office (emphasis added).

[17] Brief annotation on the Platform of Islamic Organizations, also on behalf of Cie. C.M., dated 7 September 1988. Rotterdam Municipal Council, Migrants Office.

Platform, at least provided it excluded 'one or two unacceptable mosques', and he declared himself prepared to help look for suitable premises.[18] In early September 1988 the Platform—still in the process of formation—submitted an application for a subsidy, asking for Fl. 79,170 for the remainder of that year and for Fl. 316,450 for 1989. The official who dealt with it reacted in the first instance rather sarcastically to the budget submitted. He cut it back drastically, with the comment that the Platform might do better if they passed the money on to individual organizations, as the municipality was doing.[19]

One of his colleagues was in complete disagreement with this. He wrote to the Alderman that something might perhaps be cut from a few individual items, but that Fl. 200,000 to 300,000 would be necessary if the Muslim Platform was to have a chance of success.[20] A senior official suggested in an internal memorandum that the Foundation for Foreign Workers in Greater Rotterdam could give extra support to the Platform 'by way of compensation'. Moreover, KROSBE, a Surinamese second-line institution, should perhaps be able to make a contribution in view of the participation of Surinamese Muslims. Finally he proposed making a gesture towards the Platform 'in the area of setting up services: rent, office costs, etc. (. . .), provisionally on a temporary basis, because if it goes badly you need to be able to pull out of it'. As a final consideration he mentioned the possibility of using a subsidy to counteract any potential influence of foreign powers.[21]

After consultation the officials proposed that the Platform be considered eligible for subsidy for activities which directly contributed to promoting its members' interests, such as study days, workshops and the provision of information.[22] In the meeting of the Council

[18] Ibid. The Platform of Islamic Organizations turned down the Ahmadiya movement, the alevite Hicret Mosque and the 'fundamentalist' Eyyüb Sultan Mosque. The Alderman's remarks probably referred only to the last mentioned.
[19] Brief annotation on the Platform of Islamic Organizations in Greater Rotterdam, s.a. Rotterdam Municipal Council, Migrants Office.
[20] Brief annotation on the Platform of Islamic Organization in Greater Rotterdam, s.a. Rotterdam Municipal Council, Migrants Office.
[21] Memorandum for internal consultation, dated 3 October 1988. Re: positioning of local authority with respect to subsidy application of the Platform of Islamic Organizations. Rotterdam Municipal Council, Migrants Office.
[22] Memorandum for CM staff, dated 10 October 1988. Re: subsidy of the Platform of Islamic Organizations. Rotterdam Municipal Council, Migrants Office.

Committee for Cultural Minorities it was considered that setting up the Platform of Islamic Organizations in Greater Rotterdam was 'an important development', and that it could be 'an important partner in the political debate'. It was decided to allocate a sum of Fl. 60,000.[23] This meant the *de facto* political recognition of the Platform.

An energetic start was made. Study days on education and job opportunities were held in the autumn of 1988, and a management course was organized in early 1989. The Platform also addressed the question of regulations affecting the establishment of places of worship and the introduction of Islamic religious instruction, as well as a formal advisory council for immigrants.[24] In addition it joined a co-operative structure of local immigrant organizations, the Network of Co-operative Organizations of and for New Rotterdammers, which provided the municipal council with recommendations both on request and of its own accord.[25] By the mid-1990s the Platform had developed into a full-blown structure for promoting the interests of and for Muslims and their organizations in Greater Rotterdam, and had become too important to be ignored. In late 1995 there was a split in the Platform: 12 Turkish Muslim organizations accused the Platform executive of mismanagement (Engberts 1996).

---

[23] Report on the meeting of the Committee for Cultural Minorities, dated 26 October 1988. Rotterdam Municipal Council.

[24] Letter from the Federation of Cape Verdean Organizations in Rotterdam, Platform for Foreigners in Greater Rotterdam, Platform of Islamic Organizations in Greater Rotterdam, to the Board of Mayor and Aldermen, dated 15 May 1991. Rotterdam Municipal Council. Quite soon after the advent of the Platform, discussions started between representatives of the Platform of Islamic Organizations and the Platform for Foreigners in Greater Rotterdam to see whether and how both co-ordinating organizations might be able to work together. One of the results of the discussions was an initiative to set up an advisory council for migrants in Rotterdam. In May 1991 both Platforms and the Federation of Cape Verdean Organizations submitted an application for a subsidy for the Rotterdam Advisory Council for Immigrants Foundation. However, this Advisory Council in the event never took shape: no agreement was reached either between the municipal council and immigrant organizations or among the immigrant organizations themselves on the problem of the form it should take, whereupon the idea of an official Advisory Council 'died a slow death', according to an official.

[25] For a survey of the organizations represented in the Network see: *Almanak 92/93, Samenwerkende Organisaties van & voor Nieuwe Rotterdammers*. Rotterdam Municipal Council.

Utrecht

In the 1970s Utrecht's municipal council was renowned for its progressive approach to consulting immigrants. As early as 1972 it denounced the inadequate political influence of Mediterranean and other immigrants, and it was the first in the Netherlands to set up a separate advisory council for them, the Migrants Council. In the *Outline Memorandum on Minorities Policy* (GU 1981) the council again emphasized the importance of empowering ethnic minorities, and here again they were more advanced in their policy plans than the national government.[26] Bearing in mind the developments in Rotterdam, it seemed a justifiable assumption that in Utrecht, Muslim organizations would also be smoothly involved in political decision-making. But was this really the case?

The Migrants Council

In the early 1970s there was a Working Party on International Policy in Utrecht, on which representatives of the various immigrant groups had seats, as well as Dutch nationals. The members criticized the way the Foundation for Foreign Workers in the Central Netherlands worked, and they were dissatisfied about access to Dutch political channels (Ester & Mellegers 1974: 8–9). In 1971 they organized hearings to try to assess the opinion of foreigners about the desirability of a Migrants Council. The result was positive. In March 1972 the Working Party submitted a draft proposal to the municipal council, in which the Migrants Council was assigned the function of encouraging the formation of opinion among immigrants, and of providing the government and private institutions with recommendations about foreign workers.[27] The municipal council backed the proposal a month later.[28]

In practice the new Council was engaged mainly in the problems of immigrants in the areas of education, housing and employment,

---

[26] For example, the Temporary Subsidy Arrangement for Extra Administration Costs with regard to the Minority Policy to Municipalities, which came into effect in 1981. To be eligible for this temporary subsidy from the Ministry of Internal Affairs, there had to be (amongst other things) a regulated forum for consultation with minority groups, established by the municipal council.

[27] Utrecht Municipal Council, Printed Collection, no. 76 (1972), p. 8.

[28] Minutes of the Meeting of the Municipal Council, dated 7 April 1972. Utrecht Municipal Council.

and in a few cases mediated in finding locations for places of worship. In June 1977, in a 'structural conference' between the municipality, the Migrants Council and the Foundation for Foreign Workers, it was agreed that the continued existence of two organizations for promoting the interests of foreign workers in the municipality of Utrecht should be brought to an end as soon as possible. There should be a single organizational body: a Working Party for Foreign Workers.[29] In late 1978 the Migrants Council—albeit unwillingly—decided to dissolve itself. The direct cause of this was the decision of the Minister for Culture, Recreation and Social Work to suspend the subsidy 'for the experiment of a Migrants Council' effective from 1 October 1978.[30]

The Working Party for an Islamic Services Centre

The Migrants Council, when it was in operation, was intended primarily for foreign workers, and not specifically for Muslims, even though most foreign workers were of Islamic sympathies. Some officials saw this as a deficiency, and an official working party in the municipality's General Administration Department therefore launched the idea of creating a Muslim services centre (Theunis 1979: 438). This would need to be set up 'centred on a mosque to be founded in Utrecht', and would engage in 'various activities in the social and socio-cultural fields' (ibid.). After a positive reaction from the Migrants Council,[31] the municipal council declared itself perfectly prepared to provide financial assistance for activities of a social or cultural nature. It hoped that it would be possible to bring about 'good mutual contacts between the foreigners and the other residents of Utrecht'. For its precise activities the council thought an exchange of views with representatives of Utrecht's Muslim organizations was necessary, and the Working Party for an Islamic Services Centre was finally set up on 16 March 1975.[32] Apart from the Alderman for Social Affairs

---

[29] Report of the Migrants Council 1975–1977, p. 60. Utrecht Municipal Council.
[30] The Ministry of Culture, Recreation and Social Work provided the largest part of the subsidy: 95 per cent; the municipality provided the remaining 5 per cent (Theunis 1979: 557).
[31] Letter from the Migrants Council to the Board of Mayor and Aldermen, dated 13 December 1974, on the project on behalf of Foreign Workers.
[32] Letter from the Board of Mayor and Aldermen to the Migrants Council, dated 28 January 1975, ref. 5587 AZ, on the project on behalf of Foreign Workers. Utrecht Municipal Council. In this letter the Board also claimed to have taken

and a number of civil servants, and two members of the Migrants Council, the Foundation for Foreign Workers, the Council of Churches, and a number of Muslim bodies were represented on it (Feirabend 1993: 17). The Working Party met several times, always to discuss the need for mosque space. However, nothing more was heard of this group after April 1977.

The Advisory Group for Ethnic Groups

Around 1980 neither Muslim nor Mediterranean immigrant organizations were functioning as official dialogue partners with the municipal council. In 1981, after consultation with the Foundation for Foreign Workers, the project manager for the Minorities Policy drew up a proposal to set up a working party for all nationalities.[33] In his view the target group would gain nothing by fragmentation, because common interests were involved. Nevertheless, in May 1981 a start was made with two working parties based on separate categories: the Working Party for Surinamese and Antilleans, and the Working Party for Foreign Workers, with representatives of Mediterranean groups. Participation by the target group was in principle restricted to a single, permanent representative for each nationality, and one or two representatives of the Foundation for Foreign Workers.

In early 1990, when representatives from Surinam, the Netherlands Antilles and Aruba took their seats in the Working Party, it was rechristened the Advisory Group for Ethnic Groups (Feirabend 1993: 20). Although its task was to formulate recommendations and plans for the minorities policy, in practice it functioned mainly as a sounding board for the municipality's policy proposals affecting minorities (GU 1991: 17–18).[34] In 1993 the municipal council and the immi-

---

'good note' of the indivisible nature of the services centre and the mosque, and to be confident that a reasonable solution would be found for the foundation of a mosque.

[33] *Official Memorandum on the Setting Up of a Classified Working Party on Foreign Workers*, dated 4 February 1981. Utrecht Municipal Council.

[34] Apart from this the municipal decision-making procedure offered alternative opportunities, in case the official advisory system did not live up to its promise. For instance, interested parties could present their views directly to the Administrative Co-ordination and Consultation on Minorities, in which the administrators, officials and external bodies concerned could outline and monitor the minorities policy. In practice this did not work, mainly because at that stage the administrators often did not define their position (see also: GU 1985a).

grant organizations involved carried out an assessment of the Advisory Group. It was decided that alternatives to the Advisory Group, which was not working well, would be explored.[35]

To be sure, not a single Muslim organization had ever been involved in either the Working Party or the Advisory Group. The official reason given was that only representatives of subsidized interest organizations could be accepted in either of them. Muslim organizations were not subsidized in Utrecht and therefore had no right to separate representation—an example of circular logic. In theory Muslim organizations could submit an application to the municipality for a subsidy, provided it was not for religious activities (Feirabend 1993: 20–21). When in 1984 the municipality realized that in a number of cases Muslim bodies also organized non-religious activities, they laid down a new guideline:

> If a non-religious activity signifies a complement to the package of activities of an existing non-religious organization, we are in principle prepared to subsidize that activity. In such cases it will also be necessary to review the resources of the religious organization, in order to see whether a subsidy for that activity is desirable.[36]

This much is certain: although the non-religious activities of Muslim organizations were not explicitly excluded from subsidies, the conditions imposed by the municipality effectively made subsidies extremely unlikely.

Around 1991 the Turkish Cultural Centre requested accession to the Advisory Group for Ethnic Groups; its statutes intentionally contained no explicit reference to Islamic principles.[37] Yet the Centre's request never came any further than the agenda committee, as was explained by the deputy co-ordinator for Minorities Policy at the time, who was also an ex-officio member of the Advisory Group. According to her, the request for membership was officially turned down because it did not fully comply with the conditions for ongoing subsidy provision; unofficially it was because the Turkish Democratic

---

[35] Discussion paper, co-ordinator for emancipation and minorities policy, dated 25 April 1995. Utrecht Municipal Council.

[36] *Guideline Subsidization of Organizations of Foreigners (Richtlijn Subsidiëring Organisaties van Buitenlanders)* 1984, p. 5. Utrecht Municipal Council.

[37] This was acceptable, however, because a Muslim organization was established at the same address. The treasurer of this Muslim organization was, moreover, one and the same person as the Turkish Cultural Centre's treasurer.

Workers Movement had threatened to withdraw from the Advisory Group. In fact the Turkish Cultural Centre did receive a subsidy, if only on an occasional basis.[38]

The Platform for Islamic Organizations

Though Muslim organizations were not official dialogue partners with the municipal council, they did sometimes need to be consulted, for instance in 1989 in discussions on the public call to prayer. Here, the council took the step of holding meetings with all the Muslim bodies, in order to arrive at regulations about the duration, the frequency and the maximum noise level of the call to prayer. Consultation took place on two or three occasions, but no ruling was arrived at.[39]

During the consultations the wish was expressed for more regular meetings, resulting in the advent of the Platform for Islamic Organizations. The Muslim organizations hoped that this would at last lead to political recognition. However, the Platform did not survive long. The first—and last—consultation between the municipal council and the Platform took place on 1 March 1989.[40] Subjects

---

[38] Early in January 1988 the Turkish Cultural Centre submitted an application for a subsidy to set up an association. The Board of Mayor and Aldermen turned down the request, whereupon the Centre lodged an appeal a month later. The municipal council decided in September 1988 that the refusal to grant the subsidy had been justified. The Centre then lodged an appeal with the Council of State, which found in its ruling of 14 February 1991 that the municipal council's decision was contrary to the principles of proper administration and declared the decision void; Utrecht municipality had to grant a (one-off) subsidy (Raad van State, Afdeling Rechtspraak, kenmerk RO3.88.6167, on the ruling on the dispute between the Turkish Cultural Centre and the Utrecht Municipal Council).

[39] After the introduction of the Public Manifestations Act, one mosque proceeded to broadcast an amplified call to prayer. This provoked a complaint from the people living in the neighbourhood to the police and the town hall. Although measurements showed that the sound was 'within acceptable standards', the Board of Mayor and Aldermen still wanted consultations to come to an arrangement. On account of the fact that there had never been processions in Utrecht, the Board considered that the call to prayer should only be vocal, without amplification, from an open window or door. This regulation never came into force, as the senior official concerned decided that the ban on using amplification was not sufficiently substantiated in law. The law does actually permit amplification. Nor do the police orders contain any reference to the call to prayer, and in the 1990s two mosques broadcast their call once a day, with amplification (Feirabend 1993; Groenendijk 1994).

[40] Report of a consultation between Utrecht Municipal Council and the Platform for Islamic Organizations, dated 1 March 1989, dossier 1.844.922, Care for Foreigners. Utrecht Municipal Council, Welfare Department.

on the agenda included mixed-sex swimming, the right to graves in perpetuity, Islamic religious instruction, the possible subsidization of Muslim organizations, and, more generally, the attitude of the council to these bodies. The Alderman for Welfare, Van der Sluis (Labour, PvdA), stuck to the point of view taken earlier that neither a Muslim socio-cultural centre, nor a platform of Muslim organizations, could be considered for subsidies. In effect this meant that the Platform was not viable. The representatives of the Muslim organizations argued that such a platform could promote the interests of Muslims, but the representatives of the council were not to be moved.

In 1992 the political role of Muslim organizations reappeared on the agenda, albeit to some extent disguised. A *Memorandum concerning the Policy on Mosques* underlined the possible role of Muslim organizations in promoting the interests of Muslims, and argued for more intensive contacts between these bodies and civil servants and administrators (GU 1992). In the council's Welfare Committee, Christian Democrat and Labour members (CDA and PvdA) may have acknowledged that these comments gave cause for concern, but they did not draw any conclusions from them.[41]

In short, in spite of laborious consultation and sometimes half-hearted overtures, in the mid-1990s Muslim organizations in Utrecht were still excluded from the central political stage.

Impetus for change

When a new municipal administration took office in April 1994, a change in the attitude of the municipality began to show itself. The new Alderman for Welfare, Van der Linden (Labour, PvdA), was much more open to contacts with Muslim organizations than her predecessor. So far none of the contacts has led to ongoing consultation with Muslim organizations, but there might now be opportunities for them in a new structure of advisory councils based on nationality. Whether the four advisory councils would in fact materialize, and whether Muslim organizations could really be given a place in them, was still uncertain in mid-June 1995.

---

[41] Report of the public meeting of the Committee for Welfare, dated 19 March 1992, p. 3. Utrecht Municipal Council.

Ideological concepts and arguments

Unlike in the 1970s, which were characterized by reserve, it is now-adays recognized in Rotterdam and Utrecht political circles that Muslims must be allowed to take part in official local politics in the Netherlands. This recognition, however noncommittal it may be, stems from ideas about citizenship and democracy and is above all related to the *rights of the individual*. This means that the archetypal political bodies—the parties—should be open to everyone, and so also to Muslims. The following statement by the Utrecht Alderman for Welfare, Van der Sluis (Labour, PvdA), is a good example:

> I think that people should try to be active primarily in the existing political parties. And that those parties should also have the duty to recruit people, to make them active, and that people in the municipal council should also be from these groups. As yet this happens only on a very limited scale.

The Alderman had good reason to suggest the joining of existing parties. The thought that Muslims might use their democratic rights to set up their own political associations, and so engage in politics collectively, sends cold shivers down the spines of many politicians. In Utrecht, where in 1993 there was talk of the formation of a Muslim Party, a Labour council member exclaimed: 'I don't like the sound of that at all!' But if it came to that, no politician would be prepared to ban it. The legalistic point of view takes precedence. One Christian Democrat Utrecht council member remarked:

> You can't forbid anyone to form a political party, but whether or not it is a good development is something I would like to think about or discuss.

On closer analysis many of those concerned think that Muslims have the right to take *collective* political action, but that there is a certain risk involved in these activities, which is considered specific to Islam, and which increases as Muslims start to act more autonomously.

In this view Muslim organizations are *not democratic*. More seriously, they would function as fronts for movements such as the Turkish Grey Wolves or the Moroccan Amicales. These fears were particularly strong in the 1970s and 1980s, but have by no means completely disappeared.

An extension of this thinking is that Muslim activities would be associated with the *involvement of foreign powers* in Dutch politics. It was no accident that an official of the Rotterdam Migrants Office was so heavily biased in favour of municipal support for the co-ordinating Platform of Islamic Organizations in Greater Rotterdam:

> A negative reason for the government to offer its support (. . .) without wanting to cast any doubt on the integrity of the Platform (. . .) is the possibility that foreign funding, and therefore also foreign influence, might play a role.

It is popularly assumed that Islam is a totalitarian, all-embracing, religion. The political implication of this is that Muslims are not in agreement with the separation of church and state, considered so important in the Netherlands, and will use their political influence to weaken this separation. To quote an Utrecht council member (for the Democrats 66, D66):

> . . . because the laws of the Moroccans are interwoven with their religion. (. . .) Although I consider that it must be made clear how things work in the Netherlands. We keep church and state separate, and I think that is a right we have won which should not be altered. (. . .) If that is quite clear, I think we can all live together very well. And then there are obviously also certain laws, such as compulsory schooling, which should be observed. You have to do that through making information available, and that is why contact with the mosque organization is so important, to explain it all clearly.

There is a popular view that Muslims lag behind in this respect, compared, of course, with modern, non-Muslim Dutchmen. They adhere to a pre-modern religion, in the sense that they expect an active political role from 'church leaders' and 'church' organizations. Interestingly enough, we also come across this assumption in a Christian party like the Christian Democratic Party (CDA). To quote an Utrecht council member:

> Surely, you have other links. You don't just have your imam. I am also a member of a religious community, my parish also has its minister. But I don't go to him when I have a housing problem. Then I go to the housing department, I don't go to the minister. That was how it used to be done in the old days. I mean, those days are gone.

Although in many people's eyes Muslims are obviously strangers in their midst, Dutch politics must come to an understanding with them. This produces contradictions, which people think can be resolved by 'information' and 'education', which can 'free' Muslims of their religiosity. In Rotterdam the municipality has begun a dialogue with

Muslim organizations, not an ordinary dialogue, but a 'critical' one, 'in which the differences of opinion will not be covered up'.

Both in Rotterdam and Utrecht the municipal council has to deal with *demands of Muslim organizations* to be involved in the formation of local policy. Such involvement implies political recognition as a partner in the political process. Should the local government go as far as that, and if so, should it actively promote recognition? An important principle by which those involved are guided is the *principle of equality*. However, there are several ways of interpreting this. As a Christian Democrat council member in Utrecht remarked:

> There, too, you have to be careful not to give other people the impression that you are putting them in a privileged position. In normal policy, Protestants or Catholics don't have a special voice either.

This politician apparently regards recognition as a privilege, and therefore a breach of the principle of equality. Instead of comparing Muslim organizations (of immigrants) with Protestant or Catholic ones, they are also compared with non-Muslim immigrant organizations. In a Memorandum from the Rotterdam Migrants Office we read:

> The mosques are *by far the most important interest organizations*. In order to be able to approach these groups it is important to take the mosques seriously, and to respect their perception of their identity (GR 1981b: 3; emphasis added).

The authors of that Memorandum regard *non*-recognition as a breach of the principle of equality. Another principle central to these kinds of considerations is the *separation of church and state*. Some people maintain that church organizations should have no established role in the formation of policy, certainly not where matters of more general social interest are involved. After all, the age of pillarization is past. When account is taken of the supposed risk inherent in their political activities, this would apply all the more to Muslim organizations.

Both these principles, of equality and of the separation of church and state, come into play when considering whether Muslim organizations should be eligible for subsidies. It has already been shown that eventual recognition as a partner in the political debate is dependent upon this eligibility. In Utrecht the municipal council manipulated the subsidy rules like a trap. They would only subsidize interest organizations which were not linked to a religion or political party, which was why the Platform for Islamic Organizations never became viable there. At the same time this rule was employed to exclude Muslim organizations from the Advisory Group for Ethnic Groups. The Alderman for Welfare was unmoved, and had no difficulty in shifting the responsibility onto the interest organizations:

> It is only interest organizations to which we give subsidies, and that does not include all organizations. We only give a subsidy to one organization for each nationality. And there are no Muslim groups among them, because they get no subsidies. (. . .) There is also a practical reason for this: if we had to let all the various religious clubs in, then we would have at least ten more people sitting around the table. So we don't do that. But I admit that it makes the club a very limited one at the moment. But I think that it is more their problem, how they can reach their own supporters, their own rank and file. I think that these interest organizations should be asking themselves how else they can tackle the problem.

Officialdom certainly made cautious attempts to abandon this cut-and-dried point of view,[42] but for the time being, apparently, the Alderman remained adamant:

> They want to discuss all kinds of things with the council from their little clubs, but I won't have it. It may be stated in the Memorandum, but I never wanted to endorse that, in the sense that I was prepared to turn it into a permanent consultation with the council. I am quite willing to discuss specific points with them now and then, but not really regular consultation. If they want to talk to me, let them invite me and I will go and see them.

How different the situation is in Rotterdam. There the municipality changed the subsidy rules to the advantage of Muslim organizations, and consequently opened the way to recognition (and separate subsidies) for the co-ordinating Platform of Islamic Organizations in Greater Rotterdam. This happened mainly *to increase the effectiveness of the minorities policy*. By way of explanation, the Alderman for Special Groups stated:

> . . . in the development of policy for immigrants, more and more importance is attached to these so-called interest organizations as representatives of ethnic minorities. They can be, as it were, *social partners in the process of integration*. (. . .) In this case the dominant form of interest organization is the mosque association (emphasis added).

---

[42] Cf. GU 1992.

In the end this partnership implies that Muslim organizations play a role not only in the implementation, but also in the development of the minorities policy. After all, *quid pro quo*. This emphasis on the functionality of the recognition of Muslim organizations has the effect of making discussions about the separation of church and state seem somewhat forced. Don't make things difficult, is the message. One official commented that if the Platform of Islamic Organizations in Greater Rotterdam

> started getting involved in the social interests (education/employment) of their rank and file, (. . .) the principles involved in the separation of church and state would not keep the authorities out of the discussion entirely'.[43]

To a certain extent affairs were conducted *as if religion was of no importance*. For instance, one of the officials involved remarked that it made no difference to him whether the municipality was dealing with Muslim organizations or soccer clubs. What mattered was that certain immigrant organizations became socially relevant, and 'it so happened that they transpired to be mosque associations'. At the same time religion is actually an important consideration, and not only because Muslim organizations typically make religious claims (for instance in such matters as establishing a mosque or Islamic religious instruction). The Rotterdam supporters of the recognition of Muslim organizations as dialogue partners hope in this way to tap *new sources*. In doing so they *treat them on an equal footing with interest organizations*. For instance, the Alderman for Cultural Minorities (Labour, PvdA) called on the Foundation for Foreign Workers in Greater Rotterdam to assign a permanent seat to the Platform of Islamic Organizations:

> It is also essential that the policy official enjoys the full confidence of the member organizations. The Platform has let it be known that it would like a decisive voice in the selection of such an official. I gather that you have previously granted this facility in similar cases. I would appreciate it if you were prepared to do the same in this case.[44]

---

[43] Memorandum of 3 October 1988 for internal consultation. Re: the local authority's position with respect to the subsidy application by the Platform of Islamic Organizations in Greater Rotterdam. Rotterdam Municipal Council, Migrants Office.

[44] Letter from the Alderman for Cultural Minorities to the Committee of the Foundation for Foreign Workers in Greater Rotterdam, dated 19 October 1988. Rotterdam Municipal Council.

In a certain sense Muslim organizations are here set *against* secular interest organizations and their platform. One official spoke, not without reason, of 'the old platform' and 'an alternative platform', without any attempt to disguise his preference for the latter.

CHAPTER EIGHT

THE ESTABLISHMENT AND FUNDING OF
PLACES OF WORSHIP

Financial aid for Muslim places of worship has repeatedly appeared on the national political agenda. Yet by 1995 there were no official national rules for subsidizing the running or building of such places by the government. What is the situation locally? Just as in the 1950s with Christian churches, municipalities can always make their own rules. To what extent, then, is there evidence of local financial support—whether overt or indirect—for Muslim places of worship?

Rotterdam

The 1970s: restraint

In 1972 Muslims observed Ramadan in the Ahoy complex, a huge exposition hall, which was specially hired for the occasion, and in the same year a community centre made a large room available for Friday prayers. The first permanent mosque was opened in 1975.[1] Towards the end of the 1970s the number of places of worship gradually began to increase; there were five in 1979, eight in 1980, and 13 in 1981 (Landman 1992: 290).

Their establishment was by no means problem-free. Some people—both Dutch and foreign—condemned what they saw as the fascist-like character of Muslim organizations; others opposed the coming of such places of worship for other reasons. For instance, in 1977 the Afrikaanderwijk Initiative Group fiercely opposed plans for the Kocatepe mosque, because they felt it would lead to a disproportionate increase in foreign influence within the district. In the same year the municipal council stressed in its *Memorandum on Migrants in Rotterdam* (*Nota Migranten in Rotterdam*, GR 1978: 71) that the authority bore no responsibility—financial or otherwise—for churches, and

---

[1] In 1974 the Turkish Nurcu movement in Rotterdam had already established a *medresse*, in which there was a prayer room (Landman 1992: 120, 137–138).

that it had no intention of 'favouring the Muslim community more than other church communities'. This was a rather curious statement, because the city council granted several one-off subsidies, and acted as mediator between Muslim organizations and the Ministry of Culture, Recreation and Social Work.[2] In 1976 the municipality had even asked Saudi-Arabia for support in founding a mosque.[3] In their Memorandum it acknowledged the need for places of worship, but its attitude to mosques remained as yet extremely reserved, particularly in comparison with the generosity with which it approached progressive, secular migrant organizations at the time. The annual budgets of these organizations, including their premises, were almost completely covered by subsidies from the authorities. The Muslim organizations, however, were expected to support their own churches.

The early 1980s: a U-turn in policy

In October 1981 the municipal Migrants Office questioned this policy of reservation in its *Memorandum on Mosques* (GR 1981b). Many mosques, partly as a result of inadequate municipal supervision, did not comply with the building and fire regulations, and this had to change. As a sequel to this internal Memorandum the local Urban Development Department made an inventory of the current state of the mosques and laid out its prognosis, regretting, among other things, that there was no central policy on the establishment of mosques (GR 1983: 4). Meanwhile the Migrants Office grew more anxious about the social isolation in which most mosques were thought to be operating, and in 1983 came up with a new Memorandum entitled *Mosque Groups as Interest Organizations*. This stated that the central city administration should issue appropriate directives to ensure that the foundation of places of worship could be integrated smoothly into the zoning plans of the various districts. Like other 'interest organizations', Muslim organizations should also be eligible for subsidies,

[2] For instance, the municipality paid Fl. 36,000 in 1977 as a contribution to the cost of establishing the Kocatepe Mosque in de Putselaan (Fl. 350,000); the Ministry of Culture, Recreation and Social Work paid Fl. 90,000. In the same year the Ministry also contributed Fl. 12,000 to the cost of establishing the Fatih Mosque (GR 1985b; see also GR 1981b: 2).
[3] The government of that country promised $ 300,000 in 1978, then worth about Fl. 700,000 (*Het Vrije Volk*, 19 January 1978 and 6 March 1979; *Rotterdams Nieuwsblad*, 28 July 1979). This action by the municipality was rather remarkable in view of the frequently voiced fear of interference by foreign powers in internal affairs.

and the municipality should give consideration to provisional support for the foundation costs of places of worship with some arrangement similar to the Church Building Subsidy Act (GR 1983). The Board of Mayor and Aldermen accepted this Memorandum in principle.[4]

The Working Party on Interest Organizations

In view of the proposed decentralization of welfare work for ethnic minorities, the municipality created the Working Party on Interest Organizations in the autumn of 1983. From 1 January 1985, municipalities were to take over the Ministry of Welfare, Health and Culture's task of granting subsidies to immigrant organizations, and the Working Party was to make the necessary recommendations. As well as officials and leaders of secular interest groups, a representative of the 'mosque groups' had a seat in the Working Party (GR 1984b: 2).

It took as a starting point that subsidies should not be based on immigrant organizations or nationalities, but on activities in the areas of emancipation, education, integration, participation and also identity formation, to the extent that these activities served to promote 'the integration process of foreigners in all sections of Dutch society' (ibid.: 10). Furthermore, new interest organizations applying for subsidies should do their best to join existing organizations already in receipt of subsidies. The Working Party concluded unanimously that mosques should be eligible for subsidies for activities prioritized in the municipality of Rotterdam.

The Working Party was less unanimous about subsidizing the accommodation expenses of Muslim organizations. Two mutually exclusive points of view emerged. Some members thought that these organizations should not be eligible for government subsidy because of their religious approach, fearing that they would hamper the integration process or that foreign powers would have too great an influence. Others held that they should indeed be eligible for funding, because in addition to their religious activities they carried out a number of other essential activities. Moreover, they were so placed

---

[4] Agenda of the meeting of the Board of Mayor and Aldermen, dated 16 September 1983. Rotterdam Municipal Council. This item on the agenda included a letter from the Centrum-Noord district, dated 11 July 1983, in which the Mayor was urgently asked for a well co-ordinated policy on mosques.

that they could reach very large groups of people. Adherents of this view felt that mosques, just like other meeting places, should be subsidized for a substantial share of the cost of their premises.

Decisions in principle

In the spring of 1984 Alderman Simons for Special Groups (labour, PvdA) submitted a Memorandum to the Board of Mayor and Aldermen, incorporating the views of the Working Party on Interest Organizations.[5] The Board recognized the socio-cultural function of Muslim organizations. Some members, however, were hesitant about granting financial aid, because it concerned activities of a religious nature. However, the Board finally voted in favour of subsidies 'on a very limited scale, exclusively for activities in the socio-cultural sphere directed at integration, and which were in no way at variance with municipal policy' (GR 1984a). With the exception of one member (Labour, PvdA), the Board was also prepared to grant occasional subsidies to cover the cost of premises. The majority of the Committee for Special Groups supported this fundamental change of direction (ibid.).[6]

Two months later a letter was circulated to 'the Muslim citizens of Rotterdam', in which Simons announced that a member of staff had been appointed to the Migrants Office, 'who is himself a Muslim and who will be responsible for contact with the mosques'. He added that although religious activities did not qualify for subsidies, other activities—including their associated accommodation costs—did. He spoke of his confidence that these measures would lead to a better relationship between the city council and the Muslim citizens of Rotterdam.[7] In spite of the Alderman's progressive spirit and high

---

[5] Public meeting of Co-ordinated Welfare Policy/Welfare Planning/Special Groups, dated 5 June 1984 (SG Affairs), agenda item 8. Rotterdam Municipal Council, Secretariat Department of Cultural Minorities.

[6] The speakers included the secretary of the Turkish-Islamic Cultural Federation Foundation, who referred to the report on the functions of foreigners' organizations (*Funkties eigen organisaties buitenlanders*) by De Graaf (1983). Among the papers submitted the councillors also received an abstract of De Graaf's report, which reported reasonably favourably on the social significance of Muslim organizations, while the progressive, secular organizations came off rather badly. This last group was stung by the publication and demanded a rectification of the report (Majic-Haak & Schellekens 1986).

[7] Open letter from Alderman Simons to the Muslim citizens of Rotterdam, dated 25 June 1984, Rotterdam Municipal Council.

ideals, however, the practical implementation of his new policy was
not immediately sanctioned by the city council.

In September 1984 the Committee for Special Groups supported
the draft proposal for financial support to Muslim organizations, but
with conditions on subsidies for the cost of premises. The members
first wished to see a report on current accommodation for Turkish
and Moroccan organizations, and they wanted more information
about the possible function of the mosques as 'meeting places'. The
information requested became available a few months later.[8] It stated
that Turks and Moroccans had no separate meeting places, as the
Italians had, but that mosques provided for their needs in this respect
(GR 1985b: 11).

During a meeting of the Committee a representative expressed his
satisfaction on behalf of all the Turkish Muslim organizations at the
recognition of Muslim organizations as valid interest organizations
for migrants,[9] although he regretted that subsidies were exclusively
granted for activities directed at integration. On the other hand the
Greater Rotterdam Foreigners Platform thought in that the municipality was trying to destroy interest organizations of foreigners.

Alderman Simons was then faced with the difficult task of con-
vincing his opponents and the undecided. In a comprehensive written explanation of the item on the agenda he set out his point of
view once more. He considered that this issue affected those minorities which were the least integrated, but the largest in numbers.[10]
On behalf of the Muslim organizations, the secretary of the Turkish-
Islamic Cultural Federation Foundation stated that if the municipality decided not to grant subsidies, the Federation saw no point
in further dialogue.[11] After exhaustive discussions, opinions remained
divided: the Alderman and two council members indicated that they
were prepared to cover the accommodation costs of Muslim organ-

---

[8] The report (GR 1985b) discussed the situation of 20 Turkish and 11 Moroccan
organizations.
[9] Report of the public meeting of the Committee for Co-ordinated Welfare
Policy, Welfare Planning and Special Groups (SG Affairs), dated 26 February 1985.
Rotterdam Municipal Council, Secretariat Department of Cultural Minorities.
[10] BG 3234, dated 26 March 1985, agenda item 7b. Rotterdam Municipal Council,
Committee on Special Groups.
[11] Report on the open session of the Committee for Co-ordinated Welfare Policy,
Welfare Planning and Special Groups (SG Affairs), 26 March 1985. Rotterdam
Municipal Council, Secretariat Department of Cultural Minorities.

izations—provided these were associated with activities eligible for grants—and also to subsidize their 'function as a meeting place'; three council members wanted at the most to contribute to the cost of premises; and two were against any subsidy at all.[12] Subsequently the Board of Mayor and Aldermen decided to make a contribution to the accommodation costs of activities which were eligible for subsidy, such as language courses. The Board took no decision on subsidies for the 'meeting place' function.[13]

The Official Working Party on Establishing Mosques

Meanwhile the actual establishment of mosques—in the physical sense—was still left to the free play of social forces, with the attendant problems. These included the unlawful change of use of residential property, mosques being established in conflict with zoning plans, infringement of building and fire regulations, and problems with parking and noise. Moreover, certain mosques were found to be established on sites which in the urban renewal plans were due for urgent demolition or renovation. However, there were no agreed rules for relocating places of worship (GR 1983: 4).

In 1982 the local Urban Development Department had already pleaded for a central policy on the establishment of mosques. An interdepartmental working party on this issue had been formed, but had ceased its activities after a single meeting because the municipality saw no prospect of contributing to the cost of converting mosques.[14] That marked the end of any hope for central approach. Meanwhile the tension gradually increased in a number of districts. Because of the situation in the Feijenoord district—where the establishment of four mosques led to protests by the residents organization to the city administration[15]—an official of the Urban Development Department proposed resuscitating the Official Working Party on

---

[12] Ibid.

[13] Report on the meeting of the Board of Mayor and Aldermen, dated 12 April 1985. Rotterdam Municipal Council.

[14] Memorandum resulting from discussion on the appointment of a working party of officials on the establishment of mosques in Rotterdam, dated 5 September 1985. Rotterdam Municipal Council, Migrants Office.

[15] Report on the public meeting of the Committee for Co-ordinated Welfare Policy, Welfare Planning and Special Groups (SG Affairs), dated 4 June 1985. Rotterdam Municipal Council, Secretariat Department of Cultural Minorities. On the role of the Feijenoord Residents Association see also: Sunier 1996.

Establishing Mosques.[16] It would have the task of co-ordinating the foundation and relocation of mosques, and examining to what extent financial support could be made available—for example from the funds for Urban Renewal.[17]

During initial consultations, officials of the Migrants Office, the Urban Development Department and the Project Co-ordinators Collective for Urban Renewal (PCC) decided to concentrate on problem cases, especially the establishment of the mosques in Feijenoord. To that end the Official Working Party was expanded by the addition of a member of the district welfare planning staff, and later by staff from the Urban Renewal project offices in several districts.[18]

The central problem was the almost total lack of alternative premises. Moreover, the costs of relocation rose rapidly, and most Muslim organizations were relatively impoverished. There were, admittedly, regulations for reimbursing the costs of relocating businesses and socio-cultural institutions, but the project offices considered them inappropriate to places of worship. The Official Working Party therefore concentrated on making lists of empty properties and on exploring the possibilities of subsidies for mosques.[19] For this purpose an official of the Migrants Office composed a Memorandum, attaching as an appendix a copy of an Amsterdam subsidy regulation.[20] There the

---

[16] The author had in mind the participation by the Migrants Office, City Development, the PCC Bureau, the fire brigade, the building and housing inspection department, the project offices on Urban Renewal and on Welfare Planning (Official Working Party on Establishing Mosques, Rotterdam Municipal Council, Urban Development Department, section Research and Structural Planning, dated 8 July 1985).

[17] For a proper understanding of the situation some insight into the organization of the process of urban renewal is necessary. At the time this process had been decentralized to a large degree: in each redevelopment area a project group under the direction of a project co-ordinator organized demolition, renovation and other relevant activities. The project group formed a platform within the community where residents could air their wishes and grievances about redevelopment issues. Representatives of the residents co-operated with officials of various municipal departments. The work of implementation, meanwhile, was carried out in a project development office, headed by the project co-ordinator. All project co-ordinators together formed the Project Co-ordinators Collective (PCC), a city organization in which matters of general policy were discussed. The whole operation of urban renewal was the responsibility of the Alderman for Urban Renewal and Housing.

[18] Working Party on Mosques, report of the meeting of 28 November 1985 in the Afrikaanderwijk Project Development Office. Rotterdam Municipal Council, Migrants Office.

[19] Ibid.

[20] *Memorandum on Subsidy Facilities for Mosques*, dated 3 December 1985. Rotterdam

municipality made available a financial contribution of up to Fl. 60,000 if a mosque had to move to a new location as a result of urban renewal plans.[21] The PCC consultation body next decided to make a new inventory of mosques, on the basis of which a policy proposal could be submitted to the Aldermen for Urban Renewal and Special Groups.[22] In September 1986 the locations of 18 mosques were found to be causing problems. The project co-ordinators urged the Board of Mayor and Aldermen to make arrangements for the reimbursement of the costs of relocation. Although the Board objected in principle to subsidizing places of worship, it invited the project co-ordinators, in collaboration with the Migrants Office, to produce a detailed recommendation.

In September 1987 the PCC and the Migrants Office issued their joint report, a summary of the short-term solutions (GR 1987b). The second section of the report, proposing a structural approach, followed late in October, and its composition was the exclusive responsibility of the project co-ordinators (GR 1987c).[23] The PCC stressed that the municipality had an obligation to act, and requested clarification on the possibility of financial contributions to the cost of relocating mosques, on the attitude to the establishment of new mosques, and the best geographical distribution of mosques. In addition the PCC wanted the backlog in dealing with infringements of the regulations to be dealt with (ibid.: 2–4).

In the spring of 1988 Alderman Simons, in a letter to the managements of the Rotterdam mosques, provided clarity on the first point. A financial contribution by the municipality was only possible in the case of relocation or renovation in the context of the urban renewal programme, and only 'if the mosque group itself first raises as much as can reasonably be expected'.[24] There was no possibility

---

Municipal Council, Migrants Office. In its ruling on the public call to prayer, too, Rotterdam has followed Amsterdam's example. Cf. Groenendijk 1994.

[21] This ruling was based on the Regulation on Granting Financial Assistance to Entrepreneurs in Urban Renewal Areas (Amsterdam Municipal Council, *Gemeenteblad* 1983, section 3, no. 168).

[22] Report of the Working Party on Mosques, dated 8 January 1986. Rotterdam Municipal Council, Migrants Office.

[23] From this can be deduced that the PCC and the Migrants Office held opposing views and did not work well together (GR 1987c: 4).

[24] Letter from the Alderman for Cultural Minorities, Simons, to the managements of the Rotterdam mosques, dated 23 March 1988. Rotterdam Municipal Council, Secretariat Department of Cultural Minorities.

of a standard regulation as in Amsterdam, in view of the small number of mosques having to be relocated, and the diversity of their various situations. A separate solution would have to be sought for each relocation.[25] In practice, more or less fixed routines emerged. If ownership of property was involved, the site was bought through the Estates Agency. If the property was rented, then the costs of moving were reimbursed. In addition, capital expenditure which had been incurred by mosque organizations could be reimbursed in part (GR 1992a: 21). However, it was not only these technical problems which caused difficulties in the establishment of places of worship. There was also obstruction and opposition from various sectors.

Obstruction and opposition

An attitude of obstruction to the introduction of places of worship was in itself nothing new. What was new was that now residents organizations also took up entrenched positions on the social role of Muslim organizations. In addition, since 1995 the so-called migrant community workers of the Rotterdam Institute for Community Work were seconded to various residents associations to organize Turkish and Moroccan residents (Mulder & Van Duyvenbode 1988; Van der Pennen 1988). In most cases they were welfare workers with progressive views and a secular ideology. They soon became embroiled in a conflict with Muslim organizations and with the Migrants Office over the role of mosques in the district, and about municipal policy. Particularly in the Oude Westen district, feelings ran very high. In 1987 the Dutch Islamic Federation, in other words the Turkish Milli Görüş movement, had hired the former Arena youth centre from the city for Ramadan. After Ramadan, however, the Federation continued to occupy the Arena, and negotiations started with the Municipal Buildings Service about the possible purchase of the property.[26] The presence of the mosque caused great alarm among the local residents association, the Oude Westen Action Group, particularly for the Turks in the Group, who complained vigorously. According to the Turkish migrant community workers, the presence

[25] Progress report on the relocation of mosques in the context of urban renewal, for the meeting of the Committee for Urban Renewal and Housing of 23 March 1989. Rotterdam Municipal Council.
[26] For financial reasons the purchase did not go through. The Dutch Islamic Federation left the premises on their own initiative after a few months.

of the mosque threatened to reverse within a few weeks the process of integration which the Action Group had worked so hard to get started. To make matters worse another Muslim group, the Nurcular, were squatting in a vacant commercial property in breach of local development plans.

In the summer of 1987 the residents association sent a letter to the Board of Mayor and Aldermen. They thought it high time to launch a practical exchange of ideas about the place of mosques in the urban districts of Rotterdam.[27]

The head of the Secretariat Department of Cultural Minorities— to which the Migrants Office reported—took the initiative in 1987 of discussing a 'central municipal arrangement' with the Aldermen for Urban Renewal and Cultural Minorities.[28] At the same time the Board of Mayor and Aldermen invited several residents associations and representatives of mosques to a meeting about the call to prayer and the relocation of mosques. However, the meeting never took place because several of the residents associations refused the invitation. They first wanted a meeting concerning the effects of the mosques on the community in the districts. In their view there were 'no fruitful grounds for a discussion between the districts and the mosques'. However, they pressed for a meeting with the Board *without* the mosque organizations.[29]

Attempts at a dialogue

In the early months of 1988 the municipal council held separate discussions with the residents associations and the mosque organizations. In this the council—in the best tradition of Dutch public

---

[27] Letter from the Action Group Oude Westen to the Board of Mayor and Aldermen, dated 20 August 1987. Rotterdam Municipal Council.
[28] Letter from the head of the Secretariat Department of Social Affairs, Public Health and Cultural Minorities, to the head of the Department for Town Planning, Urban Renewal and Housing, ref. CM 4145c, dated 14 September 1987. Rotterdam Municipal Council.
[29] Letter from the Action Group Nieuwe Westen, Residents Associations Oude Noorden, and Action Group Oude Westen to the Board of Mayor and Aldermen, dated 14 September 1987. Rotterdam Municipal Council. More than a week later Alderman Simons received a similar request from the Feijenoord Residents Association. The latter was worried about the consequences of an unlawful, 'very strict Turkish mosque' in the district, and requested an informal interview (letter from the Feijenoord Residents Association to Alderman Simons, dated 22 September 1987. Rotterdam Municipal Council).

administration—pressed for a dialogue between the representatives
of both parties. However, the residents associations, and particularly the migrant community workers among them, were dismissive.
They refused to sit around a table with any mosque organization
whatsoever.

The dialogue threatened to be made even more difficult by the
migrant community workers' negative publicity about the mosques
(Aksu & Dogan 1987).[30] In the first meeting between the mosque
leadership and the Aldermen, complaints were expressed from the
Muslim side about the district activists and the migrant community
workers. The latter in particular were held to be prejudiced, to have
made all kinds of accusations, and to have a great deal of influence
in the district. The mosques had too few activists of their own to
do anything to counter the residents associations.[31] Nonetheless the
mosque organizations showed themselves ready for a dialogue. When
in mid-1988 the co-ordinating organization known as the Greater
Rotterdam Platform of Islamic Organizations was formed, the dialogue accelerated. In October there was a meeting between officials,
the Platform, and some of the migrant community workers. In the
same year a 'mosque team' was formed, consisting of officials from
Urban Renewal and Cultural Minorities, and charged with resolv-
ing the bottlenecks and facilitating some new mosques.[32] A structural
agreement was quickly reached between the mosque team and the
Platform. In 1989 a full-time member of staff was appointed to the
Project Co-ordinators Collective to be responsible for mosque policy,
which was set out in a draft Memorandum of February 1991, in
which a number of proposals for a more structural policy were elaborated (GR 1991). The emphasis was on encouragement and regulation.

Faith in the future

In the draft Memorandum *Faith in the Future* (*Geloven in de toekomst*) it
was stated that there was a shortage of places of worship, which in

---

[30] See also: *Rotterdams Nieuwsblad*, 25 February 1988.
[31] Report of a meeting between Rotterdam mosque organizations and the Aldermen
for Urban Renewal and Cultural Minorities, dated 26 February 1988. Rotterdam
Municipal Council, Migrants Office.
[32] *Policy Memorandum* of the Rotterdam Municipality on mosques etc. for meetings
between Aldermen and district representatives, October-December 1987. Rotterdam
Municipal Council, Migrants Office.

view of the expected increase in the number of Muslim residents
was likely to grow larger in the future (GR 1991: 2). To avoid unlawful and dangerous situations, the municipality needed to play an
active role in the policy on mosques. A plea was made for the creation of several larger mosques on through-routes, rather than in the
centre of neighbourhoods. Experience elsewhere suggested that the
establishment of such mosques put a curb on new initiatives. However,
such plans required the co-operation of mosque managements, sufficient
financial resources and suitable sites.

Here an active role was reserved for the municipality. In particular
it had to encourage the mosque organizations to combine forces. For
the financial resources pressure would have to be put on the national
government, in co-operation with the other three major cities, to
implement the proposals of the Hirsch Ballin Committee.[33] In addition, collaborating mosque managements deserved support in the
search for locations and in obtaining the necessary authorizations. An
effort had to be made to keep the additional functions of the mosques
to a minimum, so that the places of worship would be neutral and
could be used by a variety of religious groups. Activities such as
socio-cultural work and shops should be kept outside the mosques.
In addition, active efforts should be made to negotiate the relocation of four mosques in the context of the urban renewal programme.

Faith in the Future was sent to all mosque organizations, minority
group platforms, residents associations, municipal departments and
district organizations. The Platform of Islamic Organizations reacted
with delight, and regarded the draft Memorandum as a recognition
of the importance of religious provisions.[34] They agreed that the
muncipality should take action and that something should be done
about the shortage of places of worship. However, there was also
criticism of the Memorandum. For instance, the Platform took great
exception to the exclusion of the 'additional' functions, and did not
agree with the interpretation of the concept of the separation of
church and state, on which grounds subsidies were refused.[35] Staff
of the Rotterdam Institute for Residents Support[36] also thought that

---

[33] See Chapter 3.
[34] *De Eenheid* 4 (1991).
[35] *De Eenheid* 5 (1991): 5–6; see also: Report on the public meeting of the Committee
for Education, Cultural Minorities and Emancipation, dated 19 June 1991. Rotterdam
Municipal Council, Secretariat Department of Cultural Minorities.
[36] Formerly the Rotterdam Institute for Community Work.

the municipality itself should come up with some money, particularly if mosques were forced to hive off their 'additional' functions.[37] For the national Turkish Consultation Body, this initiative was simply an example of 'interfering in religious life' (IOT 1992: 18).

Both in the Committee for Urban Renewal and that for Cultural Minorities the draft Memorandum gave little cause for discussion.[38] In late August 1991 *Faith in the Future* was accepted by the Board of Mayor and Aldermen, and the Town Planning and Housing Department was given the task of implementing it (GR 1994: 2).

The new mosque policy in practice

The definitive version of the draft Memorandum appeared a year later (GR 1992a). At first very little was done about it, partly because of a reorganization of the various municipal services. The 'mosque team' was abolished in the reorganization, which caused the Platform of Islamic Organizations to conclude: 'There is no longer any question of co-ordination or collaboration, rather the opposite.'[39] In 1993 a project leader for Mosque Policy was at last appointed, who went energetically to work and carried out various searches for sites for the larger mosques suggested in the Memorandum.

In practice there were still various obstacles. For example, there were few potential locations in the urban renewal areas of the city, the establishment of mosques was still a sensitive question, and the financial resources of the organizations involved were often limited. As the rejection of the Hirsch Ballin Committee recommendations had meant that there was little likelihood of a government subsidy,[40] encouraging joint action became all the more important. However, in Rotterdam-Zuid the mosque managements saw little advantage in working in concert.[41] Where there was a degree of collaboration,

---

[37] *Migranteninformatief* 102 (1991): 17.

[38] Notification from the Committee for Urban Renewal and Housing to the Board of Mayor and Aldermen, dated 13 June 1991. Rotterdam Municipal Council, Secretariat Department of Town Planning, Urban Renewal and Housing; Report of the public meeting of the Committee for Education, Cultural Minorities and Emancipation, dated 19 June 1991. Rotterdam Municipal Council, Secretariat Department of Cultural Minorities.

[39] *De Eenheid* 9 (1992): 9.

[40] When the Memorandum was written in 1991 it was assumed that the proposals of the Hirsch Ballin Committee would be put into effect, which turned out not to be the case.

[41] *De Eenheid* 8 (1992): 4.

the local district authorities tended to oppose the building of a new mosque.[42]

As well as searching for suitable locations, a number of sticking-points were resolved in the context of urban renewal. Meanwhile, fresh problems arose over a number of other mosques. In early 1994 there were 37 mosques, more than half of which were still struggling with accommodation problems (GR 1994).

Utrecht

The first places of worship

Around 1970 the Foundation for Foreign Workers in the Central Netherlands established a temporary place of worship, the first mosque in Utrecht. However, when the building was demolished in early 1972, the Foundation failed to secure any replacement accommodation (Theunis 1979: 381–382 and 391–404). The first Muslim organizations were founded in the same period. In 1972 some Turks started the Islamic Centre Foundation; a year later Moroccans launched the Mosque Foundation, and Surinamese formed the Netherlands Muslim Association Foundation (Landman 1992: 212).

In May 1973 spokesmen of the Islamic Centre Foundation and the Mosque Foundation acted in public together for the first time with a manifesto entitled *Islam in Utrecht*, which was in fact a long plea for a place of worship. In typical Dutch official jargon it stated that

> the lack of a central mosque confirmed the Diaspora situation of Muslims, and that because of uncertainty about their own identity contacts with the majority population were influenced adversely (Theunis 1979: 392).

The desire to meet the Dutch in a space of their own was mentioned several times (*Islam in Utrecht* 1973: 2, quoted in Theunis 1979: 395).

Both foundations united in the Mosque Working Party, which next entered into consultations with Aldermen Harteveld of Environmental Planning, and Kieboom of Community Affairs, both Labour (PvdA). Alderman Kieboom, who co-ordinated policy for foreign workers, let

---

[42] Progress report on the implementation of the Mosque Policy, February 1994, pp. 4–5. Rotterdam Municipal Council, department of Urban Development and Housing, Project Management Office.

it be known that the municipality would give no financial support
to Muslim organizations. That was a matter for the Ministry of
Culture, Recreation and Social Work. He did, however, offer to help
them in their search for suitable premises.[43] For instance, the council could buy the vacant Roman Catholic church of St Monica and
let it with a subsidy to the Mosque Foundation, provided they could
put down a deposit of several tens of thousands of guilders.[44] The
Alderman also promised to apply to the Ministry of Culture, Recreation
and Social Work for a subsidy for socio-cultural projects. When the
Working Party next met, however, Alderman Kieboom appeared to
have suddenly changed his position, and now thought that the Muslims
should buy the church themselves. Meanwhile a number of organizations had taken an interest in the maintenance of St Monica's and
in the possible establishment of a mosque: the Migrants Council, the
Foundation for Foreign Workers in the Central Netherlands, the
Pijlsweerd Neighbourhood Committee, the Restoration of the Quality
of Life Working Party, the Council of Churches, and the Gothic
Revival Working Party. In addition negotiations were started on the
conversion of other churches in Utrecht. However, these always ran
aground on the high costs of acquisition and conversion.

  Among the churches in Utrecht there were sharp differences of
opinion regarding co-operation with Muslims. The local Council of
Churches thought that Dutch society, including the churches, had
an obligation to see that foreign workers had the opportunity to hold
religious services. Other believers rallied behind the opinion of the
Utrecht Minister Van der Werf, who declared in the *Utrechts Nieuwsblad*
of 4 August 1973 that help for Muslims was not the churches' responsibility, because Christians had a quite different faith,

> and that can be stated quite briefly and to the point: the God of Israel,
> the Father of Jesus Christ, is certainly not the same as Allah. (. . .)
> The Koran is one thing and the Bible is another.

In his view it was a task for the government and the business community to see that 'these guests received what they required in the
field of religion'.

---

[43] Minutes of a meeting of officials with the mosque organizations, dated
3 October 1973. Utrecht Municipal Council.
[44] Unless otherwise stated, the information given in this section is from Theunis
1979: 395 ff.

In October 1973 three churches were temporarily made available to Muslims for Ramadan, and here and there collections were made. The collection in St John's Church raised Fl. 400, and a great deal of commotion. Many people did not agree with its purpose. The Dutch Interchurch Network used a national collection, known as the 'Wild Geese' (Wilde Ganzen), for the same cause, and raised Fl. 15,000. The Reverend Klamer afterwards revealed that they had received a large number of negative reactions. Around this time the Mosque Foundation began to contact the representatives of several Muslim countries, in the hope of financial support. Only later (in 1975 from Saudi Arabia and in 1981 from Libya) did these initiatives actually bring in money.

The Working Party for an Islamic Services Centre

In spite of various promises, no proposals for a mosque were forth-coming from the municipal council. In early 1977 Alderman Velders for Community Affairs called together the Working Party for an Islamic Services Centre, set up two years earlier.[45] The immediate cause was a request about whether an old school building could be taken into permanent use as a mosque. Alderman Velders opened the first meeting with the question of whether 'the different groups of Muslims were prepared to work together'. Representatives of these groups replied that they had promised to work jointly a long time ago, subject to the condition that the municipality would give them some support.[46] In the next meeting Alderman Velders declared that he was prepared to have a sum for the establishment of a mosque entered on the 1978 list of 'desirable projects'. The council and the Alderman took the opportunity to reiterate that they were keen to see the various groups working together.[47]

In practice, however, there was no real collaboration.[48] The Working Party for an Islamic Services Centre never met again as such, nor was there ever a common mosque.

---

[45] See also Chapter 7, 'Working Party for an Islamic Services Centre'.

[46] Report on the meeting on the establishment of a mosque, dated 16 February 1977, quoted in Theunis 1979: 402–403 and 439.

[47] Minutes of a meeting of officials with the mosque organizations and the Migrants Council, dated 5 April 1977. Utrecht Municipal Council.

[48] See the official notification to Mayor and Aldermen, dated 30 September 1977. Utrecht Municipal Council. See also: GU 1982.

Recognition of one mosque, conflict about others

In November 1977 Moroccan members of the Migrants Council founded a new association, the Moroccan Islamic Centre Association.[49] The Mosque Foundation was immediately dissolved. About a month later the Association bought a property to take into use as a services centre and mosque. Funding was made possible by the revenues from the Mosque Foundation, savings from the last two Ramadans, and by the '*Wild Geese*' campaign.[50] The Board of Mayor and Aldermen sent a congratulatory letter to the Association, by which act the mosque was recognized by the municipality. A few weeks later the Association submitted a request for a subsidy to the Ministry of Culture, Recreation and Social Work, quoting the General Regulation concerning Subsidies for Places of Worship. In May 1978, however, the Fire Department announced that fire precautions in the property were insufficient, a reason for the Association to be on the look-out for alternative accommodation.

The Turkish Islamic Centre Foundation, which had run a small place of worship in the Otterstraat since 1972, had never received any words of congratulation from the Board. On the contrary, a great deal of protest had been aroused by this place of worship, particularly by neighbouring residents, because of nuisance from noise, parking problems and unlawful building. In 1977 the Pijlsweerd Action Committee sent its first complaint to the Board of Mayor and Aldermen. In the summer of that year the municipality helped the Centre to find temporary accommodation for Ramadan and promised help in finding permanent premises. A year later they even called in the help of the Ministry of Culture, Recreation and Social Work. The Neighbourhood Committee remained active until the Centre found an alternative property, which did not happen until 1984.

Elsewhere, too, neighbouring residents registered protests against the coming of a mosque. There was even some civil disturbance during Ramadan in 1980 involving the mosque of the Moroccan Association of Adherents of El Sunna in the Narcisstraat. The police, warned by neighbours, interrupted a number of prayer meetings,

---

[49] Theunis (1979: 404, 440) refers to this organization as the Moroccan Islamic Centre Association, but also as the Moroccan Islamic Community Association.

[50] Our information about the Moroccan Islamic Centre Association and the Turkish Islamic Centre Foundation in Utrecht is from Theunis (1979: 404, 440–441).

fireworks were thrown into the mosque, and fights broke out between neighbouring residents and those going to the mosque.[51] The community centre and the Foundation for Foreign Workers in the Central Netherlands managed to calm things down. After this the municipality offered the association a former factory building as an alternative, and the controversial premises in the Narcisstraat were vacated. Although they were no longer in use, the association still had to bear the expense of interest and redemption, while they also had to pay rent for the new premises. They refused to do this, arguing that 'the municipality had chosen to side with the residents and had more or less forced them to accept the alternative' (Landman 1992: 52). After long negotiations the municipality agreed to take over the former place of worship for a sum which equalled the obligations of the association.

The first Memorandum on Mosques

In 1981 Utrecht had two Turkish mosques, two Moroccan, and one Surinamese. Two of the five mosques were too small, and the presence of three of them was producing tensions with the neighbouring residents.[52] In April that year an interdepartmental working party of officials was formed to address these problems. In 1982 they presented a Memorandum to the Welfare Committee, which was intended to give the initial impetus to a more coherent policy for mosques (GU 1982).[53] They started from the premise that 'the same rules should apply to the building of mosques as for other places of worship. This implies that the municipality does not subsidize mosques' (ibid.: 4). They also thought that mosques should fit into the Utrecht town planning structure and must comply with any regulations in force. In addition the Memorandum noted that not one of the existing mosques complied in all particulars with the essential conditions, or else they were being used in breach of the local development plan. To find a solution to these problems, the working party pressed for regular contacts between the municipality and the various mosque groups. They did not consider that a single consultation structure,

---

[51] The information on this issue is taken from: Bovenkerk *et al.* 1985: 280–284; Landman 1992: 51–52.

[52] See: Bovenkerk *et al.* 1985: 280–284; Landman 1992: 51–52; see also GU 1984.

[53] The councillors actually took this Memorandum as notification.

in which all mosque groups would be represented, would be effective because the internal differences would be too numerous. In particular, mosques in former residential premises in heavily populated areas needed to be relocated at the expense of the Muslim organizations. The separation of church and state laid down once and for all that the municipality could not grant any subsidy. The most that was possible was their mediation in finding premises (ibid.: 4–5).

In two cases (in 1982 and 1987) this mediation led to the exchange of properties without cash being involved. Within the municipal bureaucracy proposals to this effect originally raised a storm of criticism. An official of the Housing Department thought that the Islamic Centre Foundation was taking advantage 'of the difficult position of the municipality in relation to the existing problems in the neighbourhood'. The city was too ready to meet their demands.[54] According to the head of the Estates Agency an exchange without cash was in effect a direct subsidy.[55] An important reason for allowing mosques to be relocated in this manner was that the problems which had been dragging on in the neighbourhood for so many years could not be brought to an end in any other way.

Accommodation problems in the late 1980s

In the course of the 1980s the number of mosques doubled. In spite of the high-minded intentions of the 1982 *Memorandum on Mosques*, there were still problems by the end of the 1980s, and several times the municipality had to close mosques down.[56] The working party of officials which had been active in 1982 no longer had a role to play. Muslim organizations were still given guidance, but such opportunities were limited, not least because of the organizations' inadequate financial resources and the continued opposition of neighbouring residents.

When in March 1989 the municipality entered into consultations with Muslim organizations, the establishment and subsidizing of mosques was one of the important items on the agenda. The consultation took place through the Platform of Islamic Organizations,

---

[54] Internal minute to the head of the Housing Department, dated 3 October 1984. Utrecht Municipal Council.
[55] Internal minute to the head of the Department of Social Affairs, dated 26 September 1984. Utrecht Municipal Council.
[56] See *Utrechts Nieuwsblad* 9 April 1989 and 12 August 1990.

which had been especially set up for this purpose. The spokesmen for the municipality again showed little enthusiasm for taking on more responsibility for the establishment and funding of Muslim places of worship.[57]

In a later written submission the council argued that it had to maintain the principle of the separation of church and state. All religious organizations should be financed by their members; government had no role in this, nor did it want one. In addition the municipality added that it only subsidized general organizations for the common welfare. If the Muslim organizations had special wishes, they should make them known to these common welfare organizations. In addition a number of interest organizations, not associated with a religion or political party, were subsidized.[58] An official later stated that the municipality, particularly the Aldermen responsible, had adopted an extremely strict interpretation of the rules with respect to Muslim organizations. Where Christian organizations could expect favourable consideration of their requests for financial support, Muslim organizations were given a categorical refusal.

The municipality's negative attitude offered no solution for the sticking-points.[59] Although the Board of Mayor and Aldermen had announced, in its paper on welfare work for ethnic minorities (*Deelnota welzijnswerk etnische minderheden*, GU 1986) that it would implement the municipal policy on mosques, this intention had still not been carried out in 1990. Council members of the Christian Democratic Party (CDA) therefore felt obliged to submit a motion during the debates on the budget. They requested the Board to 'present policy proposals on mosques, places of worship and religious organizations in good time, and certainly before Ramadan in 1990'.[60] The motion found general support.[61] It would, however, be some considerable time before a new *Memorandum on Mosques* appeared.

---

[57] Report of a consultation between Utrecht Municipal Council and the Platform for Islamic Organizations, dated 1 March 1989, dossier 1.844.922, Care for Foreigners. Utrecht Municipal Council, Welfare Department.

[58] Brief municipal reaction to the points on Muslim organizations, dated 8 March 1989. Utrecht Municipal Council, Welfare Department.

[59] In 1992 the municipality announced that no less than nine applications for mosque premises were on the Estates Agency's waiting list. This number was as high as the number of mosques already established (GU 1992).

[60] Minutes of the afternoon session of the budget meeting of the Municipal Council, dated 25 October 1989. Utrecht Municipal Council.

[61] Mayor and Aldermen had no objections either. See: Minutes of the Municipal Council, dated 25 October 1989 evening session. Utrecht Municipal Council.

The second Memorandum on Mosques

In 1989 an official of the Welfare Department wrote a draft of a new *Memorandum on Mosques*, of which the definitive version would only appear three years later. One of the reasons it took so long were the objections by various Aldermen against its recommendations.[62]

The definitive second *Memorandum on Mosques* (*Moskee-notitie*, GU 1992: 19) was centred on three policy recommendations. The first referred to the development of a priority policy for mosques, suggesting that the municipality, 'during the period in which there was a demonstrable lack of suitable provision in any given district', should make efforts to rent out any suitable property in its control for use as places of worship, or should grant leases on available building sites for the construction of new places of worship. It should also 'extend a helping hand to the organization involved by directing them towards the private sector market'. In addition, an investigation should be made into the extent to which Muslim organizations could fulfil a role in activities concerned with the promotion of their interests and the provision of information. Finally, consideration should be given to more intensive contacts with the mosque organizations at the official and/or administrative level.

Partly as a result of the Aldermen's intervention, the municipality's attitude was hardly accommodating. During the discussion of the Memorandum in the Welfare Committee of the municipal council, members of the Christian Democratic Party (CDA) and Labour (PvdA) remarked that the last two recommendations particularly were less than robust. In spite of this the Committee accepted the Memorandum.[63] It was then sent on to the full council, where it was never even discussed.

In the end the priority policy which had been advocated did not lead to any great changes. What was available was supplied. According to an official of the Development Agency—formerly the Estates Agency—this was also the case before the *Memorandum on Mosques*. In 1995 Utrecht had 16 mosques. However, as the number of places

---

[62] Internal minute to an official of the Welfare Department, dated 8 October 1991. Utrecht Municipal Council, Welfare Department.

[63] Report on the public meeting of the Committee for Welfare, dated 19 March 1992, p. 3. Utrecht Municipal Council.

of worship rose, the number of Muslims in the town also rose,[64] and the demand for places of worship still always exceeds the supply.

A new municipal administration: a possible opening?

The advent of a change in control of the municipal council in 1994 appeared to open an opportunity for Muslim organizations. The new Alderman for Welfare, Van der Linden (Labour, PvdA), no longer simply rejected co-operation with the mosque organizations. In 1995 one Muslim organization received a subsidy from the municipality of Utrecht's Stimulation Fund for Minorities for carrying out a home-work class project in the mosque (GU 1995: 33–34). An important condition for subsidizing activities is that Muslim organizations are willing to work jointly with community welfare organizations.

Ideological concepts and arguments

Both in Rotterdam and in Utrecht the need for places of worship for Muslims was recognized. Opinions differed on the extent to which municipalities should give active support. The original attitude was very much one of reticence. The provision of support was mainly restricted to looking for suitable premises and if necessary media-tion, particularly in the case of conflict with local residents. Subsidies for places of worship were ruled out in principle, although there were plenty of special cases. The argument advanced for this restraint is in the first place the *separation of church and state*. In 1978 the Rotterdam municipality stated that the authorities had no respon-sibility whatsoever towards the church, and therefore no financial responsibility either. In addition the *principle of equality* was cited: finan-cial aid to Muslim organizations would mean favouring Muslims above other denominations. A member of the Liberal party (VVD) in Utrecht commented in this regard that mosques, like churches in the Netherlands, were not subsidized and that immigrants had to respect this ruling.

---

[64] Early in 1995 the number of Muslim residents in Utrecht was estimated at 23,500 (Interkerkelijke Stichting Kerken & Buitenlanders 1995: 1).

There is agreement that the municipal authorities should offer help in finding premises. In this regard a member of the Labour Party (PvdA) in Utrecht referred to the *disadvantaged position* of Muslims:

> I agree in theory that everyone must find their own premises for their religion, but then, in a crowded town like Utrecht this is quite difficult, and you have to help a bit. Basically the town is already complete, the infrastructure is there, the churches are there. So in those circumstances you really need a little back-up. I think it quite right to give a chance to a group which is new and so at a disadvantage.

His Democrats 66 (D66) colleague advised caution and thought that the disadvantaged position was no reason to start subsidizing places of worship:

> I don't think you should subsidize mosques because before you know where you are, and that is what happens in those North-African countries, church and state are completely mixed up. Mosque organizations should realize that here we maintain the separation of church and state, because before you know it you are on a slippery slope and then the excuse is often: oh well, they are disadvantaged.

In these arguments Muslim organizations are taken to be purely religious organizations. Not everyone shares this view. In Rotterdam the awareness grew in the early 1980s that Muslim organizations could fulfil an important role in the *integration of newcomers* into the Rotterdam community.[65] Years later a council member for Labour (PvdA) in Utrecht expressed a similar idea: 'Co-operation with the mosque organizations benefits integration.' In Rotterdam they went a step further, and in 1984 the Board of Mayor and Aldermen proposed treating Muslim organizations on equal terms with secular interest organizations. This implied that they could be eligible for subsidies for socio-cultural activities. In this perspective Muslim organizations are no longer seen as purely religious groups, but as representatives of immigrants or minorities. Important arguments for the reversal of policy in Rotterdam were *the great reach* of Muslim organizations and *minimizing* or *preventing their isolation* and its negative consquences for integration. According to a member of the Rotterdam council for the Liberal Party (VVD), a church or mosque could also fulfil an important function in the reception of immigrants. On the basis of similar arguments, the Christian Democratic

---

[65] Cf. GR 1981b, 1983.

Party in Utrecht cautiously argued for an increase in co-operation with mosque organizations:

> . . . take a careful look and don't be over-enthusiastic, but try to see how far you can go in co-operating with the mosque managements, because that, of course, covers thousands of people each week in each mosque. And of course that is a gigantically important entry point for welfare work too, so find out how far you can develop that. We are a little less aloof in our attitude to this than the other parties in Utrecht affairs.

In the discussion following the Board's proposals in Rotterdam in 1984, the *principle of equality* was again put forward, albeit now on behalf of the Muslim organizations. A council member for the Christian Democratic Party (CDA) compared Muslim organizations with other interest organizations and came to the conclusion that if the latter received 'a quite substantial subsidy for their organization expenses', the former also had a right to one.

Not everyone shared this opinion. In considering whether the socio-cultural work of Muslim organizations should be subsidized, various counter-arguments—in addition to that of the separation of church and state—were heard: the fear of the activities being *coloured by a church bias*; doubts about the *emancipatory or democratic nature* of Muslim organizations; and the *fear of involvement of foreign powers*. In addition, the potential competition with existing socio-cultural work played a role. In the Feijenoord district it was put in the following way:

> We do not reject outright the tendency to start subsidizing more interest organizations, but we do ask, which ones? We don't think mosques fit into this category. Moreover, they are not interested in integration, but in an eventual return to the homeland and the strict preservation of old norms and values. Furthermore, our experience is that the language lessons in the club houses are in a state of permanent uncertainty about their future, while mosques can be granted money just like that.[66]

In Utrecht many people categorically rejected subsidizing socio-cultural work by Muslim organizations. 'Give them a subsidy? I'm not going to start on that,' said the former Alderman for Welfare, Van

---

[66] Letter from the project group, residents associations, Kluphuis Brug/Arend-en Zeemeeuw, and community centre 't Eiland to the Alderman for Special Groups, ref. 1018/PG/is, concerning the Memorandum *Minorities Policy in a Changed Situation* (*Minderhedenbeleid in een gewijzigde situatie*), dated 3 October 1985. Rotterdam Municipal Council.

der Sluys (Labour, PvdA). His view was that Muslims should make use of the existing institutions:

> Recently a mosque in Overvecht asked us for help in teaching Dutch to Moroccan women. They were running Dutch classes on a small scale for a group of women. We said yes, we would like to help, but through the normal channels. For instance, we would be happy if they went to something like KANS [the municipal Institute for Adult Education], and if KANS would agree to arrange a bit of teaching there.

In 1992 a party colleague of the Utrecht Alderman commented, however, that on the basis of the principle of equality Muslim organizations could also invoke the existing subsidy regulations. After all, other religious organizations did so:

> We have all kinds of subsidy regulations, but what we look at are activities, and there isn't anything of that sort going on. Why don't they start doing that, something in the area of culture, emancipation, job opportunity, or whatever? I think we would look very favourably on that, and if organizations then have their applications rejected, they can always take it up politically. They can argue, we did our best, but those Catholics, they get it without difficulties.

This statement did not, however, reflect the real situation at the time. An official in Utrecht commented:

> The council leadership is not over-enthusiastic when it comes to contacts with Muslim organizations. (. . .) I can't avoid the impression that I get Aldermen ringing up when it is about Muslim organizations, but not when it is about orthodox Calvinist or Catholic ones. We are still subsidizing the summer camps, also from Welfare, of the Calvinist evangelists. But if the same club were called Muslim evangelists, there is no way it would have been agreed. We also subsidize scout groups based on ideological principles. Of course they go out exploring, so that is something else again. I know that, but sometimes I think (. . .) Hindus have arranged a special tobacco- and alcohol-free room in the Surinamese meeting centre, which they use for religious services. We don't go overboard about that either. Now we are going to subsidize a meeting centre for the Chinese, who also want to hold religious services there, with catechism and bible study classes. The same story. But for Muslims? The Crusades are not over yet.

By the mid-1990s some attempts at change had been registered. One Muslim organization has been receiving a subsidy for a homework project since 1995. Here too, arguments about the reach of the mosque organizations can be important. An official in Utrecht remarked: 'The way to contact young Moroccans especially is through the mosques.' He suggested that the best thing to do would be to set up a separate association or foundation to organize socio-cultural activities. 'We would prefer it if a mosque organization did not do that under the flag of the mosque.' The same suggestion had been made in Rotterdam 10 years earlier.

CHAPTER NINE

ISLAMIC RELIGIOUS INSTRUCTION IN STATE PRIMARY SCHOOLS

From the early 1970s onwards several Muslim organizations started exerting pressure at the national level for Islamic religious instruction to be made available in state schools.[1] At the time of writing such instruction is only provided in a few municipalities, such as Rotterdam; there is none in Utrecht. What is behind the presence or absence of its availability, and what discussion has there been about it in either municipality?

Rotterdam

Rotterdam has had a subsidy arrangement for religious or ideological instruction in state education since 1955. This was originally intended only to cover Bible classes,[2] but was amended in 1972, so that Humanist education could also be eligible for subsidy.[3] Two organizations took advantage of this, the Interdenominational Network on Schools Affairs Foundation and Netherlands League of Protestants, and the Foundation for Humanist Education.[4]

In 1981, in the discussion paper *Educative Ideas* (*Educatieve ideeën*, GR 1981a: 36), the municipal council recorded that 'there was no

---

[1] Cf. FOMON s.a.; Triesscheijn 1989b; Landman 1992: 245.
[2] Bible instruction in primary schools, *Verzameling 1955*, No. 241, litt. a, 21 October 1955. Rotterdam Municipal Council.
[3] Subsidy ruling on religious instruction and socio-cultural education, *Gemeenteblad van Rotterdam*, 103 (1972).
[4] The Interdenominational Network on School Affairs and Netherlands League of Protestants is a collaboration of various churches and religious communities, such as the Dutch Reformed Church, the (orthodox) Reformed Churches in the Netherlands, the Remonstrant Brotherhood, the General Baptist Society, the Evangelical Lutheran Church, the Union of Baptist Congregations and the Netherlands League of Protestants. Contact is maintained with other collaborating churches in the Council of Churches. The Foundation for Humanist Education originates from the Humanist League. For a concise description of the establishment, aims and method of operation of these organizations, see: VOO 1992: 19–29.

known desire on the part of Islam or Hinduism for a "spiritual orientation"',[5] in spite of which a separate section was devoted to the subject (ibid.: 36–37).[6] The sequel to the Memorandum (GR 1982a: 5) included a fundamental appraisal of education in a multicultural society, which was intended to contribute to the 'integration of all the distinguishable population groups, but with retention of "their own identity"'. Integration was here perceived as 'mutual influence in a continuous process of change'. State schools should be meeting places, where different religious denominations encountered each other, and the following procedure was proposed to achieve this: the class teacher would introduce a theme to an intercultural group, after which the pupils would separate into their various religious or ideological groups, in which the same theme would be dealt with from their own specific point of view. Finally they would all come together again after which the teacher would review the theme with the whole class. Although the reactions to this Memorandum were mixed (ibid.: 47)—Turkish teachers in particular were against the rising influence of Muslim organizations—the municipality proceeded with its implementation. In the *Memorandum on Spiritual Orientation in State Schools* (*Notitie Geestelijke oriëntatie in de openbare school*) there was one explicitly stated condition: the lessons would have to be given in Dutch (ibid.: 67).

The municipality created a federal co-operative structure, which included the Turkish-Islamic Cultural Federation Foundation, to implement this policy (ibid.).[7] This body met several times, without coming to any hard conclusions; the Muslim organizations, whose participation was essential, were apparently not able to find suitable Dutch-speaking teaching staff.[8] The Muslim organizations then made

---

[5] The Memorandum in fact stated that 'a number of groupings (that is Muslim, Hindu, etc.) definitely did have need of religious education', but that they fulfilled this 'almost entirely by separate provisions of their own, completely isolated from the regular field of education'. It also stated that the subject of Islam was included in the syllabus of Turkish and Moroccan teachers.

[6] See also GR 1982a: 67.

[7] Also included in this collaboration were the Interdenominational Network on School Affairs and Netherlands League of Protestants, the Foundation for Humanist Education, the Convent of Churches, the ASRN, the Primary Education Parents' Council and finally the Rotterdam Secretariat Department of Education, Juvenile Affairs and Socio-Cultural Work.

[8] The Turkish-Islamic Cultural Federation Foundation preferred to appoint imams. It is interesting that in the same period the municipal council's Migrants Office

vain attempts to have Koran teaching in the mosques recognized
and subsidized as a kind of 'education in community language and
culture'.[9]

In 1988 there was an acceleration in the campaign for Islamic
religious instruction.[10] First of all staff of the nascent Platform of
Islamic Organization in Greater Rotterdam held discussions with
representatives of the Interdenominational Network. Next the Platform
submitted a formal application to the municipality, immediately followed by a joint letter from the Interdenominational Network, the
Foundation for Humanist Education and the Platform with a request
to strengthen the position of state-school education vis-à-vis denominational schools. The three organizations also broached the problem
of finance. For some years the council had only made funds available up to a maximum of Fl. 300,000. Now that a third organization
was involved, the Interdenominational Network and the Foundation
for Humanist Education were afraid that they would receive even
less. The organizations would welcome more money, though they
realized that the political support for such an initiative was limited.[11]

The council's Education Committee put the Platform's application
on the agenda for their April 1989 meeting. The co-ordinator of the
Platform explained that the lessons would be informative and would
not contain any propaganda. He increased the pressure by announc-
ing that if their application were rejected, the Platform would insist
on the legally permitted maximum of three hours of religious instruc-

---

prepared a Memorandum on the recognition of Muslim organizations and the role
of imams in this process (see the previous two chapters). Furthermore, according
to officials involved, discussions took place within the Secretariat Department of
Education, on the problematic relationships between Turkish teachers of education
in community language and culture and potential Muslim teachers. The first group,
who were strongly secular, feared that conservative movements would gain influence
at their cost.

[9] In a letter to the editor of the daily *Trouw* (2 August 1988), an official of the
municipal Migrants Office suggested that the establishment of education in community language and culture had such a strong aversion to Islam that it regularly
obstructed the recognition and subsidizing of Koran teaching as a form of this education. Moreover, the teachers concerned objected strongly to working in a framework of private-sector religious organizations.

[10] In November 1987 the municipal council issued a new *Policy Memorandum on
State Primary Education* (GR 1987a). In contrast to earlier memoranda this one did
not contain any mention of religious or socio-cultural education.

[11] Verbal information provided by a representative of the Platform of Islamic
Organizations in Greater Rotterdam.

tion per week, if necessary without any municipal subsidy. Of the councillors present, the Labour (PvdA) and Liberal (VVD) members in particular supported a limited subsidy. Finally a one-off sum of Fl. 50,000 was set aside for the Platform. The councillors were not prepared to decide on future structural subsidies until they had held a fundamental discussion about the relationship of religious instruction to the curriculum subject of religious studies (*geestelijke stromingen*).[12]

This subject had been part of the curriculum since the introduction of the 1985 Primary Education Act. If it were to be considered as corresponding to religious instruction, the municipality could themselves decide on the content of the lessons, while the whole cost would be borne by the state. However, an official minute argued that two separate subjects were concerned: 'religious studies' involved the transfer of objective knowledge, whereas 'religious instruction' was mainly subjective instruction in one's own philosophy of life. The aim of one was essentially social, the other personal.[13] At the end of 1990 the council's Education Committee closed the discussion and decided to keep the budget at Fl. 350,000 (including the one-off Fl. 50,000 for the Platform).[14]

In March 1991 the municipal council adopted a new arrangement for subsidies.[15] One of the more essential innovations involved Article 2, Section 5, which stated that lessons must be given in Dutch. Although this requirement was hardly elaborated on in the official documents, it was nonetheless obviously important, for Alderman Simons of Education (Labour, PvdA), in a letter to parents and guardians of state-school children in April 1989, judged it necessary to put the announcement in capital letters: 'THE LESSONS WILL BE GIVEN IN DUTCH.'[16]

---

[12] Report of the public meeting of the Education Committee, dated 5 April 1989. Rotterdam Municipal Council.

[13] Subsidizing religious and ideological socio-cultural education in state primary and (secondary) private education. *Verzameling 1991*, no. 38, litt. a Rotterdam Municipal Council.

[14] Report on the public meeting of the Committee for Education, Cultural Minorities and Emancipation, dated 14 November 1990. Rotterdam Municipal Council.

[15] Directions for subsidizing religious education/ideological socio-cultural education, *Gemeenteblad* 22 (1991).

[16] Letter from the Alderman for Education to the parents/guardians of pupils in the 2nd to 7th year at state schools, April 1989. Rotterdam Municipal Council.

The total amount of the subsidy was divided among the three organizations in proportion to the number of applications, but proved to be inadequate, which the Platform resolved by simply paying the teaching staff a lower hourly rate.[17] To test the wishes of parents the municipality organized a survey each spring. Not all heads of primary schools co-operated wholeheartedly.[18] The survey and the religious instruction itself produced a mass of bureaucratic administration, while some heads had particular problems with Islamic religious instruction. At least twice the inspectorate had to deal with serious disputes. In one case a head denied an Muslim teacher access to the school because she was wearing a headscarf (de Volkskrant, 22 December 1990).

At the executive level relationships with the Platform now seem to be normal. Problems with school teams, such as the headscarf issue, had virtually disappeared by the mid-1990s. The Platform has good relations with the other two co-ordinating organizations, the Interdenominational Network and the Foundation for Humanist Education, and holds regular meetings with them. Within the space of a few years there has been an appreciable increase in Islamic religious instruction in Rotterdam. Whereas in the 1989–1990 school year a start was made in 17 schools with 58 hours of religious instruction a year, five years later (1994–1995) the number of schools had more than doubled to 38, and the number of hours had climbed to 134.[19] Interest in Islamic religious instruction is still growing.

Utrecht

In contrast to Rotterdam, the municipality of Utrecht has made no arrangements for subsidizing religious or ideological instruction, though this does not exclude the possibility of unsubsidized religious instruction being given (Drop 1985: 224).

The municipality has made a single official statement about the possible introduction of Islamic religious instruction. In the *Memorandum*

---

[17] Verbal information provided by a representative of the Platform of Islamic Organizations in Greater Rotterdam.

[18] Cf. Report of the public meeting of the Committee for Education, Cultural Minorities and Emancipation, dated 30 May 1990. Rotterdam Municipal Council.

[19] Verbal information received from a representative of the Platform of Islamic Organization in Greater Rotterdam.

on Primary Education (Nota Basisonderwijs) it referred to all kinds of problems for which it had no solution, such as the legal standing of the organizations, and the requirement that lessons should be given in Dutch. It was stated that the council 'needed to determine its position further' on Islamic religious instruction (GU 1985b: 36). 10 years after the publication of this Memorandum, however, the promised position had still not been determined. When asked about this, officials of the Education Department agreed that all pupils should be able to attend such instruction, and that it should be given in Dutch. It would then also be possible to monitor that it was not of a proselytizing nature. Most of the officials and politicians involved thought that Islamic religious instruction should eventually be allowed in state schools. Several of them even declared themselves expressly in favour. In practice, however, Islamic religious instruction was not encouraged in any way; rather the opposite, as was also the case with the reaction to a request from the Protestant Council for Education in the Scriptures in 1990. It asked the council to encourage religious instruction in state schools vigorously, and to draw the parents' attention by circular to the possibility of such instruction. The area managers of the Education Department thought, however, that it was unwise to take such special measures, because 'there is a strong likelihood that Muslim parents will also make use of the right to religious instruction'.[20] They produced several arguments relating to the pedagogic approach, attitudes to gender differences, and the disadvantages which foreign children already suffered in education. The area managers advised the Alderman for Education, Van Lidth de Jeude (Labour, PvdA), to reject the application, which in the end he did.

All this does not alter the fact that some years ago several heads of state schools in Utrecht had been considering the idea of introducing Islamic religious instruction. However, this coincided with the opening of a Muslim school in the Zuilen district; particularly in two districts (Kanaleneiland and Zuilen) there was fear of an exodus from the state schools. So far no concrete proposals have been submitted to the Education Department.

---

[20] Letter from the CCO representative of the area managers to Van Lidth de Jeude, Alderman for Education, dated 11 July 1990. Utrecht Municipal Council.

Ideological concepts and arguments

Those involved in the discussion about Islamic religious instruction
are armed with a long list of arguments, based on all kinds of ideological assumptions about the facts of the case.

To start with there is the *principle of equality*. The endeavour to
treat Islam on equal terms with other recognized religions may appear
a cliché, but is of no less importance for that. A spokesman of the
Christian Democratic Party (CDA) in Utrecht put it very clearly: 'If
you are a Catholic child and go to a state school, you can request
religious instruction. Well, you can also do that if you are a Muslim
child.' During the debate about the Platform of Islamic Organizations
in Greater Rotterdam, the Rotterdam councillor Muijsenberg (Liberal
Party, VVD) put it even more directly and succinctly: the Platform
has the same rights as other organizations.[21]

In Rotterdam, more than in Utrecht, various protagonists have
advanced the importance of what they called the *active pluriformity of
state education*. The Rotterdam councillor Hallensleben (Labour, PvdA),
shortly before her appointment as Alderman, even revived from the
distant past the old slogan, 'undivided to the state school', which
had been used in earlier, pillarized days to promote state education.
In this view religious instruction was a condition of 'undividedness',
because it contributed to active pluriformity. For the same reason
the Foundation for Humanist Education welcomed the Platform's
application:

> It is precisely in a state school where various ideologies are repre-
> sented, and children from different backgrounds meet each other and
> in this way are being prepared to take their place in a pluriform soci-
> ety where, through religious instruction and socio-cultural education,
> children may be put in a position to reflect about their own religion
> or ideology. (. . .) And where the Education Department of the Rotterdam
> municipal council speaks of active pluriformity in state education, and
> of strengthening its identity, these are best served by making instruc-
> tion in religion and ideological education possible in the long term.[22]

---

[21] Report on the public meeting of the Education Committee, dated 5 April
1989. Rotterdam Municipal Council.
[22] Statement Foundation for Humanist Education, PMG/WRK/89041/IB, delivered in the Education Committee, dated 4 April 1989. Rotterdam Municipal Council.

So Islamic religious instruction is in this view regarded as supportive of state education.[23]

In this respect the hope or expectation is very much alive that the introduction of religious instruction in state school *may take the wind out of the sails* of private denominational education, particularly of *Muslim private education.* In a joint letter, the Interdenominational Network, the Foundation for Humanist Education and the Platform of Islamic Organizations in Greater Rotterdam wrote:

> Supporters of state education see the importance of fulfilling the desires of ideological groups in respect of socio-cultural education; after all, in this way the flow away from state education to existing or future private denominational schools will be discouraged. This applies to both Protestant and Catholic private education; it can also apply to private education with a Humanist outlook on life, and is *even more convincing with respect to Muslim private education.*[24]

A Utrecht councillor (Liberal Party, VVD) put it as follows:

> If you are talking about the attraction [of state education], that [religious instruction] should be possible, and allowance must be made for it. (. . .) I would much rather have that than that they should set up separate schools.

The municipal council of Rotterdam has long taken a strong line on spiritual orientation, though not particularly in support of active pluriformity. On the contrary, rather than strengthening the identity of separate social groups, the municipality wanted to encourage the *meeting* of these groups. The initiative for this resulted from the endeavour to work constructively for a multi*cultural* (and so not primarily multi-*religious*) society in Rotterdam:

> Not only will the presence of various national groups with a diversity of cultural backgrounds determine the "image" of the city, but—perhaps most importantly—the mixture of cultures present, from which various new "Rotterdam" cultures emerge, will shape Rotterdam society. The city—in our view—is a pluriform social community, a meeting place for the indigenous and those from outside, for "dissimilar" people in the most literal sense of the word (GR 1901a: 1).

---

[23] Cf. VOO 1992.

[24] Letter from the Interdenominational Network on School Affairs and Netherlands League of Protestants, the Foundation for Humanist Education and the Platform of Islamic Organizations in Greater Rotterdam to Simons, Alderman for Education, January 1989; emphasis added.

Nine years later, during discussion on the application of the Platform of Islamic Organizations in Greater Rotterdam, echoes of this statement could be heard in the words of councillor Ter Kuile-Van der Hoeven (Liberal Party, VVD):

> If it is argued that as many children as possible should attend state schools, as a meeting place, then religious instruction and socio-cultural education will also have to be provided to meet the wishes of the parents.[25]

The idea that religious instruction should have as little as possible to do with *the experience of religion in the narrow sense of the words*, but all the more with the exchange of information, followed naturally from this view. It should be a way of cultivating an understanding of each other's behaviour, according to a spokesman of the Green Left Party (GroenLinks) from Utrecht:

> We don't say that nothing should be done in schools with ideology, whether it be Catholic, Protestant or Islam. Something really should be done about it in state schools, because there you have children of different denominations together, who can learn about each other's cultures. (. . .) Yes, I see it more in terms of social studies, of social orientation. (. . .) I don't see teaching the Koran as the responsibility of a state school. That is just like teaching the catechism. It should be done outside school hours.

The increased *cultural content* he allocates to religious instruction can be found in a subject such as religious studies. The Rotterdam councillor Van Veenen (Labour, PvdA) expressed similar views. Her preference was for 'a broader approach comparing several religions, than for more subsidies for all kinds of separate denominations within the religious instruction programme'.[26]

This view of religious instruction is to some extent associated with ideas about the *separation of church and state*. Some people think that religion does not belong in state schools, especially when religious organizations are involved in it. Such opinions can be heard among the native Dutch population, but also among progressive Turkish organizations.[27] Others believe that religious instruction as such does

---

[25] Report on the public meeting of the Education Committee, dated 5 April 1989. Rotterdam Municipal Council.

[26] Report on the public meeting of the Education Committee, dated 4 April 1990. Rotterdam Municipal Council.

[27] Cf. GR 1981a: 47–48; FOMON s.a.: 28–29.

not breach the separation of church and state, but they stop short
of wanting the authorities to subsidize it. Still others feel that some
attention should be paid at school to the subjective perception of
every religion, and that support by the government should be granted
as a matter of course.

A more cultural content for religious instruction is often linked to
the fear that in the process of religious instruction Muslim organizations *insulate themselves from Dutch society* or do things which *are in
conflict with Dutch norms and values*. In their letter to the municipal
administration the Interdenominational Network, the Foundation for
Humanist Education and the Platform of Islamic Organizations
stressed the need

> for sufficient competence among the staff giving Islamic religious instruc-
> tion with respect to mastery of the Dutch language and understand-
> ing of West European didactic principles.[28]

In Utrecht the area managers in their letter to the Alderman also
spoke of 'a great difference in assumptions about pedagogic methods between a Muslim spiritual leader (. . .) and Dutch teachers'.[29]
In the Koran schools—which were clearly regarded as the testing
ground for Islamic religious instruction in state schools—children
were sometimes suspected of being abused, but the area managers
also added other arguments:

> The assumptions, too, about the roles of men and women, or boys
> and girls, are very different, and often clash with ideas of emancipa-
> tion and anti-discrimination. These matters could put the specific role
> of state education at risk. The respect for each other's ideology and
> for other people's cultures would be in danger; there might be too
> much of a one-sided bias from the Muslim side. Whether or not there
> is any question of proselytizing or even of indoctrination we cannot
> say because of the language differences.

In Rotterdam in the early 1980s the council required that lessons
of a spiritual nature be given in Dutch, 'because only in that language could there be a meeting of minds' (GR 1982a: 67). When

---

[28] Letter from the Interdenominational Network on School Affairs and Netherlands
League of Protestants, the Foundation for Humanist Education and the Platform
of Islamic Organizations in Greater Rotterdam to Simons, Alderman for Education,
January 1989. Rotterdam Municipal Council.
[29] Letter from the CCO representative of the area managers to Van Lidth de
Jeude, Alderman for Education, dated 11 July 1990. Utrecht Municipal Council.

the Platform of Islamic Organizations in Greater Rotterdam produced their application in 1988, the council repeated this requirement, although in the current set-up for religious instruction there
is no question of any kind of meeting, at least not between Muslims
and non-Muslims. The Platform has actually given an interesting
twist to this requirement:

> Dutch as the medium of communication has in his [the Platform
> spokesman's] view two advantages: first all Muslim pupils can be reached
> regardless of their nationality, and secondly the children will learn to
> express their thoughts in Dutch, which should contribute to their eman-
> cipation (SLV 1992b: 2).[30]

The Rotterdam organizations which were already active in this area
said that they did not want to do anything which might obstruct
the introduction of Islamic religious instruction. Nonetheless some
ambivalence is detectable in their statements. A spokeswoman of the
Foundation for Humanist Education suggested, for instance, that
Muslims were treated far too generously:

> It is claimed that Muslims are minorities. Yes, that is quite true. But
> the Humanists are minorities too. Not ethnic ones, but if you look at
> what is known about us in schools (. . .) there are still plenty of schools
> where we simply don't get inside. (. . .) That is why I say, they may
> be minorities, but they have a lot of facilities.

The *parallel with their own position as a minority* was expressed more
robustly by the Interdenominational Network: 'The churches feel that
they are a minority in the big cities, alongside the Muslim minority. That produces a feeling of solidarity.'[31]

---

[30] Cf. SLV 1992a: 8.
[31] Interdenominational Network on School Affairs and Netherlands League of
Protestants/the Foundation for Humanist Education, Brief report on the meeting
of Wednesday 18 January 1989. Rotterdam Municipal Council.

CHAPTER TEN

THE ESTABLISHMENT OF MUSLIM SCHOOLS

In addition to the right to religious instruction in state schools, Dutch legislation and regulation provides for the possibility of setting up schools based on religious or ideological foundations. In the 1980s Muslims had recourse to this option. As indicated in the previous chapter, the advent of Muslim schools was by no means welcomed at the local level. What were the reactions in Rotterdam and Utrecht?

Rotterdam

In January 1980 the Foundation for Turkish Education in Rotterdam tried to open a school for the 'advancement of education in the Turkish language and of Turkish culture' (Landman 1992: 260). However, in 1983 the plan ran aground because the Foundation was unable to raise the necessary funds. Officially the proposal was not for a Muslim school, but the initiative did come from a Muslim organization: a member of the executive of the Dutch Islamic Federation claimed to us that his movement, the Milli Görüş, was involved.[1]

In 1987 this movement again launched an initiative to found a primary school, this time a 'real' Islamic one. The first school, Al Ghazali, opened in the 1988–1989 school year in West Rotterdam. The Islamic Foundation of the Netherlands for Education and Upbringing quickly followed this initiative, and a year later the Ibn-I Sina school opened in South Rotterdam.[2]

---

[1] Cf. Landman 1992: 260–261 (including the notes).

[2] The fact that these two organizations in particular founded schools creates the impression that part of the religious-political controversy in Turkey was reproduced here. The Dutch Islamic Federation is associated with the Milli Görüş movement, which is Islamic in the sense that their adherents aim to restore an Islamic political and economic system. In Turkey these people originally came together in the Milli Selamet Partısı (MSP, National Welfare Party), and since 1983 in the Refah Partısı (RP, Welfare Party). Their religious ideology, and particularly their degree of orthodoxy, is quite different from the official interpretation of Islam in Turkey, which is characterized by the endeavour for reconciliation with secularism. In Turkey the latter interpretation is disseminated by the Presidium for Religious Affairs (Diyanet

Since then several applications for Muslim primary schools have been submitted for approval.[3] However, for this investigation the founding of the first school, Al Ghazali, is the most interesting since all kinds of Rotterdam institutions suddenly felt it necessary to consider their position with regard to it. The foundation of the second school was much more a matter of routine.

The application for the Al Ghazali school

In the mid-1980s, adherents of Milli Görüş were involved in attempts to have Islamic religious instruction introduced in state schools and private denominational schools. The failure of these attempts confirmed their opinion that they had no voice in the established educational system. Then a Dutchman suggested the idea of starting a school of their own.[4] It seemed to be quite simple; it was just a question of collecting signatures, and at that time only 50 were needed.[5] The idea was discussed in the Iskenderpaşa mosque and during an international conference of the Dutch Islamic Federation in Rotterdam in March 1987. Both the leaders and their supporters greeted it with enthusiasm.[6] Members of the Dutch Islamic Federation executive next set up the Islamic College Foundation, and within a short time collected between 300 and 400 declarations from parents. Meanwhile those behind the initiative had assured themselves of the unofficial co-operation of the Association of Private Schools for Education on General Principles. At first there were only Turks in the executive, and the municipal authorities voiced no objection to all members of the executive having the same nationality. In spite of this, the Foundation decided after a while to include Surinamese and Moroccan Muslims in the executive. The chairman thought this would make

---

İşleri Başkanlığı), to which the Islamic Foundation of the Netherlands for Education and Upbringing is affiliated (Landman 1992: 80–82, 86–87, 101–113 and 119–127).

[3] See, *inter alia*: Appendix 6, continuous list no. 1189, Meeting of the Municipal Council, dated 21 September 1989. Rotterdam Municipal Council, Education Department; Appendix 4–1 to the Plan for new primary schools 1991–1994, Rotterdam Municipal Council, Education Department.

[4] This information is based on verbal information from members of the management of the Islamic College Foundation.

[5] Based on Article 54, Section 5, of the Primary Education Act.

[6] According to Landman (1992: 262), the conference was organized by the Müslüman Cemiyetler ve Cemaatları Federasyonu, although the organizers by then already used the name Dutch Islamic Foundation. For a brief report of the conference see: *Het Vrije Volk*, 21 March 1987.

the school more accessible to other Muslim groups, and act as a restraint on the influence of the Milli Görü', which was operating from Germany.[7]

In mid-1987 the Islamic College Foundation submitted a request to the Rotterdam municipal council for the inclusion of two Muslim primary schools in the schools plan. The Foundation would be satisfied in the short term with one, provided the municipality would fund travel costs for it.[8] In a later review of the way the decision was taken, the new Alderman for Education, Hallensleben (Labour, PvdA), suggested that the schools had been included in the plan without much argument. In her view the application was handled with 'Rotterdam common sense'. 'We have never tried to block this process, because that is just not possible. After all, everyone in this country has the right to start a school' (de Volkskrant, 22 December 1990).

The question is what exactly she meant by 'Rotterdam common sense', since at the time there was evidence of almost 'moral panic'. The Board of Mayor and Aldermen, with the support of Labour (PvdA) and the Liberal Party (VVD), made no attempt to hide its 'serious concern' and 'disappointment'. The Muslim school would be the next 'ghetto school' and promote 'apartheid'.[9] Alderman Van Veenen (Labour, PvdA) exclaimed during a council meeting: 'Mother is not angry, just sad.'[10] In her view the process of integration was being undermined, which would be to the detriment of the children. The leader of the local Liberal Party (VVD), Ter Kuile-Van der Hoeven, made a strong plea in favour of state education, where children could learn to get on with each other from a young age. In a separate discussion with a delegation from the Foundation she even went so far as to urge them to withdraw the plan.[11] In fact only the

---

[7] This finding seems to be contrary to that of Landman (1992: 262), who suggested that the initiators in fact benefited from interference from Germany or Turkey. According to him they managed to get 'support not only (...) from a national Muslim organization, but also from related organizations throughout Europe and, last but not least, from the leader of the Milli Görüş movement, Necmettin Erbakan'.

[8] Transport at government expense is possible under Article 45 of the Primary Education Act.

[9] See, inter alia: Rotterdams Nieuwsblad, 18 September 1987, 23 October 1987, 15 March 1988 and 12 April 1988.

[10] Council minutes, meeting of 17 September 1987. Rotterdam Municipal Council, Secretariat Department of Education.

[11] An interesting detail is that this politician had on an earlier occasion told the Turkish chairman about the possibility of standing as a candidate for the Liberal Party (VVD). Relations between them were clearly good.

Christian Democratic Party (CDA) took a positive view. In the end all the councillors had to acknowledge that there were no legal grounds for refusing the application, and so reluctantly voted for its inclusion in the schools plan.[12]

In the Islamic College Foundation, surprise was expressed that the founding of a Jewish school—an application being dealt with at the same time—hardly attracted any attention. Was this a case of differ-ential treatment? Alderman Simons made no bones about it in the *Rotterdams Nieuwsblad* (12 April 1988):

> The object is quite different. The acceptance of their children in the education system is not the main preoccupation of the Jewish com-munity. For them it is a matter of identity, as it is in a Roman Catholic school. But in the case of the Turks the reason is that they are much less happy about acceptance into our education. The religious aspects weigh considerably less with them.

'Rotterdam common sense' in finding premises for the school

In anticipation of approval and funding from the Ministry of Edu-cation, the Islamic College Foundation started making preparations for premises, equipment, and recruitment of staff. For the manage-ment this was an exploratory period, with a great deal of contact with officials of the Office for Private Education, in which they con-stantly had the feeling that the officials did not take them seriously and were restraining them. This impression was confirmed by a spokesman of the Association of Private Schools for Education on General Principles and the Government Inspector, both of whom declared that the officials were holding things up, for instance in allocating premises.

The school management expressed its preference for premises in the Middelland district, from which most of the parents' signatures had come. At first the municipality offered a building in that area which was listed for demolition. The management was inclined to accept the condemned building until a staff member of the Association of Private Schools took an interest and urged them to refuse the offer. For a long time the officials offered no alternative, until in March 1988 they came up with a school building in Spangen. The

---

[12] Council minutes, meeting of 17 September 1987. Rotterdam Municipal Council, Secretariat Department of Education.

property itself suited the school management, but the location, in the view of the chairman, created alarm:

> Spangen was the backwoods for us. We were aware of the composition of the population and of its racism, and we thought we would not be welcome there.

However, under pressure from the municipal council the management agreed.[13] The pre-war property had lain empty for some time and needed refurbishment, but the officials did not think it could be considered that year. The management was prepared to have the school cleaned and painted, provided the municipality could supply the materials. That was agreed, but nothing in fact was done. Meanwhile the new school year was fast approaching and the management had not even received the keys. They had to wait for ministerial authority.[14] The officials became increasingly irritated with the continuous arguments, while the school management felt increasingly powerless because the officials did not fulfil their responsibilities. Only after the intervention of the Schools Inspectorate did things being to happen. Yet it was still not until the end of July that the property was handed over to the school management.

The Schools Inspectorate had to intervene again when there were further delays in paying for furniture and teaching materials. In spite of everything the Islamic College Foundation succeeded in opening the doors in time. At that time 85 pupils were on the register. In a few years the total rose to around 300.

By the mid-1990s relations with the municipality had changed considerably for the better, but the executive of the Islamic College Foundation still looks back with bitterness on all the bureaucratic rigmarole. One member concluded:

> The Office for Private Education is like a great mill where you are driven from pillar to post like a pingpong ball. If they also know that you are not be familiar with all the rules, they can have a good game with you, and that is the kind of ball they like. But those days are gone.

The executive members suspected—without being able to prove it—that the Alderman had sanctioned the negative attitude of the officials.

---

[13] This information is based on interviews with members of the school management and officials of the municipal Education Department.
[14] Ministerial approval only came in mid-August 1988.

Local resistance

The allocation of the property in Spangen by the municipality caused
uproar in the district, first of all among the staff of the nearby state
schools. They were worried by the prospect of what they saw as the
excessive influence of orthodox Muslims and continued segregation.
Moreover, they foresaw a steep decline in pupil numbers, eventually
undermining state education. The question was raised in discussions
about the Education Priority Policy in the district, but this did not
result in any official attitude or protest being adopted.[15]

The allocation also led to a fierce clash between the Spangen residents organization and the council. Those involved assured us that
the residents organization's opposition had nothing to do with objections to Muslims or with racism. It was purely that they were irritated about the progress of the city redevelopment programme, and
the awkward attitude of the municipality. The provision of open
space in the district, the relocation of the Sparta playing ground,
the local concentration of primary schools, and similar issues had
indeed preoccupied the residents for years. The property which the
municipality had suddenly allocated to the Al Ghazali school was in
an inner area which the residents in fact wanted to see cleared for
the provision of open space and recreation. The residents organization was most upset because there had not been 'a millimetre' of
consultation. However, according to a community worker at the time
there were also other factors, such as 'anxiety about an unfamiliar
phenomenon and the reactions it might cause'.

The residents organization sent an angry letter to the municipality, but the officials did not recant. They announced that the municipality had no control over the allocation of that specific building,
and that the Ministry of Education had forced things through. The
residents organization did not react well to this. The school year
had not yet begun when complaints started in the neighbourhood
about the nuisance of noise on Saturday mornings from children
learning the Koran. According to the community worker, proper
arrangements were then made with the school to keep the noise
within bounds.

Nowadays the Islamic College Foundation has normal relations

---

[15] Verbal information from the Education Priority Policy project assistant, Spangen.

with the neighbourhood and the municipality.[16] And although the Al Ghazali school recruits most of its pupils from the district, its advent has not led to an exodus from the state schools.

Administrative acceptance

The various school managements in Rotterdam are organized in three local co-ordinating bodies, the Foundation for General Private Schools in Rotterdam, the Area School Council for Protestant Education, and the Catholic School Council of Rotterdam. State education as a whole is represented by members of the municipal Education Department. The Alderman for Education—responsible for all primary education—and these co-ordinating bodies meet regularly in the Consultative Council, where important matters affecting primary education in Rotterdam are discussed. The function of this Council is to influence and legitimize policy, comparable to the Central Committee for Consultation on Education at the national level, described earlier.

When the Islamic College Foundation was still part of the Association of Private Schools, the municipality asked the Foundation for General Private Schools in Rotterdam to represent it. According to a member of this neutral co-ordinating body the answer was a 'categorical no'. They did not wish to get involved with education organized on religious principles. Since 1990 the Islamic College Foundation has been a member of the Islamic Schools Managements Organization, which, however, has no local branches. The Foundation therefore attends meetings of the Consultative Council as an observer.[17]

Islamic education is, however, represented on the executive of the Foundation for Combatting Disadvantage in Education, an organization created in 1991 to co-ordinate and supervise the policy of removing arrears in education. Moreover, as it controls a multi-million-guilder budget, the Foundation commands great influence.[18]

---

[16] In spite of the more or less normalized situation of education in Rotterdam, the Al Ghazali school, to the dismay of those concerned, from time to time attracts unfavourable publicity in the media. The MP Franssen (Liberal Party, VVD) expressed his resistance to Muslim schools as follows: 'I was myself at a Muslim school in Rotterdam-West. What I saw there was all nostalgia, Arabic pictures, photos and texts. The Dutch influence was apparently minimal' (*NRC Handelsblad*, 13 January 1992).

[17] Verbal information from the secretary of the Consultative Council.

[18] Verbal information from a member of the Foundation for Combatting Disadvantage in Education.

Utrecht

In Utrecht, too, Muslims took the initiative to found Muslim schools. The first application was in 1988, and the second followed four years later. Both are described below.

The first application

Since its creation in 1982, the Islamic Foundation of the Netherlands has fought for the establishment of a large number of Muslim primary schools, and set up the Islamic Foundation of the Netherlands for Education and Upbringing for that purpose. Utrecht was one of the first municipalities where they wanted to open a school. To that end the Islamic Foundation of the Netherlands collected signatures in the winter of 1987–1988, and in late March 1988 submitted an application to the municipal administration for the establishment of a private primary school.

The council's Education Committee dealt with the draft proposal of the 1989–1991 primary schools plan just six months later. Hardly anyone was enthusiastic about it. According to the chairman, Education Alderman Pot (Labour, PvdA), the application did not even satisfy the requirements for the foundation of a school. The Foundation had omitted to indicate the catchment area, which was a requirement under Article 55, Section 2, of the Primary Education Act. Moreover, the application was considered to be in breach of Article 7, because the school would only be for pupils of Turkish—or at any rate of non-Dutch—nationality. Only the Christian Democratic Party (CDA) spoke in favour of approving the application.[19]

This did not augur well, as was confirmed when the primary schools plan came before the municipal council in September.[20] Members for the Christian Democratic Party (CDA) and the Democrats 66 (D66) submitted an amendment, in which they proposed including the Muslim school in the plan, and setting the starting date for funding as 1 August 1989. The amendment was rejected by 30 votes to 11. The council then approved the proposed plan for primary

---

[19] Report of the Committee for Education, Culture, Media, Sports and Open Air Recreation, dated 24 August 1988. Utrecht Municipal Council.
[20] Memorandum from the Board of Mayor and Aldermen, Utrecht, to the Council, on the Primary Schools Plan 1989–1991, dated 12 September 1988. *Gedrukte Verzameling* 1988, no. 349.

schools by a majority vote. This put the seal on the rejection of the application as being inadmissible.[21]

The Foundation appealed against this decision to the Provincial Executive of the Province of Utrecht, which in February 1989 ruled that the application had been wrongly rejected. It was not the actual pupils on the roll who determined the scope and applicability of Article 7 of the Primary Education Act, but whether the foundation of the school would comply with Dutch law and follow the regular education system.[22] In the view of the Provincial Executive, nothing—not the import of Article 7, the school management's articles of association, nor the actual situation likely to result—justified the conclusion that the school would only be intended for children of non-Dutch nationality.[23] And although there was no detailed specification of the catchment area included, the supplementary information and the fact that the proposed school would be the only one for that denomination for tens of kilometres, were for the Provincial Executive sufficient.

During the hearing Alderman Pot (Labour, PvdA) came up with a new counter-argument; the required signatures had not been collected by the institution making the application, but by the Islamic Foundation of the Netherlands, and for that reason they were invalid. Again the Provincial Executive decided otherwise, because it had not been proved that the signatures submitted had been collected with any other object than obtaining the assent of the subscribers that their children should attend the school in question.

After a closed committee session, the Utrecht municipal council appealed to the Council of State.[24] In February 1992 the Crown gave its decision in the Foundation's favour.[25] By that time the Foundation had, however, decided to withdraw its application for a school

---

[21] Council minutes, meeting of 22 September 1988. Utrecht Municipal Council.

[22] This argument was used earlier by the government during the parliamentary debate on the Primary Education Act (*Explanatory Memorandum on the Primary Education Act*, TK 1976–1977, 14428, nos 1–4, p. 41; Preliminary Report on the Primary Education Act, TK 1979–1980, 14428, no. 11, p. 36; *Memorandum in Reply to the Primary Education Act*, TK 1979–1980, 14428, no. 12, p. 24).

[23] Ruling by the Second Chamber on Disputes Hearings of the Provincial Executive of the Province of Utrecht, no. 275812'883, dated 7 February 1989.

[24] Pending this appeal under Article 52 of the Primary Education Act, the Crown was asked to rule on whether or not the Primary Schools Act was applicable to the school.

[25] *Staatsblad* 1992, no. 118.

in Utrecht, the most important reason being that it did not wish to obstruct the progress of the Utrecht Islamic Education Foundation, which had meanwhile also submitted an application. According to a spokesman of the Islamic Foundation of the Netherlands for Education and Upbringing they were also afraid that the municipality might play off the two foundations against each other. As a result, plans for a school in Utrecht were finally dropped.

The second application

In the spring of 1992 four Muslims (of Turkish, Moroccan and Surinamese origin) took the initiative of setting up the Utrecht Islamic Education Foundation. Its constitution states that as many ethnic groups as possible should be represented on its executive.[26] The Foundation soon submitted a request to the Utrecht municipal council for assistance in setting up two private primary schools for education on Islamic principles. The schools would be affiliated to the Islamic Schools Managements Organization.[27] In good time *before* they submitted the official application, members of the executive approached the Education Department of the Utrecht municipality for advice. The final application was drawn up in close co-operation with several civil servants.

The next meeting of the Education Committee discussed the outline proposal for the primary schools plan for 1993–1996. The Board of Mayor and Aldermen proposed accepting the application. Although the next day's daily *Utrechts Nieuwsblad* (16 June 1992) carried the headline, 'Parties support Muslim schools', the minutes show that not all the parties were in favour without qualification. Several objections were made that such schools would not help in the integration of the pupils.[28] However, the chairman, Education Alderman Van Lidth de Jeude (Labour, PvdA), who was Alderman Pot's successor, reported that the application had been checked against all

---

[26] Articles of Association of the Utrecht Islamic Education Foundation, 25 March 1992. Utrecht Municipal Council, Chamber of Commerce. Its executive committee has since then retained its mixed composition.

[27] Request from the Utrecht Islamic Education Foundation to the Municipal Council for the inclusion of two private primary schools for education on Islamic principles in the 1993–1996 plan for new primary schools, dated 27 March 1992. Utrecht Municipal Council.

[28] Minutes of the public meeting of the Committee for Finance and Education, dated 25 June 1992. Utrecht Municipal Council.

the legal requirements and had satisfied them. The primary schools plan was then dealt with in the municipal council and accepted more or less 'on the nod'.[29]

Procedure prescribed that the plan should next be sent up to the Provincial Executive, so that the school could start in the school year 1993–1994. However, on 1 July 1992 the Temporary Act on Funding New Primary Schools came into force, which required among other things a forecast of the school's viability. This requirement posed the Foundation a considerable problem, and it was unable to meet the 30–day deadline because the municipality could not provide the necessary data in time. The management therefore applied in writing to the Ministry of Education for an extension. The municipal Education Department also pressed for an extension to be granted.

However, this did not produce the desired result. The Foundation asked the Alderman for Education to mediate, but he explained that he had no power to do so. The management then decided to appeal to the Council of State, and also (on the advice of the Alderman) requested an interview with the Secretary of State for Education, Wallage (Labour, PvdA). In the event this proved unnecessary, since to everyone's surprise they suddenly received news that they had been granted an extension until early 1993. The department's U-turn might have had something to do with a telephone call from the Alderman to his party colleague, the Secretary of State.[30]

The appeal was then withdrawn and the forecast was ready by early December. It envisaged the Foundation being able to launch two Muslim primary schools in August 1993. In April of that year the management heard from the Ministry that they could start one school, provided they withdrew the application for the second. If they did not do this, the Ministry would reject both applications. The forecast submitted did not show that two schools would be viable in the future.[31] The management finally agreed to the condition and in May received approval for a primary school.[32] But all

---

[29] Council minutes, meeting of 3 September 1992. Utrecht Municipal Council.

[30] Interview with members of the executive of the Utrecht Islamic Education Foundation.

[31] Ibid. According to the members involved it remained unclear what this conclusion was based on because government officials did not wish to reveal their calculations in black and white.

[32] Letter of 1 June 1993 from the executive of the Utrecht Islamic Education Foundation to the authors.

the barriers were even now not yet cleared. The municipal Education
Department, which had at first been so helpful, suddenly began to
display much less enthusiasm. The officials would have liked to postpone the opening of the Muslim school for a year. It began to take
rather a long time to allocate premises. At last a (provisional) address
was announced in late July 1993. There were scarcely two weeks
left to prepare the school for the arrival of the 165 pupils, who
started the new school year in the first and so far the only Muslim
school in Utrecht, the Aboe Da'oed school.

The Foundation did not proceed with their application for a second school because they first wanted to solve the problem of premises
for the other one.[33] The site allotted to them served only as temporary accommodation and did not meet the requirements. Moreover,
the location left much to be desired; the school was situated near
the red-light district and had a lot of trouble with drug addicts. Still
in 1993, the municipality submitted an application to the Ministry
for a new building, which was then used as an excuse to do nothing to improve the current premises.[34] The application was eventually rejected, at which a new application was made. Meanwhile
various parties—including the Schools Inspectorate—declared that
the school building was not suitable for teaching children.[35]

The Foundation made various attempts to bring the question to
the attention of political circles in Utrecht. In the summer of 1995
a decision was finally taken to carry out a number of improvements.[36]
For the time being this did not include a new building.

---

[33] Unless stated otherwise, the information about the premises of the Aboe Da'oed
school is from the *Utrecht Nieuwsblad* of 20 August 1993, 28 October 1994, 31 May
1995 and 7 July 1995.

[34] Verbal information from a member of the executive of the Utrecht Islamic
Education Foundation, Utrecht. See also: letter from the Director of the Education
Department to the Inspector of Primary Education, dated 24 November 1994.
Utrecht Municipal Council.

[35] See also: letter from the Director of the Education Department to the executive of the Utrecht Islamic Education Foundation, dated 31 January 1995. Utrecht
Municipal Council.

[36] Letter from the Director of the Education Department to the executive of the
Utrecht Islamic Education Foundation, dated 21 June 1995. Utrecht Municipal
Council.

Ideological concepts and arguments

The debate about Muslim schools revolved around the central principles of *freedom of education* and *equality*. Many civil servants and politicians have put forward objections to the founding of Muslim schools,
but have finally given way before the strength of these principles.
Many people expressed dissatisfaction at the way freedom of education was interpreted. A system of denominational schools has emerged
which highlights differences between religious and ideological groups,
and stands in the way of social integration. Denominational education is regarded as a tainted legacy of the past, which should be dis-
posed of. From this point of view, any attempt to found Muslim
schools is a step in the wrong direction. On the other hand there
is a realization that the Constitution obliges the government to recognize and fund schools of all denominations. The principle of equality, moreover, lays down that Muslim schools have the right to the
same treatment as Roman Catholic or Protestant schools. In Utrecht
we found these opinions and arguments mainly among members of
the Labour (PvdA), Liberal (VVD) and Green Left parties, who were
clearly committed to state education. A Green Left council member
had this to say:

> Our basic conviction is that there should not actually be any denom-
> inational schools at all. In that sense you can say: no Muslim schools
> either. In our opinion education based on ideological principles has
> no place in this society. Education should be something the state pro-
> vides, and there should be room in it for all possible movements. There
> should not be any schools based on ideological principles and there-
> fore able to discriminate against anyone who is permitted to be taught
> there.

A colleague of the Labour Party (PvdA) added:

> It's quite unrelated to what you think of Islam. (. . .) The official view
> is simply that under the Constitution there is a right to found Muslim
> schools. So if applications satisfy the requirements of the law, as a
> municipal council we cannot formally reject an application.

Nevertheless attempts have been made in Utrecht to prevent the
foundation of a Muslim school, not by opposing freedom of education, but by resorting to all kinds of legal technicalities. However,
to judge from the decisions of various successive appeal bodies, such
moves had little substance in law, although the chicanery certainly

contributed to stopping the school ever being established. In Rotterdam, too, there was 'some raising of eyebrows', as a member of the Consultative Council euphemistically put it, but 'it was not felt necessary to start a public debate about it'. Objections to Muslim schools also came—in a more negative sense—from the *fear that there might be an exodus from state education*. In Rotterdam there were murmurs along these lines from nearby state primary schools, but also from the Education Department and in the municipal council itself. This was also the case in Utrecht, and the Schools Inspector in Rotterdam commented:

> At first the foundation of this Muslim school was seen as a serious threat, particularly to state education. Because, of course, that's where most of the Muslims were . . . and people thought, my word, what next?

In his view the objections also had something to do with the *assumption that Muslim schools were 'different'*:

> . . . because it is a Muslim school, or because it is a denominational school, but most of all because it's a different sort of school. And we don't like things to be different.

It would seem logical for adherents of religious faiths to welcome the foundation of a Muslim school with somewhat greater enthusiasm. After all, they have an affinity with institutions based on religious foundations. To a certain extent this was in fact the case. In the Utrecht municipal council, the Christian Democratic Party (CDA) was the only party to support the introduction of a Muslim school from the start. Their party members saw a certain *parallel with their own past history*:

> In the course of time we have seen that Protestant and Catholic schools worked together in the process of emancipation. They had been at a disadvantage, particularly the Catholics. But their emancipation was advanced by the fact that they had the opportunity to develop their identity through denominational schools. So I had a faint hope that this might also be the case with Islamic education. Their identity would be better developed by it, and afterwards they would fit better into society. That was the inherent reasoning that we in the Christian Democratic Party shared.

In spite of this they still had some reservations. To quote a member of the Christian Democratic Party:

My position was strictly formal. Look, of course you can say, we would rather not have [muslim schools], for we believe that integration, if possible at all, is more important. You could say that, but I didn't go that far, because it wasn't relevant. What was relevant was that they were entitled by an article of the Constitution to found a school like that. Otherwise you would have to close down all those Catholic and Protestant schools. If you support denominational education, then you also have to support a Muslim school, provided it meets all the conditions. If it doesn't meet these conditions, well then there's an end to it.

A Party colleague added:

In 1988 we took a fairly straightforward stance, in the sense that the Constitution provides for freedom of education. So if there is a demand for it within that community they have the right to it. At the time we also said we would not encourage it, because we thought that it was in the best interests of children to be in an integrated school where there would be indigenous children as well as foreign ones.

Apparently the *'possible segregation tendency'*[37] caused the Christian Democratic Party (CDA) considerable concern. And they were certainly not alone. A councillor from D66, the second party in Utrecht to support the initial application for a Muslim school, formulated her concerns as follows:

We are not particularly in favour of sending children to segregated schools. And with the problems of immigrant children and their adaptation to Dutch society, the best idea is to put all children into the same school, so they can get to know each other, and also learn to appreciate each other's culture. I think that if you start from that basis you will never be happy about the foundation of a separate school, whatever its denomination. (. . .) It's a pity to split up young children again in this way, so that they set off on separate school careers, which means you are naturally making the gaps between them larger, rather than smaller.

This concern is fairly widespread. In the Rotterdam council, some members used strong terms such as 'ghetto schools' and 'apartheid'. The advent of a Muslim school clearly touches a nerve; not so much because it is based on religious principles—objections on those grounds

[37] This phrase is from the Secretary of State for Education Ginjaar-Maas (Liberal Party, VVD) (Foundation of Primary Schools on Hindu or Islamic Principles, TK 1988–1989, 21110, no. 1, pp. 1–8).

would be constitutionally indefensible—but because of the supposed
social and cultural effects of such education. The expectation is that
Muslim schools will take most if not all their children from immigrant families, and no indigenous Dutch children. This would make
it very hard for these categories to encounter each other, let alone
exchange ideas or customs. It was precisely these encounters and
exchanges which many people considered essential, not only for the
success of the local minorities policy, but above all for the development of an integrated society. A spokesman for the Labour Party
(PvdA) in Utrecht put it in the following way:

> We think it is rather regrettable that people want to proceed with
> founding these schools, because we fear it compromises their integra-
> tion into society. (. . .) In a multicultural society where several cultures
> have to encounter each other, and therefore in education as well, new
> situations emerge in which certain groups cut themselves off again.
> (. . .) Those contacts involve doing things together, such as sharing cer-
> tain festivals at school. But in lessons, too, it can receive some atten-
> tion; for example by giving some space in Dutch books to sections of
> the history or the culture of Moroccans, Surinamese or Turks. Just
> look at *Sesame Street*, to give just one example. (. . .) And I also think
> that a multicultural society also implies that people should maintain
> certain values of their own, and that we should get to know about
> such things from each other.

When the issue of Muslim schools comes up, the 'contact hypothe-
sis' is often referred to again. It holds that more contact automatically leads to more understanding and tolerance, and possibly more
co-operation. However, practical experience within existing education, where people have been trying to create this utopia for years,
teaches us that the real world is appreciably more stubborn than the
televized world of *Sesame Street*. Worries about the 'possible segrega-
tional tendency' indicate a lack of confidence in the quality of Muslim
schools, which would not prepare their pupils adequately for a society perceived as ideal, integrated and tolerant. An Utrecht councillor (Liberal Party, VVD) was afraid that one thing or another could
result in 'too little emphasis being placed in their upbringing and
education on the norms and values which our legal system guarantees'. Some were also afraid that pupils would be taught wrong ideas,
particularly regarding the relationships between men and women,
and between parents and children.

Others, however, saw some benefits. For example, it was felt that specific groups of Muslim children could gain temporarily by having their own school. The children in mind were those whose way of life was very different from the Dutch one, and who might be disoriented or lose contact with their roots in the existing schools. Alderman Van Lidth de Jeude (Labour, PvdA) in Utrecht had this to say about this 'feeder route' into Dutch culture:

> I think that there is a small group who will indeed do better in a Muslim school, where they will have a slightly longer cultural grounding in their own group and a more gradual transition into Dutch culture and society. I think that this is the group which, if things go too fast for them, produces drop-outs from the shock. I believe the great majority derive much more benefit from being grafted into Dutch language and culture in the ordinary Dutch schools, and not in Muslim schools. If they were to go to Muslim schools then their emancipation and integration would in fact be delayed. By emancipation I mean having a reasonable chance of getting work and participating in social organizations.

Within the Christian Democratic Party in Utrecht, the view was expressed that Muslim schools might make a positive contribution to the school career of girls:

> Another argument was that girls were often withdrawn from school when they started to menstruate. Although they are then still below the official school-leaving age, some fathers are ready to pay thousands of guilders in fines as a result, whereas if they had gone to a Muslim school they could have carried on. (. . .) I think that for these girls a Muslim school is one answer.

Even among the opponents of Muslim schools there are some who allow them the benefit of the doubt on one point: parents who send their children to a Muslim school are after all making a deliberate choice, an indication of self-confidence which augurs well for their social progress. Moreover, the demand for Muslim schools certainly does not indicate faith in the quality of existing education.

As we have seen, certain individuals are strongly against Muslim schools, because in their view they spread *deviant norms and values*. In spite of this, others plead for more room for 'other cultures' in existing schools, in this case state primary schools. For instance, an Utrecht councillor (Labour, PvdA) wondered why so little publicity was given to Islamic religious instruction. A councillor for Democrats 66 (D66) remarked:

> If you want people to understand each other, to have respect for each
> other's convictions, then you must let them grow up together and you
> must inform them about the nature of each culture. That means that
> you must create space in education for such cultural matters. And that
> implies that you must do much more in general education about phi-
> losophy and religion, but then for all children.

One consideration occasionally voiced against Muslim schools, both
in Rotterdam and in Utrecht, is that they would encourage *racism
in non-Muslim Dutch people*. In Rotterdam this fear increased when the
first Muslim school was allocated its premises in Spangen, which in
earlier plans was to have been the site of a small park. The Spangen
residents organization was afraid that the advent of the school would
increase existing tensions between population groups, and this was
one of their reasons for opposing it. They also justified their opposition with the formal argument that there had been no prior consultation, and that the area needed more open space. Elsewhere,
too, opponents of Muslim schools muted their objections to some
extent, for fear of racist reactions from other people.

CHAPTER ELEVEN

CONCLUSIONS AT THE LOCAL LEVEL

Institutionalization at the local level has occurred in a variety of fields and with varying results. We have singled out the cities of Rotterdam and Utrecht for closer examination, and concentrated on developments in the three spheres of politics (recognition of Muslim organizations as partners in the political debate), religion (establishing and funding places of worship), and education (Islamic religious instruction in state primary schools and the establishment of Muslim schools). In terms of our three central research questions, what are the conclusions we can draw from our findings at the local level?

Range and density

Several Muslim organizations have been set up in recent years in Rotterdam and Utrecht, mostly with a religious objective. Some of these maintain contacts with the municipality and wish to be involved in the process of political dialogue. To this end most organizations in Rotterdam have joined forces under the umbrella of the Platform of Islamic Organizations in Greater Rotterdam. Quite soon after its formation, the city acknowledged this co-ordinating organization. Although there is still no regular pattern of consultation with the municipality, the Platform has since then taken its place in the structure of political decision making. There is no comparable mechanism in Utrecht. There Muslim organizations may carry on incidental consultation with the local authority, but they are outside the political decision-making process. If it was up to the municipal council, Muslim organizations would only be able to communicate with the authorities through secular immigrant organizations. In the real world, this is not a practical option.

In both cities there are many places of worship for Muslims of various nationalities and religious groups, but their establishment has never been without controversy. In the mid-1990s in Rotterdam, after years of ad hoc decisions, this institution was regulated as best as could be managed. The municipality negotiates and grants facilities within the narrow limits allowed by the government for religious organizations. This does not prevent a number of organizations still struggling with problems of accommodation. Although some Muslim organizations have received funds to establish places of worship in the past, there is now no longer any question of a subsidy system. However, the municipality meets part of the organizations' costs when a place of worship has to be relocated, purchased or sold. They are in fact treated as far as possible on an equal footing with secular interest organizations, which means that for specific activities (including the cost of premises) they can apply in similar terms for subsidies.

In Utrecht, Muslim organizations which have (or wish to have) a place of worship in use are still not eligible for regular attention or support from the municipality, and certainly not financial support. The municipal council gives priority in word and deed to secular interest organizations.

In 1995 there were two Muslim primary schools in Rotterdam, and one in Utrecht. The establishment of the first Muslim school in Rotterdam was accomplished with extreme difficulty. Officially the municipality provided no obstacles and there was euphemistic talk of 'Rotterdam common sense'. However, certain politicians campaigned against it, and officials delayed matters. The opening of the second school went much more smoothly. Both have been integrated into the Rotterdam education management system. Within the provision for religious and ideological education—which is funded by the municipality—it is also possible to take Islamic religious instruction in Rotterdam state primary schools.

In Utrecht the municipality opposed the first application to open a Muslim school there. An embittered legal battle then flared up, which was ended only after the initiators of the application had withdrawn from the process. The most important reason for the withdrawal was the submission of an application by another organization, which in fact involved two Muslim schools, which under pressure from the national government was reduced to one. In Utrecht no Islamic religious instruction is offered in state primary schools.

All in all the process of institutionalization in these two large municipalities shows surprising differences. In Utrecht, the first reactions were negative across the board, and so were subsequent responses; to that extent the local authority has been remarkably consistent. In Rotterdam positions shifted with time, but once the decision had been taken that Muslim organizations should be recognized in principle as immigrants' interest organizations, the consequences must have been foreseen. There was a dominoes effect, as institutions were set up and recognized in one social sphere after another. In hindsight, there would have been no Islamic religious instruction without the Platform of Islamic Organizations in Greater Rotterdam, no Platform without the subsidization of Muslim organizations, and no subsidization without recognition in principle. Before that stage was reached, the dominant attitude, as in Utrecht, was one of reserve, and sometimes opposition. Whenever possible, politicians and officials were all too anxious to avoid Muslim entanglements.

Factors and agents

Neither in Rotterdam nor in Utrecht can the existing situation be called self-explanatory. It is the result of consultation and sometimes conflict between the authorities and individual interest groups, and between sections of the authorities themselves. Up to a certain point these differences resulted from the extent and the force with which *Muslim initiatives* were pursued. The determination with which they had tried to open their own schools or, in Rotterdam, to obtain Islamic religious instruction, appears to have been an essential condition for their success. That there is no provision for Islamic religious instruction in Utrecht is mainly because Muslims have made no real efforts for it there. We should add that the municipality has also done its best to prevent Muslims proposing the idea.

But not every initiative is automatically rewarded with success. In Utrecht the request to take part in the political process fell on deaf ears, and it rendered no tangible results. Nor is it the case that all institutions are the result of Muslim initiatives. The formation of a co-ordinating organization in Rotterdam, for example, can by no means be credited entirely to Muslim efforts.

Foreign powers and *international Muslim organizations* have played only a limited role in the process of institutionalization either in Rotterdam or in Utrecht. There was some degree of influence from abroad on the formation and policy of certain Muslim organizations, and in a single case money was also transferred for the establishment of places of worship. But the *fear* of such influences, which was used as an argument in the debate, does not correspond to the reality. For instance, the subsidy of Muslim organizations in Rotterdam is based partly on the belief that it is better to provide this support than to leave it to foreign powers to do so. However, the municipality has not always been consistent in such matters: a few years earlier they had invited Saudi Arabia to put up large sums of money for the Islamic Diaspora in the Dutch polders. Moreover, it is not only the indigenous, non-Muslim administrators who attempt to neutralize external influences. For instance, the articles of association of the first Muslim school in Rotterdam were drawn up from the start so that the original Muslim organization in Germany would not be able to interfere in the running of the school in any way.

Legislation and regulation has determined issues in diverse ways. To the extent that there are national rules, they have acted as guidelines. This applies most particularly to the rules for funding schools. Without their detailed provisions, and therefore without legal guarantees, the Muslims in neither Rotterdam nor Utrecht would have succeeded in founding their schools. Municipal councillors and officials, or at least many of them, did nothing to hide their antipathy to Muslim schools, but legally had no leg to stand on. It took much longer for this realization to dawn in Utrecht than in Rotterdam, and only after all kinds of legal devices—such as trying to claim that it was a school based on nationality—had been employed in vain to prevent a school being founded.

In addition to this legislation and regulation, *national policy guidelines* have also played a role. These may not have had the formal status of the law, but were treated as if they did. The rule that Islamic religious instruction must always to be delivered in Dutch is an example. This was set down in writing somewhere (in Amsterdam), and has since been followed unswervingly by municipal administrators, the Association of Dutch Local Authorities, the Ministry of Education, and others. In local practice the absence of national regulation was used as an excuse for doing nothing, and sometimes for creative accounting as well. Civil servants and politicians in Utrecht defended their refusal to support mosques financially with the argument that the national government no longer had any arrangements for subsidies. Although this argument was also used in Rotterdam, we saw that there the Alderman and his officials did all they could to widen the parameters of the national policy.

On a few occasions Muslims were able to take advantage of existing *municipal regulations*. The request in Rotterdam for the provision of Islamic religious instruction was based on a ruling accepted by the municipal council in 1955.

The *local authority* is always the pivot upon which everything moves. It grants or refuses subsidies to Muslim organizations, recognizes or spurns them as partners in the political debate, includes or rejects Muslim schools in the schools plan, and gives or refuses financial support for the establishment of mosques. In a number of cases the municipalities have taken an extremely active part, albeit with varying objectives.

In Rotterdam it was civil servants who proposed treating Muslim organizations on an equal footing with secular organizations. That was in part the result of calculated self interest, in order to avoid abuses and to create 'partners' for their policy. Once this had become the accepted strategy, officials worked on Muslim organizations in such a way that by all appearances they formed their own co-ordinating body. A different attitude could be perceived in Rotterdam towards attempts to establish the first Muslim school; at that time officials were hardly falling over each other in their efforts. In fact the municipal authority does not always speak with one voice. While in Rotterdam the officials of the Migrants Office and their Alderman displayed the necessary energy, other members of the municipal council (including the Board of Mayor and Aldermen) remained unresponsive. Only at the very last moment did they come around.

When it came to the political participation of Muslim organizations, the Utrecht municipality behaved in a very passive manner, quite unlike its attitude in the debate about the Muslim school or the introduction of Islamic religious instruction, where it did everything possible to prevent the advent of these institutions.

The *authority of the courts* was only sporadically invoked; strictly speaking only in Utrecht, where the fight about whether the application to include a Muslim school in the schools plan should be honoured went up to the highest legal authorities. In the end the organization concerned was not able to profit from it, but each time won its case. In Rotterdam the courts were never involved, but the national Schools Inspectorate had to lend a hand in persuading the officials to co-operate in the founding of a Muslim school.

Organizations based on religious or ideological principles were involved to varying degrees in the institutionalization process, for instance concerning schools management associations. When the Muslim school was opened in Rotterdam the management enjoyed the full support

of the national Association of Private Schools for Education on
General Principles. However, its local branch did not feel that it
could represent this school in the management system, and invoked
the incompatibility of principles. The initiative to offer Islamic religious instruction forced the existing Protestant and Humanist organizations for religious and ideological education to decide their position,
especially because support for the Muslim initiative would probably
result in a cut in their own subsidies. The organizations nevertheless took the point of view that there was a common interest, and
supported the initiative. They soon decided to work closely together.
In Rotterdam, church organizations also co-operated with Muslim
organizations sporadically, for instance by offering temporary premises
for places of worship.

It is difficult to discover why the school organizations involved in
Utrecht did not form an association, as they did in Rotterdam.
Religious organizations sometimes supported the funding of mosques,
and sometimes not. In Utrecht collections were made in some churches
for the establishment of mosques. This produced not only some
money, but also dispute: why should a *Christian* organization involve
itself with the advancement of a non-Christian religion? Though the
Christian Democratic Party (CDA) gave its approval from the start
to the founding of Muslims schools, the support of the Christian parties for the other Muslim initiatives—and that applied to both municipalities—was by no means automatic.

Naturally a number of *organizations not based on religious or ideological principles* were also interested in the institutionalization. First of
all there were the secular immigrant organizations. In both Rotterdam
and Utrecht they did their utmost to thwart the development of
Islamic religious communities. They were at their most vociferous in
the discussions about subsidizing Muslim organizations, and their
recognition as partners in the political debate, perhaps because this
was where their own interests were most at risk. Sometimes they
were supported by welfare organizations, such as the Foundation for
Foreign Workers in Greater Rotterdam, or the Rotterdam Institute
for Residents Support. Other parties entering the lists from time to
time were residents associations, particularly against the founding
and potential nuisance of mosques, or in Rotterdam the Muslim
school. They rarely campaigned for the interests of their Muslim
neighbours; for the most part they acted as the mouthpiece of the
non-Muslim local residents.

As for *other relevant institutions*, the role of the media should be recorded, particularly the local daily press and the district journals. Their reports helped to put the interests of Muslims on the political agenda and keep them there. Special mention should be made of the '*Wild Geese*' campaign of the Dutch Interchurch Network, which raised funds in 1973 to found a mosque in Utrecht.

Ideological concepts and arguments

Neither in Rotterdam nor in Utrecht did we find organizations or individual administrators who denied Muslims the legal right to establish mosques, to engage in political activities, to organize Islamic religious instruction, or to found their own denominational schools. All acknowledged these rights, though with varying degrees of conviction. The enduring existence of these ideas was shown in practice when they were put to the test. Unanimity then dissolved into a palette of distinctions and contrasts; some wanted to pay no more than lip service to these rights, others wanted to recognize them only subject to specific conditions, while others still threw themselves vigorously into the fray as advocates.

The debate evoked numerous arguments in principle, and practical considerations in favour of particular policies. One was the principle of the *separation of church and state*. Those who supported the development of a more secular society, and who consequently had reservations about the Muslim claims, advanced this argument. Some even claimed that incidental or formalized contacts with Muslims might endanger the current application of the separation of church and state. Although to invoke this separation is legitimate in itself, certainly since the 1983 constitutional amendment, some attributed an absolute significance to this principle, and consequently it became somewhat divorced from everyday reality. For instance, the municipality of Rotterdam invoked it in 1978 to demonstrate that the authorities bore no responsibility whatsoever towards Muslim organizations, a position which suggested that they should have nothing to do with any of the churches. It is remarkable that in the same period the muncipality paid out tens of thousands of guilders to Muslim organizations in subsidies towards the costs of founding places of worship, as did the Ministry of Culture, Recreation and Social Work. In addition, they gave strong political support to the advent

of a large mosque, and went so far as to forestall the opposition of
the local residents organizations. It looks therefore as if invoking the
separation of church and state was being used in some cases as an
opportunistic argument for shuffling off responsibility in advance.

The argument of *freedom of religion* was only used a few times, as
in Rotterdam when the question arose of whether to proceed against
places of worship which did not comply with the fire and safety regulations, or caused a nuisance. The officials were aware that too rig-
orous an attitude would mean depriving Muslims of an important
opportunity to practise their religion. In other discussions this argument was rarely used explicitly, except as the standard statement
that Muslims in the Netherlands should also be able to practise their
religion. Usually the question has rather been whether the constitutional freedom of religion obliges the local authorities to provide
facilities. Some thought that this was not the case, and referred to
the social process of secularization. Exponents of this view could be
found in Utrecht, but also in the Rotterdam council. Others took a
more generous view, and talked about the social disadvantages of
Muslims.

These considerations are closely associated with the *principle of equality*, which has been paraded whether relevant or not, sometimes to
plead for a cautious approach, and sometimes to encourage intervention. However, as it does at the national level, the reference group
varies. The most likely to adopt this attitude are other religious communities or churches. In the 1990s, Roman Catholic and Protestant
churches no longer receive government support for new buildings;
nor do they take part in regular consultation with the council authorities on general policy matters. A strict application of the principle
of equality would therefore mean that mosques would get no subsidy, nor would Muslims have any claim to separate consultation
provisions because this would constitute discrimination in favour of
Muslims. In Utrecht the municipality keeps the consequences of the
principle of equality clearly in mind, but in a negative sense. For
instance, they rejected a request by a Protestant organization for
Bible classes on the grounds of a supposed precedent for Muslims.
On the other hand, others took a more historical point of view, and
argued that the Roman Catholics or orthodox Calvinists had only
achieved their position in the history of the nation after they had
already organized themselves on their own principles. If the principle of equality is perceived in this way, it places an obligation on

the authorities to do something to help Muslims to catch up, which is an idea aired now and then, particularly by Protestant groups, but is certainly not widely held.

The reference group for the application of the principle of equality can also be rather different. In practice Muslims are often equated with immigrants (or ethnic minorities) and their organizations. The reasoning is then that the municipality is dealing with the same categories of people in the provisions of the minorities policy, which does not please certain secular immigrant organizations and their representatives, who emphasize rather the enormous differences, and stress the social dangers which the presence of Muslims may produce, such as reinforcing the social isolation of immigrants and undermining the unity of the nation. These secular forces sometimes refer back to political and social conflicts in the countries of origin. Some Turks, for instance, defend the secularization promoted by Atatürk. They make their views known on various fronts and in various roles: as immigrant workers in the districts, as teaching staff for the education in community language and culture-programme, or as political leaders of interest organizations. In both Rotterdam and Utrecht they opposed the establishment of Muslim institutions. But in Rotterdam they achieved a contrary effect. The establishment of the Platform of Islamic Organizations in Greater Rotterdam can in one sense be regarded as a reaction, albeit belated and indirect, to the exclusion of Muslim organizations from public administration in Rotterdam. In Utrecht, these secular forces have so far had the best of it.

The idea that the application of the principle of equality leads to giving support to Muslims on an equal footing with ethnic minorities seems to have struck a particular chord in Rotterdam. Two aspects, indissolubly linked to each other, are involved here: the *fear of isolation* and the *support for integration*. We are concerned here with an ideologically determined assessment of the position of Muslims or of Islamic immigrants. The fear that Muslims might cut themselves off from Dutch society is a recurring motif in all the reactions from the municipality. In Rotterdam the threat of social isolation was one of the more important driving forces behind the municipal decision to subsidize the activities of Muslim organizations, to make facilities for religious instruction in state primary schools dependent upon the requirement that Dutch would be the language of instruction, and to act as a brake on the foundation of the first Muslim school. This social isolation is considered such a problem because of the Muslim lifestyle, which is thought to be completely at variance with what is perceived as typically Dutch. In orthodox circles they are considered to be obsessed by their religion, not to treat women as equal to men, to use incorrect pedagogic methods, to be open to influence by foreign powers, and to have pre-modern and sometimes even undemocratic political customs.

Countering the fear of social isolation is the endeavour to help Muslim immigrants to integrate, which would consist above all in the adoption of Dutch values and norms, as a result of personal contacts and dialogues. In both cities Muslim schools were regarded as a problem mainly because they prevented these desirable personal contacts. To that extent, Islamic religious instruction gained more support in Rotterdam, provided it was perceived not as teaching a religious faith, but as a form of providing information on religion in general. The readiness to help Muslims integrate is generally present in both Rotterdam and Utrecht, provided they are prepared to accept the terms of Dutch society, which—with some exaggeration—comes down to Muslims behaving as little as possible in an Islamic way.

Comparison of Rotterdam and Utrecht

Why have reactions in Rotterdam been so different from those in Utrecht? The municipalities were operating within the same national political system and legal framework, and were dealing with Muslims from more or less the same regions, with comparable histories of migration and socio-economic positions. The Aldermen with whom Muslims first came into contact were even members of the same political party. In part the explanation lies in the amount of energy with which those involved pressed their cases and eventually forced them home. We received the impression that in this respect the Rotterdam Muslims had more to offer. The enthusiastic reaction of Migrants Office officials, when faced with Turkish Muslim leaders who 'had got the right idea', is telling. However, in practice Muslim initiatives only produced something when the society around them was prepared to make room for them.

We could discover no perceptible difference between civil servants and politicians in Rotterdam and in Utrecht in their assumptions about Islam and its adherents. There is agreement that Muslims should be offered opportunities. The debate is about different norms, values and behaviour. The crucial contrast between Rotterdam and Utrecht is that in Rotterdam the implementation of the minorities policy had taken a different shape, and that opinions there gradually changed. Muslims are no longer categorized and judged so much on the basis of their religious characteristics, but rather on their socio-cultural and socio-economic behaviour—as is customary with ethnic minorities. The partnerships extended to Muslims by Rotterdam first became possible after strict Islamic features were ideologically side-tracked or played down, and greater significance was given to their aspects as a minority.

PART THREE

AN INTERNATIONAL COMPARISON

INTRODUCTION

In the previous chapters we have discussed at length the process of institutionalization in the Netherlands. In this part of the study we move outside the Dutch national borders and examine the situation elsewhere, in the assumption that an international comparison can add an important dimension to the material assembled in the Netherlands. It can illustrate those aspects in which the Dutch context differs from other countries, and those in which there are parallels, which should deepen our understanding of the process of institutionalization.

As mentioned in Chapter 1, Belgium and the UK (specifically England) were selected for comparison. Our description of the process of institutionalization of Islam in these countries is based mainly on the use of secondary literature, with the limitations this implies. The information on specific aspects or areas is not evenly distributed. The British case, for instance, supplies a spate of information about the town of Bradford, where a great deal has taken place. The question remains to what extent the situation there is representative of the rest of the country. Moreover, existing studies did not enable us to devote the same systematic attention to the ideological views and arguments in the debate about Islam as we had in the Netherlands.

Again we centre our attention on three spheres: religion, education, and political life. Within these we will concentrate on the same subjects, but on a rather wider scale in the sphere of politics. Both the Belgian (Chapter 12) and the British (Chapter 13) examples start with a discussion of the recognition of Islam in a general sense, coupled with that of Muslims as partners in the political debate. Then follow the subjects of places of worship, Islamic religious instruction in primary schools, and Muslim schools. In these accounts we make no clear distinction, as we did in the case of the Netherlands, between the national and local level. In Chapter 14 we compare the situations in Belgium and England with the Netherlands, and consider the central issues of the coverage and density of the institutions, and the factors and agencies involved.

CHAPTER TWELVE

BELGIUM

A historical outline

Belgium, unlike most other European countries, had no previous experience of Islam, even in the colonial period. Only in the 1960s, with the arrival of an increasing number of Muslim immigrants, did Belgian society come face to face with this religion.[1] These immigrants came mainly from Turkey and Morocco.[2] As in the Netherlands, in the course of time Muslim institutions emerged in Belgium. In this process of institutionalization, and the reactions to it, particularly by the authorities, three periods can be roughly distinguished.

The first period runs up to 1974. The 'new' religion only really became visible with the opening of the Islamic and Cultural Centre (ICC) in Brussels in 1969; this is often regarded as the first step towards the recognition of Islam in Belgium.[3] However, legal recognition, or the granting of equality with other religions which were already recognized, only took place in 1974 (Blaise & De Coorebyter 1990: 29).

This formal recognition ushered in the second period, which lasted till the end of the 1980s. The number of places of worship grew, and Islamic religious instruction was introduced in education. With financial support from the government several imams were appointed for the spiritual care of Muslims held in penal institutions. In public cemeteries in Liège and Farciennes space was made available for burials according to the Islamic rite.[4] In other areas, however, efforts towards institutionalization were frustrated. The ICC played a key

---

[1] In the 1950s there were only about 10 Muslims living in Belgium, most of them students. In 1992 the number of Muslims in Belgium was estimated at 250,000 (Leman *et al.* 1992a: 44).

[2] These are also the countries with which Belgium signed recruitment agreements in 1964 and 1965 respectively (Dassetto 1990: 15).

[3] Cf. Dassetto & Bastenier 1985: 3.

[4] See Commissie-Hirsch Ballin 1988: 190; Dassetto 1990: 20; Tamarant & Omar 1990: 4; Leman *et al.* 1992a: 56, 71–72.

role in the whole process and had a monopoly of contacts with the government, a development which had negative consequences, resulting in a number of missed opportunities.[5] For a long time Islam did not exist on genuinely equal terms.

In the mid-1980s broad sections of the population became aware of the presence of Islam. Extreme right-wing parties which saw their support growing, and several politicians of the established parties, made the 'battle against integrism' a major political issue. In the media they labelled each manifestation of Islam as either 'Khomenism' or 'integrism'.[6] Events such as the demonstrations against the American bombing of Tripoli and Benghazi in 1986, and the Rushdie affair three years later, kept Islam in the centre of public as well as media attention.[7]

The third period started at the end of the 1980s. A series of events—the opening of a Muslim school, disputes about the wearing of headscarves in school, and the legal enforcement by parents in Schaarbeek and Sint-Gillis (in the Brussels area) of the provision of Islamic religious instruction—led to a wide political and social debate about the place of Islam in Belgian society.[8] From that time onwards the Belgian authorities, particularly the Royal Commission on Migrants Policy set up in 1988,[9] were actively involved in the organization of Islamic worship, and the ICC lost its monopoly position. These developments culminated in a provisional recognition of an Executive of Muslims in Belgium in the autumn of 1994 (Leman & Renaerts 1996: 176). Whether this recognition will result in real equality for Islam is still an open question.

---

[5] Cf. Dassetto & Bastenier 1985: 14; Leman *et al.* 1992a: 49–52.

[6] Dassetto 1991: 14–15; cf. Luyten 1992: 14; Leman & Renaerts 1996.

[7] Cf. Dassetto 1991; Leman & Renaerts 1996.

[8] See, *inter alia*, Blaise & De Coorebyter 1990; Dassetto 1991: 18–19.

[9] The Royal Commission on Migrants Policy was set up after the October 1988 municipal elections, which were marked by a substantial gain in votes by the extreme right, particularly in Flanders. The Royal Commission was charged with research into the immigrant problem and with making proposals for essential measures. Although the Royal Commission has no special competence to deal with religious affairs, it has also made a number of concrete recommendations for setting up a representative body and for dealing with the associated problems. In the opinion of Leman *et al.* (1992a: 53) this was in fact one of the important items on the Royal Commission's agenda.

Recognition of Islam and of Muslims as partners in the political debate

Towards recognition

Belgian Muslims had attempted to organize themselves politically and gain recognition since the 1960s. The situation in Belgium is organized rather differently from elsewhere in Europe. On the strength of current legislation the Belgian government is able to give formal recognition to a religion with a single stroke of a pen. After that an Act of Parliament or Royal Decree can set up a committee to supervise the property used for worship, which acts as the official channel of communication with the authorities. Next local religious committees can request official recognition by Royal Decree, for which the criteria to be applied by the authorities are not laid down in law and can vary,[10] so there is scope for political and ideological manoeuvring.

Recognition brings a number of advantages for the religious communities in question. The government provides the person administering the religious rites not only with a salary but also with accommodation. The community also qualifies for consideration for subsidies for part of the cost of buying, building or converting places of worship, for favourable fiscal treatment, and for free postage. In addition, state and municipal schools are obliged to offer instruction in the religion of the recognized community. The necessary staff qualified to teach religion are appointed on the advice of a recognized representative and paid by the government.[11]

The thought lying behind this far-reaching government involvement, with its considerable financial commitment, is that worship represents a social and moral interest and so makes a contribution to the general interest (Commissie-Hirsch Ballin 1988: 144–145). According to the law, involvement should be limited to 'temporal' aspects of the religion: the authorities should not intervene in matters concerning the content of its practice. Articles 14, 15 and 16 of the Belgian Constitution guarantee freedom in the practice of religion and of religious organization (Leman *et al.* 1992b: 46).

---

[10] Cf. Commissie-Hirsch Ballin 1988: 143–146; Blaise & De Coorebyter 1990: 21 ff.

[11] See Roovers & Van Esch 1987: 107; Blaise & De Coorebyter 1990: 24–25; Leman *et al.* 1992b: 46–47.

However, in reality this is sometimes not so straightforward, as the process of the recognition of Islam shows.

A first step in this direction was taken in 1968. By Royal Decree of 16 May that year the Islamic and Cultural Centre (ICC) acquired the Oriental Pavilion in the Brussels Parc du Cinquantenaire for its use for a period of 99 years. This complex would serve as place of worship, cultural centre and co-ordination point for mosques (Dassetto & Bastenier 1985: 3). The ICC initiative did not originate from local Muslim communities, but from the official representatives of 'Islamic' countries, who were also represented in its management.[12] The Centre maintained particularly close links with Saudi Arabia.[13] From the late 1960s onwards the ICC had a monopoly of contacts with the Belgian government, and the Ministry of Justice consulted the ICC's Imam-Director, Alouini, about the formal recognition of Islam.[14]

It would nevertheless be several years before this recognition acquired a legal basis. Smet, Heylen and Vandewiele of the Christian People's Party (CVP) tabled a first bill in 1971. The initiative ran aground when parliament was dissolved. Three years and several bills later, Islam was given equality with other recognized religions with unanimous parliamentary support, and legal recognition followed in mid-1974.[15] This prescribed that supervision of the Islamic rite should be organized in the same way as for the other recognized religions, but on a provincial basis. This last aspect was unusual; the organization of other recognized religions was conducted at a municipal level. The consequence of this deviation from the rules was that Muslim supervision committees had to be set up at the provincial level and at the cost of the provincial authorities.

This specific form of organization for the Islamic rite was the result of a recommendation by Alouini, the Imam-Director of the

---

[12] The first elected management council consisted of four ambassadors: those of Saudi Arabia (chairman), Morocco (general secretary), Pakistan (treasurer) and Senegal (vice-chairman). Day-to-day management was in the hands of a director who acted in the name of the Islamic World League (Tamarant & Omar 1990. 3 4; see also Roovers & Van Esch 1987: 102).

[13] For instance, on 13 June 1969 King Faysal accepted the keys of the Oriental Pavillion from the Belgian Minister of Justice, Wigny (Dassetto 1990; Leman *et al.* 1992a: 50).

[14] Cf. Dassetto & Bastenier 1985: 4; Tamarant & Omar 1990: 4.

[15] Act of 19 July 1974 covering recognition of the bodies charged with control of the temporal aspects of Islamic worship (*Belgisch Staatsblad*, 23 August 1974; see also Blaise & De Coorebyter 1990: 25–29; Tamarant & Omar 1990: 4–5).

ICC. The reasons behind it are not entirely plain. The literature gives the impression that the ICC, which was orthodox and Saudi-oriented, thought that this would better enable it to retain its hold on the Muslim community. Other Muslim variants, particularly those from Turkey and Morocco, were much stronger in some local communities.[16]

It is also far from clear why the Belgian government chose to grant recognition in 1974. Several reports from the Justice Commission referred to the number of people—around 100,000—who were thought to be Muslims and to the increasingly permanent nature of their residence in Belgium. Humanitarian arguments also played a role: recognition of Islam would offer Muslims the opportunity of feeling better integrated into Belgian society.[17] According to Foblets (1991: 92), recognition could also have served as political compensation for the general ban on immigration imposed by the Belgian government in 1974. Moreover, this change in the law was 'coincidentally' simultaneous with the first oil crisis and with commercial negotiations between the Belgian government and various oil-producing countries, including Saudi Arabia. Dassetto and Bastenier (1985: 12) suggested that the Belgian state, by its recognition of Islam and the role assigned to the ICC, assured itself of 'a permanent religious supervision of the popular masses successively transplanted into the country'. In their view recognition had little to do with any such aim as 'the integration of Muslim immigrants'. Be that as it may, the Islamic religion was formally recognized in 1974 and placed on an equal footing with the Roman Catholic, Jewish, Protestant and Anglican religions.

De facto *recognition of the Islamic and Cultural Centre*

In 1975 a circular from the Ministers of Education indicated the Imam-Director of the ICC as the person to whom applications for the appointment of teaching staff for Islamic religious instruction should be directed (Foblets 1991: 93). In addition, supplementary legislation assigned an important role to the ICC in the further proceedings for the legal recognition of Islam. In 1978 a Royal Decree was issued in which the principle of provincial organization was

---

[16] See, *inter alia*, Tamarant & Omar 1990; Dassetto 1990: 18–19; Leman *et al.* 1992a: 52.

[17] Cf. Dassetto & Bastenier 1985: 3–4; Blaise & De Coorebyter 1990: 26.

developed.[18] The first elections for the provincial committees which had official recognition were to take place under the auspices of the ICC. In January 1981 an Act followed, regulating the salaries of ministers of the Islamic religion.[19] In an arrangement analogous to that for the Protestants, a hierarchic distinction was made between Imam, Chief Imam, and the Imam-Director of the ICC (Dassetto & Bastenier 1985: 6). There was in fact no legal basis for the *de facto* recognition of the ICC as the exclusive spokesman for Islam in discussions with the Belgian government.

The monopoly position of the ICC soon aroused strong opposition among the overwhelmingly Turkish and Moroccan local Muslim communities. The political authorities in the countries supporting the ICC had the reputation of being mainly conservative (Billiet & Dobbelaere 1976: 21). Moreover, in the eyes of many Muslims the centre represented the 'Islam of the powerful' (Bastenier 1988: 40). Countermovements emerged, such as the Association for Islamic Culture and Religion, the Committee for Religion in Belgium, the Islamic Federation, and the Turkish Islamic Federation, each of which in their own way tried to undermine the position of the ICC. However, they were unable to achieve much success.[20]

The Belgian authorities, too, were not entirely in agreement regarding the *de facto* recognition of the ICC as the representative body. Though the Ministry of Education recognized the Centre as the authorized institution for Islamic religious instruction, the religions department of the Ministry of Justice did not go so far, and even denied the ICC a subsidy. In their view recognition would only be possible if elections were held for councils which could then act as representative bodies which would represent all the nationalities and Muslim variations presently in Belgium (Tamarant & Omar 1990: 7). Two municipal authorities in Brussels also questioned the official recognition of the ICC and refused to organize Islamic religious instruction.[21]

In the 1980s various attempts were made to achieve a representative body for the Islamic religion.[22] In 1983 elections were organized

---

[18] Royal Decree of 3 May 1978, setting up committees charged with control of the temporal aspects of recognized Muslim communities (*Belgisch Staatsblad*, 6 May 1978).
[19] For the regulation of salaries see Tamarant & Omar 1990: 6.
[20] Cf. Dassetto & Bastenier 1985: 15–17; Roovers & Van Esch 1987: 102.
[21] See the section on 'Islamic religious instruction' in this chapter.
[22] Cf. Blaise & De Coorebyter 1990: 35; Leman *et al.* 1992a: 52.

to set up an Interlocutory Committee of Civil Authorities, which was not, however, recognized by the Belgian government. Two years later the Minister of Justice, Gol, submitted a draft decree for the establishment of a High Council of Muslims of Belgium to the Council of State, which decided that there were no grounds for the draft in the 1870 law on the temporal aspects of worship, at which point the draft was withdrawn.

In the summer of 1986 the ICC itself took an initiative in setting up a council. However, it was not democratically constituted, nor was it representative of all Muslims in Belgium. It was an 'improvised transitional council' consisting of the five ambassadors of Morocco, Turkey, Pakistan, Senegal and Saudi Arabia, three representatives of the Islamic World League, and four imams of Turkish and Moroccan origin (Tamarant & Omar 1990: 7). Again the Ministry of Justice did not recognize the council, and the impasse continued.

ICC initiatives and active government involvement

The High Council for Muslims in Belgium
In 1989 the issue came to the forefront again. The new Imam-Director, Radhi, took several steps immediately on his appointment which earned the ICC a great deal of publicity. As well as setting up a Muslim school in Brussels, Radhi took the initiative of setting up a High Council for Muslims in Belgium. In September, at a meeting of representatives of Belgian mosques and other Muslims, a Committee to Prepare Elections for the High Council was assembled. It consisted of 13 members: four Moroccans and four Turks, chosen during the meeting; two members of the ICC, one of them the Imam-Director; and three Muslims of Belgian origin. The Committee would stand down as soon as the High Council was set up.[23] In late October a deputation from this Committee met with the Royal Commission on Migrants Policy and administrators from the religions department of the Ministry of Justice. According to the members of the deputation, the Royal Commission indicated that it was in favour of the elections for the High Council 'having a fundamentally religious character, being carried out in a peaceful manner, with as little publicity in the media or politicizing as possible, and on the basis

---

[23] *Islamitische Nieuwsbrief* 2 (1990) 5: 9–10.

of the Royal Decree of 3 May 1978'. In addition the registration of electors should take place by January 1990 at the latest.[24]

Shortly after this, however, the Premier (at the request of the Brussels District Executive) announced the convening of an 'inter-ministerial conference' to discuss the official representation of Islam in Belgium (Blaise & De Coorebyter 1990: 17). Almost by return of post the Royal Commissioner on Migrants Policy, D'Hondt, produced a first report, recommending the government to set up a High Council of Belgian Muslims, which should consist of elected representatives of mosques and of co-opted members (KCM 1989: 394).

Reactions to the recommendation varied. The Brussels District Executive rejected D'Hondt's proposal (Blaise & De Coorebyter 1990: 18), while the ICC reacted with delight:

> ... our hopes that there should be an end to the untenable situation in which the Islamic and Cultural Centre has found itself since its inception have been answered. It should be remarked that the ICC, in consultation with the Commission, has itself made proposals for democratic elections based on mosques.[25]

In December 1989 the ICC invited representatives of various mosques to a meeting to discuss the organization of elections for the High Council. The Royal Commision reacted more cautiously than before and indicated that neither the Commission nor the government had given the ICC a mandate. They also made reference to the decision of the interdepartmental conference to set up a working party to address the representation of Muslims, and therefore thought it premature to start organizing elections (Blaise & De Coorebyter 1990: 17–18). In spite of this the Committee to Prepare Elections for the High Council organized three information sessions in which representatives of more than 120 Arabic and Turkish mosques expressed agreement with the aims and the realization of the proposed council.[26] Just before the new year the Imam-Director of the ICC confirmed that he was ready to organize open elections, to which he added that this involved purely religious matters, which as such did not concern the government (Blaise & De Coorebyter 1990: 18). The

---

[24] According to an account of an internal memorandum of the Commission in the same *Islamitische Nieuwsbrief*.

[25] *Islamitische Nieuwsbrief* 1 (1989) 4: 37.

[26] *Islamitische Nieuwsbrief* 2 (1990) 5: 9.

elections were originally planned for mid-January 1990, but were
then postponed 'in a spirit of consultation'.[27]

Two months later the Minister of Justice, Wathelet, officially informed the Imam-Director that the government thought it premature to organize elections and that Belgium would in no way consider
itself bound by their results. In spite of this, the Committee to Prepare
Elections decided to put its plans into action. All Muslims of 18
years and above with Belgian nationality, or who had lived in Belgium
for at least one year, were invited to register as voters. Altogether
more than 30,000 potential voters responded.[28]

In March there was a meeting between Imam-Director Radhi and
Minister Wathelet.[29] The Minister explained the Belgian government's
point of view, which only led to a hardening of positions. Wathelet
even asked for the election process to be halted. After a further appeal for voters by the preparatory Committee, the government repeated
its request in a formal letter. They suggested instead that Radhi
should become a member of a Provisional Council of Wise Men,
consisting of 17 individuals, three of them representatives of the ICC.
This council would be charged with formulating proposals for the
organization of the Islamic religion. Radhi was not interested, arguing that the government should not interfere in religious affairs.

The Provisional Council of Wise Men
The Council of Ministers took little notice of this and established the
Provisional Council in July 1990. Six months later the Minister of
Justice received a first report, with proposals for the way in which
the representation of Islam in Belgium should be arranged. A sec-
ond report appeared in November 1991. Most of the Turkish mosques
managed by the Diyanet supported the proposals. Mosques of other
Turkish persuasions, such as the Milli Görüş, were not consulted.
The proposals were rejected almost everywhere by the Moroccans
(Leman *et al.* 1992a: 54).

On a proposal by the Provisional Council it was also decided to
set up a Technical Committee for the appointment of teaching staff

---

[27] *Islamitische Nieuwsbrief* 2 (1990) 5: 10.

[28] Blaise and De Coorebyter (1990: 18) considered this a remarkably high figure,
in view of the appeal by the Turkish and Moroccan Embassies for the elections to
be boycotted.

[29] On this issue and its consequences see Blaise & De Coorebyter 1990: 18–19;
Leman & Renaerts 1996: 173.

for Islamic religious instruction.[30] This deprived the ICC of its function as the only official mouthpiece and representative of Islam in Belgium.[31]

Meanwhile the ICC had gone ahead and held elections for a General Council for Muslims in Belgium, which in its turn chose a High Council.[32] However, this was not recognized by the Belgian authorities. Moreover, a boycott of the elections by the Turkish Embassy meant that no adherents of the Diyanet were represented. Turkish participation in the Council consisted predominantly of members of the Milli Görüş (Leman 1992: 13).

In the autumn of 1992 the Provisional Council of Wise Men was disbanded because its task—the formulation of recommendations—had been completed, and negotiations with the various Muslim communities had reached an impasse (Leman *et al.* 1992a: 55).[33] This could be put down to the lack of credibility and legitimacy in the Muslim communities of the members of the Provisional Council, together with the attempts by some of them to project themselves as 'pseudo-head of the religion' (ibid.: 54). After it was disbanded, negotiations continued within the Muslim communities to achieve a compromise as quickly as possible, and to create a solution to the problem of a representative body (ibid.: 55).

The Executive of Muslims in Belgium

In the spring of 1994 the High Council for Muslims in Belgium requested Minister of Justice Wathelet to recognize an Executive of Muslims in Belgium. Six months later he replied that he was prepared to accept 16 of the proposed members of the Executive as official spokesmen. He requested that one seat should be reserved

---

[30] See also the section on 'Islamic religious instruction' in this chapter.

[31] See Leman *et al.* 1992a: 54 and 58. Otherwise the Islamic and Cultural Centre retained its position as the representative authority in a number of other areas, such as the spiritual care of Muslims in penal institutions and the granting of slaughter licences (ibid.: 68, 71; ibid. 1992b: 51–52).

[32] Van den Broeck (1992: 21) states that the elected General Council for Muslims in Belgium consisted of 43 Moroccan, 25 Turkish and 10 Belgian Muslims, with 11 Muslims of other nationalities. The High Council for Muslims in Belgium consisted of 7 Moroccans, 4 Turks, 3 Muslims of other nationalities, one representative of the Islamic and Cultural Centre and two co-opted members. The High Council was chaired by one of the co-opted members.

[33] Van den Broeck (1992: 21) remarks that the government dropped the Provisional Council 'like a hot brick'.

for someone of Turkish origin, who would be independent of '*mouve-ments opposés*'.[34] The composition also needed to comply with 'our democracy and with the rules and customs of our constitutional state'; in no case could anyone be accepted who was not willing to adhere to these principles. Recognition of the Executive was for the moment of a temporary nature: for a period of a single year. Moreover, its powers were limited to such matters as the appointment of teaching staff for Islamic religious instruction, and of imams for the spiritual care of Muslims in hospitals and penal institutions (Leman & Renaerts 1996: 176).

Until the year of the temporary recognition of the Executive, the active participation of Muslims in local and regional councils had been very limited. Moreover, Muslims who were not of Belgian nationality had no right to vote in national or local elections. 1994 marked the beginning of a cautious change in active participation, when for the first time a number of individuals with a Muslim background were elected to several municipal councils.

Places of worship

The first Muslim places of worship in Belgium date from the 1960s. From then on their numbers increased rapidly. They are often located in old workshops, stores or former dwelling houses.[35] In the period 1970–1981 their number increased tenfold and in 1990 Belgium had 209 Muslim places of worship and mosques (Bastenier 1988: 135). Most of them were organized as non-profit-making associations. Their activities consisted mainly of worship and teaching the Koran. However, in the course of time several mosques widened their provision to include socio-cultural activities such as discussion evenings, educational opportunities for women and children, social services and sporting activities (Leman *et al.* 1992a: 65–66).

Apart from the rules for building permits and safety regulations, there is no specific legislation in Belgium affecting the establishment of places of worship. A Mayor can close a building if he thinks it is not suitable for certain activities, but there are no clear guidelines

[34] Letter from Minister Wathelet to the proposed members of the Executive, dated 27 October 1994.
[35] See, *inter alia*, Dassetto 1990: 20; Van Oers 1992: 6.

for this. The general criteria of public order, health, and safety leave room for diverse interpretations. As head of the police, the Mayor can prescribe municipal regulations. Policy on mosques is therefore in practice a matter for the local authorities, who take a variety of attitudes. For instance, in 1988 a planning application by the Moroccan community in Antwerp was rejected because there were plans for a place of worship in the proposed cultural centre. The Mayor of Antwerp, Cools, thought that 18 mosques in the city was sufficient. In other municipalities, such as Schaarbeek and Beringen, mosques could only be used as a place of worship and not as a social or cultural centre (ibid.).

Most of the Muslim places of worship were financed by money collected among the faithful, sometimes supported by the local Catholic clergy or the management of a local factory. Several mosques were built with the help of local reception centres, community centres and action groups, such as those in Hoboken and Borgerhout in 1966 (Van Oers 1992: 6). Only the accommodation of the Great Mosque in Brussels in the buildings of the Islamic and Cultural Centre was allocated by the national authorities in the 1968 Royal Decree mentioned earlier. Although Muslims, by reason of the recognition of Islam in 1974, have the right to partial subsidy for the purchase, building or conversion of places of worship, none of the Muslim communities has as yet received any financial support. Nor has the Belgian government paid out any salaries or pensions to the spiritual leaders of the Islamic religion (Leman *et al.* 1992a: 49, 64). The reasons for this are the problems described earlier of setting up and recognizing a representative body.

Islamic religious instruction

Legislation

The Belgian education system recognizes public education organized by the authorities (linguistic communities, provinces or municipalities) and subsidized 'free' education or private schools. Education provided by the state has to be neutral, a criterion which proceeds from the principle of the separation of church and state. There is an unequivocal obligation in the Constitution for the government to provide neutral education, and within it, to organize instruction on religion and/or non-confessional ethical teaching. However, there are limitations on this obligation: instruction must be provided only in those religions recognized by the state at government expense, whenever a parent of a child of school age requests it (Foblets 1991: 90).

Private schools are authorized to offer a single religion, for example instruction in just the Catholic religion. If a Catholic school wants to offer instruction in Islam as well as in Catholicism, then with regard to paying its teaching staff, it comes under the same regulations as public or state education (Roovers & Van Esch 1987: 114).

The introduction of instruction in the Islamic religion was made possible by the recognition of that religion in 1974. Four years later, by an Act of 20 February 1978, this right was formally confirmed by an amendment to Article 8 of the School Pact Act of 29 May 1959. The Islamic religion was then added to the four religions recognized earlier: Roman Catholic, Protestant, Anglican, and Jewish. All schools organized by the state are obliged to devote at least two hours a week to instruction in religion or non-confessional ethics. When a child is registered, the head of the family has to sign a declaration giving his choice of religious instruction (and which religion) or the course in ethics. The law also lays down that the head of the family must be left to make an entirely free choice, and that 'it is strictly forbidden to exercise any pressure on him in this respect'.[36]

The appointment of teaching staff is regulated by Article 9 of the School Pact Act, as is the inspection of religious instruction. The instruction concerned must be given by 'ministers of the religion, or their representatives, who are appointed by the governing body on the recommendation of the head of the religion concerned'.[37] Hence the appointment of teachers of religion is on the recommendation of the head of that religion. This also applies to the inspection of the religious instruction.

Practical results

Instruction in the Islamic religion goes back quite some time in Belgium. Even before 1974 there were municipalities in which such classes were provided (Van Loock 1989: 13), but the national govern-

---

[36] Act of 20 February 1978 containing amendments of Article 8 of the Act of 29 May 1959 with regard to the School Pact (*Belgisch Staatsblad*, 11 March 1978).

[37] Act of 29 May 1959 to amend some provisions of the legislation on education (*Belgisch Staatsblad*, 19 June 1959).

ment first took steps to ensure that instruction in the Islamic religion
was available in 1975. Anticipating the changes to the legislation on
education, the Ministers of Education Humblet (Francophone) and
De Croo (Dutch language) sent a circular to head teachers, asking
them to offer a course in Islamic religion and ethics to children
whose parents requested this, starting the next school year (Blaise &
De Coorebyter 1990: 39–40). There followed a period of experimen-
tation. The circular did not mean that the Belgian government was
particularly anxious to organize this instruction; it was simply a consequence of the Belgian legislation. The Director of the Centre for
Equal Opportunities and the struggle against Racism[38] called these
religious instruction classes 'the holy cow' of Belgian education:

> It is an ideological compromise that everyone should have the right
> to religious instruction in the official curriculum. This is one of the
> most onerous obligations imposed by the state. (...) even some Catholic
> schools, which are not obliged to teach Islamic religion, do so. Why?
> Because here it is so much a matter of common sense that a child
> should be allowed to follow his own life-philosophy, and every phi-
> losophy agrees with that.

From 1975 onwards Islamic religious instruction increased steadily
in Belgian schools. In the 1988–1989 school year 23,162 children in
primary schools took these lessons, and in secondary education 12,569.
In all, 453 staff were appointed in both types of schools (Tamarant
1989: 42). In spite of this increase a great number of practical problems arose, closely associated with the lack of an officially recognized
head of the Islamic religion, which had its repercussions on the
appointment of teaching staff.

The circular mentioned above referred to the Islamic and Cultural
Centre (ICC) as the chief religious authority of the Islamic religion
in Belgium. All applications for the appointment of teaching staff for
Islamic religious instruction had to be referred to the Imam-Director
(Foblets 1991: 93). In 1981 the ICC, with financial support from
the Islamic World League, set up an educational secretariat, which
was charged with various administrative and pedagogic tasks: recruiting teaching staff; development of a curriculum for Islamic religious
instruction in primary, secondary and technical schools; publication

---

[38] This Centre is the successor to the Royal Commission on Immigrants Policy.
The current Director of the Centre for Equal Opportunities and the struggle against
Racism was formerly the *chef de cabinet* of the Royal Commission.

of text books; training teaching staff; and organizing pedagogic con-
ferences (Dassetto & Bastenier 1985: 10–11). From 1975 to 1990 the
ICC appointed Turkish and Moroccan teachers, though not without
the inevitable problems.

Moroccan teachers were mainly recruited from students and teaching staff in the Muslim community in Belgium; Turkish teachers
were recruited from Turkey for a period of four or five years through
the Turkish Embassy. Problems arose among this last group after
1982: several teaching staff protested against the appointments policy and authority of the Turkish Embassy. They were joined in their
opposition by a number of Moroccan teaching staff. Nevertheless the
Turkish Embassy applied so much pressure that Turkish teaching
staff continued to be recruited from Turkey. In June 1989 17 teaching staff broke with the ICC and set up the Association of Islamic
Teachers in Flanders (Souissy 1993: 25). The ICC also came up
against opposition from other quarters.

Three years earlier the Brussels municipalities of Sint-Gillis and
Schaarbeek had refused to organize Islamic religious instruction
because there was no competent authority to appoint teaching staff.
Both municipalities questioned the legitimacy and unofficial recognition of the ICC (Blaise & De Coorebyter 1990: 15). Some 20
Muslim parents of children in Schaarbeek municipal schools refused
to accept this and in October 1989 started proceedings against the
local authority. They demanded the immediate introduction of Islamic
religious instruction in their children's schools, invoking the constitutional principle of freedom of religion and the European Convention
on Human Rights (ibid.). The court allowed their demand, referring
among other things to the current situation in other municipal schools
where Islamic religious instruction had effectively been introduced
and the local authorities had complied with the constitutional requirements. A case was also brought against the Sint-Gillis municipality,
with a similar result (Foblets 1991: 90).

The same year D'Hondt was appointed Royal Commissioner on
Migrants Policy. She immediately started informal consultations with
the Association of Islamic Teachers in Flanders, which recommended
that the appointment of religious teaching staff be entrusted to an
independent democratic organization; that fixed rules be laid down
for the staff involved; and that within a period of two years an
inspectorate be set up at the provincial level with democratically
elected staff (Souissy 1993: 25).

In November 1989 the Royal Commission put forward proposals for setting up a representative body for the Islamic religion.[39] It was considered advisable that this body be elected and recognized before the end of the 1989–1990 school year, 'so that the appointment of teaching staff for Islamic religious instruction could be made before the start of the 1990–1991 school year' (KCM 1989: 395). At first the ICC was enthusiastic about the proposal; the Centre hoped that by this means an end would finally be made of the 'unsound situation in which Islamic education found itself'.[40] In practice things did not turn out as expected. In the summer of 1990 the Provisional Council of Wise Men was established, separate from the ICC. On its recommendation it was decided at the same time to recognize a Technical Committee, which should effect the appointment, or confirmation, of teaching staff for the 1990–1991 school year (Leman *et al.* 1992a: 58). With the appointment of this Committee, the ICC lost its powers of appointment of religious teaching staff. In fact, in taking this route, the government was interfering in the organization of the Islamic religion, since officially only the head of a religion had the power to propose religious teachers. For this reason Radhi, the Imam-Director, addressed a letter to the Ministers involved, asking what specific measures they proposed to take to 'prevent disarray at the start of the school year',[41] and also pressed for consultation with the ICC. In a press release the *Islamitische Nieuwsbrief*[42] reacted as follows to the Technical Committee's proposals:

> Freedom of education is a constitutional right in this country. It behoves us that policy does not trespass on the territory of the religious communities. The larger communities would not accept anything else. The measure currently being introduced as the procedure for nominating/ appointing teachers of Islamic religious instruction applies double standards. The policy trespasses to an extent on the territory of the religious community and the secretariat recognized *de facto* for that purpose within this community, without the least consultation of those involved and apparently without urgent reason. In this way the constitutional

---

[39] See the second section of this chapter.
[40] *Islamitische Nieuwsbrief* 1 (1989) 4: 37.
[41] *Islamitische Nieuwsbrief* 2 (1990) 7: 21.
[42] The *Islamitische Nieuwsbrief* is an independent non-profit-making association, which receives no financial support from the ICC and is anxious to emphasize its independent operation. Admittedly one of the chief editors of the *Islamitische Nieuwsbrief* is a member of the ICC staff.

order is being unnecessarily compromised. We expect, certainly at the policy level, a more cautious approach, grounded in democracy.[43]

This criticism did not prevent the establishment of the first Technical Committee, consisting of four delegates from the Provisional Council of Wise Men, and six teachers of Islamic religious instruction (KCM 1990: 67–68). In June 1991 the Interministerial Conference on Migrants Policy decided that the Committee should also be charged with the appointment or reappointment of teachers of Islamic religion for the 1991–1992 school year. The complaints soon began to pour in. The Committee was alleged to have left requests for teaching staff unanswered for months. In the spring of 1992 the activities of the Committee were suspended, and six months later the MP Sleeckx of the Socialist Party (SP) asked in parliament for the state of affairs to be clarified. The upshot was that, again with the aid of the Royal Commission, a new Committee was set up with similar tasks to those of the first. Its remit was once again limited to a single school year (1992–1993) (Leman *et al.* 1992a: 59).[44]

At a study day on Islamic religious instruction in Flanders in June 1993, the chairman of the Association of Turkish Islamic Religious Teachers in Belgium, Özkan, complained that the second Committee was not working correctly either. It was appointing teachers not for their pedagogic and theological competence, but acting on 'a political basis'.[45] Moreover, teachers were being appointed—some of them unqualified—without reference to the Committee. One of the members of the Committee admitted that not everything was going as it should, mainly due to a lack of resources and powers. The Committee was saddled with volunteers working alongside their full-time occupation, so that it could not get to know the teaching staff it was appointing or reappointing (Janssen 1993: 35).

At the end of 1994 the Executive of Muslims in Belgium—the provisional contact body between Muslims and the government— replaced the Technical Committee. Its powers were, however, limited to the nomination of teachers. Many other matters were left with little or

---

[43] Press release from the *Islamitische Nieuwsbrief* concerning Islamic education in Flanders (*Islamitische Nieuwsbrief* 2 (1990) 7: 21).

[44] Cf. *Islamitische Nieuwsbrief* 4 (1992–1993) 16/17: 26–27.

[45] See paper issued by the Association of Turkish Islamic Religious Teachers in Belgium for the workshop in Hasselt, dated 16 June 1993, p. 2.

no regulation, such as training courses for Islamic religious teachers, establishing a curriculum, questions regarding residence and work permits, and the inspection of education.[46]

The Muslim school

Legislation

The establishment of a private school, subsidized by the state, is possible in Belgium by reference to the School Pact Act of 29 May 1959, provided a number of conditions are satisfied. These are laid down in Article 24.2, and involve the organization of the teaching, the curriculum, acceptance of inspection, the number of pupils, teaching resources, and the qualifications of the teaching staff. In addition the premises must satisfy health and hygiene requirements. The education inspectorate checks whether all the legal requirements are satisfied, after which a subsidy is granted. Conversely, if a school no longer complies with all the requirements, the subsidy can be withdrawn (Article 24.3). The funds made available are intended for the salaries of the teaching staff and allowances for running costs and equipment. Those founding the school are themselves responsible for providing the actual accommodation.[47]

The Al Ghazali school in Brussels

The first and so far the only school in Belgium based on Islamic principles is the Al Ghazali school in Brussels. This Francophone school was set up on the initiative of the Islamic and Cultural Centre (ICC) and particularly of Radhi, its Imam-Director, who took up his post at a difficult period for the ICC,[48] and was resolved to fight resolutely for the rights of Muslims in Belgium within the framework

---

[46] See, inter alia, Leman et al. 1992a: 56–60; Janssen 1993; Karagül 1994: 147 150; Limburgs Mozaïek 4 (1995) 33: 2–4; Demirci 1995: 385–387.

[47] Act of 29 May 1959 amending some provisions of the legislation on education (Belgisch Staatsblad, 19 June 1959).

[48] His predecessor, Al Ahdal, together with a colleague, was murdered in 1989 in the Great Mosque. The Organization of Soldiers of the Law in Lebanon claimed responsibility for the murders, which were probably connected with the moderate attitude adopted by Al Ahdal during the Rushdie affair (Dassetto 1991: 16; Van den Broeck 1992: 20).

of the law. The establishment of a Muslim school was one of his most important objectives.[49]

Apart from the Director of the ICC, parents had been campaigning for the opening of the school. An important motive was their wish to give their children an education which would contribute to 'a cultural and religious formation of their personality in the spirit of Islam' (Leman *et al.* 1992a: 63). In addition the education currently available in the 'concentration schools' (schools with a high percentage of foreign children) was regarded as problematic. The parents hoped that a Muslim school would achieve two aims: strengthening their own identity and improving the quality of education.[50]

The application for recognition and subsidy for the school was submitted in August 1989 to Minister Grafé of Education for the Francophone Community. A month later the Al Ghazali school, in the absence of a proper school building, was set up in the ICC building in the Cinquantenaire Park in Brussels. After several visits by the inspectorate, recognition and subsidy followed.[51] Originally there were also plans for a Dutch-language school in Antwerp, but practical (financial) problems and the fear of hostile reactions caused this to be abandoned.[52]

The project to set up the school caused a certain amount of political upheaval. The application coincided with attempts by the Royal Commission on Migrants Policy to form a representative body for the Islamic religion. By its application the ICC thwarted this plan, 'for it would render impossible any calm discussion about the place of Islam' (Leman 1992: 12). According to Leman, a former *chef de cabinet* of the Royal Commision, Radhi was well aware of the situation, but gave priority to another interest, the restoration of a consensus within the Muslim community. And Leman thought that Radhi had been successful in that objective:

> However one judges the actions of Sheikh Sameer (Radhi), his actions in the affair of the Muslim school in Brussels and his "unofficial" elections have led to a greater collective awareness and increased homogeneity among the Muslims living in Belgium (ibid.: 13).

---

[49] Interview with a representative of the ICC. Cf. Dassetto 1991: 18–19; Leman 1992: 12–13.
[50] Interview with a representative of the ICC.
[51] Ibid.
[52] Ibid. Cf. *Het Volk De Nieuwe Gids*, 8 September 1989.

In the same year the school was set up, Radhi set in motion elections to the High Council for Muslims in Belgium. According to a representative of the ICC, this was the indirect reason for the Centre's loss of its status as the principal negotiator with the Belgian authorities, and of its power to organize Islamic religious instruction.

The debate about the Al Ghazali school

The arrival of the Muslim school also evoked considerable public debate.[53] On 24 August 1989 *Le Soir* announced the ICC's application in a brief report; nothing would now stand in the way of a Muslim school provided the application met all the requirements. This was also the position of the cabinet of Minister Grafé of Education (Social Christian Party, SCP), who from the start had indicated that there would be no political interference.[54] The application was within the competence of the education service, and that service alone could determine whether the legal requirements were met, and whether a subsidy should be granted.[55] The report in *Le Soir* was followed by a large number of reports, interviews, articles and letters about the approval of the Al Ghazali school.

The discussion soon took on the nature of a moral panic. The first reaction from the world of politics came on 29 August from Anciaux ([Flemish] People's Union, VU), the Secretary of State in the Brussels region responsible for the co-ordination of policy on migrants. He had written to the Imam-Director of the ICC to deter him from the idea of setting up a Muslim school, and the Belgian press had received a copy of his letter.[56] Anciaux recognized the right to found Muslim schools, but thought that such a school would be an obstacle to the desired integration. In his letter he demanded a meeting with the Imam-Director, which was in his view the only way of exercising sufficient pressure for the project to be abandoned. The next day the Royal Commissioner D'Hondt (Christian People's Party, CVP), announced in a BRT radio programme that she agreed

---

[53] For a summary of the coverage on the Al Ghazali School, see Blaise & De Coorebyter 1990.

[54] Cf. *Het Volk De Nieuwe Gids*, 25 August 1989.

[55] Cf. *De Financieel Ekonomische Tijd* and *Vers l'Avenir*, 25 August 1989; *De Morgen*, 2 September 1989.

[56] Among the papers in which this was published were *Het Belang van Limburg*, *Het Volk* and *Le Soir*, 29 August 1989.

with Anciaux's views. She wondered whether a religious leader who
had only been in Belgium a few months, spoke no Dutch or French,
and had very little familiarity with the situation in Belgium, was well
advised to take such an initiative. In her view it showed little sense
of responsibility. She also pointed out in *Het Nieuwsblad* (30 August
1989) that no comparison could be made with Jewish schools, because
the Belgians and the Jews had lived together for many centuries
before these schools were built, whereas in the case of the Muslim
school 'the problems of living together were yet to be solved'.

In September the spokesmen of social organizations and of other
political parties joined in the discussion.[57] MP Vogels of the Agalev
Ecology Party was not happy about the way Anciaux and D'Hondt
had reacted to the ICC's plans; the Imam-Director had meanwhile
replied in the negative to the request from the powers that be to
postpone setting up the school (*Het Volk De Nieuwe Gids*, 1 September
1989). The People's Union (VU), in a press release from their chairman, Gabriëls, reacted indignantly to the Imam-Director's answer to
Anciaux and D'Hondt: 'Both of them are anxious to encourage integration. The Imam's initiative is clearly a step in the opposite direction' (quoted in *De Morgen*, 1 September 1989). The People's Union
asked the Flemish and Francophone Community Ministers of Education
to join D'Hondt in taking steps to prevent the establishment of the
Muslim school in Brussels.

The issue was next discussed in a meeting of the Brussels government, which decided to take no steps, but to continue monitoring
the affair closely (*Het Laatste Nieuws*, 5 September 1989). The same
evening Picqué (Socialist Party, PS), chairman of the Brussels government and Mayor of Sint-Gillis, also explained on RTBF (the francophone media) that he would oppose the school with all the means
in his power.[58] In an ICC press conference, Radhi reacted to the
discussion which had arisen, and particularly to Picqué's statements,

> When Charles Picqué threatens 120 children that he will use *all the
> means in his power* to close their school, it is our view that he has lost
> all human feelings, all legal logic, and all civility and respect. His words
> make us realize that he is not concerned about the legal status of the

---

[57] See, *inter alia*, *De Morgen* and *Het Laatste Nieuws*, 2 September 1989.
[58] Cf. *De Standaard*, 8 September 1989.

school, but only about its closure by all possible means, including illegal ones.[59]

A few hours after this statement Picqué responded with a 'counter-press-conference'. He called Radhi's utterance plainly insulting and uncalled for: 'The position of power which the Islamic and Cultural Centre has arrogated to itself is completely unjustified.' He continued, 'I do not oppose freedom of religion, nor Islamic education, but I am against the power which has wrongfully been assigned to the Great Mosque' (quoted in *De Morgen*, 8 September 1989). This was the reason why Picqué also refused to allow Islamic religious instruction in schools in his municipality. In the *Gazet van Antwerpen* of the same day he announced that he was also against the opening of a Muslim school in principle. Moreover, he did not want to hold discusssions with anyone 'who was controlled by foreign embassies'.

The first politician from one of the traditional parties to speak out in favour of the Muslim school in Brussels was Sleeckx of the Socialist Party (SP), which until then had not taken part in the discussion. In *De Morgen* (9 September 1989) he said he was incensed by Picqué's statement and found Anciaux's and D'Hondt's arguments misplaced. After a meeting of his party leadership, the SP chairman, Vandenbroucke, expressed himself in much the same way in *Het Volk De Nieuwe Gids* (12 September 1989). He argued for consultation between Belgian and Muslim representatives, and thought that this should all have been done before any statements had been made.

On the other hand, the chairman of the Christian People's Party (CVP), Van Rompuy, was strongly opposed to the school. He announced in *Het Laatste Nieuws* (12 September 1989) that his party was working on a legal document to prevent the establishment of a Muslim education network. If no legal measures were possible, then there must at least be guarantees that Muslim schools would work towards integration. Dewinter (Flemish Block, VB) explained in a press conference the letter which he had sent in early September to around a 100 schools, appealing to them to boycott Islamic religious instruction for the time being. By doing so the extreme right-wing Flemish Block wished to protest against the Flemish community having no control over the manner in which this teaching took place

---

[59] Quoted in the *Islamitische Nieuwsbrief* 1 (1989) 3: 5; italics printed in bold in the original.

or who delivered it. Dewinter also proposed that recognition of the Islamic religion should be withdrawn, and finally he let it be known that he was opposed to the opening of a Muslim school in Brussels (*Het Belang van Limburg*, 21 September 1989).

Until mid-October, reports continued to appear in the press in which politicians or people working in immigrant organizations expressed their views on the opening of a Muslim school. On 19 October 1989 the Al Ghazali school organized an open day, and there was enormous press interest. After that everything went quiet round the school in the Cinquantenaire Park.

CHAPTER THIRTEEN

THE UNITED KINGDOM

A historical outline

The United Kingdom, unlike Belgium, has been familiar with Islam for centuries. The presence of Muslims in the country is closely linked to British expansion and to its colonial presence in the Indian sub-continent. More than three centuries ago the East India Company began recruiting seamen there, including Muslims. In the mid-nineteenth century such people were among the first Muslims to settle temporarily in the United Kingdom. After the opening of the Suez Canal in 1869, Muslim seamen from the Yemen and Somalia followed. Muslims also emigrated to the United Kingdom because of trade, and to follow higher education, and Muslim centres grew up, particularly in London, Liverpool and Woking. Towards the end of the nineteenth century the first mosques were built for these partly temporary, urban communities (Lewis 1994: 10–13).

From the 1950s onwards the nature of these Muslim communities changed with the arrival of an increasing number of labour migrants from the Indian subcontinent, particularly from what are now East and West Pakistan.[1] In the late 1960s their wives and children followed. With the settlement of these labour migrants and their families, more permanent Muslim communities gradually came into being, and the need for places of worship and religious instruction increased. Most of these communities are to be found in a number of English cities, such as London, Birmingham and Bradford (Nielsen 1992: 42).

As in the Netherlands, the presence of a growing number of Muslims and the process of institutionalization following in its wake remained more or less unnoticed by British society for a long time.

---

[1] In particular the prospect of the 1962 Commonwealth Immigrants Act—which put an end to the free entry of immigrants from the Commonwealth—created a sudden rise in the number of immigrants from the Indian subcontinent (Nielsen 1992: 39–40). In 1991 they made up more than 75 per cent of the total number of Muslims (1,000,000) in Great Britain (Peach & Glebe 1995: 34).

Only in a few areas, such as education, did Muslim initiatives occasionally attract the attention of the national authorities.[2] At the local level, on the other hand, the authorities frequently had to deal with initiatives to set up Muslim institutions. Local authorities reacted in a variety of ways; in some places Muslims met with co-operation, in others not.[3]

It was not until the 1980s that Islam appeared on the national political agenda. The number of claims for government support of Muslim schools increased. Demonstrations and school strikes in Bradford, with the object of achieving the introduction of *halâl* food for Muslim schoolchildren, and a publicity campaign against a certain headmaster, Honeyford, in the same area, attracted the attention of the media for months.[4] These events led not only to a national debate, but also to the involvement of the national government. The outcome of the protests was what Nielsen (1992: 58) called, 'the first major public campaigning victory of any Muslim community in Britain': Honeyford took early retirement. It was abundantly clear that Muslims wanted recognition of their religious identity.

In the late 1980s the Rushdie affair ushered in a new phase. Wide sections of the British populace then realized that a substantial group of Muslims had settled in their midst. The Muslims adopted a higher profile and advanced their claims openly.[5] This was particularly plain in two areas: requests for voluntary-aided status for Muslim schools, and the protection of Islam against blasphemy and discrimination.

Recognition of Islam and of Muslims as partners in the political debate

The legal position of Islam

Unlike the situation in Belgium, British legislation does not rest on the concept of formal recognition. Both England and Scotland have an established church. Its position is reflected, among other things, in the status of church law, in the procedure for appointment to

---

[2] To a large extent this is linked to the decentralized character of British government policy in many of the areas relevant to our subject; cf. Nielsen 1986: 6.

[3] See, *inter alia*, Nielsen 1986.

[4] On these issues see, *inter alia*, Kaye 1993: 237–238; Lewis 1994: 2, 149–153; see also the section on Islamic religious instruction in Bradford, later in this chapter.

[5] See, *inter alia*, Modood 1993: 513; Husbands 1994: 193–195.

high ecclesiastical offices, in the organization of the ecclesiastical courts, and in the representation of the church in the House of Lords. In addition the head of state is also the head of the church. Other religious communities have a separate, usually less privileged, status. There are special Acts of Parliament for the older Christian denominations and the Jews. The rest are free to function within the bounds of the law.[6]

In practice all kinds of arrangements made for the Church of England are also available to other denominations, although it is not explicitly stated. This applies, for instance, to the area of spiritual care (Commissie-Hirsch Ballin 1988: 39). Most legal provisions are, however, implicitly based on the Christian faith or Christian ethics, and can therefore sometimes hamper the free observance of the worship of other religions.[7] One of the few laws which applies exclusively to the Christian faith is the prohibition of blasphemy. This law only protects Christianity or the particular doctrines of the Church of England (Poulter 1990: 118-119). A possible amendment to this situation could be interpreted as a form of recognition of Islam.

In order to achieve this recognition, Muslims have been taking political action in a variety of ways. At first they limited their participation in politics to the local level, but this started to change in the 1990s.

The great majority of Muslim immigrants are British citizens and therefore enjoy active and passive suffrage in both local and national elections. And they make use of those rights, particularly at the local level.[8] The number of Muslims on Bradford's municipal council increased sharply in the 1980s: in 1981 three of the 90 councillors were Muslims, but by 1993 there were 12 (Le Lohé 1993: 536). According to Lewis (1994), the arrival of Muslims in the body politic has worked to the benefit of those Muslim organizations which made claims on specific provisions.

Recognition of co-ordinating bodies

Apart from participation in party politics, Muslims have engaged in political activity by taking their seats in bodies such as the Community

---

[6] See Commissie-Hirsch Ballin 1988: 168; Nielsen 1992: 43; Rath *et al.* 1993: 62.

[7] Cf. Poulter 1989: 124; Rath *et al.* 1993: 63; Shadid & Van Koningsveld 1995: 82.

[8] This active and passive suffrage is a consequence of the fact that most immigrants hold a Commonwealth nationality (Nielsen 1992: 49-50).

Relations Council (CRC), and by setting up co-ordinating bodies which could act as a mouthpiece and promote the interests of Muslims in the course of dialogue with the authorities. Initiatives for setting up these co-ordinating organizations first bore fruit at the local level.

The Bradford Council for Mosques (BCM) is a good example. It was set up in 1981, to the great satisfaction of the Bradford municipal council, which a few months earlier had identified a lack of political representation for ethnic minorities. The municipal council and other public institutions therefore welcomed the initiative. They regarded the Council of Mosques as an organization which could be consulted on a whole range of issues. In their turn the Muslims who had taken the initiative hoped that the platform would improve their negotiating position with the local authorities, but also that it would strengthen their hand in obtaining financial support from local and central government. The municipal council supported the establishment of the BCM with a Community Programme subsidy of £ 13,000, so that it could afford its own premises. The BCM devoted itself to promoting the interests of Muslims in a variety of fields, particularly in the area of education, and received support from the local government in such activities. Contact was made easier by the fact that certain Muslim municipal councillors were also members of the Bradford Council for Mosques and of the Community Relations Council (Lewis 1994: 143 ff.).

A first attempt to establish a co-ordinating body at national level dates from 1970, when the Union of Muslim Organizations of the UK and Eire (UMO) was set up, with as its principal object the national promotion of the interests of Muslims. However, the UMO never achieved the aims it had set for itself upon its foundation, for two reasons. In the first place those taking the initiative had not quite realized that many decisions and matters of policy directly affecting Muslims took place not at a national but at a local level. Secondly, the establishment of the UMO was premature: Muslim communities did not apparently need a national organization to promote their interests as yet. When the need did arise in the mid-1980s, the UMO had become just one of many organizations in the UK (Nielsen 1992: 47).

Since the late 1980s, Muslim organizations have played an increasingly important part on the national political stage. This was a result of events in Bradford. In January 1989, during a demonstration against the publication of Salman Rushdie's *Satanic Verses*, a copy of

the book was publicly burnt. This incident was not totally unex-
pected. Immediately after the book's publication an action committee had been set up, the UK Action Committee on Islamic Affairs
(UKACIA), on which several of the most important Muslim organizations were represented. In early October 1988 this Committee
appealed to the governments of several Muslim countries to take
action. In December of that year a group of ambassadors staged a
demonstration at the Ministry of Internal Affairs and asked that the
publication be banned. These actions did not produce the desired
result, and attracted very little attention outside a restricted circle.
This all changed after the Bradford book-burning, which sparked off
a fierce debate. Khomeini's *fatwa*, condemning Rushdie to death,
was issued a month after the demonstration and gave an international dimension to the affair: the *fatwa* led to diplomatic relations
between the United Kingdom and Iran being broken off. Nevertheless
the demonstrations continued, and discussion on possible legal solutions concentrated on the possible amendment of the law on blasphemy (Nielsen 1992: 156 ff.).

In Kaye's view (1993: 241), one consequence of the Rushdie affair
was a growing awareness within the Muslim community that they
were not represented in the political arena. This caused both the
UKACIA and a number of Muslim leaders and organizations to
adopt a higher profile and try to mobilize their adherents to cham-
pion their interests more strongly.[9] Besides putting Islam on an equal
footing with Christianity in the context of the law on blasphemy,
such issues as the religious requirements of Muslim children in state
schools and government subsidies for Muslim schools were also on
their agenda.

These matters were raised at a meeting to discuss the Rushdie
affair in June 1989, between a number of Muslim leaders and the
Minister of Internal Affairs (Hurd) and the Secretary of State (Patten),
both Conservatives.[10] A month later an open letter from Patten to
the Muslim leaders revealed that the British government had little
inclination to meet the leaders' wishes. Some enlargement of the law
on blasphemy was indeed given serious consideration, but in the end

---

[9] Cf. Nielsen 1992: 161–162; Le Lohé 1993: 534.
[10] In the UK the Secretary of State is the head of the Ministry. In the Netherlands
and Belgium the Secretary of State (*staatssecretaris*) is a deputy minister, junior to
the Minister him/herself.

rejected by the Church of England. Attempts by the UKACIA to get the law amended in the courts failed in May 1990. The High Court decided that the law on blasphemy could not be applied to Islam. This negative attitude caused a number of leaders to form their own political movements; the Islamic Party of Britain was set up in September 1989, and a few years later the Director of the pro-Iran Muslim Institute took the initiative of setting up a Muslim Parliament.[11]

The Islamic Party proved in practice to have little significance, and in the 1992 parliamentary elections it collected only a handful of votes (Kaye 1993: 243). However, the establishment of the Muslim Parliament in January of that year made a bigger impression. The radical utterances of Siddiqui, the man behind it, evoked particularly strong reactions.[12] He urged Muslims to reject any British law which clashed with their own interests. Secretary of State Patten reacted immediately, stating that

> every British citizen, and everyone resident in our country, must observe the law of the land. That is my message to every community in our country, Muslim or not (quoted in *de Volkskrant*, 6 January 1992).

Next Siddiqui called for a tax boycott, as a protest against the refusal to subsidize Muslim schools. At a meeting to celebrate the first birthday of the Muslim Parliament, it became apparent that the number of members had not yet reached the planned 200, and that relations with the authorities left much to be desired (Le Lohé 1993: 536).

Neither the Islamic Party nor the Muslim Parliament were able to raise much support among the communities they claimed to represent. In 1992 *Muslim News* reported that several Muslim leaders were working to set up a single co-ordinating body, in which all British Muslims would be represented (Kaye 1993: 243).

It is clear that the Rushdie Affair was an important turning point. It not only made wide sections of British society aware of the presence of Muslims, but also led to an increased political awareness among Muslims, who since that time have promoted their interests much more forcefully.

---

[11] See Nielsen 1992: 157; Kaye 1993: 242; Husbands 1994: 194.
[12] For a discussion of reactions in the media, see *Runnymede Bulletin* 3 (1992): 2–3.

Places of worship

We remarked earlier that the first mosques in Great Britain were established in the nineteenth century. However, the expansion of their numbers is of more recent date and closely related to the stages of immigration. There were 13 registered mosques in 1963. From 1966 onwards, as a consequence of the immigration of families, there were on average seven new mosques every year. Particularly after 1975 there was a substantial increase in the number of registered mosques, up to 338 by 1985 (Nielsen 1992: 44). We can reasonably assume that the total number is higher, since registration is not mandatory.

Religious organizations, including mosques, can be registered as charities under the Places of Worship Registration Acts of 1852 and 1855,[13] and are then included in an official list at the General Registration Office (GRO).[14] Recognized charities can qualify for reduced taxes. In Nielsen's view (1986: 10) this was the decisive factor for many organizations applying for registration.

Religious organizations wanting to use a building as a place of worship or for education have to apply for planning permission, in accordance with the Town and Country Planning Act of 1971. These applications are dealt with at the local level by the Local Authority Planning Committees (LAPCs), who are guided by established plans for the neighbourhood, the appearance of the building (whether or not it has minarets), the degree of nuisance expected from such things as traffic and loudspeakers, and the possible effects on what is termed racial integration in the immediate surroundings. The use of mosques for social and cultural ends can also be a consideration for the LAPC in deciding whether or not to grant planning permission. The procedure usually takes a long time and there is no guarantee that permission will be granted. Many religious organizations therefore establish their mosques in buildings which other religious denominations have used as places of worship, for which no separate approval is required from the local authorities.[15]

---

[13] A trust or foundation whose main object is the practice or propagation of a religion can be registered as a charity (Poulter 1990: 114). If a mosque is used for the contraction of legally valid marriages, it must be registered (Nielsen 1992: 51).

[14] At least in England and Wales; there is another system in Scotland (Nielsen 1986: 10).

[15] See Poulter 1990: 14; Hodgins 1981; Rath et al. 1993: 64.

In practice, policy on the establishment of places of worship varies
considerably from one authority to the next. In addition, Muslim
organizations have not automatically been treated on an equal footing with Christian organizations. Nielsen (1986) investigated how the
policy functioned in 79 local authority areas. When asked, spokesmen declared that applications from Muslims were treated in the
same way as others, but Nielsen remained unconvinced.[16]

Some authorities laid down special guidelines for the establishment
of mosques. Birmingham was one of the first authorities to have a
detailed, initially rather restrictive policy: planning permission was
only temporary; the use of the building was restricted to the hours
between 8.00 a.m. and 10.30 p.m.; it had to be a detached building;
no structural changes could be made; and sufficient parking space
had to be available (Nielsen 1986: 13).[17] As a result of the new guidelines many applications were refused. After various organizations had
successfully appealed to Secretary of State against the decisions of
the Birmingham local authority, their policy became more flexible
in 1981 (ibid.). Several authorities followed their example, but a number continued to carry out a restrictive policy (Nielsen 1988).[18]

There is no government subsidy for religious communities in Great
Britain, and consequently none for Muslim organizations either. Sometimes, however, Muslim centres receive financial support from ministries or local authorities for such things as the maintenance of buildings,
or providing instruction in community languages. In Bradford several mosque organizations received grants in 1983 from the Department
of the Environment for carrying out essential maintenance to supplementary schools. Five years later the local authorities of the same
town made £ 100,000 available to enable these schools to comply
with new fire regulations. Since the early 1980s three Bradford
mosques have received grants for organizing instruction in community languages. Usually, however, the mosque organizations are dependent upon their own funds (Lewis 1994: 124).

---

[16] Cf. Nielsen 1988: 58.
[17] Cf. Joly 1988: 36.
[18] For other examples, see *British Muslims Monthly Survey* (*BMMS*) III (1995) 3:
19–20.

Education

The United Kingdom has three separate educational systems: England and Wales share the same system, while Scotland and Northern Ireland each have their own. Here we confine ourselves to England.

Since 1870 England has had a twofold system. There are county schools (state schools) run by the local authorities, and voluntary schools, founded by religious organizations and wholly or partly financed by the authorities. This last type of school can again be subdivided into schools with controlled, special agreement, or voluntary-aided status. This last status most closely approaches that of the Dutch private schools. About a quarter of the schools in England have voluntary-aided status. They are mostly church schools (Church of England or Roman Catholic) and a small number of Jewish schools. In addition there are also private or independent schools, which have to finance themselves.[19]

Islamic religious instruction

Legislation

Since the 1944 Education Act, the provision of education in religion has been obligatory in both state and voluntary schools. There are two components to this education: collective worship and religious instruction. In accordance with Section 25.4 of the Act, parents have the right to withdraw their children from one or both of these. School governors may also offer facilities to religious communities to give religious instruction outside normal school hours. They are not, however, obliged to do so. The Act also lays down that local authorities, or Local Education Authorities (LEAs), should not concern themselves with religious instruction in schools with voluntary-aided status.[20]

In state schools, religious instruction must follow an agreed syllabus. A committee assembled by the LEA, known as the Agreed Syllabus Conference (ASC), draws up this syllabus. The ASC is made up of representatives of various bodies, such as the teaching unions,

---

[19] See Roovers & Van Esch 1987: 53–55; Wagtendonk 1991: 157.
[20] *Education Act 1944*. London, HMSO; cf. Roovers & Van Esch 1987: 56–58.

the various religious groups in the region, the Church of England,
and the LEA itself. The LEA has the casting vote and responsibility for the content of the programme.

Although the 1944 Education Act made religious instruction obligatory, it allowed scope for flexibility in the way in which it should
be taught. At first it was strictly based on the Christian faith and
the Bible. The Birmingham 1962 syllabus included the statement:

> We speak of religious education but we mean Christian education (. . .)
> the aim of Christian education in its full and proper sense is quite
> simply to confront our children with Jesus Christ . . . (quoted in Nielsen
> 1986: 25).

In the 1960s, influenced by changes in the school population, more
attention was paid in a number of syllabuses to religions other than
Christianity. Moreover, in some places representatives of Muslim
organizations were included in the committees drawing up the syllabuses. In 1975 a multi-faith syllabus was drawn up in Birmingham
for the first time; it gave official recognition to other religions besides
Christianity. Several LEAs, such as Hampshire and Bradford, followed Birmingham's lead. In these multi-faith syllabuses, teaching
was usually conceived as providing information about Christianity
and other religions, rather than confessional instruction. This view
was also propagated by the Swann Committee, which at the request
of the British government issued a report (DES 1985) on the education of children from ethnic groups.[21]

In conservative Christian circles there was increasing opposition
to the multi-faith character of the syllabuses on the grounds that the
schools simply made a hotch-potch of them.[22] Although the 1944
Education Act did not state explicitly that religious education should
be Christian in nature, this had, they maintained, always been the
intention, and this opposition eventually led to new definitions in the
1988 Education Reform Act.[23]

---

[21] See LEA Bradford 1983; Roovers & Van Esch 1987: 58; Nielsen 1986: 25,
1989: 228–229; Cox & Cairns 1989: 18; Karagül 1994: 157.
[22] The arguments are listed in, for example, Burn & Hart 1988; Hart 1991: 8.
For that matter some Muslims also raised questions about multi-faith religious education: they thought it too secular and too relativist, and preferred to have someone from their own community giving the instruction (Nielsen 1989: 230; Wagtendonk
1991: 162; Karagül 1994: 157–158; Dwyer & Meyer 1995: 44).
[23] *Education Reform Act 1988*, London, HMSO.

The new Education Act meant a step backwards from the existing practice, in that it brought an end to freedom in carrying out religious instruction. This time it was explicitly stated that 'collective worship shall be wholly or mainly of broadly Christian character', and 'any agreed syllabus shall reflect the fact that the religious traditions in Great Britain are in the main Christian'. All LEAs were required to review their agreed syllabus for religious education in the light of the 1988 Act. Standing Advisory Councils for Religious Education had to advise local authorities on collective worship and religious instruction. Schools with a substantial percentage of pupils of another religious background could request permission from the Advisory Councils to hold alternative acts of collective worship (Parker-Jenkins 1991: 572).

In July 1992 the government issued proposals for new educational legislation. As regards religious education, where local authorities had not yet adapted their agreed syllabus according to the terms of the 1988 Education Act, they were urged to do so. Moreover, they were reminded again of the emphasis in the Act on Christianity:

> Proper regard should continue to be paid to the nation's Christian heritage and traditions in the context of both the religious education and collective worship provided in schools.[24]

As we have observed, schools with voluntary-aided (VA) status do not have to keep to the agreed syllabus. They may take their own decisions on what their programme looks like. Moreover, the governors of such schools are free to set the qualifications which their religious teaching staff must hold. Until 1995, there were no Muslim schools with VA status, which means that no Islamic religious instruction was given within the regular system. The situation in Bradford, however, will show that the need for such instruction was very much present among British Muslims.[25]

---

[24] *Choice and Diversity, a new framework for schools 1992*, London, HMSO.
[25] The following case study is based on the following sources: LEA Bradford 1982, 1983; MPA 1982; Lodge 1983: 10; Nielsen 1986: 28–29; Roovers & Van Esch 1987: 65–67; Halstead 1988: 231–242; Parker-Jenkins 1991: 578; Samad 1992: 513–514; Dwyer 1993: 146–147; Lewis 1994: 2, 69–70, 148–153; Shadid & Van Koningsveld 1995: 117.

Islamic religious instruction in Bradford

In Bradford the number of labour migrants from India, Pakistan and Bangladesh increased rapidly in the 1960s, and with it the number of Muslim children. As early as 1965 there were schools where more than a quarter of the children were Muslim. Two mosques gave Koran lessons, which by the end of the 1960s were attended by most Pakistani children for some 15 to 20 hours each week outside normal school hours.

From the start education (including religious instruction) formed a potential source of friction between Muslim communities and the Bradford local authorities. In October 1969 the Bradford Muslim Association submitted a request for Islamic religious instruction in secondary schools. The head of the Education Department felt that this would go against Bradford's policy of integration, and refused the request. Two years later there was a fresh request, this time also supported by the Muslim Educational Trust, an organization set up especially to promote Islamic religious instruction in state schools. In July 1972 the Local Education Authority (LEA) gave permission for religious instruction to be provided in secondary schools in Bradford, but outside normal school hours.

Two years later, in 1974, the LEA set up an education committee to take another look at the curriculum for religious education, and to guarantee that the agreed syllabus reflected the variety of religions in Bradford.[26] In the same year a Muslim father set up the Muslim Parents Association (MPA) in Bradford, which drew up a list of the wishes of Muslim parents for the education of their children in the existing schools. One of their wishes concerned the legal right to withdraw Muslim children from collective worship and from religious instruction. The head of Bradford's Education Department subsequently confirmed this right.

In a report in February 1982 the MPA complained that the local authority had not abided by the 1974 agreements, and pressed for the resignation of the chairman of the Education Committee. At the same time they put forward plans for setting up five Muslim schools with voluntary-aided status.[27] At this point the LEA, in late 1982,

---

[26] This resulted in the *Guide to religious education in a multi-faith community* (ESC 1974).
[27] See also the next section.

sent all schools in Bradford a policy document about provisions for the education of ethnic minorities. It included, among other things, that Friday prayers, led by an imam, might be held for Muslims in schools, that permission for absence should be granted for religious festivals, and that parents could withdraw their children from religious instruction and collective worship. In 1983 a new agreed syllabus appeared, which emphasized a multi-faith approach to religious instruction. It was also announced that the LEA was considering the introduction of *halâl* meat in school meals, which in fact took place soon afterwards.

The introduction of ritually slaughtered meat on school menus provoked strong reactions, particularly from animal protection organizations. In February 1984 the municipal council gave way to requests for a full debate on the subject. This decision caused an uproar among the Muslim residents of Bradford, who feared that they would lose their recently acquired right to *halâl* meat. As a result the Council for Mosques called upon all Muslim parents to boycott the schools, and to demonstrate with their children in front of the town hall, and indeed a majority of the parents complied with the call. The municipal council then decided to keep *halâl* meat on the school menus.

The debate had hardly subsided when a second controversy arose—the Honeyford affair. This erupted as a consequence of the negative comments of head teacher Honeyford about Bradford council's anti-racist and multicultural policy, and about residents of Pakistani origin. This gave reason for collective action. The Drummond Parents Action Committee (DPAC) was set up and pressed for the dismissal of the head teacher, and in addition the Pakistan Community Centre set up an alternative school. The DPAC proclaimed 15 October 1985 as a day of action, and Muslim parents were again called upon to boycott the schools. The agitation eventually led to the headmaster taking early retirement.

Meanwhile the council had financed the establishment of an Interfaith Education Centre, in which all religious denominations in Bradford were represented. After the Education Reform Act came into force in 1988, the LEA still tried to meet the wishes of Muslim parents. For instance, an agreement was reached about facilities for Islamic prayers, and on Fridays schools could invite an imam to lead prayers. Muslims were also admitted to the Standing Advisory Council for Religious Education.

All things considered, the 'Bradford affairs' led to more support among Muslims for the establishment of Muslim schools in England.

Muslim schools in England

The lack of opportunities for the provision of Islamic religious instruction within the existing regular education system was a reason for Muslims to make efforts to set up their own schools.[28] In theory there were two possibilities for doing this within the existing school system: founding an independent or private Muslim school, or acquiring voluntary-aided status.[29]

Legislation

In the early 1990s there were around 20 private Muslim schools.[30] Although the authorities do not finance any private schools, they do exercise control over them. The 1944 Education Act lays down that these schools must be registered. To achieve this, they must comply with specific criteria for accommodation, suitable teaching staff and the quality of education. These are checked by inspection by Her Majesty's Inspectorate (HMI). A school can be struck from the register if it does not meet all the requirements, which leads automatically to its closure.

In addition to the founding of private schools, British educational

---

[28] Cf. Ashraf 1988: 1–7; Sarwar 1991; Dwyer & Meyer 1995.

[29] The 1988 Education Act offers a third possible alternative: application for *grant maintained* (GM) status. This means that schools no longer come under the authority of the LEA, but directly under the Ministry of Education. Any school can apply for this status; state schools can decide to withdraw from the control of the local authority (opting out), while private schools can opt for direct control by the central government (opting in). The relevant procedures are laid down in Articles 60–72 of the 1988 Education Reform Act. A school must retain its original form for at least five years after gaining GM status before the governors can apply for a different status. Until 1995 it was not clear whether applying for GM status is a practical option for anyone wanting to start a Muslim school financed wholly or partly by the state. In Birmingham a school with a preponderance of Muslim pupils gained GM status in 1990. In 1995 it had still not altered its status, so that it remained a state school open to all comers (Cumper 1990: 386; Knight & Hedegüs 1994; *BMMS* III (1995) 3: 18; Dwyer & Meyer 1996: 226).

[30] Estimates vary from 15 (Wagtendonk 1991: 162) to between 20 and 25 (*The Times Educational Supplement*, 9 November 1990; *Q-News* 2 (1993) 21: 6; Karagül (1994: 161) records that in 1994 there were 28 Muslim schools in total.

legislation offers the option of government financing, which an existing private Muslim school can obtain by applying for voluntary-aided status. It is also possible to take over a state school with a high proportion of Muslim pupils, and then apply for voluntary-aided status.[31]

This status has several advantages. The founding board only bears a small proportion of the initial costs,[32] but even so has a great deal of say, particularly in the areas of staffing and the content of the curriculum. Two thirds of the governors come from members of the foundation or the religious community, with the remaining seats reserved for the local authority. In primary education, secular teaching comes under the supervision of the LEA, but the content of religious instruction is controlled by the governors. In secondary education both secular and religious instruction are the responsibility of the school governors (Roovers & Van Esch 1987: 54–55).

There have been several attempts in the past to gain voluntary-aided status for Muslim schools,[33] but by late 1995 not a single application had been successful. The next section describes the struggle for voluntary-aided Muslim schools.[34]

The struggle for a Muslim school

What was probably the first attempt to establish a private Muslim school dates from 1974. In that year Bradford opted for co-education in secondary schools, giving every reason for two Muslim fathers to withdraw their daughters from school. The matter was given a

---

[31] As stated earlier, in addition to VA status there are two others: 'special agreement', and 'controlled'. The difference between the three is related to the degree of autonomy of the school and funding by the government or local authority. 'Controlled' status is not attractive to Muslims wanting to start up a Muslim school, because control is then in the hands of the LEA. The same applies to 'special agreement status', which involves the school and the local authority coming to an agreement about splitting the finances. Moreover, agreements also have to be made about who bears responsibility for the teaching. The governors have control of religious education and must be consulted about the appointment of staff for it. The other subjects and their staff are entirely the responsibility of the LEA (Roovers & Van Esch 1987: 54–55).

[32] The governors are responsible for 15 per cent of the costs of the premises and 5 per cent of the running costs of the school (Wagtendonk 1991: 157).

[33] Cf. Nielsen 1986: 29; Dwyer 1993: 148–149.

[34] This section is based on the following sources: Bhatti & Kanitkar s.a.; Mack 1979; 762–765; *Muslim Educational Review* 1 (1982) 1; Lodge 1983: 10; Halstead 1988: 233.

wide airing in the press.[35] One of the two fathers set up the Muslims
Parents Association (MPA), which we have already encountered, and
which approached the Bradford council on issues which gave Muslim
parents cause for dissatisfaction. The council met the MPA half way
on a number of points. For instance, decently covering clothes could
be worn for sports, and there would be no mixed swimming lessons.
The request for single-sex schools, and therefore the retention of separate teaching for girls, was not accepted. The MPA then started
initiatives for founding a Muslim girls school, but because of insufficient
support from Muslim parents it never came into being.

In 1978 the Union of Muslim Organizations set up the National
Muslim Education Council of the United Kingdom, which one year
later covered around 130 organizations. This Council set itself the
goal of setting changes in motion in existing state schools, as well
as establishing voluntary-aided Muslim schools. To start with, however, its efforts were concentrated primarily on private schools. The
first private Muslim school was established in Coventry in 1979—
the Daral Uloom Al Aribiya Al Islamiya, a secondary boarding school
for boys.

In December 1978 in London, the Islamic Cultural Centre and
the Central London Mosque organized the first conference for Muslim
teaching staff in Great Britain. The organizer, a former Schools Inspector in the Inner London Education Authority (ILEA), emphasized
that the time had come for Muslims to develop plans for their own
schools, in the same way that Jews and Roman Catholics had done.
This conclusion was also reached at an international educational conference organized by the Muslim Educational Board (MEB) in 1981,
at which the MEB presented their ideas for a model school in Batley.
The school in question, the Zakariya Muslim Girls high school, was
actually opened a year later. After that the number of private Muslim
schools gradually grew, and the subject of state-financed Muslim
schools with voluntary-aided status returned to the agenda. One case
is worth examining in detail—the Islamia primary school in Brent
(North-West London).[36]

---

[35] One daughter was sent back to Pakistan; the other was kept at home until
she was no longer of school age (Halstead 1988: 231–242).
[36] For an account of the attempts of Muslim organizations to gain VA status for
schools in Bradford, see Khan-Cheema 1984; Halstead 1988: 231–242; Dwyer 1993;
Lewis 1994: 148.

The Islamia primary school in Brent

This school opened in 1982.[37] A year later the founding organization, the Islamia Schools Trust, submitted an application for voluntary-aided status to the Education Committee of the Brent municipal council. In 1984 the Committee decided in principle to support the application,[38] but before coming to a final decision the council members asked for a report on the education for Muslim children in state schools. They also wished to consult the Muslim community in Brent. In June 1985 there was a meeting between the governors of the school and representatives of the Muslim community. A decision would be taken on the application after collecting information on finance and curriculum, and sampling the reactions of the Brent community.[39] Meanwhile members of the Education Committee visited the school. They reported positively, and it seemed as if the Committee would have no objections on educational grounds to granting voluntary-aided status.[40]

When it became known that there was a reasonable chance of the application being granted, the reactions set in. *Education*, a journal read by all LEAs, forecast that if Brent LEA were to support the application, Muslim groups in other towns would be encouraged to submit their own applications for separate provisions. That was also the message given to Labour-controlled LEAs by the education advisory service of the Labour Party.[41] In a letter to the head of the Education Department of the Brent council this body also suggested that supporting the application would be in conflict with the recommendations of the Swann Committee's report,[42] which had pronounced against the establishment of separate religious schools.[43]

---

[37] Where original sources have not been consulted (see notes), information on this school has been obtained from the following sources: *Education* 8 (1985): 161–162, 8 (1990), 3 (1991); Lodge 1986: 1; Dalrymple 1988: 14–15; *Islamia* 13 (1990): 4, 19 (1992): 1, 5; Weston 1990; Bates 1992; Dwyer & Meyer 1995: 45–46.

[38] Letter from the Brent Deputy Director of Education to three mosques in Brent, the Pakistani Community Centre and the Pakistan Workers' Association, dated 12 March 1985; letter from the Deputy Director of Education to Yusuf Islam, dated 4 April 1985.

[39] Minutes of a meeting of representatives of the Education Committee and the governors of the Islamic Primary School, dated 3 June 1985 and 25 July 1985.

[40] *Memorandum from the Brent Deputy Director of Education*, dated 20 August 1985; Report no. 27/85 to the Policy & Estimates Sub-Committee, dated 17 September 1985.

[41] Letter from the General Secretary of the Socialist Educational Association to the Brent Director of Education, dated 23 August 1985.

[42] See also the section on Islamic religious instruction in this chapter.

[43] Six members of the Committee—all from ethnic minority groups—formally

The Conservatives (32 seats) who with the three Liberal seats had a narrow majority on Brent's municipal council, were in favour of supporting the application. However, the Labour Party, with its 31 seats, was against separate schools for Muslim children, and wanted to provide facilities in the existing state schools.[44]

The promised decision on the application was not forthcoming that year. Time and again, in meetings of the Education Committee and of the Education Policy and Estimates Sub-Committee, additional information was requested about the need for such a school, the secular curriculum, the staff, the governors, and the criteria for admission.[45] In early February 1986 the governors of the school decided to publicize their application for voluntary-aided status.[46] A vote was finally taken in a meeting of the Subcommittee: the Conservatives, Liberals, and several independents voted in favour of giving support; the Labour Party abstained. The proposal was carried by a 10 to one majority.[47] In March the full Brent Education Committee ratified the decision, and a month later the council formally declared its support.[48]

Islamia Primary School could now submit an application to the Ministry of Education which, however, rejected it on the grounds that the school was too small to be viable. Attempts to expand the school by buying adjacent empty school buildings or by erecting new ones were initially delayed by the Brent Planning Subcommittee. However, in October 1988 planning permission for the expansion was finally granted.

---

dissociated themselves from this position and issued a minority statement in which they said: '. . . it's unjust at the present time not to recommend that positive assistance should be given to ethnic minority communities who wish to establish voluntary schools in accordance with the 1944 Education Act' (DES 1985: 515).

[44] London Broadcasting Company, 19 August 1985; BBC Radio London, *Inside London*, 2 November 1985.

[45] See letter from the Brent Deputy Director of Education to the Department of Education and Science, dated 18 September 1985; Report no. 27/85 to the Policy & Estimates Sub-Committee, 17 September 1985; Report no. 41/85, Education Policy & Estimates Sub-Committee meeting, 25 November 1985; letter from Brent Deputy Director of Education to all members of the Education Committee, dated 28 November 1985.

[46] Letter with copy of a press release from Yusuf Islam to the Brent Deputy Director of Education, dated 6 February 1986.

[47] Minutes of the meeting of the Education Policy & Estimates Sub-Committee, dated 17 February 1986.

[48] Letter from the Deputy Director of Education to the Department of Education and Science, dated 10 April 1986; see also Boseley 1986: 3.

The Ministry then received a fresh application for voluntary-aided status, after which two years passed before the Secretary of State for Education came to a decision. In May 1990 the school's application was again rejected, now with the argument that there were empty places in other Brent schools, which had to be filled first.[49] The school governors then went to court, and were granted leave to appeal against the Secretary of State's decision. At the same time the governors started lobbying to get as many members as possible of both Houses of Parliament to support their application, and they were particularly successful among the Conservatives. Baroness Cox, for instance, tried several times to have the procedure for obtaining voluntary-aided status simplified.

In May 1992 the High Court decided that the Secretary of State's decision to reject the school's application was an example of 'manifest unfairness' and that it should be reconsidered. The Brent council announced their support.[50] Nevertheless a further rejection followed on the grounds that sufficient places were available at other schools in Brent. The chairman of the Islamia Schools Trust reacted indignantly:

> It's an outrage. We have come to expect a great deal of injustice. We get the impression that the Government just does not want to see a Muslim school and is pursuing a policy of starving us of funds (quoted in *The Times Educational Supplement*, 27 August 1993).

The Secretary of State for Education denied that the application had been treated any differently from those of other schools. A new application would have to be submitted, this time for a site in a region without empty places.

During the 10 years or more in which vain attempts were made to obtain voluntary-aided status for the Brent school, a number of applications from the governors of other Muslim schools had also been rejected. The reasons given included the quality of the accommodation of the school in question, empty places in schools in the neighbourhood, the presence of girls' schools in the neighbourhood, the fact that such applications were contrary to the adopted multicultural

---

[49] Letter from the Department of Education and Science to the Chairman of the Islamia Schools Trust, dated 24 May 1990.

[50] Minutes of the meeting of the Education, Arts and Libraries Committee, dated 7 July 1992, Part 1, Decisions of the Committee, p. 3.

policy, and the additional financial burden they would impose on
the local authority's budget (Shadid & Van Koningsveld 1995: 125).

The debate on Muslim schools

As far back as the early 1970s, the possible advent of Muslim schools
financed by the government raised questions about their desirability. For instance, the National Secular Society (NSS)—traditionally
a supporter of public education—commented in 1970 that some
Muslims had raised the question of why there were no subsidized
Muslim schools when there were subsidized Methodist, Catholic,
Jewish, and Church of England schools. The NSS warned that if
the government were to start subsidizing Muslim schools and those
of other 'oriental religions', this could lead to segregation based on
race and colour (Tribe 1970: 13). Up to that point there had hardly
been any public debate on the question.

   That all changed when Bradford's council wanted to introduce
co-education, and the Muslim Parents Association attempted to found
a Muslim girls school. As a result a debate started about Muslims
and education, with various organizations and individuals adopting
firm positions. At first the debate was limited to the desirability of
Muslim schools for girls. In response to a paper on the subject published by the Union of Muslim Organizations (UMO) (Iqbal 1975),
the London Community Relations Commission declared itself in
favour of single-sex schools.[51] The Association of LEAs, on the other
hand, talked of the 'threat of sectarianism'. They considered that as
long as the demand for single-sex schools was based on educational
and social benefits, it should be respected. However,

> ... the danger (...) is that claims are made in the name of religious
> rights and freedoms which mask sectarian beliefs and which cannot
> be in the wider interest of the Muslim community in the context of
> British society.[52]

There were other organizations, too, which spoke out against separate education based on religion or sex, such as the British Secular
Society, which stated that 'the policies of some of the Muslim relig-

---

[51] *Islamic education booklet welcomed by Community Relations Commission*, London: Community Relations Commission, Press Release 57/75, 12 June 1975.
[52] *Education* 10 (1975): 430.

ious leaders in the North could lead to social disaster later on'
(Cumper 1990: 382).

Since the early 1980s, when the first applications for voluntary-
aided status for Muslim schools were submitted, all kinds of organizations have joined in the debate. Many spoke out against the
introduction of Muslim schools, their objections often based on the
fear of possible segregation and division. The World Council of
Churches (WCC) considered that separate ethnic schools would lead
to educational apartheid,[53] and Lord Scarman—who viewed the introduction of Hindu and Muslim schools with 'absolute horror'—warned
of a situation like that in Northern Ireland, which in his view could
be blamed on the fact that Protestant and Catholic children were
educated separately (Bayliss 1982: 10). The National Union of Teachers
(NUT 1984) made a stand against Muslim schools because it would
sow division, and at the local level, too, there was fear that Muslim
schools would foster racial prejudice (Cumper 1990: 383–384).

The Socialist Education Association (SEA), the Labour advisory
body on education, contended that a multicultural education system
should educate members of all races and religions collectively and
that separate schools were therefore not the way forward.[54] This
opinion was also encountered in the Swann Committee's report (DES
1985: 515). Five years later, however, the Commission for Racial
Equality (CRE)[55] pointed out that the growing demand for Muslim
schools was directly connected with the failure of existing multicultural education:

> We would estimate (. . .) that the demand for voluntary status would
> substantially diminish if existing state provision offered and delivered
> (. . .) schools with a genuine, active commitment to multi-cultural, anti-
> racist and non-discriminatory education, including facilities to meet
> needs for prayer, diet and dress requirements, as well as particular and
> organizational matters, and especially with regard to procedures for
> dealing with racial harassment (CRE 1990: 20).

---

[53] *Christians and Education in a Multi-faith World*, Papers from the Joint World
Council of Churches and the Centre for the Study of Religion and Education in
the Inner City, meeting held at Salford, United Kingdom, 1–8 July 1981; see also
Rogers 1982: 6–13.

[54] Letter from the General Secretary of the SEA to the Brent Director of Education,
dated 23 August 1985.

[55] The CRE is a government committee set up to monitor the observance of the
1976 Race Relations Act.

The CRE considered that the role and the future of all religious schools should be examined, and appealed for wide discussion within the community.[56]

There were also arguments against the introduction of Muslim schools founded on alleged aspects of Islam. Pat Guinan of the Labour Party in Blackburn was an opponent of such schools because the aim of education based on Islamic principles would be

> to produce women prepared for docile and devout acceptance of a reactionary family and social structure where women are possessions (quoted in *The Guardian*, 19 July 1989).

Guinan was not the only one to take this view about women's position in Islam.[57]

In addition to objections to the establishment of Muslim schools, arguments were also advanced in favour of their being granted voluntary-aided status. These were mainly heard from church circles. In February 1986 the Bishop of London informed the Education Select Committee of the House of Commons that the Church of England had no objections to subsidies for Muslim schools, provided these were open to all children in the community, as were existing religious schools.[58] A few years later both Roman Catholic and Church of England bishops also expressed their support for granting voluntary-aided status to Muslim schools,[59] and in this regard some of them drew parallels with their own history. The Catholic Bishop of Leeds told a conference on education:

> The experience of my own community (which has been a persecuted minority) is that having our own school within the state system helped us to move out of our initial isolation so as to become more confident and self-assured. The effect of the separate schools has been integration not divisiveness (quoted in *The Times Educational Supplement*, 4 January 1991).

Others appealed to the principle of equal treatment, which was also the argument put forward by the Labour Party (1990: 49) for granting voluntary-aided status to Muslim schools:

---

[56] *CRE calls for religious schools review*, London: CRE, Press Release, 8 August 1990; see also CRE 1990.
[57] Cf. Dwyer 1993: 156.
[58] *Education* 2 (1986).
[59] *Education* 1 (1991): 1–2.

The right to such status already exists in law and it has been exercised and enjoyed in practice by Anglicans and Roman Catholics. In equity, that right cannot be denied to others.

To date, however, appeals on grounds of equal treatment have produced few concrete results. By 1995 not a single Muslim organization had been successful in obtaining voluntary-aided status for a school.

CHAPTER FOURTEEN

CONCLUSIONS AT THE INTERNATIONAL LEVEL

To determine how far the situation in the Netherlands is specific to that country, the previous chapters have discussed the institutionalization of Islam in two neighbouring countries, Belgium and the United Kingdom, or more precisely, England. In several aspects the situation in Belgium is comparable to that in the Netherlands. There are, for instance, many similarities between the Muslim population of both countries, most of whom come from Turkey or Morocco. In both countries they have been settled for much the same time and for the same reasons, and have come to be in a similar situation. Moreover, Belgium, like the Netherlands, has a history of 'pillarization', a compartmentalization of society along ideological lines; however, this developed differently in Belgium, which makes a comparison useful. The United Kingdom was chosen by way of contrast. The Muslim population there has a different composition, migration history, and background. The largest group comes from the Indian subcontinent and indeed holds British citizenship. Another important feature in the British case is that there is an established church. Other religions, including Islam, therefore obviously have a different, usually less privileged status.

In broad terms, the process of institutionalization in the Netherlands, Belgium and the United Kingdom appears to have undergone a similar pattern of development. In all three countries the presence of Muslims and their institutions went more or less unnoticed for a long time. This gradually changed with the arrival of increasing numbers of migrant workers who settled permanently with their families. Not until the late 1980s did Islam really become the subject of wide political and social debate. In England Muslim organizations adopted a higher profile and advanced their claims more emphatically. In Belgium a number of initiatives by the Islamic and Cultural Centre produced the necessary shake-up and the government started to take an active interest in the organization of the Islamic religion. In the Netherlands a debate took place at the national level about the scope the Muslim newcomers should have to establish their own institutions.

When this process of institutionalization is examined more closely, it becomes clear that important differences exist alongside the similarities. Here we have limited ourselves to four areas: recognition of Islam in the general sense and the participation of Muslims in politics, places of worship, Islamic religious education, and the establishment of Muslim schools financed by the government.

Range and density

As in the Netherlands, Muslim organizations in Belgium and Great Britain tried to gain *recognition* for their religion, and organized themselves politically. This did not occur in the same way everywhere. For example, in Belgium, unlike the other two countries, there is a system for the formal recognition of religions, which has repercussions on the way in which political participation occurs. The Belgian government formally recognized Islam in 1974, thereby placing it on an equal footing with other recognized religions. In theory this meant that from that moment on, Muslims qualified for a number of facilities, such as partial subsidies for the establishment of mosques, the funding of accommodation, salaries and pensions for ministers of the Islamic religion, some fiscal benefits, and the implementation of Islamic religious instruction in state schools. In practice, however, many of these facilities have still not been realized. The way in which the Belgian government granted recognition was problematical. Difficulties arose particularly around the question of which body could claim to be representative of the Islamic religion. As early as 1975 the Ministry of Education recognized the Islamic and Cultural Centre (ICC) *de facto* as the head of the Islamic religion, but there was no legal basis for this recognition. Neither the Muslim communities in Belgium nor the national government were convinced about the monopoly position of the ICC.

In the 1980s several attempts were made to agree on an officially recognized representative body, but the Belgian government continued to withhold recognition. In 1989 the issue once again came into the spotlight: the Imam-Director of the ICC organized elections and at the same time the Belgian government started to become actively involved. All this led to a High Council for Muslims being set up under the auspices of the ICC, while the Belgian government installed a Provisional Council of Wise Men. Whereas the High Council lacked recognition, the Provisional Council proved inoperable, so that it was dissolved in the autumn of 1992. Meanwhile there was still no solution to the impasse which had arisen. In late 1994 the Minister of Justice, at the request of the High Council for Muslims, provisionally recognized a Muslim Executive. Whether this recognition has produced a definitive solution is far from clear. Until 1995 the powers of the Executive were limited, and there was no question so far of Islam being placed on an equal footing with other recognized religions.

We have already remarked that formal recognition does not exist in the United Kingdom, although, as in the Netherlands, there may be implicit recognition based on a number of separate regulations in particular fields. British Muslims first came into the public eye mainly in the local political arena. For instance, they achieved representation on the Bradford municipal council, and in bodies such as the Community Relations Council. They also set up a co-ordinating organization to promote the interests of Muslims. Since the early 1990s Muslim organizations have been presenting their claims with increasing emphasis to the national government, albeit without direct results. Government subsidies for Muslim schools have been refused for years, and after opposition from the Church of England, Islam has been denied the protection of the law on blasphemy.

In the Netherlands contacts between Muslim organizations and the national government were limited at first and concentrated mainly on practical matters. When in the 1980s it was realized that Muslim organizations could fulfil a role in the implementation of the minorities policy, contacts were intensified. Moreover, the government involved Muslims in the process of the separation of church and state, and in the negotiations preparing for the impending revision of the Constitution.

In the Netherlands, as well as in Belgium and in England, numerous *places of worship* have come into existence. The practical issues of establishing and financing these institutions show many parallels in the three countries. The establishment of Muslim places of worship proved to be a matter for the local authorities. Although local councils differed in their points of view, the establishment of mosques was not an automatic process in any of the three countries. In a number of cases there was a definite restrictive policy.

Currently there is no general government support for the establishment of Muslim places of worship. There are some general regulations on this subject in Belgium, but the lack of a representative body means that in practice they have not been followed up. There have been various regulations for subsidies in the Netherlands, but after the last one expired (in 1983), proposals for a new arrangement have come up against political opposition. Since then Muslim organizations have once more been dependent largely upon their own resources for the establishment of mosques. In the United Kingdom, on the other hand, there has been no general government subsidy for places of worship throughout the whole period.

Important differences are encountered when we look at the *sphere of education*. In Belgium Islamic religious instruction now exists on a relatively large scale, while there is no such instruction in state schools in England, and very little in the Netherlands. In all three countries Muslims have campaigned for the establishment of Muslim schools financed by the government, but here, too, the results of their efforts vary. In the Netherlands 29 Muslim primary schools have been set up in a relatively short period; in Belgium there is one Muslim school financed by the government, whereas in England most applications have been rejected by the government.

England has therefore shown the least results, although there were Muslim children in the British education system in relatively large numbers as early as the 1960s; most of their parents possessed British nationality and had agitated from the start for changes to the existing curriculum. The Dutch and Belgian education systems had hardly any Muslim children in the 1960s. In spite of their later arrival in the education system, in 1995 it appeared that the efforts of Muslims in these two countries had in this respect delivered substantially more results than in the United Kingdom.

Factors and agents

To some extent the diversity in the process of institutionalization in the three countries can be explained by the extent to which the Muslims have developed their own *initiatives*. In Belgium, for example, after the establishment and recognition of the first Muslim school, there were no further applications, partly for fear of arousing more negative reactions. In the Netherlands, on the other hand, Muslims energetically promoted the establishment of such schools; applications were submitted within a short time in a number of places. In other fields, however, the different results of the process can in no way be blamed on a lack of initiative. Indeed, in all three countries Muslims have attempted to have Islamic religious instruction included in the regular educational curriculum, but only in Belgium have they been successful.

Foreign powers and *international Muslim organizations* have also played an important part in the process of institutionalization, albeit in differing degrees. In Belgium, at the instigation of the authorities, official representatives of 'Islamic' countries were involved from the start in the process of institutionalization and recognition of Islam. The Islamic and Cultural Centre, which for a long time had a monopoly of contact with the Belgian government, maintained close links with Saudi Arabia. In the United Kingdom ambassadors from a number of countries were involved at the time of the Rushdie affair. In the Netherlands, however, ambassadors and other official representatives played no visible part in the process of institutionalization. The Netherlands also seems to have been much more reluctant to accept the influence of foreign powers. This does not mean that there was no involvement on their part. In particular the Turkish Presidium for Religious Affairs, the Diyanet, was involved in numerous initiatives, such as the appointment and training of imams and the establishment of three Muslim schools. There was also some involvement on the part of the Turks in Belgium. Teaching staff for Islamic religious instruction were recruited through the Turkish Embassy, and the Diyanet called for a boycott of the elections to set up a High Council for Muslims. While the Belgian government appears at first to have given foreign powers every chance to get involved in discussions about Islam, the *fear of interference* was later used by some people engaged in fierce opposition against the advent of certain Muslim institutions. A particular example is the debate that broke out at the prospect of the opening of the Muslim school in Brussels.

Another influential factor in the process of institutionalization is the existing pattern of *legislation and regulation*, which varies on important points in the three countries, and to some extent this also explains the different results of the institutionalizing process. For instance, this becomes clear from the extent of the inclusion of Islamic religious instruction in the normal curriculum. In the British system religious instruction is obligatory in schools financed, wholly or in part, by the government. Apart from a number of Jewish schools, this is normally instruction in Christianity. The Muslim variant is officially only possible in state-financed Muslim schools, and this materialized only very recently. In the Netherlands, on the other hand, it is not a question of an obligatory subject, but of the competent authority, in this case the municipality, enabling education in whatever religion the parents consider desirable. The subsidization of it is, however, discretionary. Moreover, religious education is regulated only in general terms and leaves much room for maoeuvre on the part of the local authorities, which have tended to be unresponsive when it comes to Muslim initiatives in this field. In Belgium the situation is different again. Instruction in recognized religions is regarded as an important state obligation; it is the 'holy cow' of Belgian education. According to law, instruction in one of the recognized religions is a set part of the curriculum in state schools in that country. Every child has to take these lessons. If just one parent of a child of school age asks for religious instruction in a recognized religion, this must be arranged and subsidized, as a matter of principle. Since the recognition of Islam in 1974, this has also applied to Islamic religious instruction.

As far as other institutions are concerned, the influence of legislation is less clearly attributable. In both the United Kingdom and the Netherlands it is legally possible to establish Muslim schools wholly or partly financed by the state. In both countries Muslims have launched initiatives to do so, but only in the Netherlands have such schools actually come into being on a relatively large scale. Although British Muslims repeatedly appealed to the existing legislation, the government for a long time refused to subsidize Muslim schools, even after the High Court had described this as 'manifest unfairness' in a case brought by a Muslim organization.

The *national government* is also an important agent. Unlike the Dutch or British governments, the Belgian seems at first sight to be remarkably active, for as early as 1974 it went ahead with the official recognition of Islam. Why it decided to do so is not entirely clear, although it seems as if the recognition had more to do with the government's own economic interests than with those of the Muslims. In the light of developments since 1974, it does not appear that *de facto* recognition of Islam had a particularly high priority for the Belgian authorities. For a long time they did little to break through the impasse which had developed around the recognition of a representative body. Time after time, possible solutions were turned down. In 1989 the Belgian government, in the shape of the Royal Commission for

Migrants Policy, took the matter into their own hands. However, their efforts have not yet resulted in a definitive solution.

The lack of a recognized representative body has been used in Belgium as an argument to deny Muslims a number of facilities enjoyed by other recognized religions; for instance, imams receive no emoluments or pensions and there is no general government subsidy for Muslim places of worship. The only exception to this pattern is Islamic religious instruction. By 1975, three years before such instruction became officially possible, Ministers of Education were putting pressure on head teachers to make something of the kind available. The establishment of the Muslim school in Brussels, on the other hand, came up against bitter opposition from various members of the government. However, the Minister of Education whose responsibility it was applied the law strictly, and in due course there followed recognition, and eventually subsidies.

All in all it is difficult to define the attitude of the Belgian government, or for that matter, of the Dutch. In some cases they tried to delay the advent of Muslim institutions, in others they remained neutral, and in other cases they encouraged them. The Dutch were particularly welcoming with provisions which were thought important for the minorities policy, and which might contribute to the process of integration. In Belgium this consideration seems to have played hardly any role, with only the Royal Commission's brief involvement pointing in that direction.

Nor did such considerations carry much weight with the national government in the United Kingdom. The British government usually showed itself to be inflexible, and in some areas even appears to have systematically opposed the recognition of Islam. They repeatedly rejected applications for Muslim schools, refused to put Islam on an equal footing with Christianity with respect to the law on blasphemy, and in 1988 emphasized that religious education should bear a primarily Christian stamp, which meant that the space which had gradually been set aside in some syllabuses for Islamic religious instruction was abolished. At the local level, on the other hand, the authorities took a less rigid attitude, and some Muslim initiatives were supported. For example, in Bradford the formation of a coordinating organization was encouraged, and the authorities in Brent gave their support (albeit after much vacillation) to the application for a Muslim school.

Nevertheless, in none of the three countries does the government form a monolithic block. The Belgian Ministry of Justice, for example, would pay no salaries or pensions to ministers of the Muslim faith because of the lack of a representative body, but at the same time the Ministry of Education regarded the Islamic and Cultural Centre as a representative body for the organization of Islamic religious instruction. In the United Kingdom a substantial part of government policy is devolved to local authorities, which can sometimes adopt a different attitude to claims by Muslims than the national government. The Islamia Schools Trust's application for voluntary-aided status, for example, was supported by the local authorities, but repeatedly rejected by the Secretary of State for Education.

As in the Netherlands, Muslims in Belgium and the United Kingdom have sometimes called on the *judiciary* to add strength to their claims. In Belgium Muslim parents were successful in legal actions when two local councils in Brussels refused to organize Islamic religious instruction. In England, too, Muslims have had recourse to the courts; in 1992 the High Court ruled that the claim by a Muslim school in Brent for government financing had been wrongly refused by the British government. Nevertheless the application failed once again.

Organizations based on religious or ideological principles are also of importance in the process of institutionalization. In Belgium, Catholic organizations sometimes offered financial support for establishing mosques. In England the attitude of religious organizations was ambivalent, particularly that of the Church of England. Sometimes they opposed the recognition of Islam. It was, for instance, at the insistence of the established church that the British government refused to put Islam on an equal footing with the Christian religion with respect to the law on blasphemy. It is remarkable that in other areas the Church of England has shown support for initiatives by Muslims, for example for the establishment of government-financed Muslim schools. In that matter support was also forthcoming from Catholic bishops in Great Britain.

Organizations based on general principles have also been involved with the advent of Muslim institutions. In Belgium reception centres and action groups supported the establishment of Muslim places of worship, while in England the National Secular Society and the National Union of Teachers opposed the establishment of Muslim schools.

Other relevant institutions which have indirectly influenced the process of institutionalization include the media. As in the Netherlands, it contributed significantly in Belgium and in Great Britain to alerting the great majority of the host society to the presence of Muslims and their institutions. Moreover, in some cases it was able to ensure that the interests of Muslims reached the political agenda. On a number of occasions the political debate was in fact conducted primarily in the media; this is particularly true of the whole issue of Muslim schools in Belgium.

In summary, the process of institutionalization developed differently in each of the three countries. Looking at the concrete results, the situation in the Netherlands seems the most favourable for Muslims. Although the Belgian government granted official recognition to Islam as early as 1974, in practice there are important areas where there has proven to be no *de facto* recognition. In the Netherlands and the United Kingdom there is no official recognition, only a series of separate regulations on particular issues. In these matters Muslims in England have repeatedly come up against an uncompromising stance from the national government, while in the Netherlands a more pragmatic attitude has been adopted. To a large extent the Dutch attitude resulted from the ideology and the implementation of the minorities policy, which in a variety of different fields had furthered the institutionalization of Islam.

CHAPTER FIFTEEN

CONCLUSIONS

Immigration from North and West Africa, Asia, the Caribbean and elsewhere has brought with it a massive influx of Islam into Western Europe. For a long time it led a rather 'concealed' existence, but Islam has proved to be an important mobilizing power. More and more institutions were established in public life, and gradually the outlines of a Muslim 'community'—assuming that there is such a thing—became visible. Requests were repeatedly heard from Muslim circles for recognition of their religion and its institutions. The replies of the host societies however, were rarely unequivocal, despite constitutional freedom of religion, legislation and the resulting regulation. Some institutions emerged without opposition, others only after struggles with the government or other interested parties, or even sometimes with their support. Relatively little is known about the precise reactions of society, what obstacles to the advance of Muslim institutions it throws up or removes, or how these reactions can be explained.

Western European countries are all democratic nation states which place a high value on respect for human rights, such as freedom of religion. At the same time these are societies in which there has been a certain degree of secularization and where the separation of church and state is largely a fact. The question is, to what extent are Muslims being given the opportunity to set up their institutions according to their own agenda in this particular arena? How are the politics of recognition worked out in Western Europe?

Our interest is in the process of institutionalization in so far as the established society is involved or experiences its effects. In such cases Muslims and their organizations—whether on their own initiative or at the instigation of others—will engage in consultation with the established society, or sometimes even generate conflicts concerning the recognition of their institutions. This struggle for recognition can have both positive and negative effects for Muslims. Society can attach conditions to certain decisions on the recognition of Muslim institutions, depending on its institutional context: some institutions seem to fit in relatively easily because, for example, other groups or churches have comparable institutions; others prove more difficult to place because they require new decisions or regulations.

In this book we have looked at the process of the institutionalization of Islam and have examined the extent to which there has been an increase in the emergence of Muslim institutions in Europe—more specifically in the Netherlands, Belgium and Great Britain. In what spheres of life has this occurred, what factors and agents have played a role in it, in what way has the debate on Muslim institutions unfolded, and how does it relate to the political operations of those involved? The concern is therefore not so much with Muslims or the mobilization of Islam, or indeed with any other process localized in Muslim communities. The primary concern is with these European societies themselves, their characteristics, potentials and limits.

We present first the conclusions for the Netherlands, to be followed by those for the other two countries.

The Netherlands: the emergence of Muslim institutions in a depillarizing society

Society in the Netherlands has undergone many drastic social changes in recent decades, one of which is *depillarization*. Before the Second World War and in the 1950s, pillarization produced a society in which religion and ideology were among the most important social determinants, and people were organized accordingly. In the developing welfare state, the emerging organizations were closely involved in the formation and implementation of government policy. First and foremost they were concerned with the distribution of social resources and services to citizens. This state of affairs was embedded not only in social and political practice, but also in legislation and regulation. There were admittedly alternative forces present during the development of this pillarized system, but their effect was limited; it was not until the 1960s, partly as a result of the diminishing influence of the church and secularization, that they gained in influence. Organizations based on religion and ideology gradually lost their monopolistic position. Some even ceased to exist. Their self-evident involvement in the formation and implementation of policy declined. Legislation and regulation were correspondingly adjusted in a number of areas, the provisional milestone being the 1983 amendments to the Constitution.

It was no longer the religious or ideological collective, but the individual, around which things now revolved.

More or less simultaneously, with this process of depillarization a new religious community emerged in the Netherlands, although until recently it attracted very little attention. Particularly since the 1960s, substantial numbers of Muslims had settled in the Netherlands as immigrants, and from the start they had begun to develop their own institutions.

Although these two processes more or less coincided, they were in a certain sense opposed to each other. Historical accident played Muslims false, not least because the general acceptance that religion had a recognized place in Dutch society was being eroded. On the other hand, the depillarization process is not yet complete, if in fact it ever could be. Many social, political and legal practices and structures dating from the peak period of pillarization are still at least partly intact. In spite of the separation of church and state, the constitutionally guaranteed equality of citizens—irrespective of their religious or ideological convictions—and freedom of religion, have survived untouched. But what does that mean in practice when Muslims are knocking on the door?

The range and density of Muslim institutions in the Netherlands

In the first chapter we distinguished seven spheres in which the process of institutionalization can take place: the spheres of religion, law, and education; the socio-economic, socio-cultural and political spheres; and that of health and social care. A distinction was also drawn—at least in the case of the Netherlands—between the national and local level, with special attention to the situation in the municipalities of Rotterdam and Utrecht. The first and second parts of this book were therefore in the form of a report, though always concentrating on the key questions of which institutions have emerged, and how and when this occurred. Here we restrict ourselves to a summary.

So far Muslims have been active mainly in the *sphere of religion*. Almost immediately after their arrival in the Netherlands, they sought premises for collective prayer, and set up places of worship. At first these were unofficial (in private houses or business premises), but separate foundations or associations were gradually formed to run 'real' mosques.

Now there are almost 400 places of worship or mosques in the Netherlands, though many of them are still facing accommodation problems.

With the establishment of official places of worship, the question of the admission of imams trained abroad arrived on the agenda. In this early period the availability of ritually slaughtered meat was another priority. Within a few years official rules were laid down for this, by identifying butchers and negotiating agreements about the practice of ritual slaughter. Only at a later stage, particularly once the reunion of families hade taken off, were practices such as the circumcision of boys and time off work for religious festivals officially regulated. In addition, Muslim cemeteries were opened in several places, and the public call to prayer was integrated into local regulations.

In the *sphere of politics*, very little happened at first. Contacts between Muslim organizations and the authorities were limited to practical matters, such as ritual slaughter or the foundation or funding of places of worship. In the course of the 1980s this began to change. Contact became less incidental and informal in character, particularly after Muslim organizations in some municipalities and at the national level were included in advisory bodies set up by the government to implement the minorities policy. In due course Muslims participated more regularly in social organizations such as political parties, although it was not always immediately clear whether they were doing this as Muslims or in some other capacity. Separate Muslim parties or trade unions did not appear to be viable. In a few places, and also at the national level, federated leagues of Muslim associations and foundations were set up to operate as dialogue partners with the government on certain policy matters.

In virtually all local Muslim organizations, Koran classes were given from the start. However, there was no real breakthrough in the *sphere of education* until the 1980s, when a Muslim broadcasting organization began transmitting; training courses were arranged for imams; and the first Muslim primary schools were opened. By the late 1990s there were approximately 30 such schools. In various municipalities, steps were also taken to offer Islamic religious instruction in state primary schools, an initiative which was only successful on an extremely limited scale.

In the *legal, socio-economic and socio-cultural spheres*, and those of *health and social care*, hardly any Muslim institutions have been set up. At the local level it has mainly been a matter of commercial operations in a number of mosques and Muslim butchers, or socio-cultural activities such as language and computer courses, which Muslim organizations have occasionally provided, with or without subsidies.

By looking at all the spheres, the conclusion can be drawn that the formation of Muslim institutions has occurred rather selectively. In view of the model of Dutch pillarization, we might have expected the formation of a Muslim daily and weekly press, trade unions and pressure groups, political parties, housing associations, maternity clinics and other medical institutions, secondary schools, universities and polytechnics financed by the government, and perhaps even Muslim emigration foundations. However, none of these have been established.

Some general patterns

In our examination of the range and density of Muslim institutions, we have encountered certain regular features, or patterns, in the way in which Dutch society has coped with Islam.

Firstly, we discovered that *few claims by Muslims have been categorically rejected*. Usually Muslims are given scope and occasionally also support for their institutions, though often only after long negotiations. The automatic and unconditional recognition of Muslim institutions, on the other hand, is rare. In important cases, the authorities can apparently be persuaded. During negotiations, the majority often tries to steer institutionalization towards more liberal and 'Dutch' practices, that is to say away from orthodoxy; aimed at dialogue and integration; and organized in a way that is familiar to the Netherlands. If this does not work immediately, some of the policy makers and administrators may try to delay Muslim initiatives. We are left with the impression that time is needed to get used to Muslim claims before granting them, with mixed feelings. On the other hand, in a few cases the recognition of Muslim institutions has run smoothly.

Secondly, claims based on *equal treatment* with existing groups seem to evoke *fewer objections* than claims which require *special group-specific measures* or reactions. Anyone denying Muslims something which is already allowed to other religious groups is manoeuvring himself into an awkward corner. Or in a more positive light, the strategy of including Muslim institutions in existing arrangements is more likely to bring results, as in the area of medicine, with circumcisions. Muslims invoking equal rights also have more opportunities to form coalitions. Partly for these reasons, Rotterdam's municipal council has granted subsidies for Islamic religious instruction in state primary schools, while Utrecht has not. When this question came up in Rotterdam, there was already an arrangement in place, and the two existing organizations began co-operating with the Muslim one. There was no such arrangement in Utrecht, nor was there any co-operation.

Thirdly, we found great *differences between municipalities*. What was completely unacceptable in one municipality was tolerated in another, or even encouraged. In the municipalities investigated we encountered two opposite practices. The Rotterdam municipal council granted subsidies to Muslim organizations for certain activities, encouraged them to play a role in politics, provided facilities for Islamic religious instruction in primary schools, and assisted in the founding of a Muslim school (not wholeheartedly, but there was no official obstruction). On the other hand, the Utrecht municipal council was adamantly against recognizing (let alone subsidizing) Muslim organizations, to say nothing of Muslim involvement in local politics. Islamic religious instruction was not encouraged, while by a series of legal processes they tried to prevent the foundation of a Muslim school.

That these two municipal administrations should adopt such different attitudes should of itself cause no surprise. All they were doing was making use of the powers allotted to them. In Dutch constitutional law, certain powers are decentralized to subsidiary authorities, so that they can take account of local circumstances. Such differences can be difficult for the Muslims involved to accept, especially since the reasoning behind them is not always made clear. From their point of view, the demand for a uniform regime is entirely justified. There are in fact visible indications that from the early 1990s the Utrecht council has been exchanging its discouraging attitude for a more accommodating one.

Fourthly, the *complex relationship between ideologically inspired debate and practical politics* is very obvious. To start with there is the historical paradox that a broad and fundamental public discussion about the place of Islam in Dutch society, and about the general recognition of Muslim institutions, did not start until the process of institutionalization was already well underway. The fierce debates in the early 1990s were in that sense too late. There is also a noticeable contrast between the various levels of authority. In so far as weighty and ideologically driven discussions may take place at the national level, they often concern issues for which practical solutions have long ago been found at the local level.

Of course, this does not mean that there were no such discussions in an earlier period, or that there is no connection at all between ideological discussions and practical politics. The point is that the connection between them is neither direct nor clear. Municipal policy makers have to deal more directly with concrete claims, and problems requiring a solution. Abstract views about the future direction of society are in these circumstances a luxury which they cannot allow themselves, which produces in consequence a more pragmatic attitude. Thus secular parties in the Second Chamber have since 1983 repeatedly and emphatically rejected a subsidy arrangement for Muslim places of worship, on the grounds that the national government no longer pays out money for the establishment of religious premises because of the separation of church and state. Municipalities faced with the problem of having to devise solutions for the establishment or relocation of mosques—because of such things as neighbourhood parking problems or planned urban renewal—saw little point in such principled stances. In practice all kinds of financial provisions were made, including subsidies for specific activities, inflated purchase prices for properties, or direct exchange of properties.

Fifthly, it is striking that the conflict about the institutionalization of Islam has to a large degree been played out in two *specific areas of policy*, one involving the *separation of church and state*, and the other the *minorities policy*. In the political, ideological, and also in the organizational sense, these two constantly prop up whenever the claims of Muslim immigrants come up for discussion. Both policy areas offer special opportunities to Muslims, but also problems, of which more will be discussed later.

Factors and agents

After these remarks about the degree and form of institutionalization, and particularly its presence and density in the different social spheres, the question of factors and agents becomes relevant. In the first chapter we started from the assumption that institutionalization is the result of an interaction between initiatives by Muslims, links with foreign powers and international Muslim organizations, legislation and regulation, government, the judiciary, private organizations—whether or not based on religious or ideological principles—and other institutions.

These factors and agencies are not monolithic entities with unchanging and consistent attitudes to the presence of Islam and the claims of its adherents. In theory they can react in one of three different ways: the active promotion or support of new religious institutions; adopting a more or less neutral or passive attitude; or taking active steps against the development of new institutions, for example by applying the letter of the law and delaying implementation, or by setting up new restrictive rules.

It will arouse little surprise that Muslim institutions often result from *initiatives by Muslims*. Yet they cannot take all the credit. The establishment of the co-ordinating Platform of Islamic Organizations of Greater Rotterdam, or the organizations of Muslim school managements, were partly the result of the involvement of third parties. Although Muslims often take the initiative, it should not be assumed that they have been able to arrange the Muslim institutional landscape entirely of their own accord. After all, not all initiatives produced the desired results. For instance, there is still no government-funded training course for imams in the Netherlands, and in state primary education only lip-service is paid to offering Islamic religious instruction. Moreover, Dutch society also takes an interest in the formation of these institutions, and exercises a guiding influence.

Although we have paid little attention to processes within the category of Muslims itself, it is clear that they have not always spoken with one voice. There has sometimes been bitter rivalry, as in the allocation of broadcasting time or the creation of primary schools and national co-ordinating bodies, though on other occasions they have worked closely together. This confirms once again that the Muslim community forms an imagined unity, rather than a real one.

In the discussion about Muslim institutions, repeated reference has been made to the *interference of foreign powers and/or international Muslim organizations*. It is indeed the case that they have intervened in the fortunes of the diaspora along the North Sea, for instance by helping to fund of places of worship, or by training and recruiting imams. Such action has been taken occasionally by Saudi Arabia or Libya, but more often by Turkey through the Presidium for Religious Affairs (the *Diyanet*).

However, the intervention was less frequent than has been alleged;

more striking perhaps was the *fear of intervention*. Dutch protagonists
opposed certain institutions on these grounds, such as the Member
of Parliament who tried to prevent the founding of Muslim schools.
Other agents were equally motivated, but in support of Muslim initiatives, because by supporting local organizations, or making arrangements in the Netherlands for training imams, the Dutch government
might be able to neutralize foreign powers or organizations. In fact
the policy makers are often remarkably inconsistent on this point.
Partly for fear of fundamentalist influences from abroad, the Rotterdam council adopted a policy of subsidizing Muslim organizations,
while only a few years earlier they had cordially invited fundamentalist Saudi Arabia to fund a mosque. Organizations associated with
the *Diyanet* were also given a more favourable reception because
they were thought to follow a more liberal type of Islam than other
organizations.

Legislation and regulation impresses its stamp firmly on the institutionalization of Islam in the Netherlands. It influences the way Muslims
formulate their claims, and also provides the legal framework in
which they are assessed. Dutch legislation contains numerous provisions which give religions and ideological bodies and their members
the right to specific facilities. Muslims can successfully invoke these
rules, particularly if they are worked out in detail. This applies, for
example, to the foundation of Muslim schools, where the constitutional principle of freedom of education works to the advantage of
Muslims. The objections of officials, politicians and others can be
rendered ineffective by purely legal arguments.

It is more complicated in cases where the existing rules are broadly
formulated, and where it is not immediately clear how and to what
extent these 'open' rules should apply to Muslims. The same is true
of cases where the existing rules state explicitly which religious organizations they apply to. In the armed forces, for instance, there is a
ruling that Jewish servicemen have the right to opt for a rest day
other than Sunday. To what extent this right also applied to Muslims
only became clear when a new ruling was published. In such cases
the practical solution is usually favoured. Sometimes amendments
are only made to regulations after Muslims have broken the existing, restrictive rules. For Muslim butchers who carried on their trade
without valid written qualifications, a more pliable transitional ruling
was made.

Some general changes to legislation and regulation have been very decisive for Muslims. The 1983 constitutional amendment, which put the seal on the separation of church and state, made the subsidization of places of worship more difficult. But paradoxically it also forced the government to formulate new rules about churches, Sunday as a day of rest, church bells, and spiritual care in prisons and the army. Thus the legal equivalence of the public call to prayer to ringing church bells fell straight into the Muslims' lap, as did the opportunity for Islamic spiritual care in the armed forces.

General policy processes can also work against the institutionalization of Islam. For example, new legislation to expand the scale of primary education—which itself had little to do with Muslim schools—turned out to be against the interests of Muslims.

In a number of cases where the parties involved could not reach agreement, an appeal was made to the *judiciary*. In some cases Muslims find themselves forced to follow this route because the rules are unclear, or even completely lacking; because they feel that there is unwillingness to apply the rules to them; or because they have reached a dead end. A judge's ruling often also provides the political solution to a problem, because it can be regarded as applying to similar cases, or else forces the parties involved into closer consultation. This was the case with the recognition of Islamic religious festivals by businesses and by the government.

In the vast majority of cases, *national and local government* forms the pivot on which the process of recognition turns. However, their role is by no means unequivocal or consistent. At one moment the authorities may actively encourage the formation of Muslim institutions, but then adopt a neutral, legalistic attitude, delay the advent of institutions, or even make things impossible. The general label of 'government' has proved to be misleading, since different departments can adopt different attitudes. This is partly because they have different interests, powers and regular contacts, and partly because of variations in the political and legal context. It is often a question of differences between individuals; some interpret the rules very narrowly, while others are more flexible. What people find desirable also varies. For instance, one directorate of the Ministry of Culture was quite co-operative with regard to subsidies for Muslim places of worship, while another adopted a very negative attitude to a Muslim broadcasting channel. For a long time the Rotterdam municipal council maintained a somewhat ambivalent policy on mosques because the two departments involved (the Migrants Office and the Secretariat for Urban Redevelopment) could not agree with each other. The application of the rules varied for each subject from individual to individual and from department to department.

If the authorities do grant facilities, they usually urge Muslims to organize themselves in the way which is customary in the Netherlands and most efficient for the authorities. In practice this comes down to Muslims being encouraged to unite in co-ordinating organizations with 'responsible' leaders, who can act as spokesmen for the rank and file. In Rotterdam the municipality played an active role in this process, which meant that Muslims had to organize themselves, as Roman Catholics and Protestants had done in an earlier period. The intention was to avoid politicians and civil servants having to deal with an amorphous and constantly changing group of minor leaders, or getting entangled in internal squabbles; moreover, it would enhance the legitimacy of their own political actions. The requirement of representativeness was not actually applied very consistently. Sometimes it was written in as a strict requirement (for example, for spiritual care in the armed forces, and at first for broadcasting), while other times it was interpreted more pragmatically (for instance for ritual slaughter, training for carrying out circumcisions, or the admission of imams to prisons). Sometimes the requirement could amount to a straightforward ban on granting facilities. There is every indication that this is precisely what some people intended.

One category of civil servants is very emphatically involved with Muslims: those whose departments are charged with the development and implementation of the minorities policy. From the early 1980s onwards they have found a place in that policy for most of the interests of Muslims. They have been supported by the official statements in the 1983 *Minorities Memorandum*, for it concerns organizations of categories of the population defined as minorities policy target groups. However, these same officials show great reluctance when it comes to forming a single representative body for Muslims, or new rules which might question the separation of church and state. Apart from exceptions such as Utrecht, where Muslim organizations are excluded in principle from consultation arrangements for ethnic minorities, the minorities policy serves as a catalyst for the recognition of Islam. To be sure this means institutionalization is steered in a specific direction, to fit in with the objectives of the minorities policy.

We have remarked that the officials, politicians and private organizations involved at the national level tend towards discussing the problem, while at the local level they are more inclined to look for practical solutions. A comparable difference in approach can be observed between politicians and civil servants, certainly at the local level. Both in Rotterdam and in Utrecht, civil servants have been more committed, and at an earlier stage, to the interests of Muslims than were the council members. In Rotterdam, officials of the Migrants Office changed their negative attitude towards Muslims into a more co-operative one as early as 1981; the council only followed four years later. In Utrecht the politicians reprimanded the officials for their inclination to get closer to Muslims.

The way in which the policy rules were applied to Muslim institutions reveals a certain insecurity on the part of those implementing the policy. In several cases a solution of one local council, which was pragmatically intended but sometimes arbitrary, was adapted as a norm in another, for example, in drawing up local regulations for the public call to prayer.

Organizations based on religious or ideological principles have been involved in the formation of Muslim institutions to a varying extent, and with divergent objectives. It may not always be obvious in the sense that one can talk of a 'natural' alliance between related organizations. This does not alter the fact that such agents as the Council of Churches, and ministers and priests, have sometimes sprung to the aid of Muslims, on issues like Islamic religious instruction and the employment of imams in penal institutions. We saw such coalitions forming, particularly around the issue of severing the financial links between church and state. Leading politicians of the Christian Democratic Party (CDA), including the Prime Minister and the Minister of Welfare, Health and Culture, paid official visits to Muslim institutions on several occasions, and a number of Muslim leaders, influenced in part by the invitation of the party, joined the Christian Democrats. These manifestations of solidarity produced some internal discussion within Christian organizations about whether or not they should be working for the Muslims' cause. Within the Christian Democratic Party (CDA), this was one of the questions raised in discussions about Muslims becoming party members. The orthodox Calvinist parties on the extreme right had a simpler answer: they usually strongly opposed what they saw as Muslim heresy.

Organizations not based on religious or ideological principles have been involved in the institutionalization of Islam to a limited extent, for instance in the founding of Muslim schools and places of worship, in decisions on whether to subsidize Muslim organizations, and in ritual slaughter. The Association of Dutch Local Authorities and the animal protection organizations have made their point of view widely known at times. In many issues, secular and often left-wing immigrant organizations joined in the fray, sometimes in alliance with residents associations, charitable foundations or left-wing political parties. Their involvement usually amounted to putting obstacles in the way of Muslim institutions. On the other hand, the Labour Party (PvdA) argued in favour of granting facilities to Muslims, originally on the grounds of the principle of equality.

Of the *other organizations*, a limited number of academics, and particularly the media, have had their say in the debate on Islam. Their contributions, which sometimes support Muslims and sometimes are against them, have ensured that the interests of Muslims reached the political agenda, and stayed on it.

Ideological concepts and arguments

Now that we know what legal and political processes have played a role in the institutionalization of Islam, and which agents and agencies were involved, it is time to draw some conclusions about the ideological background to the behaviour of those involved.

In the first chapter we noted that the ideological conceptions and arguments relevant to our subject could be reduced to three dominant ideologies about the nation state, the rights and obligations obtaining within it, and the distribution of social goods and services: we distinguished an ideology of citizenship, an ideology of residence, and an ideology of the plural society. A second dimension concerns the question of the place in public life allotted to religion in general, and to Islam and its institutions in particular. A third dimension involves assumptions about the ethnic and cultural position of immigrants in society, whereby the emphasis is sometimes laid on the individual, but at others on the collective they are thought to form. These assumptions, propositions and arguments can be placed on a single axis, with at its two extremes an assimilationist and a pluralist ideology. Between these ideal-typical contrasting ideologies we find a large number of variants; for these hybrid forms we use the collective term, 'integrationism'. To what extent did we encounter these ideological positions? We will start by following our main analytical framework.

The *ideology of citizenship* only rarely comes to the surface. It was observed a few times in the views of the small Protestant parties when, for example, they argued that Muslims (like other non-Dutch immigrants) could only acquire political rights if they were naturalized as Dutch citizens. In fact these parties had Muslims in mind who, to put it bluntly, would trade their faith in Allah for one in Jesus Christ. Occasionally the foreign nationality of Muslims has formed an obstacle to the recognition of Muslim institutions. The admission of non-Dutch imams is a case in point. The authorities used their foreign nationality to deny certain imams entry to the Netherlands. By doing so they hoped to prevent religious conflicts. On the other hand, in the regulation of ritual slaughter it was accepted that it was required not only by Muslims of foreign nationality resident in the Netherlands, but also by Muslims of Dutch nationality. In so far as the practice of the Islamic religion and the establishment of its associated institutions are concerned, the prevailing view is that citizenship should play no role.

The *ideology of residence* is rather more frequently expressed. This maintains that all individuals who find themselves on Dutch soil, regardless of nationality, enjoy the constitutional right of freedom of religion. This tendency to equal treatment is widely adhered to (orthodox Calvinist circles excepted). In practice this amounts to individual Muslim residents being allotted the same rights and being able to make the same claims on government as the adherents of established religions or ideologies. However, there seems to be no unanimity about the practical application of this principle of equality, and it is sometimes applied with limitations. In that respect there is a gap between this particular view and the actions based upon it.

The *pluralist ideology* is disputed. It meets both support and opposition. Some people have warmly applauded the formation of Muslim communities with their own institutions. They believe that the Muslim diaspora must be allowed to flourish, or they see in the formation of Muslim communities a powerful instrument for the emancipation of the immigrants belonging to them. The formation of such communities is also encouraged because it is likely to strengthen the negotiating position of other religious communities (for example, with respect to private or denominational schools). There are, however, large bodies of opinion which object to such reasoning. Some emphasize depillarization, and no longer see any social role reserved for religion in the 'modern 1990s'. Others consider the combination of pre-modern and culturally alien elements, as in Muslim immigrant associations, as being undesirable and perhaps even damaging for Muslims and for society as a whole.

In practice we encounter these opinions in all kinds of hybrid forms. The same agents may promote the activities of one institution (for instance, for the practice of Islamic worship), but block others (such as Muslim schools). Even in cases where an institution is supported, there are still ambivalences. Thus the Christian Democratic Party (CDA), contrary to what many perhaps expected, has certainly not always supported Muslim schools with complete conviction.

To what extent is there a place in this context for *religious or ethnic-cultural identity*? In so far as the discussion relates purely and exclusively to the place of religion or of Islam in public life, often—and probably inevitably—the fundamental principle of *freedom of religion* is raised. With only slight exaggeration, we can say that the general view is that 'even' Muslims must be able to practise their religion. Great—if not absolute—value is attached to this principle, and in many cases it is weighed up against other principles or interests, such as the protection of animals (in ritual slaughter), the integrity of the body (in female circumcision), the policy of restricting entry (for imams), the regulation of economic activity (Muslim butchers), fire and safety regulations for buildings (places of worship) and the integration of ethnic minorities.

The willingness to allow freedom of religion to apply also to Muslims is greater when it involves individuals, rather than Muslims collectively. In the same way individual Muslims are encouraged to take part in Dutch politics, but the idea that they might form their own parties evokes great opposition. This is undoubtedly the result of the prevailing image of Muslims. Many of the agents encountered in our research tended to assume that Muslims have an exaggerated need to stick together and to keep themselves separate from the rest of society. They are also presumed to have an unreasonable preference for traditional leadership; not to have developed enough feeling for democratic attitudes; not to treat women as equals; to be susceptible to influence from—probably arch-conservative—foreign organizations and powers; and finally, to undermine the separation of church and state. Following this reasoning they should be given little opportunity to establish their strongholds within Dutch society. That Muslims form tight communities and need to establish strongholds is something that exists principally in the heads of non-Muslims.

Without the hindrance of knowledge about the actual nature and extent of Muslim communities and their institutions, Muslims are conveniently presented as a fixed and homogenized entity.

Discussion about freedom of religion often concentrates on the more practical question of the extent to which the government should actively guarantee the exercise of this constitutional right. The background is the disadvantaged social position of Muslim immigrants, which would justify a generous approach by the government. But few of the agents encountered in our research shared this view. Since 1983 the government should not have had to provide support for the development of religious communities—for instance, by subsidizing places of worship—because it was incompatible with the process of secularization, which many saw as being far advanced. The principle of the *separation of church and state* was eagerly embraced and sometimes took on almost the character of an article of faith. In the country that still observes Sunday as a day of rest, that has the words *God zij met ons* (God Be with Us) engraved on its coinage, and a head of state who always ends the speech from the throne with a prayer, many people still act as if the separation of church and state were an accomplished fact and taken for granted.

The argument that other church communities have been able to build up an extensive infrastructure, whether or not with government support, is also taken into consideration. The principle of the separation of church and state is then set against another constitutional right, the *principle of equality*. To the extent that other religious communities and churches are seen as reference groups, most of the agents involved are prepared in the final analysis to apply the principle of equality quite strictly; in other words, Muslims should acquire rights or facilities because similar rights have been granted to Protestant, Roman Catholic, Humanist or Jewish groups. The historical recognition of Jewish practices, such as ritual slaughter, or circumcision, as well as the arrangements for Jewish spiritual care in the armed forces and penal institutions, taking oaths, and religious festivals, works to the advantage of Muslims. It is considered fair that they should profit from similar rules. In other cases in which it is thought equitable to give Muslims facilities (for instance, dietary arrangements in the armed forces), the new rules have been drawn up in such a way that all those involved, including non-Muslims, are beneficiaries.

The question is often whether the principle of equality is only valid in the here and now, or whether a longer historical period should be taken into consideration. This was particularly the case in the debate about subsidizing places of worship. Partly as a result of donations from the government, Christian congregations have been able to build a large number of churches. However, by the time Muslims started invoking the Church Building Subsidy Act, the arrangement expired. If the principle of equality is applied in today's conditions, that would mean that mosques should have to manage without state support. In that case, so claim the supporters of more generous assistance, the historical disadvantage which Muslims have will never be eroded. Nevertheless, secular parties are uninterested in focusing on historical disadvantages, because it weakens the confirmation of secularization in the law and regulations.

It is striking that in the early stage of amendments to legislation, as in the discussions on the Church Building Subsidy Act, or the Public Demonstrations Act, it was not the Christian parties who invoked the principle of equality, but in fact the secular parties (the Liberal Party (VVD), Labour (PvdA), and the left-liberal Democrats 66 (D66)). Politicians from Christian parties, including the Christian Democratic Party (CDA), tended to emphasize the differences between the 'old' and 'new' religions, with the implication that the latter do not have the same rights. In a number of cases—the public call to prayer or private education—they were in the end prepared to share their rights with the new religions, particularly when the security of their own rights was reinforced by doing so.

What positions were adopted with respect to the scope immigrants should have for the expression of their ethnic-cultural identity? We encountered no pure *assimilationists or pluralists*. Most were prepared to allow Muslim immigrants a certain amount of singularity, though they varied in the amount. Integrationism is dominant, although within this hybrid form the more assimilationist variants are more prominent than the pluralist ones. As the manifestations of identity assume a more collective form, or have consequences for the functioning of society as a whole, so the willingness to offer scope for it declines. There is great fear of Muslim immigrants being socially isolated on the grounds that their way of life deviates from the Dutch norm. The perception is as follows: the Dutch do not identify themselves very strongly with their religion but observe it in a quiet and liberal way, they treat men and women alike, follow modern methods in education, and do not allow themselves to be dragged along by foreign fanatics, in short: the Dutch are modern and enlightened. In

Utrecht, officials put forward all these arguments against the introduction of Islamic religious instruction in state primary schools.

The fear of isolation has its counterpart in the efforts towards integration, which in the eyes of many consists of adopting Dutch norms
and values, as well as social contacts and dialogue. The minorities
policy, aimed at an 'integrated' society, justifies such opinions.

In practice the debates about Muslims and ethnic minorities become
blurred, and a new image arises; for example the ideological premise
of the customs and behaviour of Muslim immigrants, and the concerns about other, sharply delineated and more or less closed collectivities. In particular we find articulated an aversion to the formation
of Muslim strongholds, and support for an Islam oriented more
towards Dutch society. Some people think that Muslims should be
given as little room as possible to be Islamic, and to the extent that
a display of Islam is unavoidable, this should be solely in terms set
by Dutch society. This explains why many prefer the subject of religious studies, aiming at the transfer of knowledge about Islam as one
among other faiths, to instruction which is centred on the practice
of Islam. Where the latter does occur, state schools are favoured
more than separate Muslim schools. Many wonder whether Muslim
schools do not encourage the segregation of ethnic minorities, and
whether they are not contrary to the aims of the integration policy.

It is evident that such a view, even if sanctioned by the minorities policy, can cause tensions. For not only do Muslims have their
own views about the arrangement of their lives in the Netherlands,
but also, like the adherents of any other religion, they have certain
rights. Legal and political circumstances sometimes oblige people to
swallow their own opinions and to act in a manner which does not
always reflect their views, as many a civil servant or politician who
has had to co-operate in setting up Muslim schools knows from his
or her own experience.

International perspective: Belgium and Great Britain

In the third part of the book we investigated how the Dutch reaction to the institutionalization of Islam display specific features associated with the nature of Dutch society, by means of a comparison
with Belgium (which like the Netherlands is well acquainted with
pillarization) and with Great Britain (which is not). We concentrated

on the recognition of Islam, political representation, the establishment and funding of places of worship, Islamic religious instruction and Muslim schools. The comparison is mainly based on secondary sources, which entails several limitations.

At first, the three countries appear to have undergone a similar development. In all three the presence of Islam and its adherents went largely unnoticed for a long time. This gradually changed, until in the late 1980s and early 1990s their position in society became the subject of heated general debate. Yet on closer examination, there were important differences.

As far as *religions and their relationship to the state* are concerned, Belgium, Great Britain and the Netherlands are very different countries. Unlike the Low Countries, Britain has an *established church*, which has a privileged status. As in the Netherlands, the other religious communities have had to acquire recognition through a range of separate regulations in separate areas. In Belgium on the other hand, recognition of a religion is arranged by passing a law, but this has yet to come into force. Adherents of a recognized religion are in principle eligible for a number of facilities from the government, at least in theory.

The way in which the Belgian government has tried to steer the institutionalization of Islam, since formal recognition in 1974, has produced substantial problems across the board. The formal recognition even now no more than a hollow shell. The greatest obstacle in Belgium was the absence of a nationally recognized representative body. In 1975 the Belgian government granted the Islamic and Cultural Centre this position, but it had no legal standing, nor any legitimation within the Muslim communities. Since then things have been at an impasse. In Great Britain, Muslims made their presence most felt on the local political scene. Only in recent years have they turned their attention to the central government, without direct results as yet. In the Netherlands recognition of Islam, both nationally and locally, has taken place in stages and in one area at a time. There has been less political and other resistance, and lower requirements have been set as regards representativeness. In the Netherlands Muslim organizations fulfil a political or proto-political role in the implementation of the minorities policy in a number of local areas and at the national level. They are also involved in the renewed relationship between the state and the churches. Officially they are only granted facilities for such things as spiritual care if they form a representative body. Although they have never been successful in doing so at the national level, this failure has not proved to be an insuperable obstacle to the provision of most facilities.

The *establishment of places of worship* in all these countries is a matter for the local authorities. This in practice involves long deliberations about the sites, and the disruption they may cause in the neighbourhood. Moreover, the authorities sometimes apply a plainly restrictive policy. Despite formal recognition in Belgium, the authorities there provide no subsidy for places of worship. In the Netherlands such support was given for a number of years, while Great Britain has no national arrangement for funding Muslim places of worship.

Although British Muslims have been trying for a considerable time to make arrangements in the field of education, their Belgian and Dutch co-religionists seem to have been more successful. In England there are several dozen *Muslim schools*, but only very recently and after endless official procedures have a few of them become funded by the government. All the applications were rejected. Nor is there any *Islamic religious instruction*, while the content of the existing officially authorized instruction has a strong Christian bias. In Belgium Islamic religious instruction is provided on a wide scale in state primary schools. In addition one government-funded Muslim school has opened its doors there. In the Netherlands there is little specific instruction, but there are approximately 30 Muslim primary schools.

The differences can only partly be attributed to the degree to which *Muslims take initiatives*. The relatively small number of Muslim schools in Belgium is related to the fact that after the foundation of the first school, Muslims refrained from making more applications. They did not want to add fuel to the fierce opposition to Islam. This is in contrast to England, where one application after another was submitted for the recognition and funding of Muslim schools. There was certainly no lack of initiatives there. The obstacles lay elsewhere, namely with the central government. In the Netherlands a number of Muslim schools were founded within a relatively short time, despite all the opposition.

Foreign powers and international Muslim organizations play a role in all three countries, but in different ways. In Belgium official representatives of Saudi Arabia and other Muslim countries were involved from the start in the process of institutionalization, by invitation of the Belgian government. In addition the Turkish Diyanet exercised considerable influence in some cases, as in the appointment of teaching staff for religious instruction. In Great Britain the ambassadors of Muslim countries supported their co-religionists at the time of the Rushdie affair. There has never been any evidence of that degree of involvement in the Netherlands. The Diyanet was involved in sending imams and in setting up Muslim schools, but that was largely without consultation with the Dutch government. Financial support from Saudi Arabia and Libya for the establishment of mosques usually occurred at the invitation of Muslims themselves. In all three countries the foreign interventions raised objections.

In some cases *legislation and regulation* help to explain the differences between the countries. We have already referred to the general procedures affecting the recognition of religions. The privileged position of the *established church* in England is founded in the law, as is the official recognition of Islam in Belgium. In the Netherlands it is particularly the legal position of private schools which is important. This to some extent explains the relative ease with which Islamic religious instruction can be given in Belgium, or a Muslim school founded in the Netherlands, but also the problems in England in establishing similar schools. There legislation has even been adjusted in response to the presence of Muslims, in such a way that the creation of certain Muslim institutions has been seriously hindered or even rendered impossible. The most prominent example would be the curtailment of the existing opportunities for Islam in the compulsory religious education curriculum. At the same time we must qualify the importance of legislation and regulation. The general, legal recognition of Islam in Belgium has for the most part given Muslims only the semblance of advantages.

This is partly because of the special *role of the government* in the process. In comparison to the Dutch or British central government, the Belgians have been remarkably active, at least since 1989, and particularly so in arranging for a representative body for Muslims. But their active involvement has so far still not delivered a recognized body, only a series of conflicts, with the result that Muslims are still deprived of all kinds of facilities. The Dutch government has adopted alternating points of view, varying from active support to delaying tactics. Provisions which may promote the integration of Muslim immigrants into Dutch society can count on support. The success of the minorities policy is a priority. The British central government is more dismissive in this respect, but local authorities display much less rigidity and are sometimes even co-operative. In all three countries it is striking how divided the authorities are: there are great differences between central and local levels of government, and between and within departments.

In a number of cases Muslims have had recourse to the *judiciary*. When the courts have ruled in their favour, their subsequent claims have usually been honoured by the government; only in England has the government brushed aside the pronouncements of the courts, and the Secretary of State for Education has obstinately refused to finance Muslim schools.

Organizations, based on religious or ideological principles or otherwise, have in all three countries been actively involved in the institutionalization of Islam. Sometimes this has been to the benefit of Muslims. For instance, the authoritative leaders of the Church of England spoke in favour of government funding for Muslim schools, but opposed amending the law on blasphemy to cover the deity of Islam.

The *media* are also often active. They ensured that Muslims and their institutions were placed on the political agenda and stayed there. Sometimes the political debate has been conducted exclusively in the media, as in Belgium when it came to the setting up of Muslim schools.

Our comparison shows that the situation favours Muslims most in the Netherlands, where they have certainly achieved, *de facto*, the greatest scope for building up a religious infrastructure. In Belgium this scope is very limited, in spite of legal recognition more than 20 years ago. In Great Britain the central government has repeatedly shown itself to be inflexible and dismissive.

Conclusion

In recent decades Muslims have established their own religious communities in Europe, and in doing so have created a range of institutions. In the Netherlands this has mainly been in the spheres of religion, politics and education; other areas were hardly affected. An international comparison has shown us that the pattern of institutionalization has, up to a point, a specifically national character. In the course of the development of Muslim institutions, authorities and other organizations have continuously had to adjust their attitudes to institutionalization and to the structure of society as a whole.

The creation of room for Muslim institutions to operate is certainly not an automatic process. How Muslims formulate their claims and how society accepts them is largely determined by *current legislation and regulation*. The legal scope for Islam is greater in the Netherlands than in Great Britain, where Islam is at a disadvantage in relation to the Church of England. Compared to Belgium, however, the legal scope is restricted: in the Netherlands there is no provision for one-off, general recognition of a religion, and the recognition of Islam has therefore taken place by stages. Limits have been set: for instance, there has been no question of Muslims being allowed their own courts. Islamic family law, when it is incorporated in the national law of their countries of origin, can only be exercised within the limits of Dutch public law and order; thus repudiation of a wife, or polygamy, are not permitted in the Netherlands.

Much legislation incorporates rules which reflect the dominant Christian religion, for instance concerning Sunday as a day of rest, Christian festivals, and bell-ringing. Most of the legislation relevant to the recognition and support of religious institutions is, however, phrased in general terms, which do not explicitly favour any particular religion. Much of this 'pillarized' legislation, stemming from a period when religion and faith were important criteria for the distribution of social goods and services, has been replaced by new rules, or is now more tailored to individual needs and rights. The amendments to the Constitution in 1983 are a demonstrable culmination point in this trend. Even so, the legal system in the Netherlands does not in itself seem to operate against the interests of Muslims. The 'depillarization' of legislation and regulation is after all a slow process, and (paradoxically) new rules have sometimes been introduced to benefit religious or ideological groups. Muslims can benefit from this process not just in spite of, but also because of the separation of church and state.

The scope given to Muslims for the formation of their own institutions is also heavily dependent on the *conventions of political practice*, which vary not only from country to country but for each locality. It is to be expected of government and other social organizations that they will conform to current legislation—and will keep to the basic principles of freedom of religion and equality—but that does not mean that the outcome is determined in advance. Not only can the rules sometimes be interpreted in a multitude of different ways, but political and ideological circumstances and traditions also have a role to play. In this the government is of decisive importance, as was made clear in the international comparison. We saw how the British government deliberately and consciously (and sometimes even against judicial rulings) acted in own interest. On the other hand the Belgian and Dutch governments have, after some hesitation and resistance, followed the rules. Within the Netherlands, with its more or less uniform regulatory framework, differences still occur between the central government and local authorities, who often (though not always) tend to take a more pragmatic course. Moreover, there are clear differences between local authorities.

While the administration of Rotterdam has supported the formation of Muslim institutions since the early 1980s, and from time to time has even encouraged them, the municipality of Utrecht has adopted a negative attitude. This discrepancy can partially be ascribed to differences in local regulations. It has far more to do with the way in which those responsible for policy use their powers and the freedom of action of their office. Some issues are primarily determined by their perception of the institutionalization of Islam: as supporting the implementation of the minorities policy (in Rotterdam), or as a threat to existing traditions, arrangements, and power positions (in Utrecht).

We have put forward several different explanations for the variation in the actions of the government bodies involved. Which, in our considered view, is the most essential? In the first place comes the *political arena* in which the struggle for the recognition of Muslim institutions must take place. In Dutch politics great store is set on the *principle of equality*—for a variety of reasons, including social and historical ones: the pluralist system of pillarization is a manifestation of it. The application of this basic principle is more automatic in the Netherlands than in Great Britain. For instance, in the discussion about Rushdie's *Satanic Verses*, the question arose in both countries whether the existing legislation against blasphemy also extended to protecting Muslims against offence to their religious feelings. The reaction of the British government was that the criminal law only protected the Christian religion. In the Netherlands the answer was that the existing regulation offered equal protection to all religions. To allow rights to one religious group which are withheld from another is in the Netherlands evidently considered repugnant, not least because it might affect the political and ideological basis of the social system itself.

In Belgium and Great Britain in equal measure, we encounter *conventions* which govern the practice of Islam. In Great Britain one such convention is that new religions must be satisfied with a less privileged position than that of the Church of England. They certainly contribute to a climate in which members of the government can ignore a judicial pronouncement on the allocation of rights to Muslims, and can even carry through new, restrictive legislation. This incidentally is also an indication of the relationship between the central government and the judiciary in Great Britain. In Belgium, too, the control of religious education is also related to the conventions of society. It is taken for granted that religious instruction is offered in state schools, and that Muslims can take advantage of this even before the completion of all the legal formalities.

In the political arena all manner of developments take place, which at first sight have nothing to do with Muslims, but which do have an important effect on the process of institutionalization. Examples are the separation of church and state, the decentralization of responsibility from central to local government, increases in the scale of education, the maintenance of good relations with oil-producing countries, and above all the implementation of government policy on immigrants. In addition to such general considerations a role is also played by shifts in the balance of power between and within parties: cabinet changes, new ministers, and at the local level new Aldermen with their own ideas on policy.

The Netherlands has adopted a more coherent policy than either Belgium or Great Britain for the *integration of ethnic minorities*. It attaches great importance to socio-economic and ethnic-cultural characteristics. In practice, Dutch policy makers have shown a tendency to view and treat elements of the Islamic faith and the associated behaviour as elements of the ethnic culture of the relevant group of immigrants. The majority of the target groups of the minorities policy are made up of followers of Islam, and they are mobilized by Muslim organizations. To reach them, and to increase the effectiveness of their policy, the civil servants concerned increasingly involve Muslim organizations in drawing up their plans. Similar considerations are sometimes encountered in Great Britain, particularly at the local level, and mainly formulated in terms of good 'inter-racial relations', but their sociological significance seems in the end more restricted. In Belgium the appointment of a Royal Commissioner on Migrants Policy acted as a catalyst in the awkward relations between Muslim organizations and the national government. So far, however, the historical problems remain unresolved.

At the national level, it is often possible to discuss conflicting principles and take action on the long term, but at the local level the immediate *involvement of the local authorities* is unavoidable. They are confronted with actual demands for places of worship, the call to prayer, the content and funding of religious instruction, and Muslim primary schools. They have no choice but to take direct action. The minorities policy, formulated nationally but decentralized in its implementation, encourages local councils to involve its target groups in that policy. If Muslim organizations can gain a place in this process, the institutionalization of Islam can become a matter with which the leaders of various constituencies are involved, a development which is to the advantage of Muslims.

A common administrative practice is to do business, if possible, with delegates of interest groups who have been mandated by their rank and file in a democratic way. This *requirement of representativeness* is understandable, both from the democratic point of view and from that of administrative efficiency. However, its selective application has given rise to the impression that this requirement is sometimes advanced to prevent, or to counter, the claims of Muslims. This is particularly the case when after many years it has become plain that the diversity of countries of origin, religious beliefs and organizational tradition of the groups involved stands in the way of any enduring representative organization of Muslims at the national level. Developments in Belgium are a good illustration of this. In the Netherlands too, however, it is difficult to understand why a pragmatic solution has been found for ritual slaughter and the Muslim broadcasting network, while the formal arrangements for spiritual care in penal institutions and in the armed forces were frustrated by the strict requirements for representativeness.

The different reactions of the national and local authorities can also be explained by the way in which *Islam and its adherents are ideologically positioned*. In most cases it is rather negative. These reactions are usually produced by negative images: the alleged religious fanaticism of Muslims, their collectivism, rigid male-female relations, old-fashioned teaching methods, lack of sympathy for democratic relations, traditional leadership, susceptibility to political extremism and the influence of foreign powers, and their indifference to the separation of church and state. Islam is generally associated with the past, with backwardness and pre-modernity, and even with an aversion to modernity. These notions are in a sense mirrored in the positive interpretation which is placed on the host society. The fear is widespread that Muslims form sharply demarcated enclaves, which frustrate the enlightened and modernist development of society; this also explains the opposition to Muslim institutions. Muslims are therefore heavily dependent on the legal protection which legislation offers, or should offer them. They are often presented as part of a collective, while the societies we have examined tend to deal more with individual citizens, which is a remarkable phenomenon. Sometimes Muslims anticipate the negative perceptions and the opposition which their claims will arouse, and withdraw them. In Belgium they submitted no new plans after achieving their first primary school in Brussels. In the Netherlands there is also some evidence that in a few cases, like the public call to prayer, Muslims refrain from making claims, or limit them in advance, so as not to arouse opposition.

Ideological notions about Islam and its followers are shot through with other images, mainly concerned with *disadvantaged categories* of the population (like immigrants), who moreover are likely to possess *deviant social or ethnic-cultural features*. We encounter these ideas in the Dutch minorities policy from the 1980s onwards, and their interpretation can vary a great deal, especially in the emphasis on two elements—a policy for disadvantaged groups based on equality, and a parity-based policy aimed at the formation of a multicultural society. Particularly since the end of the 1980s there has been a noticeable shift towards the first element. The cultural 'otherness' of the policy's target groups is increasingly perceived as a problem, as a factor encouraging isolation and threatening integration. The practical measures aimed at integration now bear more resemblance to a policy of assimilation than they did previously. They are intended to encourage the adoption of Dutch values and norms, partly by fostering contact and dialogue. In a certain sense this implicit form of 'liberal assimilationism' is the reverse side of the great importance which is placed on the principle of equality in the Netherlands, both in theory and in practice.

What is relatively unusual in the Netherlands, but common in Belgium and particularly in Great Britain, is for Muslims to be regarded as foreign nationals, and their religion therefore as an alien religion, a *corpus alienum*. It might be expected that in Great Britain, where the vast majority have British nationality, Muslims would start

from a much more favourable position than in Belgium or the Netherlands, where most of them have the status of foreigners. In practice,
however, the ambassadors of their countries of origin can be required
to act as the representatives of their interests in Great Britain. This
is also the case in Belgium, originally even at the invitation of the
authorities. In the Netherlands there is a preference for solving problems internally or domestically.

In the process of institutionalization and the recognition of Islam
in the Netherlands, the different ideological lines converge in a specific
way. Sometimes this hinders the recognition of institutions, as with
Muslim schools being seen as expressions of segregation, but it can
also work to their advantage, as in the funding of places of worship
or recognition as a dialogue partner. In a number of cases, as in
the U-turn in the policy to support Muslim organizations in Rotterdam,
receptiveness to the claims of Muslims can be ascribed in large measure to a shift in the ideological debate. For example, those involved
are seen less and less as 'Muslims' who, because of the separation
of church and state, can expect no intervention from the authorities, but increasingly as 'ethnic minorities', who deserve support and
recognition in the context of the minorities policy.

However, the significance of ideologies is not absolute. In many
situations those responsible for policy choose solutions which do not
entirely match their ideological views, because the legislation make
it desirable, or because certain problems make a pragmatic solution
essential.

In comparison with Belgium and Great Britain, the institutionalization of Islam in the Netherlands is relatively advanced. This does
not mean, however, that the Netherlands has become the 'European
Mecca' for Muslims. Indeed, we should not overlook the fact that
the dominant reaction in the established population has been one
of fear and unfamiliarity. It is mainly in the nature of the institutionalization that the Netherlands differs from the other two countries: partly by means of the instruments of the minorities policy, the
Netherlands is steering a course firmly in the direction of an Islam
which is oriented towards Dutch society, regardless of whether this
is what Muslims want.

With this knowledge, how should we regard the discussion about
the position of Islam in the Netherlands? Although Muslims have
been busily setting up their own institutions since the 1960s, the
recognition in principle of these institutions was only discussed nation-

ally and publicly in the early 1990s. From a historical point of view this breakthrough came relatively late. The protagonists in the debate have exchanged all kinds of views on the question of what Dutch society should look like and how Islam should fit into it. Their contributions are primarily highly normative in character, and seem to take very little account of a process that has been going on for decades: the government is recognizing these institutions one after the other, even if Muslims have to plead for it. It seems as if only in the early 1990s were eyes opened to a development that had been underway for a long time. Those who actively opposed the 'new' reality, and who wanted to resist institutionalization in any way, for the most part gained only Pyrrhic victories. At most they were successful in imposing certain conditions. How could it be otherwise, in a country in which freedom of religion is anchored in the Constitution, and where everyone supports the principle of equality? Those wanting to deprive Muslims of their rights are striking at the foundations of their own society. Most politicians, civil servants and other policy makers realize this too, and so have at long last created room for Muslim institutions.

In conclusion, the idea is widespread that Islam and the form it takes in Europe is primarily a matter for Muslims themselves. In this analysis of the history of the origin of Muslim institutions in various countries, and the opportunities and obstructions Muslims have experienced, we have shown that the outcome of the process of institutionalization is to a far greater degree determined by the societies in which Muslims settle, than by Muslims themselves. In this sense, every society gets the brand of Islam it deserves.

LIST OF ABBREVIATIONS FOR POLITICAL PARTIES

The Netherlands

ARP	Anti Revolutionaire Party	Anti-Revolutionary Party
BP	Boerenpartij	Farmers Party
CDA	Christen Democratisch Appel	Christian Democratic Party
CHU	Christelijk Historische Unie	Christian Historials
CP	Centrumpartij	Centre Party
CPN	Communistische Partij van Nederland	Communist Party of the Netherlands
D66	Democraten '66	Democrats 66
GPV	Gereformeerd Politiek Verbond	Reformed Political League
KVP	Katholieke Volkspartij	Catholic People's Party
PPR	Politieke Partij Radicalen	Radical Party
PSP	Pacifistische Socialistische Partij	Pacifist Socialist Party
PvdA	Partij van de Arbeid	Labour Party
SGP	Staatkundig Gereformeerde Partij	Political Reformed Party
VVD	Volkspartij voor Vrijheid en Democratie	Liberal Party

Belgium

CVP	Christelijke Volkspartij	Christian People's Party
PSC	Parti Social Chrétien	Social Christian Party
SP	Socialistische Partij	Socialist Party
VB	Vlaams Blok	Flemish Block
VU	Volksunie	[Flemish] People's Union

REFERENCES

Akkermans, P.W.C.
1986 'Onderwijs en recht', in: J.A. van Kemenade, N.A.J. Lagerweij, J.M.G. Leune & J.M.M. Ritzen (eds), *Onderwijs: bestel en beleid 1. Onderwijs in hoofdlijnen*, 359–433. Groningen: Wolters-Noordhoff.

Aksu, M. & O. Dogan
1987 'Een moskee in de wijk', *Traverse* 4 (3): 4–17.

Anwar, M. & R. Garaudy
1984 *Social and Cultural Perspectives on Muslims in Europe*. Research Paper no. 24. Birmingham: Centre for the Study of Islam and Christian-Muslim Relations, Selly Oak Colleges.

Ashraf, S.A.
1988 'Education of Muslim children in the UK. Some aspects', *Muslim Education Quarterly* 5 (3): 1–7.

Bakelen, F.A. van
1984 *Recht van de islam*. Teksten van het op 3 juni 1983 te Leiden gehouden Symposium. Groningen: RIMO.

Bakker, E.S.J. & L.J. Tap
1985 *Islamitische slagerijen in Nederland*. Mededelingenreeks nr. 40. Utrecht: Onderzoekers kollektief Utrecht.

Bastenier, A.
1988 'Islam in Belgium. Contradictions and perspectives', in: T. Gerholm & Y.G. Lithman (eds), *The New Islamic Presence in Western Europe*, 133–143. London: Mansell.

Bates, S.
1992 'Patten ordered to review Muslim case', *The Guardian*, 16 May 1992.

Bayliss, S.
1982 'Scarman gives warning for future', *Times Educational Supplement*, 29 January 1982.

Beckeringh, H. *et al.*
1986 *HVO verlangd onderwijs. Een antwoord op de verzuiling*. Utrecht: Stichting Humanistisch Vormingsonderwijs.

Beerling, R.F.
1978 'Institutie/Institutionalisering', in: L. Rademaker (ed.), *Sociologische Encyclopedie*, 293–295. Utrecht/Antwerpen: Het Spectrum.

Beets, G.C.N. & J. Oudhof
1982 'Een schatting van de aantallen islamieten en Hindoes/Boeddhisten in Nederland, 1971–1981', *Sociaal-Cultureel Kwartaalblad* 4 (1): 8–14.

Berg-Eldering, L. van den
1978 *Marokkaanse gezinnen in Nederland*. Alphen aan den Rijn: Samsom.

Beune, H.II.M. & A.J.J. Hessels
1983 *Minderheid—Minder recht? Een inventarisatie van bepalingen in de Nederlandse wet- en regelgeving waarin onderscheid wordt gemaakt tussen allochtonen en autochtonen*. Den Haag: Ministerie van Justitie (WODC).

Bhatti F.M. & H.A. Kanitkar
s.a. *British Muslims. Their Role and Contribution*. London: The Islamic Cultural Centre.

Bierlaagh, C.J.C.
1988 'Leerlingen met een ander geloof in de katholieke basisscholen. Streven naar samen katechese doen', *Samenwijs* 9 (3): 90–91.

Billiet, J. & K. Dobbelaere
1976   *Godsdienst in Vlaanderen. Van kerks katolicisme naar sociaal-culturele Kristenheid?*
        Leuven: Davidsfonds.
Blaise, P. & V. de Coorebyter
1990   *L'islam et l'école. Anatomie d'une polémique.* Courrier Hebdomadaire nos 1270–1271.
        Bruxelles: Centre de Recherche et d'Information Socio-Politique (CRISP).
Boer, H.A. de
1982   *Toespraak door de minister van Cultuur, Recreatie en Maatschappelijk Werk*, H.A. de
        Boer bij de opening van het Islam-symposium te Rotterdam op 28 sep-
        tember 1982 om 10.00 uur. Rijswijk: Ministerie van Cultuur, Recreatie en
        Maatschappelijk Werk, Voorlichtingsdienst. (Ook gepubliceerd in *De Nederlandse
        Staatscourant* 1982, nr. 190).
Bolkestein, F.
1991a   *Address to the Liberal International Conference at Luzern.* (Friday 6 September).
        Den Haag: Volkspartij voor Vrijheid en Democratie, Tweede-Kamerfractie.
1991b   'Integratie van minderheden moet met lef worden aangepakt', *de Volkskrant*,
        12 september 1991.
Bolten, J.J.
1984   *Verstotingen naar Nederlands Recht.* Nemesis.
1987   *Verstotingen in Nederland.* Nemesis.
Boseley, S.
1986   'Islamic school backed', *The Guardian*, 11 April 1986.
Bosma, O.
1983   'Islamitische godsdienstlessen op openbare scholen', *Inzicht* 117 (7): 23.
Bovenkerk, F., K. Bruin, L. Brunt & H. Wouters
1985   *Vreemd volk, gemengde gevoelens. Etnische verhoudingen in een grote stad.* Meppel/
        Amsterdam: Boom.
Broeck, L. van den
1992   'De islam in België, gesprekspartner gevraagd?', *Fonds Informatief* 14: 19–22.
Brugman, J.
1991   *De Alphense hoofddoekjesaffaire. Kledingvoorschriften in de islamitische wet.* Recht van
        de Islam 8. Maastricht: RIMO.
Buiks, P. & G. van Tillo
1980   *Het sociologisch perspectief. Een ontmoeting met de sociologische benaderingswijze.* Assen:
        Van Gorcum.
Burn J. & C. Hart
1988   *The Crisis in Religious Education.* London: The Educational Research Trust.
Centraal Bureau voor de Statistiek (CBS)
1994   *Statistisch Jaarboek 1994.* Den Haag: SDU.
1996   *Statistisch Jaarboek 1996.* Den Haag: SDU.
Choenni, C.E.S.
1995   *Kleur in de krijgsmacht. De integratie van Surinaamse jongen mannen in Nederland.*
        Proefschrift Universiteit Utrecht.
Chorus, A.
1981   'De Nederlandse volksaard', in: S.W. Couwenberg (ed.), *De Nederlandse natie*,
        33–43. Utrecht/Antwerpen: Het Spectrum.
Commissie Doelmatigheid Landelijke Minderhedenorganisaties
1992   *Stenen voor een nieuw gebouw. Advies van de Commissie Doelmatigheid Landelijke Min-
        derhedenorganisaties.* Rijswijk: Ministerie van WVC.
Commissie-Hirsch Ballin
1988   *Overheid, godsdienst en levensovertuiging. Eindrapport criteria voor steunverlening aan
        kerkgenootschappen en andere genootschappen op geestelijke grondslag.* Den Haag:
        Ministerie van Binnenlandse Zaken.

Commissie-Sassen
1957   *Rapport regeling bijdragen kerkenbouw*. Den Haag: Staatsdrukkerij- en uitgeversbedrijf.
Commission for Racial Equality (CRE)
1990   *Schools of Faith. Religious Schools in a Multicultural society*. London: CRE.
Coppen, H. & I. Ural
1982   'Het onderwijs aan moslims in Nederland', *Qiblah* 6 (2): 39–40.
Coppes, R.
1994   'Niet zomaar een stukje stof. Hoofddoekjes-affaires in Frankrijk, Nederland en Groot-Brittannië', *Sociologische Gids* 94 (2): 130–143.
Cox E. & J.M. Cairns
1989   *Reforming Religious Education. The Religious Clauses of the 1988 Education Reform Act*. London: Kogan Page/Institute of Education, University of London.
Couwenberg, S.W.
1982   'Discussie over minderhedenvraagstuk moet worden ontdaan van demagogie', *de Volkskrant*, Open Forum, 16 oktober 1982.
Cumper, P.
1990   'Muslim schools. The implications of the Education Reform Act 1988', *New Community* 16 (3): 379–389.
Dalrymple, W.
1988   'The teaching of Islam', *The Independent Magazine*, 20 October 1988.
Dassetto, F.
1990   'Twintig jaar Islam in België', *Islamitische Nieuwsbrief* 2 (8): 15–23.
1991   'Twintig jaar Islam in België', *Islamitische Nieuwsbrief* 3 (9): 14–25.
Dassetto, F. & A. Bastenier
1985   *The Organisation of Islam in Belgium*. Research Paper no. 26. Birmingham: Centre for the Study of Islam and Christian-Muslim Relations, Selly Oak College.
Dekker-Van Bijsterveld, S. den
1988   *De verhouding tussen kerk en staat in het licht van de grondrechten*. Zwolle: Tjeenk Willink.
Demirci, K.
1995   'Waar waren betrokkenen? Studiedag "Islam in Vlaanderen"', *Samenwijs* 15 (9): 385–387.
Department of Education and Science (DES)
1985   *Education for All*. London: HMSO.
Doğru, R.
1990   'TEB benadrukt belang van OETC', *Migranteninformatief* (Thema: Islam) 94: 16–17.
Donselaar, J. van
1993   'Post-war fascism in the Netherlands', *Crime, Law and Social Change*, 19: 87–100.
Doomernik, J.
1991   *Turkse moskeeën en maatschappelijke participatie. De institutionalisering van de Turkse islam in Nederland en de Duitse Bondsrepubliek*. Proefschrift Universiteit van Amsterdam.
Drop, H.
1985   *Algemene inleiding onderwijsrecht*. Zwolle: W.E.J. Tjeenk Willink.
Dungen, N. van den
1993   *Masallah. Een exploratief onderzoek naar de ontwikkeling van moslimbesnijdenissen onder Turkse migranten in Nederland*. Doctoraalscriptie. Amsterdam: Vrije Universiteit, Faculteit der Sociaal-Culturele Wetenschappen, Etnische Studies en Minderheidsvraagstukken.
Dwyer, C.
1993   'Constructions of Muslim identity and the contesting of power. The debate over Muslim schools in the United Kingdom', in: P. Jackson & J. Penrose (eds), *Constructions of Race, Place and Nation*, 143–159. London: UCL Press.

Dwyer, C. & A. Meyer
1995   'The institutionalization of Islam in The Netherlands and in the UK. The case of Islamic schools', *New Community* 21 (1): 37–54.
1996   'The establishment of Islamic schools. A controversial phenomenon in three European countries', in: W.A.R. Shadid & P.S. van Koningsveld (eds), *Muslims in the Margin. Political Responses to the Presence of islam in Western Europe*, 218–242. Kampen: Kok Pharos.
Educational Services Committee (ESC)
1974   *Guide to Religious Education in a Multi-Faith Community*. Bradford: ESC.
Elst, L.A. van der
1989   'Islamitisch godsdienstonderwijs bij Surinaamse gebedsruimten in Den Haag', *Samenwijs* 10 (4): 151–154.
Engberts, M.
1996   'SPIOR staat op springen', *Contrast* 3 (3): 1–2.
Ergün, C.
1982   'Nogmaals de Koranschool', *Samenwijs* 2 (8): 252–253.
Ester, P. & O. Mellegers
1974   *De Migrantenraad (een tussentijdse evaluatie)*. Utrecht: Sociologisch Instituut.
Exter, J. den
1990   *Diyanet. Een reis door de keuken van de officiële Turkse islam*. Beverwijk: Centrum Buitenlanders Peregrinus.
Federatie Moslim Organisaties Nederland (FOMON)
s.a.   *Rapport 1975–1978*. FOMON.
Feirabend, J.
1993   *Islam in de lokale politiek. De politieke participatie van islamitische organisaties in Utrecht*. Nijmegen: Katholieke Universiteit Nijmegen, Instituut voor Rechtssociologie.
Feirabend, J. & J. Rath
1996   'Making a place for Islam in politics. Local authorities dealing with Islamic associations', in W.A.R. Shadid & Van Koningsveld (eds), *Muslims in the Margin. Political Responses to the Precense of Islam in Western Europe*, 243–258. Kampen: Kok Pharos.
Foblets, M.C.
1991   *De erkenning en de gelijkstelling van de islam in België. Enkele actualiteitsvragen in de afwachting van een definitieve wettelijke regeling*. Recht van de Islam nr. 8. Maastricht: RIMO.
Gemeente Rotterdam (GR)
1978   *Nota Migranten in Rotterdam*. Rotterdam: Gemeente Rotterdam.
1981a   *Educatieve ideeën. Rotterdam op weg naar een multiculturele samenleving*. Rotterdam: Gemeente Rotterdam, Secretarieafdeling Onderwijs, Jeugdzaken en Vormingswerk.
1981b   *Moskeeën*. Rotterdam: Gemeente Rotterdam, Bureau Migranten.
1982a   *Educatie in de multi-culturele samenleving van Rotterdam*. Vervolgnota nr. 1. Rotterdam: Gemeente Rotterdam, Secretarieafdeling Onderwijs, Jeugdzaken en Vormingswerk.
1982b   *Evaluerende notitie over de hoofdlijnen van het gevoerde migrantenbeleid in Rotterdam 1981–1982*. Rotterdam: Gemeente Rotterdam.
1983   *Moskeegroepen als zelforganisaties*. Rotterdam: Gemeente Rotterdam.
1984a   *Beleid ten aanzien van moskeeën—april 1984*. Rotterdam: Gemeente Rotterdam, Bureau Migranten.
1984b   *Nota inzake het gemeentelijk subsidiebeleid vanuit de sector Bijzondere Groepen vanaf 1 januari 1985 met betrekking tot zelforganisaties en vrijwilligersorganisaties van en voor migranten*. Rotterdam: Gemeente Rotterdam, Bureau Migranten.
1985a   *Minderhedenbeleid in een gewijzigde situatie*. Rotterdam: Gemeente Rotterdam.
1985b   *Rapportage Accommodaties Zelforganisaties Turken en Marokkanen*. Rotterdam: Gemeente Rotterdam, Bureau Migranten.

1987a   *Kwaliteit aan de basis. Kansen voor en ontwikkelingen in het Rotterdams openbaar basisonderwijs.* Rotterdam: Gemeente Rotterdam.
1987b   *Rapportage Moskeeën in stadsvernieuwingswijken. Deel 1: korte termijn oplossingen.* Rotterdam: Gemeente Rotterdam, Bureau Migranten/PCC.
1987c   *Rapportage Moskeeën in stadsvernieuwingswijken. Deel 2: op weg naar een structurele aanpak.* Rotterdam: Gemeente Rotterdam, PCC.
1988   *Memorandum inzake het minderhedenbeleid in de jaren '90* (aangeboden door gemeentebesturen van 18 pcg-gemeenten). Rotterdam: Gemeente Rotterdam.
1991   *Geloven in de toekomst. Moskeeën in Rotterdam.* (Concept beleidsnota). Rotterdam: Gemeente Rotterdam, DROS-PCC.
1992a   *Moskeeën in Rotterdam.* Rotterdam: Gemeente Rotterdam, dienst Stedebouw + Volkshuisvesting.
1992b   *De nieuwe Rotterdammers.* Rotterdam: Gemeente Rotterdam.
1994   *Moskeeën en Mandirs.* Rotterdam: Gemeente Rotterdam, dienst Stedebouw + Volkshuisvesting.

Gemeente Tiel
1986   *Verordening subsidiëring godsdienst- en vormingsonderwijs.* Tiel: Gemeente Tiel, Afdeling OW.

Gemeente Utrecht (GU)
1980   *Nota Organisatiestructuur coördinatie minderhedenbeleid.* Utrecht: Gemeente Utrecht.
1981   *Rompnota minderhedenbeleid.* Utrecht: Gemeente Utrecht.
1982   *Moskee-notitie.* Utrecht: Gemeente Utrecht.
1984   *Overzicht van de ontwikkelingen rondom de moskee in de Otterstraat.* Utrecht: Gemeente Utrecht, Bureau Maatschappelijke Aangelegenheden.
1985a   *Evaluerend eindverslag 'Kernproject Minderhedenbeleid'.* Utrecht: Gemeente Utrecht.
1985b   *Nota Basisonderwijs.* Utrecht: Gemeente Utrecht.
1986   *Deelnota welzijnswerk etnische minderheden.* Utrecht: Gemeente Utrecht.
1991   *Nota Zelforganisaties.* Utrecht: Gemeente Utrecht.
1992   *Moskee-notitie.* Utrecht: Gemeente Utrecht.
1995   *Steuntje in de rug. Zes jaar Stimuleringsfonds Minderheden Utrecht, een balans.* Utrecht: Gemeente Utrecht, dienst Welzijn.

Geneeskundige Hoofdinspectie van de Volksgezondheid (GHI)
1994   *Informatie over vrouwenbesnijdenis.* GHI-bulletin. Rijswijk: GHI.

Gerholm, T. & Y.G. Lithman (eds)
1988   *The New Islamic Presence in Western Europe.* London: Mansell.

Gerritsen, J.H.
1991   *Aanzetten tot een leerplan 'Islamitisch godsdienstonderwijs in de basisschool'.* Enschede: SLO.

Graaf, H. de
1983   *Funkties eigen organisaties buitenlanders.* Den Haag: Nederlands Instituut voor Maatschappelijk Werk Onderzoek (NIMAWO).
1985   *Plaatselijke organisaties van Turken en Marokkanen.* Den Haag: Nederlands Instituut voor Maatschappelijk Werk Onderzoek (NIMAWO).

Graaf, H. de, R. Penninx & E.F. Stoové
1988   'Minorities policies, social services, and ethnic organizations in the Netherlands', in S. Jenkins (ed.), *Ethnic Associations and the Welfare State. Services to Immigrants in Five Countries,* 203–238. New York: Columbia University Press.

Groen van Prinsterer Stichting
1984   *Van bijwoner tot burger. Minderheden en overheidsbeleid.* Amersfoort: Groen van Prinsterer Stichting.

Groenendijk, C.A.
1994   'De openbare oproep tot gebed. Een voorbeeld van tolerantie van de overheid', *Cultuur en Migratie* (1): 17–26.

Groenendijk, C.A. & A.H.J. Swart
1989   *Rechtspraak Vreemdelingenrecht 1988.* Nijmegen: Aers Aequi Libri.

Halstead, M.
1988   *Education, Justice and Cultural Diversity. An Examination of the Honeyford Affair, 1984–85.* Lewes: The Falmer Press.
Hampsink, R.
1991   *Steunverlening aan islamitische gebedsruimten. Een rechtssociologisch onderzoek.* Doctoraalscriptie. Nijmegen: Katholieke Universiteit Nijmegen, Faculteit der Rechtsgeleerdheid.
1992   *Nederland en de islam. Steunverlening aan islamitische gebedsruimten. Een rechtssociologisch onderzoek.* Reeks Recht & Samenleving nr. 5. Nijmegen: Katholieke Universiteit Nijmegen, Faculteit der Rechtsgeleerdheid.
Hart, C.
1991   *Religious Education. From Acts to Action,* Newcastle upon Tyne: CATS Trust.
Häussler, U.
1998   *Integration. Religion and Teaching.* Paper presented to the Fall 1998 seminar of the UC Comparative Immigration and Integration Programme, 9–10 October, University of California, Davis.
Hilhorst, H.
1985   'Etnische minderheden en de identiteit van het confessionele onderwijs. Dilemma of nieuw perspectief', in: A. Simons et al. (eds), *Van vreemdeling tot medeburger. Over het omgaan met etnische minderheden,* 19–36. KTHU-Reeks Theologie en Samenleving nr. 7. Hilversum: Gooi en Sticht.
Hirsch Ballin, E.
1983   'De scheiding van kerk en staat in verband met het overheidsbeleid ten aanzien van de godsdienstbeleving van minderheden', *Christen-Democratische Verkenningen* 5: 271–276.
Hodgins, H.
1981   'Planning permission for mosques. The Birmingham experience', in: J.S. Nielsen (ed.) *Islam in English Law and Administration. A Symposium,* 11–27. Research Paper no. 9. Birmingham: Centre for the Study of Islam and Christian-Muslim Relations, Selly Oak Colleges.
Hoffer, C.B.M.
1990   *Moslimbesnijdenissen in Nederland.* Leiden: Lidesco.
Huntington, S.P.
1997   *The Clash of Civilizations and the Remaking of World Order.* New York: Simon & Schuster.
Husbands, C.T.
1994   'Crises of national identity as the "new moral panics". Political agenda-setting about definitions of nationhood', *New Community* 20 (2): 191–206.
Inspraak Orgaan Turken in Nederland (IOT)
1992   *De vrijheid van godsdienst en de islam in Nederland.* Den Haag: IOT.
Interkerkelijke Stichting Kerken & Buitenlanders
1995   *Moskeebrochure Utrecht.* Utrecht: ISKB.
Iqbal, M.
1975   *Islamic Education and Single Sex Schools.* London: Union of Muslim Organisations of UK & Eire.
Islamitische Stichting Bevordering Integratie (ISBI)
1994   *Jaarverslag 1993.* Capelle aan den IJssel: ISBI.
Janssen, D.
1993   'Islamonderwijs beter. De stand van zaken in Vlaanderen', *Samenwijs* 14 (1): 35–36.
Joly, D.
1988   'Making a place for Islam in British society. Muslims in Birmingham', in: T. Gerholm & Y.G. Lithman (eds), *The New Islamic Presence in Western Europe,* 32–52. London: Mansell.

Karagül, A.
1994   *Islamitisch godsdienstonderwijs op de basisschool in Nederland. Theorie en praktijk in vergelijking met enkele Europese en Moslimse landen.* Amsterdam: Centrale Drukkerij UvA.

Karagül, A. & K. Wagtendonk
1994   *De Imâms. Hun taak, hun functie en hun opleiding.* Den Haag: Islamitische Raad Nederland.

Kaye, R.
1993   'The politics of religious slaughter of animals. Strategies for ethno-religious political action', *New Community* 19 (2): 235–250.

Khan-Cheema, A.
1984   'Islamic education and the maintained school system', *Muslim Education Quarterly* 2 (1): 5–15.

Klop, C.J.
1982   'De Islam in Nederland. Angst voor een nieuwe zuil?', *Christen-Democratische Verkenningen* 11 (82): 526–533.

Knight, K. & U. Hedegüs
1994   'UK: arguments for voluntary-aided schools', *Dialogue*: 7.

Knippenberg, H.
1992a   *De religieuze kaart van Nederland.* Assen/Maastricht: Van Gorcum.
1992b   'Moslims in Nederland', *Demos* 9 (1): 5–7.

Komitee Marokkaanse Arbeiders in Nederland (KMAN)
1989   *Manifest inzake islamitische scholen.* Amsterdam: KMAN.
1994   *Jaarverslag 1983.* Amsterdam: KMAN.

Koninklijk Commissariaat voor het Migrantenbeleid (KCM)
1989   *Integratie(beleid). Een werk van lange adem.* Brussel: KCM/INBEL.
1990   *Opvolging van de voorstellen november 1989 en mei 1990.* Cahier nr. 1. Brussel: KCM.

Koolen, R.
1993a   '78 Toeren', *Buitenlanders Bulletin* 18 (5): 4.
1993b   '"Voor een zaak die u aangaat ...". De mantelorganisatie van Koning Hassan II', *Buitenlanders Bulletin* 18 (4): 5–8.

Kriens, J.
1981   'De hodja zegt dat ik u niet aardig mag vinden. Koranscholen in Nederland', *Samenwijs* 2 (5): 160–161.

Labour Party
1990   *Meet the Challenge, Make the Change. Good Education for All.* Final report of Labour's Policy Review for the 1990s. Labour Party.

Lal, B.B.
1997   'Ethnic identity entrepreneurs. Their role in transracial and intercountry adoptions', *Asian and Pacific Migration Journal*, 6 (3/4): 385–413.

Lammers, M.
1989   *De stichting van een islamitische basisschool in Eindhoven.* Amsterdam: Vrije Universiteit, Theologische Faculteit.

Landelijk Aktie Komitee Anti Fascisme (LAKAF)
1980   *De Grijze Wolf en de halve maan. Turks fascisme en religieus extremisme.* Nijmegen: LAKAF.

Landman, N.
1992   *Van mat tot minaret. De institutionalisering van de islam in Nederland.* Amsterdam: VU Uitgeverij.

Latuheru, E.J., E.M. de Vries & M.J. de Jong
1994   *Integratie belemmerd? Een onderzoek naar belemmerende factoren bij de integratie van Turken, Koerden en Marokkanen in Nederland.* Rotterdam: Erasmus Universiteit Rotterdam, Rotterdams Instituut voor Sociologisch, Bestuurskundig en Milieukundig Onderzoek (RISBO).

Leeuwis, J.
1988   'School met de koran. Programma is net zoals dat van Nederlandse basis-scholen', *Stimulans* 6 (8): 3–5.
Le Lohé, M.J.
1993   'Political Issues', *New Community* 19 (3): 530–538.
Leman, J.
1992   'Ontmoeting op het terrein met moslims in België', in: J. Leman (ed.), *De integratie van de islam in België anno 1993*, 7–24. Reeks Cultuur & Migratie 1992–2.
Leman, J. & M. Renaerts
1996   'Dialogues at different institutional levels among authorities and Muslims in Belgium', in: W.A.R. Shadid & P.S. van Koningsveld (eds), *Muslims in the Margin. Political Responses to the Presence of Islam in Western Europe*, 164–181. Kampen: Kok Pharos.
Leman, J., M. Renaerts & J. van den Bulck
1992a   'De rechtspositie van de Islamitische Praxis in België', in: J. Leman (ed.), *De integratie van de islam in België anno 1993*, 43–78. Reeks Cultuur & Migratie 1992–2.
1992b   *Islam en islamitisch recht in België*. Recht van de Islam nr. 10. Maastricht: RIMO.
Lewis, P.
1994   *Islamic Britain. Religion, Politics and Identity among British Muslims*. London: I.B. Tauris & Co. Ltd.
Liefbroer, A.
1985   *Op elkaar aangewezen 3. Wat valt eraan te doen? Handreiking voor parochies en gemeenten om te komen tot contacten met migranten*. Driebergen: Werkgroep Pluriforme Samenleving van de Raad van Kerken.
Lijphart, A.
1975   *The Politics of Accommodation. Pluralism and Democracy in the Netherlands*. Berkeley, California: University of California Press. [1968]
1982   *Verzuiling, pacificatie en kentering in de Nederlandse politiek*. Amsterdam: J.H. de Bussy.
Lkoundi-Hamaekers, A.
1987   'Islam en het Nederlandse onderwijs', in: K. Wagtendonk (ed.), *Islam in Nederland. Islam op school*, 97–110. Muiderberg: Coutinho.
Local Education Authority Bradford (LEA Bradford)
1982   *Education for a Multi-cultural Society. Provision for Pupils of Ethnic Minority Communities*. Bradford: LEA.
1983   *Religious Education for Living in Today's World*. Agreed Syllabus. Bradford: LEA.
Lodge, B.
1983   'Putting their money where their faith is', *Times Educational Supplement*, 25 February 1983.
1986   'Muslim plan moves a step nearer', *Times Educational Supplement*, 7 March 1986.
Loock, L. van
1989   'De situatie van de islam-leraars', *Islamitische Nieuwsbrief* 1 (1): 11–18 and 31–32.
Luyten, R.
1992   'Moslims in Brussel', *Begrip* 18 (107): 12–14.
Mack, J.
1979   'The Muslims get a school of their own', *New Society*: 762–765.
Majic-Haak, Z. & H. Schellekens
1986   *Onze kritiekpunten op het rapport van het onderzoek 'Plaatselijke organisaties van Turken en Marokkanen' van NIMAWO*. Rotterdam: Platform Buitenlanders Rijnmond.

Marrewijk, C. van
1993 *Vestiging en financiering van moskeeën in Utrecht.* Nijmegen: Katholieke Universiteit Nijmegen, Instituut voor Rechtssociologie.
Mesman Schultz, K. & G. Methorst
1976 *Buitenlandse gedetineerden in Nederland.* Den Haag: WODC.
Meyer, A.
1993 *Islam en onderwijs in Utrecht. De oprichting van islamitische scholen en islamitisch gods-dienstonderwijs op openbare scholen.* Nijmegen: Katholieke Universiteit Nijmegen, Instituut voor Rechtssociologie.
1994 *Islam in het Nederlandse en Belgische onderwijs.* Doctoraalscriptie Algemene Letteren. Utrecht: Universiteit Utrecht.
Ministerie van Binnenlandse Zaken (BiZa)
1980 *Regeringsreactie op het rapport 'Etnische Minderheden' van de Wetenschappelijke Raad voor het Regeringsbeleid.* Den Haag: Ministerie van BiZa.
1981 *Ontwerp-Minderhedennota.* Den Haag: Ministerie van BiZa.
1982 *Reacties op ontwerp-minderhedennota.* Den Haag: Ministerie van BiZa.
1983 *Minderhedennota.* Tweede Kamer 1982–1983, 16102, nrs. 20–21.
1992 *Maatschappelijk debat integratie. Brief van de minister van Binnenlandse Zaken aan de voorzitter van de Tweede Kamer der Staten-Generaal.* Den Haag: Ministerie van BiZa.
Ministerie van Justitie
1976 *Rapport van de Werkgroep buitenlandse gedetineerden.* Den Haag: Ministerie van Justitie.
Ministerie van Onderwijs en Wetenschappen (O & W)
1992 *Onderwijsemancipatienota.* Den Haag: Ministerie van O & W.
Modood, T.
1993 'Muslim views on religious identity and racial equality', *New Community* 19 (3): 513–519.
Moore, S.F.
1973 'Law and social change. The semi-autonomous social field as an appropriate subject of study', *Law and Society Review* 7: 719–746.
Mulder, H. & S. van Duyvenbode
1988 *Projekt migranten, stadsvernieuwing en opbouwwerk in Rotterdam. Voortgangsrapportage.* Rotterdam: Rotterdams Instituut voor Bewonersondersteuning (RIO).
Mulder, J., et al.
1988 *Van medelanders naar Nederlanders? Staatkundig gereformeerde visie op de migranten-problematiek in Nederland.* Den Haag: Stichting Studiecentrum SGP.
Muslim Parents Association (MPA)
1982 *The Transformation of Muslim Children.* Bradford: MPA.
National Union of Teachers (NUT)
1984 *Religious Education in a Multi-faith Society. A Discussion Paper by the National Union of Teachers.* London: NUT.
Niedekker, D.
1992 'De integratie van islamitische scholen', *Migrantenaktief* 6: 10–11.
Nielsen, J.S.
1986 *A Survey of British Local Authority Response to Muslim Needs.* Research Paper no. 30/31. Birmingham: Centre for the Study of Islam and Christian-Muslim Relations, Selly Oak Colleges.
1987 *Islamic Law and its Significance for the Situation of Muslim Minorities in Europe. Report of a Study Project.* Research Paper no. 35. Birmingham: Centre for the Study of Islam and Christian-Muslim Relations, Selly Oak Colleges.
1988 'Muslims in Britain and local authority response', in: T. Gerholm & Y.G. Lithman (eds), *The New Islamic Presence in Western Europe*, 53–77. London: Mansell.

1989   'Muslims in English Schools', *Journal Institute of Muslim Minority Affairs* 10 (1): 223–245.
1991   'A Muslim agenda for Britain. Some reflections', *New Community* 17 (3): 467–475.
1992   *Muslims in Western Europe*. Edinburgh: Edinburgh University Press.

Oers, B. van
1992   'Moslims in Vlaanderen', *Begrip* 18 (107): 5–11.

Onderwijsraad
1994   *Advies van de Onderwijsraad over de opleiding van islamitische geestelijken (imams) in relatie tot het voortgezet onderwijs*. Den Haag: Onderwijsraad.

Ooijen, H. van, *et al.*
1991   *De islam in West-Europa, in het bijzonder in Nederland. Een bibliografie m.b.t. de islam en islamitische immigranten en de reactie van de samenleving, 1970–1991*. Reeks Recht & Samenleving nr. 4. Nijmegen: Katholieke Universiteit Nijmegen, Faculteit der Rechtsgeleerdheid.

Parker-Jenkins, M.
1991   'Muslim matters. The educational needs of the Muslim child', *New Community* 17 (4): 569–582.

Partij van de Arbeid (PvdA)
1992   *De Partij van de Arbeid en allochtonen. Beleidskeuzes voor de negentiger jaren*. Amsterdam: Partij van de Arbeid.

Peach, C.
1990   'The Muslim population of Great Britain', *Ethnic and Racial Studies* 13 (3): 414–419.

Peach, C. & G. Glebe
1995   'Muslim minorities in Western Europe', *Ethnic and Racial Studies* 18 (1): 26–45.

Pennen, T. van der
1988   *Migrantenwerk in de stadsvernieuwing. Een studie naar de betekenis van een participatiebevorderende maatregel voor allochtonen*. Leiden: Rijksuniversiteit Leiden, Onderzoekscentrum Ruimtelijke Ontwikkeling en Volkshuisvesting (ROV).

Pennings, P.
1986   *Migranten en de Amsterdamse deelraadsverkiezingen van 30 october 1985*. Amsterdam: Gemeente Amsterdam, Afdeling Bestuursinformatie/Universiteit van Amsterdam, Vakgroep Collectief Politiek Gedrag.

Penninx, R.
1979   'Politiek extremisme onder Turken', in: M. Sint & T. Nijzink (eds), *Tussen wal en schip*, 61–70. Amsterdam: Intermediair. (Overdruk van *Intermediair* 15 (1/2)).

Poulter, S.
1989   'The significance of ethnic minority customs and traditions in English criminal law', *New Community* 16 (1): 121–128.
1990   *Asian Traditions and English Law. A Handbook*. Stoke-on-Trent: Runnymede trust with Trentham Books.

Rabbae, M.
1993   *Naast de Amicales nu de UMMON. De mantelorganisaties van de Marokkaanse autoriteiten in Nederland*. Utrecht: Nederlands Centrum Buitenlanders.

Rath, J.
1981   'Turkse en Marokkaanse eilanden in het Hollandse politieke vaarwater. Migrantenkiesrecht in de praktijk', *Sociologische Gids* 28 (3): 202–227.
1982   'Wijkverkiezingen in Amsterdam en Rotterdam', *Buitenlanders Bulletin* 6 (10): 9–15.
1985   *Migranten, de Centrumpartij en de deelraadsverkiezingen van 16 mei 1984 te Rotterdam*. Uitgave 20. Leiden: Rijksuniversiteit Leiden, Centrum voor Onderzoek van Maatschappelijke Tegenstellingen (COMT).

1986   'Een verwaarloosd electoraat', *Intermediair* 22 (5): 59–63.
1988   'La participation des immigrés aux élections locales aux Pays-Bas', *Revue Européenne des Migrations Internationales* 4 (3): 23–36.
1990   'Deelname migranten aan gemeenteraadsverkiezingen. De stemming slaat om', *Namens* 5 (11/12): 46–51.
1991   *Minorisering. De sociale constructie van 'etnische minderheden'.* Amsterdam: Sua.
1993   'The ideological representation of migrant workers in Europe. A matter of racialisation?, in: J. Wrench & J. Solomos (eds), *Racism and migration in Western Europe*, 215–232. Oxford/Providence: Berg.

Rath, J. & F. Buijs
1987   'Migranten en werklozen in de electorale strijd', *Namens* 2 (3): 135–140.

Rath, J., K. Groenendijk & R. Penninx
1991   'The recognition and institutionalization of Islam in Belgium, Great Britain and the Netherlands', *New Community* 18 (1): 101–114.
1992   'Nederland en de islam. Een programma van onderzoek', *Migrantenstudies* 8 (1): 18–38.
1993   'De erkenning van de islam in België, Groot-Brittannië en Nederland', *Tijdschrift voor Sociologie* 14 (1): 53–75.

Rath, J. & A. Meyer
1994   'Ruimte voor islamitisch godsdienstonderwijs op openbare scholen', *Migrantenstudies* 10 (1): 33–53.

Rath, J. & Th. Sunier
1993   'Angst voor de islam in Nederland?', in: W. Bot, M. van der Linden & R. Went (eds), *Kritiek. Jaarboek voor socialistische discussie en analyse 1993–1994*, 53–62. Utrecht: Stichting Toestanden.

Ree, E. van
1995   'Immigratie is op termijn wel degelijk een reden tot zorg', *de Volkskrant*, 4 januari 1995.

Rijsewijk, T. van
1984a   'Islamitisch godsdienstonderwijs op Nederlandse lagere scholen. Verdeelde meningen bij christelijk en openbaar onderwijs', *Samenwijs* 4 (7): 196–198.
1984b   'Koranscholen in Nederland. Veel variatie in godsdienstonderwijs voor moslim kinderen, *Samenwijs* 4 (7): 183–187.

Rogers, R.
1982   'Church schools', *Where*: 6–13.

Rombout, H.
1990   *De 'choel' in Pakistan. De vele gezichten van het islamitische recht.* Nemesis.

Roosblad, J.
1991   *Het politieke discours rond de vestiging van een dependance van een islamitische basisschool in Amsterdam.* Doctoraalscriptie Politicologie. Amsterdam: Vrije Universiteit, Faculteit der Sociaal-Culturele Wetenschappen.
1992   *Nederland en de islam. Het politieke discours rond de vestiging van een dependance van een islamitische basisschool in Amsterdam.* Reeks Recht & Samenleving nr. 5. Nijmegen: Katholieke Universiteit Nijmegen, Faculteit der Rechtsgeleerdheid.

Roovers, W. & W. van Esch
1987   *Islamitsch godsdienstonderwijs in Nederland, Engeland, Duitsland en België.* Nijmegen: Instituut voor Toegepaste Sociale Wetenschappen (ITS).

Samad, Y.
1992   'Book burning and ethnic relations. Political mobilisation of Bradford Muslims', *New Community* 18 (4): 507–519.

Samenwerkingsverband Levensbeschouwelijk Vormingsonderwijs (SLV)
1992a   *Actuele plaatsbepaling godsdienst- en levenbeschouwelijk vormingsonderwijs.* Rotterdam: SLV Rotterdam.
1992b   *Verslag van het symposium over 'waarde, belang en relevantie van het godsdienst- en*

levenbeschouwelijk vormingsonderwijs in het openbaar basisonderwijs' op 15–4–'92 in de Pauluskerk te Rotterdam. Rotterdam: SLV Rotterdam.

Samuels, E. & P. Gransbergen
1975 *Behoeftenonderzoek moslims.* Rijswijk: Ministerie van Cultuur, Recreatie en Maatschappelijk Werk (CRM).

Sarwar, G.
1991 *British Muslims and Schools. Proposals for Progress.* London: The Muslim Educational Trust.

Schendelen, M.P.M.C. van (ed.)
1984 'Consociationalism, pillarization and conflict-management in the Low Countries', *Acta Politica* XIX January: 1–178 (Special Issue).

Shadid, W.A.R.
1994 *Beeldvorming. De verborgen dimensie bij interculturele communicatie.* Inaugurele rede. Tilburg: Tilburg University Press.

Shadid, W.A.R. & P.S. van Koningsveld
1985 'Hoofddoekjes in de klas. Lessen in acculturatie', *De Nederlandse Gemeente* 16: 275–277.

1989a 'Bijzondere scholen voor etnische groepen in de lokale politiek', *Samenwijs* 9 (5): 155–157.

1989b 'School en religie. Etnische groepen en godsdienstonderwijs', in: *Handboek voor Intercultureel Onderwijs*, 1310–1323. Alphen aan den Rijn: Samsom.

1990a *Moslims in Nederland. Minderheden en religie in een multiculturele samenleving.* Alphen aan den Rijn: Samsom Stafleu.

1990b *Vooroordelen, onbegrip en paternalisme. Discussies over de islam in Nederland.* Utrecht: De Ploeg.

1991 'Islamic primary schools', in: W.A.R. Shadid & P.S. van Koningsveld (eds), *Islam in Dutch Society. Current Developments and Future Prospects*, 107–123. Kampen: Kok Pharos.

1992a 'Islamitische scholen. De verschillende scholen en hun achtergronden', *Samenwijs* 10 (5): 227–233.

1992b *De mythe van het islamitische gevaar. Hindernissen bij integratie.* Kampen: Kok.

1995 *Religious Freedom and the Position of Islam in Western-Europe. Opportunities and Obstacles in the Acquisition of Equal Rights.* Kampen: Kok Pharos.

Sikkes, R.
1989 'Emancipatie of isolement. Buitenlanders stichten eigen scholen omdat bestaande onderwijs tekort schiet', *Het Schoolblad* 2: 26–29.

Slomp, J.
1983 'De Islam in Nederland. Angst voor een nieuwe zuil?', *Christen-Democratische Verkenningen* 2 (83): 106–108.

Souissy, Y.
1993 'Islamonderwijs', *Islamitische Nieuwsbrief* 4 (16/17): 24–26.

Spalburg, I.
1993 'Moslimbesnijdenissen', *De Eenheid* 12: 7.

Stichting Platform Islamitische Organisaties Rijnmond (SPIOR)
1989 *Werkplan 1989.* Rotterdam: SPIOR.
1995 *Jaarverslag 1994.* Rotterdam: SPIOR.

Strijp, R.
1990 'Witte vlekken op de landkaart. Recente publikaties over islam en moslims in Nederland', *Migrantenstudies* 6 (4): 19–36.

Struijs, A.
1995 'Neutraliteit en Gelijkheid. Liberaal Overheidsbeleid ten aanzien van Minderheidsgroepen', in: R. Kranenborg & W. Stoker (eds), *Religies en (on)gelijkheid in een plurale samenleving*, 225–243. Leuven/Apeldoorn: Garant Uitgevers.

Stuurman, S.
1983   *Verzuiling, kapitalisme en patriarchaat. aspecten van de ontwikkeling van de moderne staat in Nederland.* Nijmegen: SUN.
Sunier, Th.
1994   'Islam en etniciteit onder jonge leden van Turkse islamitische organisaties in Nederland', *Migrantenstudies* 10 (1): 19–32.
1996   *Islam in beweging. Turkse jongeren en islamitische organisaties.* Amsterdam: Het Spinhuis.
Tamarant, H.
1989   'Statistieken Islamonderwijs 1988–1989', *Islamitische Nieuwsbrief* 1 (4): 42–44.
Tamarant, H. & Omar
1990   'Geschiedenis van de erkenning van de Islam in België. Of hoe men van alle markten thuiskomt', *Islamitische Nieuwsbrief* 2 (5): 3–8.
Taylor, C.
1994   'The politics of recognition', in: C. Taylor *et al.*, *Multiculturalism. Examining the Politics of Recognition* (edited and introduced by A. Gutman), 25–73. Princeton, New Jersey: Princeton University Press.
Tennekes, J.
1991   'Een antropologische visie op de islam in Nederland', *Migrantenstudies* 7 (4): 2–22.
Teunissen, J.
1990   'Basisscholen op islamitische en hindoeïstische grondslag', *Migrantenstudies* 6 (2): 45–57. Themanummer 'De etnisch-culturele samenstelling van scholen. Oorzaken en gevolgen' (Edited by R. Penninx & J. Rath).
Theunis, S.
1979   *Ze zien liever mijn handen dan mijn gezicht. Buitenlandse arbeiders in ons land.* Baarn: Wereldvenster.
Theunissen, H., A. Abelmann & W. Meulenkamp (eds)
1989   *Topkapi en Turkomanie. Turks-Nederlandse ontmoetingen sinds 1600.* Amsterdam: De Bataafsche Leeuw.
Thomä-Venske, H.
1988   'The religious life of Muslims in Berlin', in: T. Gerholm & Y.G. Lithman (eds), *The New Islamic Presence in Western Europe*, 78–87. London: Mansell.
Tribe, D.
1970   *The Cost of Church Schools.* London: National Secular Society.
Triesscheijn, T.J.M.
1989a   'Stichting van islamitische scholen door ISNO voor een jaar opgeschort. Ouders laten het afweten, tegenstand groeit', *Samenwijs* 10 (3): 82.
1989b   'Verdere groei islamitische scholen. School op islamitische grondslag is van betekenis', *Samenwijs* 9 (8): 292–293 en 303.
Triesscheijn, T.J.M. & E. Geelen
1991   'Islamitisch Pedagogisch Studiecentrum in oprichting. Nuttig voor onderwijs', *Samenwijs* 12 (4): 160–161.
Tunderman, B.
1987   'Concurrentie onder islamslagers. Nieuwe opleiding', *Buitenlanders Bulletin* 12 (4): 22–24.
Verburgh, A.J.
1989   'De islam als een van de politieke factoren in ons land', *Ons Burgerschap* 4: 58–59.
Vereniging van Openbaar Onderwijs (VOO)
1992   *Tijd voor identiteit. Godsdienst- en vormingsonderwijs op de openbare school.* Kaderreeks nr. 26. Almere: VOO.
Vestdijk-Van der Hoeven, M.
1991   *Religieus recht en minderheden.* Arnhem: Gouda Quint.

Voorbij, A.
1987 'Geestelijke stromingen. Probleem en uitdaging', in: K. Wagtendonk (ed.), *Islam in Nederland. Islam op school*, 131–138. Muiderberg: Coutinho.
Waardenburg, J.
1983 'The right to ritual. Mosques in the Netherlands', *Nederlands Theologisch Tijdschrift* 37 (3): 253–265.
1986 'Iets over onderzoek betreffende islam bij etnische minderheden', *Migrantenstudies* 1 (1): 39–48.
1988 'The institutionalization of Islam in the Netherlands, 1961–1986', in: T. Gerholm & Y. Lithman (eds), *The New Islamic Presence in Western Europe*, 8–31. London: Mansell.
Wagtendonk, K.
1982 'De islam buitenshuis', in: R. Peters (ed.), *Van vreemde herkomst. Achtergronden van Turkse en Marokkaanse landgenoten*, 118–143. Bussum: Wereldvenster.
1990 'Imams in Nederland. Waar staan zij voor?', in: J.G.J. ter Haar & P.S. van Koningsveld (eds), *Schriftgeleerden in de moderne islam*, 102–119. Muiderberg: Coutinho.
1991 'Islamic schools and Islamic religious education', in: W.A.R. Shadid & P.S. van Koningsveld (eds), *The Integration of Islam and Hinduism in Western Europe*, 154–173. Kampen: Kok Pharos.
Wartna, F. (ed.)
1991 *Integratie en dialoog. Verslag van een studieconferentie*. Visies op Onderwijs nr. 7. Utrecht: Stichting Humanistisch Vormingsonderwijs.
Weerts, F.
1989 'Wachten is op behandeling Kameradvies "Hirsch Ballin". Subsidie moskee-activiteiten ook in migrantensteden uit den boze', *Binnenlands Bestuur* 10 (14): 11.
Werkgroep-Waardenburg
1983 *Religieuze voorzieningen voor etnische minderheden in Nederland. Rapport tevens beleidsadvies van de niet-ambtelijke werkgroep ad hoc*. Rijswijk: Ministerie van Welzijn, Volksgezondheid en Cultuur (WVC).
Weston, C.
1990 'Muslim schools get opt-in hope', *The Guardian*, 2 August 1990.
Wetenschappelijke Raad voor het Regeringsbeleid (WRR)
1979 *Etnische minderheden*. Den Haag: Staatsuitgeverij.
1989 *Allochtonenbeleid*. Rapporten aan de Regering nr. 36. Den Haag: SDU.
Yar, H.
1993 *Om de plaats van de Islam. Een studie naar de opstelling van de Belgische en de Nederlandse nationale overheden inzake de institutionalisering van de islam*. Doctoraalscriptie Politicologie. Amsterdam: Vrije Universiteit, Faculteit der Sociaal-Culturele Wetenschappen.

INDEX